THE PROJECT WORKOUT

Don Gr

THE PROJECT WORKOUT

SECOND EDITION

A toolkit for reaping the rewards from all your business projects

ROBERT BUTTRICK

London · New York · San Francisco · Toronto · Sydney
Tokyo · Singapore · Hong Kong · Cape Town · Madrid
Paris · Milan · Munich · Amsterdam

Pearson Education Limited
London Office:
128 Long Acre
London WC2E 9AN
Tel: +44 (0)171 447 2000
Fax: +44 (0)171 240 5771
Website: www.business-minds.com

First published in Great Britain in 1997
Second edition published 2000

ISBN 0 273 64436 X

British Library Cataloguing in Publication Data
A CIP catalogue record for this book can be obtained from the British Library.

10 9 8 7 6 5 4

Typeset by Pantek Arts, Maidstone, Kent
Printed and bound in Great Britain by Redwood Books, Trowbridge, Wiltshire

The Publishers' policy is to use paper manufactured from sustainable forests.

About the Author

Robert Buttrick currently works in one of the world's fastest growing industrial sectors, communications. He is accountable for creating and running a project-based framework for managing change within Cable and Wireless's UK operating company, enabling it to plan for, and develop, new systems, products, services, and capabilities to meet the ever growing needs of its customers. Prior to this he was a member of the management team which was accountable for managing the company's UK residential sector, acting as coach to sponsors and project managers, enabling them to succeed in a wide range of business projects.

Before joining Cable and Wireless in 1993, Robert was with PA Consulting Group, a management and technology consultancy. There, he specialized in business-led project management, advising clients such as TSB Bank, National Rivers Authority, Property Services Agency, Avon Industrial Polymers, National Westminster Bank, and RHM.

His early career was as a civil engineer. After graduating from the University of Liverpool with a first class honors degree, he joined Gibb Ltd, who provide consulting, design, and management services for infrastructure projects worldwide. He has lived and worked in countries as diverse as Kenya, Mauritius, Yemen, Senegal, and Sudan on the evaluation, design and supervision of a number of marine and water resource projects. He has also worked with the World Bank in Washington DC on investment appraisals for major development projects. Following this, he became Gibb's manager for marketing strategy and analysis.

Robert is a Master of Business Administration (Henley Management College), a Member of the Chartered Institute of Marketing, and a Member of the Institution of Civil Engineers.

His main pastime is watercolor painting. His one, unknown, claim to fame is that he once stopped a column of Russian tanks dead in its tracks.

FOR RHODRI,

my six-year-old son, who said,

"Dad, if you have too much work, do it in sections

and then you'll have time to play with me."

Contents

Part Four: Making Projects Work For You

Part Five: Implementing the Framework

List of Project Workouts

List of Project Workouts

Foreword

The forward progress of companies has always depended heavily on the management of projects. New plants, new products, new organizations, new methods, new ventures – all required dedicated teams working to strict timetables and separate budgets. But today there's a vital difference. The project management mode has broadened and evolved to the point where managers may spend as much time in interdisciplinary, cross-functional, interdepartmental project teams as they do in their normal posts.

Many factors have contributed to this unstoppable development – among them the increased complexity of all businesses, the closer interrelationships within companies and with customers and suppliers outside, and the mounting pressure for speed. The latter demands synchronous working. Companies can no longer afford to play pass-the-parcel, with each department or function waiting for the others to finish. There simply isn't enough time to waste.

That pressure demands not only speed but effective delivery, on time, on specification, and on budget. That will not happen by accident – and Robert Buttrick's book, based on his extensive experience, much of which was at Cable and Wireless, is an invaluable, lucid, and practical guide to a crucial area of management which has been crying out for the treatment it receives in these pages. Unlike management in general, project management is self-contained and dedicated to clearly defined ends. The companies and the managers who best master the methods and maxims in this book will not only achieve their specific objectives, they will win the whole game.

Robert Heller

Acknowledgments

This book is built on the experience and knowledge of many people I have worked with over the years. If I named them all the list would be as long as the credits at the end of an epic film! Here are a few mentions for those who have gone the extra mile with me.

I would like to thank my former colleagues at Gibb Ltd who took me on as a graduate and turned me into an engineer. Thanks, too, to those at PA Consulting Group who took on an engineer and gave me my grounding in business-led project management. Also I thank their clients with whom I worked and who presented me with such valuable challenges. Nick Warrillow, of TSB Bank, is just one I want to mention. Tim Smith is a particular person I worked with at PA Consulting Group and in Cable and Wireless. His rigor and precision are exceptional. He was a mentor, a friend, and he gave me a nudge when I needed it!

Unlike many books, this one was written by one of the 'infantry': I am not an academic. I would like to thank Jim Reynolds, formerly the Products and Services Director of Cable and Wireless's and UK subsidiary, Mercury, and William Hoyle, Director of Projects and Planning, for giving me the opportunity to write the book and to share my experiences with you. Bob Faulkner, also from Cable and Wireless, has provided me with endless constructive criticism, helping to shape the book into what you see today. My thanks also to Dr Eddie Obeng for introducing me to his frameworks and concepts relating to project types, and to Oded Cohen of the Goldratt Institute who opened my eyes to the Theory of Constraints.

Thank you also to the companies who took part in the benchmarking.

Putting a business-led project framework in place is a challenging and difficult task. Having the ideas is not enough – it is what you do with them that counts. During 1995, I worked with Anatoli Kaminov from Bain & Company. He looked at what I was doing and added his own spark of intelligence and practicality. He also said to me, 'Bob, you've done the ground-work; why don't you write the book?' So, thanks

Anatoli, for giving me a push to produce the first edition. . . and now here is the second edition.

Most important of all, I would like to thank my wife, Sandra, for hours of proof-reading and the solid support she has given me to ensure this venture succeeds.

And after all this, am I satisfied with what has been achieved? No – there's always more to do!

Bob Buttrick, October 1999

Preface to the Second Edition

'Nothing is impossible to him who has not got to do it!' How often do our managers complain about having to balance the apparently conflicting priorities presented to them by their leaders? But those same leaders today are under increasing pressure to deliver value to their stakeholders and the pace of change being experienced by organizations is putting more and more strain on their processes and systems.

How does the company manage complex demands on resources most effectively? How does it implement a long-term infrastructure investment programme while at the same time seeing sweeping change in the marketplace demanding the launch of brand-new technologies and products to very short timescales? This involves far more than just recruiting project managers and planning projects properly.

As this book shows, companies can never rely on a single project to achieve their aims; they need many projects. Companies need to have a common way of managing a portfolio of projects and a way of selecting and choosing which should go ahead and which should not. It means functions giving up their "rights" over their own resources to a decision-making body that will put the company's interest first. It means striking a balance between formal and informal working. It means creating a planning culture that can be flexible enough to deliver strategic initiatives while managing short-term imperatives. This takes time and effort and most large, complex organizations are still on the steep learning curve to success.

This book is all about the hard business issues of increasing customer satisfaction, creating a happier, empowered workforce and ultimately increasing profits. If we no longer have a stable playing field, the least we can do is give ourselves a stable way of managing change.

I commend Bob Buttrick's book to all leaders who lie awake at night wondering how they can process a mass of conflicting priorities through a system which will deliver.

Greg Clarke
Chief Executive Officer, Cable & Wireless Communications

Introduction

This book is about driving change in your organization by selecting the right projects and managing them in the right way. The approach is to keep to some basic principles supported by only a few formal 'rules.' In this way the likelihood of success is increased dramatically and you, as an executive, director, or manager, will have the freedom to manage.

Ian Gibson, Chief Executive of Nissan Motor Manufacturing in Britain said:

> *"As organizations we must become increasingly able to change quickly and easily. This means building on and around people's abilities rather than limiting them for the convenience of recognizable roles."*

He recognized the need for a new way of managing our businesses; one that is flexible and not tied to specific departments; one where people can be used to the best effect; where what they do counts more than the department or function they come from. In his company, the structures are flat, there are no job titles, and most personnel moves are sideways. This applies from top to bottom and no one can ever say, 'I won't do that, it's not my job!' Change is built into the way they work.

Some companies have attained this vision, but most have not. This book looks at one aspect of this, the part which relates to implementing change in your business. A 'new way' of doing this has been with us for a long time, buried within the bowels of our technical and engineering departments, but it is now being recognized by business and governments alike. It is **project and program management**.

Unfortunately, the discipline of project management is generally made to look too complicated, is frequently misunderstood, and often poorly practiced at a business level. Consequently, it does not always deliver the promised rewards. Whether you are a senior executive, manager, project manager, or 'one of the infantry,' I aim to make the 'art of project management' clearer to you in this book by:

- explaining the challenges faced by many companies;
- outlining some lessons and advice from leading companies;
- proposing a staged framework for managing individual projects;
- explaining the key roles which need to be fulfilled;
- showing how a business can manage and track all its projects as a portfolio through their life cycles;
- providing best practice for managing projects.

Reading this book will benefit you as:

- having read it, you can really start doing it!
- the 'mystique' of projects is exposed, making it simple to understand and accessible to finance, sales, marketing, customer services, administrators, and technologists alike.
- it gives practical, immediately usable methods for directing and managing complete portfolios of projects as well as individual projects.
- the content is not tied to any formally published 'methods' but is positioned as 'common sense' which overrides them all.

Part One covers the challenges and lessons. Part Two looks at a typical project life cycle. Part Three looks at dealing with the many projects you have in your company. Part Four proposes a control framework for your projects. Part Five contains some thoughts on how you can implement a projects framework in your company.

Many of the key points will be restated in different sections throughout the book. This is intentional, to reinforce the key points and allow you to dip into separate sections without the need to follow up multiple cross-references, simply to understand the basic message. Successful project management is a complete system and to describe elements of it in isolation would be deficient.

If much of the book seems to you to be 'mere common sense' then I have succeeded in relaying an important message. It is common sense; however, while it is obvious common sense to state it, the common sense of doing it is rare.

If much of the book seems simplistic, I have succeeded in relaying it to you in a form that can be understood by anyone in your organization. Everyone involved in a project, be he/she a top executive or a line worker, needs to be able to understand the basic principles. If they don't, you shouldn't be surprised if things go wrong.

Project management is an 'art.' To be effective it requires both powerful interpersonal skills (soft skills) and structured management (hard skills).

I have concentrated on the latter as this is where the myth of project management most needs exploding. I do, however, refer throughout to the soft skills needed, but this book is not aimed at being a handbook on motivation, leadership, enrolment or management style. If you want a good book which does cover the softer aspects, try Dr Eddie Obeng's *All Change!, the Project Leader's Secret Handbook* (London: Pitman Publishing, 1994).

> ***Project management is an 'art.' To be effective it requires both powerful interpersonal skills (soft skills) and structured management (hard skills). I have concentrated on the latter as this is where the myth of project management most needs exploding.***

THE PROJECT WORKOUTS

The book contains a number of exercises, problem posers, and techniques to help you put the 'book work' into practice. They will be both a stimulant and a practical help.

Case studies

The case studies are derived from real-life incidents, but some have been amended to make them more concise to convey the particular message being illustrated.

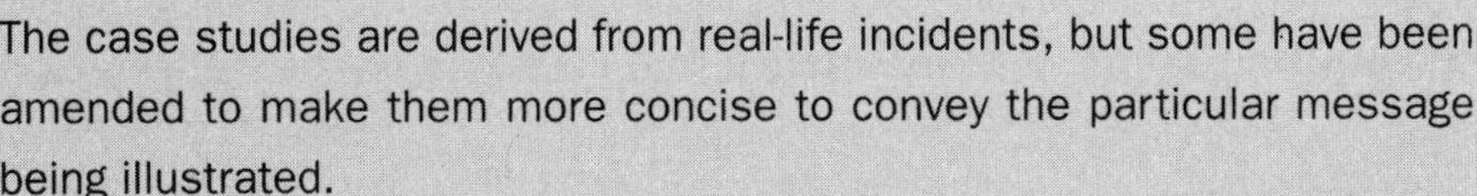

'Change the name and it's about you, that story.'

HORACE 65–8BC

Points of interest

Throughout the book I have included a number of points of interest which relate to the core theme of each chapter. These may be passed over on first reading so that you are not diverted from the main message. They may, however, provide you with some greater understanding of the subject. If this book were a presentation, these would be the questions which interrupt the presenter or the anecdotes the presenter may use to help bring the story to life.

Definitions

The way we use words is important. In the field of project management there is a converging consensus on what words mean but there are still instances where people have differing opinions. You will find a number of words which may be new to you or have been used in a new way. Appendix B comprises a jargon-busting glossary. So, if you come across a new word, look it up.

> *'How often misused words generate misleading thoughts.'*
>
> HUBERT SPENCER

Principles

These are the basic principles you need to apply if your projects are to succeed. You should ensure that any "rules" or procedures you develop and use within your organization are compatible with these.

Key points

Key points are short checklists which will keep you on the right track.

Cartoons

In many of the chapters I have used cartoons to emphasize a point. The cartoons are all set 2,000 years ago in the Roman Empire and show how, if the Romans had run their affairs as many modern companies do, they would have failed miserably. This drives home the point that project management is essentially no more than applying the common sense that has been with us for thousands of years.

The question 'why' is very powerful

CD-ROM

You are probably a very busy person and the last thing you want to do is struggle with a photocopier, trying to produce a clean copy of a useful page for a project workshop you are running. The CD-ROM enclosed with this book contains all the Workouts, ready for you to print out and use with your team. You can find them either by reference number (as given in the book) or through a context sensitive framework which collects together all the workouts relevant to a particular stage or point in your project.

We have also included a number of the templates described in Part 4 of the book including the Health Check, MS Project views and project logs. These can be downloaded to your desktop ready for use.

Finally, when you come to Part 5 and you want to put enterprise-wide project management in place in your company, the content of this CD may give you an idea or two about the design of your own project management website.

To use the software included, please refer to readme.txt on the CD.

Part One

CHALLENGES TO BE FACED

'Minds are like parachutes; they only work when open.'

LORD DEWAR

In this part of the book I set out the challenges many organizations are facing in driving through the changes they need to make in pursuit of their strategic objectives. This is followed by a review of good practice being used by many of the world's leading companies.

How to use Part One

Part One is for you to read and learn from. When first reading it, you should forget about your own situation and the problems in your company. Open your mind to what others are saying and doing. If you find yourself saying ' . . . but we don't do it like that, we are different!,' pull yourself back – LISTEN. You are different. So is everyone else. Other people's experience may give you a clue to dealing with issues confronting you.

The project workouts in Part One are designed to help you think about 'projects' in your company, and to prompt action or discussion on the parts you feel will benefit you.

Challenges We Need to Face

Problems, more problems

Initiatives fail, are canceled, or never get started – why?

In our new world of the twenty-first century no organization is immune from 'shut down' if it fails to perform.

"Facts do not cease to exist because they are ignored."

ALDOUS HUXLEY

Problems, more problems

All organizations have problems with the way they undertake their work and tackle frequent change within their businesses. Problems may be related to any aspect, be it technology, people, processes, systems, or structure. There is always something, somewhere that needs to be created or improved. Throughout the later part of the twentieth century a variety of techniques and offerings has been available to business leaders to enable them to do this, including:

- O&M;
- Total Quality Management;
- Added Value Analysis;
- Business Process Reengineering.

All these have contributed greatly to the performance of a significant number of organizations but it is a sad fact that many organizations have failed (and continue to fail) to secure the enduring benefits which were initially promised. Something has gone wrong. It would seem that we are not all as good as we should be at managing and controlling change in order to achieve sustained benefits from such initiatives.

'Grand' initiatives of the kind just mentioned are not the only ones that can fail; organizations must continually strive to solve particular problems or achieve specific objectives. For example:

- new products are developed, old ones are enhanced;
- supply chains are changed;
- manufacturing processes are altered to take account of new methods and technologies;
- sales channels are developed;
- new plant and offices are opened, old ones are closed;
- key business functions are out-sourced;
- businesses are disposed of;
- acquisitions are integrated into the mainstream business;
- computer systems are built to give greater efficiency and add to the overall effectiveness of the operation.

Again, many of these initiatives fail. Either they:

- cost too much;
- take too long;
- are inadequately scoped and specified;
- or simply don't deliver the expected benefits.

Something has gone wrong. It would seem that we are not all as good as we should be at managing and controlling change in order to achieve sustained benefits from such initiatives.

This amounts to failure on a scale which costs billions every year and for some organizations results in their demise. It happens in both private and public sectors, small undertakings and major multinational enterprises. In our new world of the twenty-first century no organization is immune from 'shut down' if it fails to perform.

Initiatives fail, are canceled or never get started – why?

A review of a representative cross-section of large companies reveals a common pattern of cause and effect.

A review of a representative cross-section of large companies reveals a common pattern of cause and effect. Figure 1.1 shows that the fundamental reasons are twofold:

- Organizations don't know HOW to control change. There is no 'company-wide' way of undertaking business change initiatives.
- Organizations don't know WHAT they should be doing. There is no clear strategy driving decision making.

This book concentrates on how you can solve the first of these root causes (how to do it) but, as Figure 1.1 shows, successful projects rely heavily on the latter (what to do) being in place. You will, therefore, see frequent references to business planning and strategy throughout the book. For a practical approach to developing your strategy, read and use Cyril Levicki's *Strategy Workout* (Financial Times Prentice Hall, 1997).

If any of the problems identified in this chapter or drawn out from Figure 1.1 are familiar to you and recognizable in your organization, there is clearly scope for improving your performance:

- The solution to issues relating to single initiatives in isolation I refer to as **project management**.
- The solution to issues relating to groups of connected projects I refer to as **program management**.
- The solution to issues relating to the undertaking of a large number of projects I refer to as **portfolio management**.

If a company is to reap the full benefits, it must be competent at all three.

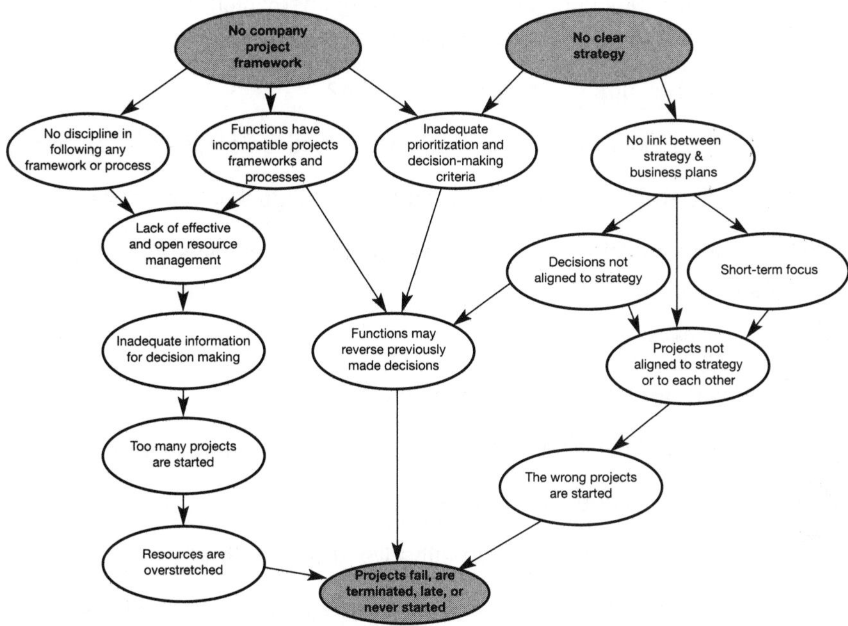

Figure 1.1 Problem analysis
A cause and effect analysis of the reasons for the failure of business change projects shows two fundamental reasons: (i) a lack of clear strategy, (ii) a lack of a rational way of managing the required changes.

SELF-DIAGNOSIS

This Workout is best done with a group of executives, directors, or managers.

1. Use the following questions as prompts to help you establish the areas of competence you may need to address.

   - ❑ Can you establish a clear link between your current strategy and business plan and all the initiatives you have underway?
   - ❑ Is it always clear what you should be doing and why?
   - ❑ Do you find middle management passes on communications and instructions accurately?
   - ❑ Do you find it easy to get decisions made?
   - ❑ Do you have any documented criteria against which decisions on whether or not to undertake initiatives are tested?
   - ❑ If so, do they apply to all your initiatives?
   - ❑ Is there a disciplined way of managing initiatives across your company?
   - ❑ Is there always enough time to do those things which must be done?
   - ❑ Do your managers and employees commit themselves to and meet the targets set for them?

   Do you really KNOW:

   - ❑ What your resources are working on?
   - ❑ When you will have spare resources to start new initiatives?
   - ❑ Who is managing each initiative?
   - ❑ Who wants the benefits each initiative should create?
   - ❑ The sum total of the costs and benefits from all your initiatives?
   - ❑ Who makes the decisions on each initiative?
   - ❑ Who makes the decisions when initiatives are competing for resource?

2. Build a cause and effect diagram similar to Figure 1.1 for your company. Start with 'Projects fail, are terminated, late, or never started' written on a Post-it Note at the bottom of a flip chart. Ask yourself why this happens. Write each possible reason on a Post-It Note and place these on the flip chart. Again, for each Post-It Note, ask the reason why, writing these on more Post-It Notes. Eventually, if you are honest, you will discover a core reason(s), picking up many symptoms on the way.

Advice the Best Companies Give Us

The advice in this chapter is based on a benchmarking exercise undertaken by the author, coupled with his own experience of working with a number of major companies.

"Example moves the world more than doctrine."

HENRY MILLER

The study

The problems outlined in the previous chapter are significant and far reaching. Finding solutions you can trust, and have confidence in, is itself difficult. The advice in this chapter is based on a benchmarking study undertaken by the author with Cable and Wireless, coupled with his own experience of working with several major companies across a number of industries.

The benchmarking questions were not directly related to project management but to "product development." In a business context, a project is a project, regardless of whether it is technology based, for cultural change, complex change, or whatever. As the development and launching of new products and services touches almost every part of a company, projects in this field are an excellent medium for learning about complex, cross-functional projects and how companies address them. If a company cannot develop new products and services efficiently, it is probable that it cannot tackle any other form of cross-functional project effectively either. The full set of questions is on the CD-ROM. The study had the following characteristics:

In a business context, a project is a project, regardless of whether it is technology based, for cultural change, complex change, or whatever.

- It covered a wide range of industries, not just that of the commissioning organization.
- It was predominantly qualitative with only a few quantitative questions added to obtain such "hard data" as were available. It was considered more important to find out how people worked rather than collect statistics.

The objective was to "learn from the best," hence the inclusion of a number of industries in the study:

- aerospace;
- construction;

- computer hardware;
- telecommunications;
- manufacturing;
- systems integrators.

The companies chosen for the study were those which had clearly demonstrated success in their own fields and markets. Despite the diverse industries, we found a marked similarity in approach taken by all those companies interviewed. They are all using or currently implementing a "staged," "cross-functional" framework within which to manage their product development projects (Figure 2.1). The number of stages may differ from company to company, but all have the characteristic of investing a certain amount of the company's resources to obtain more information across the full range of activities which impact a project and its outcome, namely:

Despite the diverse industries, we found a marked similarity in approach taken by all those companies interviewed. They are all using or currently implementing a "staged," "cross-functional" framework within which to manage their product development projects.

- market;
- operational;
- technical;
- commercial and financial.

The additional finding was that some of the companies did not confine their approach to product development only, but applied it to business change projects generally, i.e. to everything they did which created change in the organization. In other words, they had a common business-led project framework for managing change generally.

The companies did not confine their approach to product development only, but applied it to business change projects generally, i.e. to everything they did which created change in the organization.

There, however, the similarities between companies end as the individual culture and the nature of the different industries take over. Figure 2.2 illustrates that any process (including project management) sits within a context of culture, systems, and organization structure; alter any one and it will affect the others.

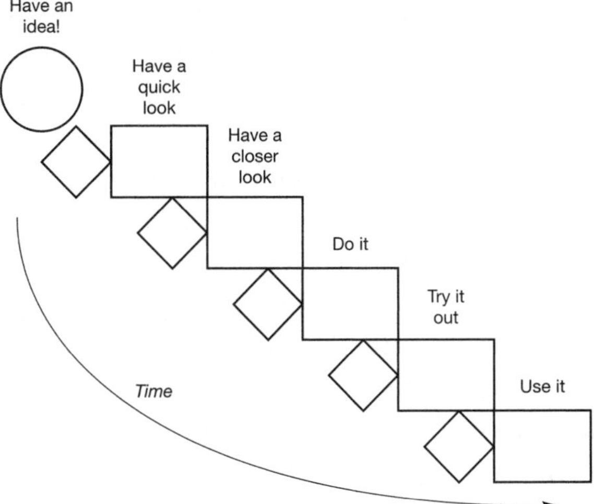

Figure 2.1 A typical staged project process framework
A staged approach to projects starts with a preliminary look at the objectives and possible solutions and results, via more detailed investigation, development, and trial, in the release of the outputs into the business' operational environment. You do not start any stage without meeting the prescribed criteria at the preceding gate. This includes checks on strategic fit and "do ability" as well as financial considerations.

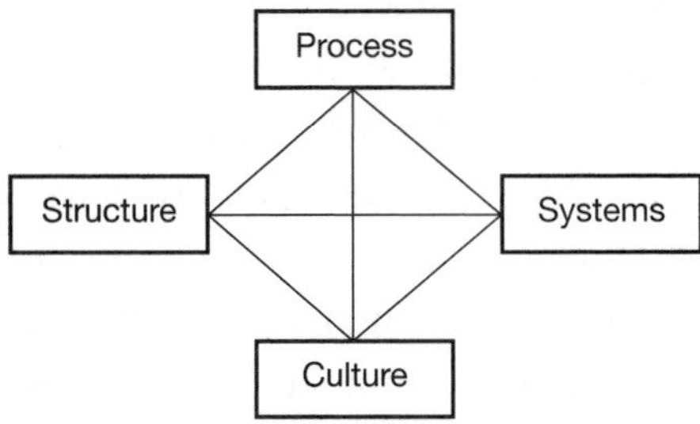

Figure 2.2 The organizational context for project management and other processes
No process sits in isolation. How you are organized, the systems you use to support the process, and the prevailing culture of the organization all affect how well any process works.

This single observation means that although the basic project management processes in many companies may be similar in principle, the infrastructure which makes them work is different. Logically, if an already proven process appears to break down, the fault may lie outside the process itself in one of the other aspects of the organization. One company told me. "We know our process is logical; if it isn't working we first look at the people trying to make it work rather than at the process itself." This company had a well established project management process in which it had a very high degree of confidence. However, it still maintained the good practice of continually improving its processes by promoting feedback and having regular quarterly reviews. This observation also means that a process which works fine in one organization will not necessarily work in every organization.

Also notable was that certain industries were excellent in particular aspects of managing projects as a result of the nature of their business. Often, they took this for granted. For example:

"Concentrate on the early stages" was a message which came across loud and clear, but it was the companies that relied on bids or tenders for their business which really put the effort in up front as the effect of failure was immediately obvious – they lost business or won unprofitable business. In companies where "bidding" is not the rule, the effects of poor upfront work are not so immediately obvious and may take a long time to become apparent. Too long.

"Manage risks" was another message. The only company to tell me, unprompted, that it was excellent in risk management was in avionics, where the consequences of failure can be painfully obvious – aircraft fall out of the sky. Interestingly enough, the company does not claim to use very sophisticated risk-management techniques, but rather has designed its whole approach with a risk-management bias. It cites its staged process as a key part of this.

"Measure everything you do." Companies which need to keep a track of man hours in order to bill their customers (e.g. consultants, system development houses) also have the most comprehensive cost and resource planning and monitoring systems. These provide not only a view of each individual project, but also enable them to collate and summarize the current status for all their projects giving them a quantum leap in management information which most other companies do not have.

The lessons and their implications

The lessons learned are summarized below and are described more fully on the following pages. The quotations are taken from the study notes.

The first seven lessons apply throughout the life of a project:

1 Make sure your projects are driven by benefits which support your strategy.
2 Use the same, simple, and well defined framework, with a staged approach, for all projects in all circumstances.
3 Address and revalidate the marketing, commercial, operational, and technical viability of the project throughout its life.
4 Incorporate selected users and customers into the project to understand their current and future needs.
5 Build excellence in project management techniques and controls across the company.
6 Break down functional boundaries by using cross-functional teams.
7 Use dedicated resources for each category of development and prioritize within each category.

The next three lessons apply to particular stages in the project:

8 THE START
Place high emphasis on the early stages of development.
9 THE MIDDLE
Build the business case into the company's forward plan as soon as the project has been formally approved.
10 THE END
Close the project formally to build a bridge to the future, to learn any lessons, and to ensure a clean handover.

1. Make sure your projects are driven by benefits which support your strategy

All the companies were able to demonstrate explicitly how each project they undertook fitted their business strategy. The screening out of unwanted projects as soon as possible was key. At the start, there is usually insufficient information of a financial nature to make a decision regarding the viability of the project. However, strategic fit should be assessable from the beginning. Not surprisingly, those companies which had clear strategies were able to screen more effectively than those which didn't. Strategic fit was often assessed by using simple questions such as:

- Will this product ensure we maintain our leadership position?
- Will the results promote a long-term relationship with our customers?

The less clear the strategy, the more likely projects are to pass the initial screening: resulting in the company losing focus.

The less clear the strategy, the more likely projects are to pass the initial screening: so there will be more projects competing for scarce resources resulting in the company losing focus and jeopardizing its overall performance.

2. Use the same, simple, and well defined framework, with a staged approach, for all projects in all circumstances

As discussed earlier, use of a staged framework was found to be well established. Rarely is it possible to plan a project in its entirety from start to finish; there are simply too many unknowns. By using defined project stages, it is possible to plan the next stage in detail, with the remaining stages planned in summary. As you progress through the project from stage to stage, your end-point becomes clearer and your confidence in delivery increases. It was apparent that companies were striving to make their project frameworks as simple as possible, minimizing the number of stages and cutting down the weight of supporting documentation. Further, the same generic stages were used for all types of project (e.g. for a new plastic bottle, and for a new manufacturing line; for a project of £1,000 cost to one of £10m cost).

This makes the use and understanding of the framework very much easier and avoids the need for learning different frameworks and processes for different types of project. This is particularly important for those sponsoring projects or who are infrequently involved in projects. By having one basic framework they are able to understand their role within it and do not have to learn a new language and approach for each situation.

What differs is the work content of each project, the level of activity, the nature of the activity, the resources required, and the stakeholders and decision makers needed in each project.

A common criticism is that a staged approach slows projects down. This was explored in the interviewing and found not to be the case. In contrast, a staged approach was believed to speed up desirable projects. One relevant point is the nature of the gates. Some companies used them as "entry" points to the next stage rather than the more traditionally accepted "exit" point from a previous stage. This simple principle has the effect of allowing a stage to start before the previous stage has been completed. In this way stages can overlap without increasing the risk to the business.

The existence of so-called "fast-track" processes to speed up projects was also investigated. In all cases, the companies said that their "usual process" was the fast track. Doing anything else, such as skipping stages or going ahead without fully preparing for each stage, increases the risk of the project failing. The experience of some companies was that "going fast" actually slowed the project down; the amount of rework required was nearly always much greater than the effort saved.

A common criticism is that a staged approach slows projects down. This was explored in the interviewing and found not to be the case. In contrast, a staged approach was believed to speed up desirable projects.

What's the point of speeding if you're on the wrong road?

3. Address and revalidate the marketing, commercial, operational, and technical viability of the project throughout its life

"We are very good at slamming on the brakes very quickly if we see we cannot achieve our goals."

All the companies address all aspects throughout the life of a project. No single facet is allowed to proceed at a greater pace than the others as, for example there is little point in:

- having an excellent technological product which has no adequate market rationale relating to it and cannot be economically produced;
- developing a superb new staff appraisal system if there are no processes to administer it and make it happen.

As the project moves forward, the level of knowledge increases and hence the level of risk should decrease. The only exception is where there is a particularly large area of risk and this work may be brought forward in order to understand the problems and manage the consequences as part of a planned risk-management strategy.

Coupled with this, the ability of companies to stop (terminate) projects was seen to be important. Some expressed themselves to be experts at this. A problem in any one aspect of the project (e.g. market, operations, technology, finance) can lead to termination. For example one company, which has a product leadership strategy, killed a new product just prior to launch as a competitor had just released a superior product. It was better to abort the launch and work on the next generation product, than to proceed with releasing a new product which could be seen, by the market, as inferior. If the company had done so, its strategy of product leadership would have been compromised.

Naturally, the gates prior to each stage are the key checkpoints for revalidating a project. The best companies also monitor the validity of the project between gates and are prepared to stop it if their business objectives are not likely to be met. At all times, the project timescale, cost, scope, and benefits must be kept in balance (Figure 2.3).

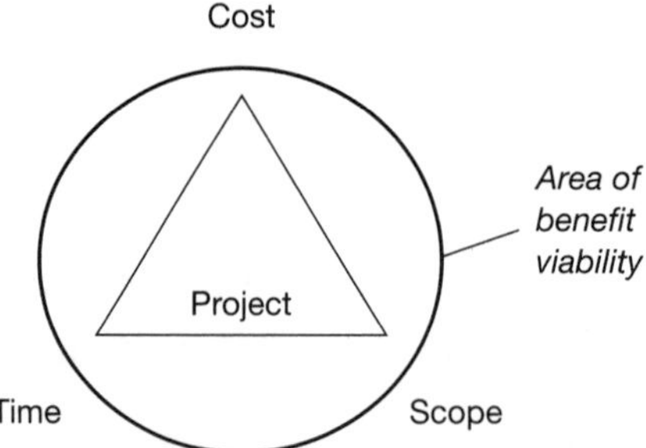

Figure 2.3 The project balance

A project comprises a defined scope (deliverables), to be delivered in an agreed timescale, at an agreed cost. These must be combined in such a way to ensure that the project is always viable and will deliver the expected benefits. If any one of these falls outside the area of benefit viability, the others should be changed to bring the project back on target. If this cannot be done the project should be terminated. (Copyright © PA Consulting Group, London)

4. Incorporate stakeholders into the project to understand their current and future needs

"The front line customer interface has been and is our primary focus."

The involvement of stakeholders, such as users and customers, in projects was seen to add considerable value at all stages of a project. Usually, the earlier they are involved, the better the result.

The more "consultancy-oriented" companies must, by the nature of the work they do, talk to customers to ascertain their needs. But even these companies said they often misinterpreted the real needs of the customer despite great efforts to avoid this. Where project teams are more removed from their users or customers, there is even greater scope for error.

Many innovative ways have been used to obtain this involvement including:

- focus groups;
- facilitated workshops;
- early prototyping;
- simulations.

Involving the stakeholders is a powerful mover for change, while ignoring them can lead to failure. When viewed from a stakeholder's perspective, your project may be just one more that the stakeholder has to cope with as well as fulfilling his or her usual duties; it may even appear irrelevant or regressive. If the stakeholders' consent is required to make things happen, you ignore them at your peril!

5. Build excellence in project management techniques and controls across the company

"Never see project management as an overhead."

All the companies I interviewed see good project management techniques and controls as prerequisites to effecting change in their companies. Project management skills were most obvious in the engineering-based companies, particularly those which have a project/line matrix management structure. However, other companies had taken, or were taking, active steps to improve this discipline.

There must be project management guidance, training and support for all staff related to projects, including senior managers who sponsor projects or make project-related decisions. Core control techniques identified in the companies included planning and managing risk, issues, scope changes, schedule, costs and reviews.

Planning as a discipline is seen as essential. If you have no definition of the project and no plan, you are unlikely to be successful. It is virtually impossible to communicate your intentions to the project team and stakeholders. Further, if there is no plan, phrases such as "early," "late," and "within budget" have no real meaning. Planning should be seen to be holistic, encompassing schedule, cost, scope, and benefits refined in light of resource constraints and business risk (Figure 2.4).

Risk was particularly mentioned: using a staged approach is itself a risk management technique with the gates acting as formal review points where risk is put in the context of the business benefits and cost of delivery. Projects are risky and it is essential to analyze the project, determine which are the inherently risky parts and take action to reduce, avoid or, in some cases, insure against those risks.

Despite good planning things will not always go smoothly. Unforeseen issues do arise which, if not resolved, threaten the success of the project. Monitoring and forecasting against the agreed plan is a discipline which ensures events do not take those involved in the project by surprise. This

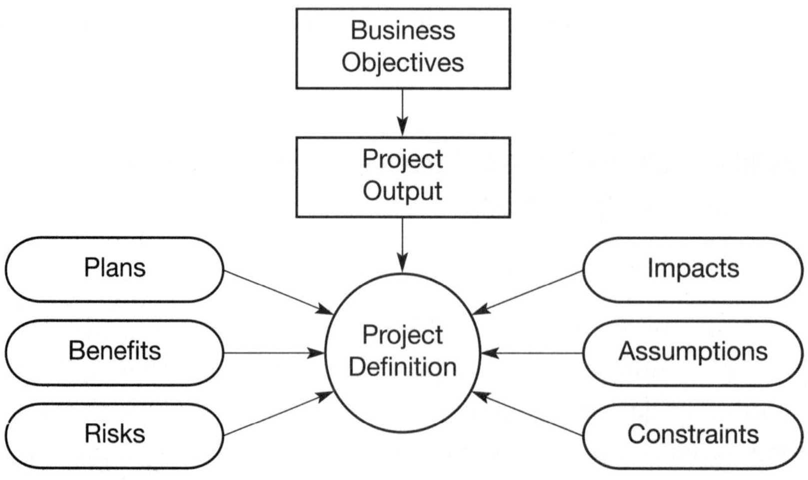

Figure 2.4 Planning

Planning should be seen to be holistic, encompassing schedule, cost, scope, and benefits refined in light of resource constraints and business risk.

is illustrated by the "project control cycle" in Figure 2.5. The appropriate frequency for the cycle depends on the project, its stage of development and inherent risk. Monthly is considered the most appropriate by many of the companies although in certain circumstances this is increased to weekly.

Such monitoring should focus more on the future than what has actually been completed. Completion of activities is evidence of progress but not sufficient to predict that milestones will continue to be met. The project manager should be continually checking to see that the plan is still fit for its purpose and likely to deliver the business benefits on time. Here, the future is more important than the past.

> ***Completion of activities is evidence of progress but not sufficient to predict that milestones will continue to be met.***

It is a sad fact that many projects are late, or never reach completion. One of the reasons for this is "scope creep." More and more ideas are incorporated into the project resulting in higher costs and late delivery. Managing change is a technique which is critical to ensuring that benefits are achieved, and that the project is not derailed by "good ideas" or "good intentions." Changes are a fact of life and cannot be avoided. Good planning and a staged approach reduce the potential for major change but cannot prevent it. Changes, even beneficial ones,

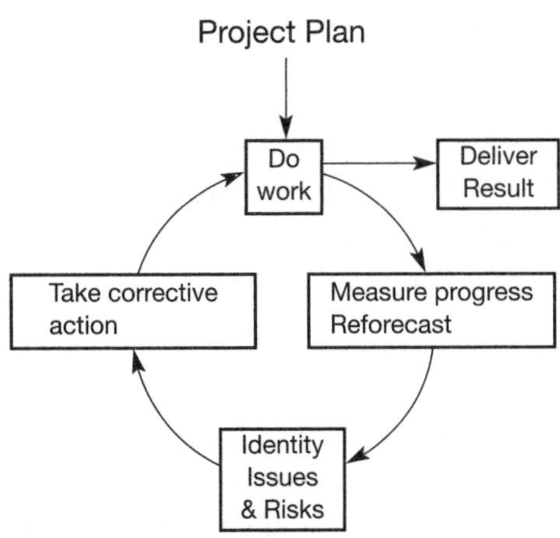

Figure 2.5 Project control cycle

The project control cycle comprises doing the work as set out in your plan, measuring progress against that plan, identifying any risks, opportunities or issues, and taking corrective action to keep the project on track. From time to time, results, in the form of deliverables, are generated. (Copyright © PA Consulting Group, London) must be managed to ensure that only those which enable the project benefits to be realized are accepted. Contracting industries are particularly good at managing change as their income is directly derived from projects – doing "that bit more" without checking its impact on their contractual obligations is not good business. Why should it be any less so when dealing with "internal projects?"

THE FULL PROJECT ENVIRONMENT

This finding says use "good project management tools and techniques," BUT it is only one of ten findings which provide the full environment for projects to work. Is this why some companies say "we do project management, but it doesn't work for us?"

6. Break down functional boundaries by using cross-functional teams

The need for many projects to draw on people from a range of functions means that a cross-functional team approach is essential. Running "projects" in functional parts with coordination between them always slows down progress, produces less satisfactory results, and increases the likelihood of errors. All the companies in the study recognize this and have working practices which encourage lateral cooperation and communication rather than hierarchical (Figure 2.6). In some cases this goes as far as removing staff from their own departmental locations and grouping them in project team work spaces. In others, departments which frequently work together are located as close as practical in the company's premises. Generally, the closer people work, the better they perform. Although this is not always practical, closeness can be compensated for by frequent meetings and good communication.

Cross-functional team working, however, is not the only facet. It was also seen that decision making has to be on a cross-functional basis. Decision making and the associated processes was an area where some of the companies were less than satisfied with their current position. Either decision makers took too narrow a view or insufficient information was available.

Another requirement of cross-functional working is to ensure that both corporate and individual objectives are not deliberately placed in

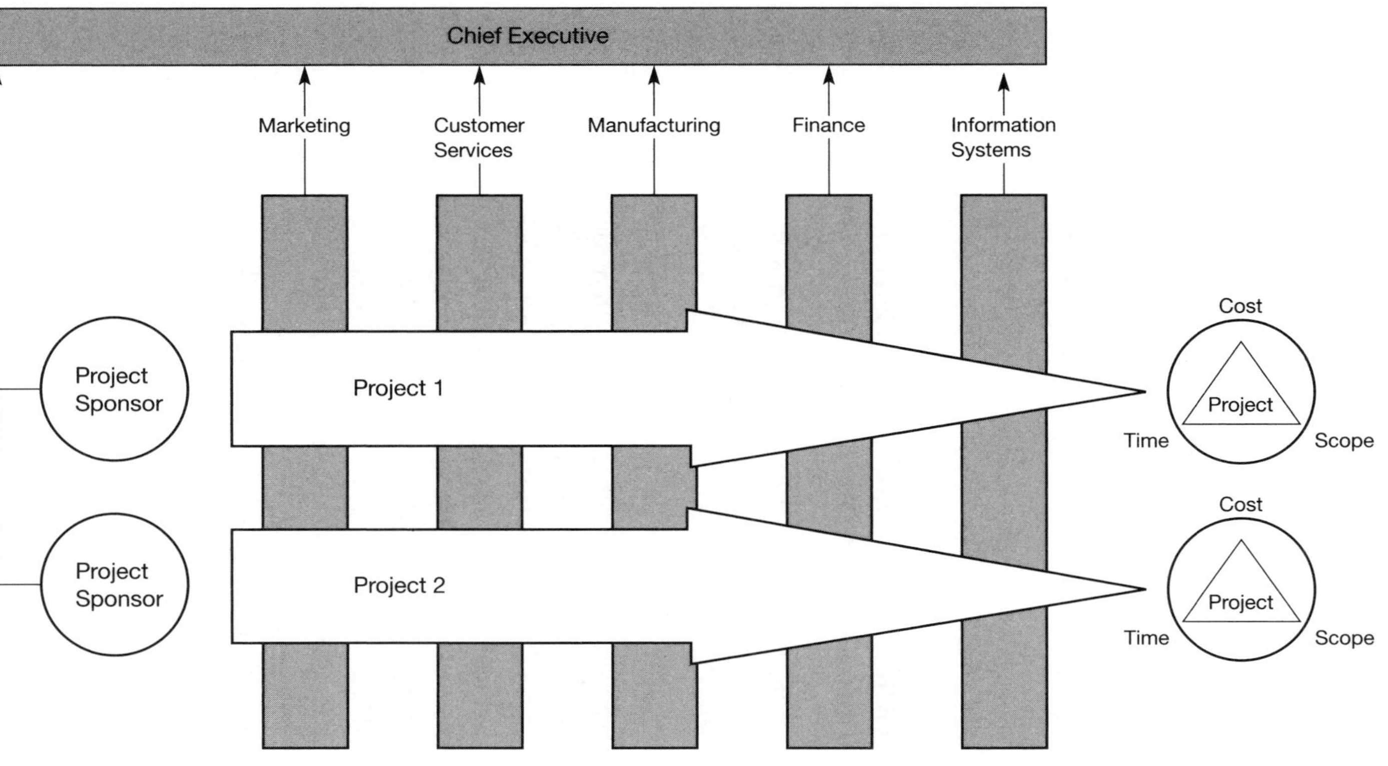

Figure 2.6 Working across functions
A project is a set of activities aligned to achieve a defined result. It draws in people from across the company who provide their particular expertise and knowledge.

conflict. For example, one company found that team members on the same project received different levels of bonuses merely because they belonged to different departments. They also found the key performance indicators for departments were no less problematic and had built-in conflicts.

The more functionally structured a company is, the more difficult it is to implement effective project management.

The more functionally structured a company is, the more difficult it is to implement effective project management. This is because project management, by its nature, crosses functional boundaries. To make projects succeed, the balance of power usually needs to be tipped toward the project and away from line management. (See Figure 2.11.)

7. Use dedicated resources for each category of development and prioritize within each category

> *"We thought long and hard about ring fencing (dedicating) resources and decided, for us, it was the best way to minimise internal conflict."*

The management and allocation of resources was acknowledged by many companies to be a problem. There is often continual competition for scarce resources between projects. One company said that at one time this had reached such a level that it was proving destructive. The impact was often that too many projects were started and few were finished.

I discovered that this problem was dealt with in two separate ways, both of which have their merits.

The first (Figure 2.7) is to apply dedicated (separate) resources for each category of project (say, aligned around a business unit) and take this principle as deep as possible into the company. In this way the potential conflicts are limited and the decisions and choices are more localized. In fact, the more separate and dedicated you make your resources, the more local your decision making can be, providing a project only needs to draw resource from that single pool. The down side of such an approach is that you will have to continually reorganize and resize your resource pools to meet demand. In a fast moving industry this can mean you may have the right number of people but they may be deployed in the wrong places. It can lead to continuous, expensive reorganizations. Most traditional, functionally organized companies follow this approach.

The second extreme is to have all staff in a single pool (shared) and to use effective matrix management support tools for resource allocation and forecasting (Figure 2.8). This method was adopted by the consulting

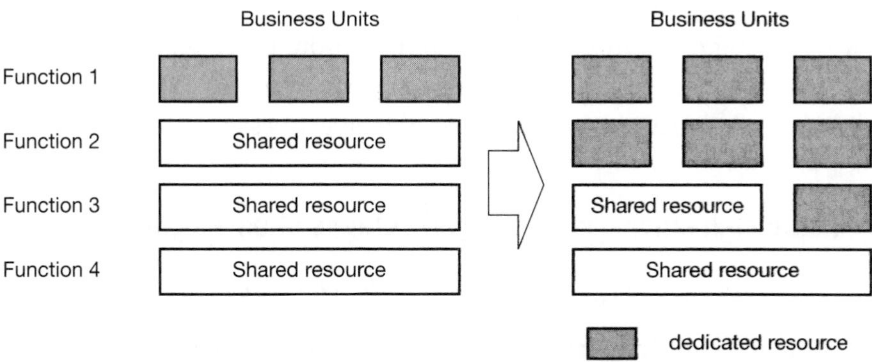

Figure 2.7 Apply dedicated resource to each project portfolio (e.g. by strategic business unit, market sector) as deeply as possible
Some companies, as a result of their organizational structure, share most of their resources across a number of categories. This allows them to deploy the most appropriate people to any project regardless of where they are in the organization. It also ensures that there is little duplication of functions within the company. Other organizations separate their resource to a greater extent, and confine it to working on a single business unit's projects. This allows quicker and more localized resource management but can lead to duplication of functional capabilities.

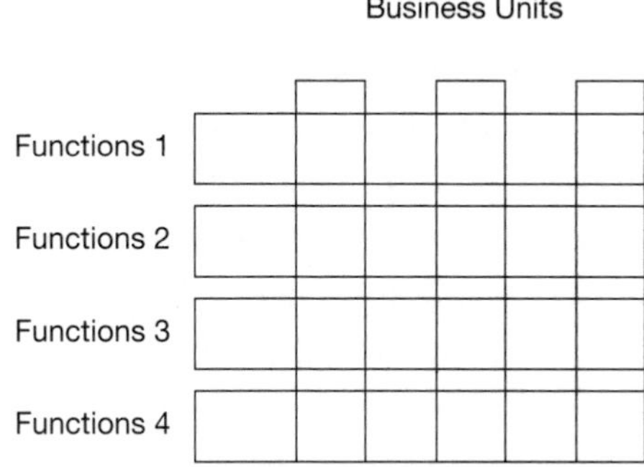

Figure 2.8 Resources from all functions are applied anywhere, to best effect
In this model anyone from any function can work on any project. It is the most flexible way of organizing but, without good control systems, is the most complex.

and engineering companies. In one case a person may work on up to ten projects in a week and there may be 300 projects in progress at any one time. It is very effective, conceptually simple, and totally flexible. Major reorganizations are less frequent but it is also the most difficult to implement in a company which has a strong functional management bias.

In practice, a hybrid between the two extremes will provide the simplicity of purely functionally based companies with the flexibility of full matrix-managed companies. The implication is, however, that the resource management and accounting systems must be able to view the company in a consistent way from both perspectives.

8. Place high emphasis on the early stages of development

"Skipping the first stage is a driver for failure."

All companies see the early stages of a project as fundamental to success. Some could not stress this enough. High emphasis for some meant that between 30 to 50 percent of the project life is spent on the investigative stages before any final deliverable is physically built. One American company had research data explicitly stating that this emphasis significantly decreased time to completion. Good investigative work means clearer objectives and plans; work spent on this is rarely wasted. Decisions taken at the early stages of a project have a far reaching effect and set the tone for the remainder of the project. In the early stages, creative solutions can slash delivery times in half and cut costs dramatically. However, once development is under way, it is rarely possible to effect savings of anything but a few percent. Good upfront work also reduces the likelihood of change later, as most changes on projects are actually reactive to misunderstandings over scope and approach rather than proactive decisions to change the project for the better. The further you are into the project the more costly change becomes.

All companies see the early stages of a project as fundamental to success.

Despite this, there is often pressure, for what appear to be all the right commercial reasons, to skip the investigative stages and "get on with the real work" as soon as possible. Two companies interviewed had found

Two companies interviewed had found through bitter experience that you can't go any faster by missing out essential work.

through bitter experience that you can't go any faster by missing out essential work. One told me that "skipping the investigative stages led to failure"; the other: "Whenever we've tried to leave a bit out for the sake of speed, we've always failed and had to do more extensive rework later which cost us far in excess of anything we might have saved."

9. Build the business case into the company's forward plan as soon as the project has been formally approved

Projects are the vehicles for implementing future strategic change and revenue generation for a company. The best companies are always sure that the projects they are undertaking will produce what they need and that they fit the company's wider objectives. In all cases, companies had far more proposals for projects than they could handle. It is, therefore, essential to know what future resources (cash, manpower, etc.) have already been committed and what benefits (revenues, cost savings, etc.) are expected. Unless this is done the "gap" between where the company is now and where it wants to be is not known and so the choice of projects to fill the gap is made more difficult (Figure 2.9).

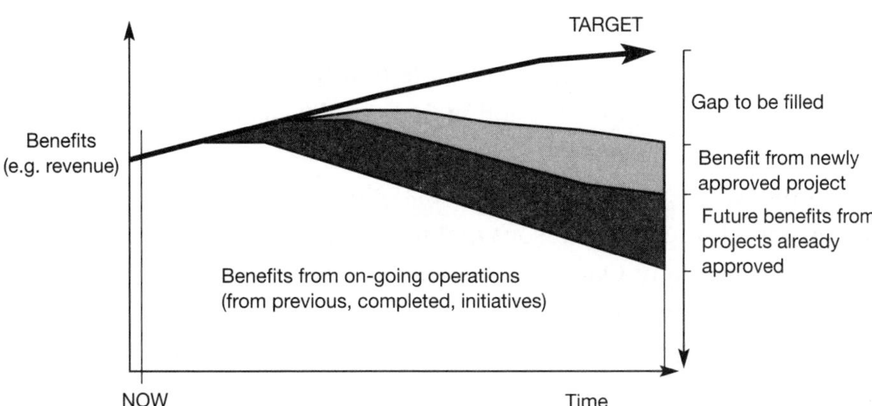

Figure 2.9 Build the project into your business plan as soon as it is authorized

The figure shows the revenue which will be generated by the company if no new projects are started. It then shows the revenue which will be generated by projects which are currently in progress. The gap between the sum of these and the target revenue needs to be filled. This can be by starting off new projects which will cause this to be generated or/and by starting initiatives in the line which will deliver the extra revenue to fill the gap.

Companies handle this by having set points in the project life cycle at which cost and benefit streams are built into the business plan. This is usually as soon as each project is authorized.

Clearly, financial planning, and resource systems must be able to be updated at any time as projects do not recognize fiscal quarters as relevant to start or finish dates. Also, any such project systems must be seen as a part of the business and not be seen as an "add-on" outside the usual pattern of planning, forecasting, and accounting.

10. Close the project formally to build a bridge to the future, to learn any lessons, and to ensure a clean handover

Closing projects formally is for some companies essential. For example, architectural companies must close the project accounts down to ensure that no more time is spent working on projects which are finished, no matter how interesting! Their margins simply won't allow this luxury. Similarly, component products in an aircraft can be in service long after the project team has dispersed or even well after some team members have retired! Not to have full records (resurrection documents) on these critical components for times of need is unthinkable.

All the companies interviewed either have a formal closure procedure or were actively implementing one. This usually takes the form of a closure report which highlights any outstanding issues, ensures explicit handover of accountabilities, and makes it quite clear to those who need to know that the project is finished.

Another key reason given for formal closure was that it provides an opportunity for learning lessons and improving the processes and workings of the company. One company left "closure" out of its process in the original design, but soon realized it was vital and added it in. It simply found that if it did not close projects, the list of projects it was doing was just growing by the day.

REVIEW OF THE TEN LESSONS

1. As a management team for the business, review the ten lessons given in this chapter and ask yourself how well you apply them in your organization at present. Agree a mark out of 10 and mark the relevant column with an "X."

   10 = we currently apply this lesson fully across our company and can demonstrate this with ease.

   0 = this is not applied at all.

2. Ask the project managers of, say, five of your projects to answer the same questions. Plot their answers with "P."

3. Ask the line managers of a number of your functions to answer the same questions. Plot their answers with "L."

4. Discuss, as a management team, the responses. Compare the answers you receive from the different stakeholder groups. Are there differences? If so, why do you think this is? Which lessons are not being applied? Why not?

5. What do you propose to do about this?

	POOR									EXCELLENT
Lesson	0	1	2	3	4	5	6	7	8	9	10
1 Make sure your projects are driven by benefits which support your strategy.											
2 Use the same, simple, and well defined framework, with a staged approach, for all projects in all circumstances.											
3 Address and revalidate the marketing, commercial, operational, and technical viability of the project throughout its life.											
4 Incorporate stakeholders into the project to understand their current and future needs.											
5 Build excellence in project management techniques and controls across the company.											
6 Break down functional boundaries by using cross-functional teams.											
7 Use dedicated resources for each category of development and prioritize within each category.											
8 Place high emphasis on the early stages of development.											
9 Build the business case into the company's forward plan as soon as the project has been formally approved.											
10 Close the project formally to build a bridge to the future, to learn any lessons, and to ensure a clean handover.											

But we're different!: organization context

Project processes only work if they are supported by compatible structures, culture, and systems (Figure 2.10). The previous sections in this chapter described how many companies used or were moving toward a staged project framework, but that the environments in which they operate are entirely different. So, when you hear the plaintive cry of "this won't work here, we're different!," you can confidently answer "yes, we are different but we can make it work if we really want to."

The following sections describe some of the wide range of approaches taken by different companies. Because of the intimate inter-relationship between process, systems, structure, and culture it not always easy to categorize this discussion into those "subjects"; this serves to underline the main message.

Structure

Organization structures vary from pure project to pure functional; this impacts the ease of cross-functional working and project management. Figure 2.11 shows the range of organization shapes and the effect they tend to have on project management. In heavily functionally driven companies, project managers are generally very weak, disempowered, and at the mercy of the functional heads of department. They are often called "project coordinators" which is very apt. In full project organizations, the project managers have greater power and influence over and above heads of department. In the middle is matrix management. This is a much maligned structure but one which can be very effective in organizations

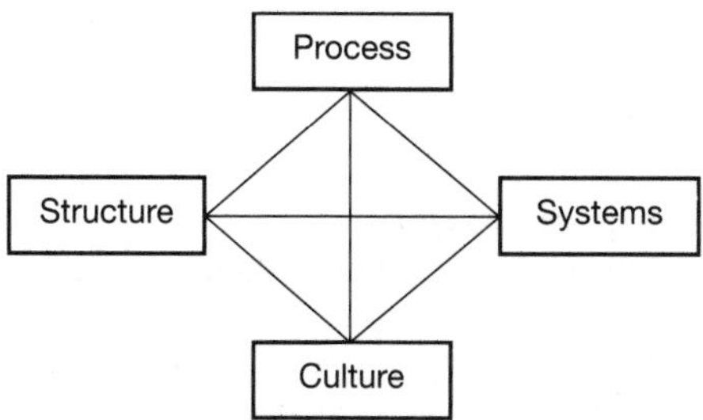

Figure 2.10 The organizational context for project management and other processes

which require a relatively stable functional structure but still need to have the advantages of a cross-functional project approach. It has often been said "matrices don't work, they just confuse." Yes, that's probably true if they are attempted in an environment with no suitable controls, and incompatible line and project processes. Generally, those companies which have moved the balance of power away from the line and towards the project, have found project management and cross-functional working more effective and reap greater rewards.

The acceptance of clear definitions of roles, accountabilities and relationships for the key players are most apparent with those companies which are comfortable with their processes. Further, the separation of "role" from job description is seen as crucial to maintaining simplicity as, in cross-functional, project environments, the role a person takes (e.g. as project sponsor or project manager) is more important than the job title or position in the functional hierarchy.

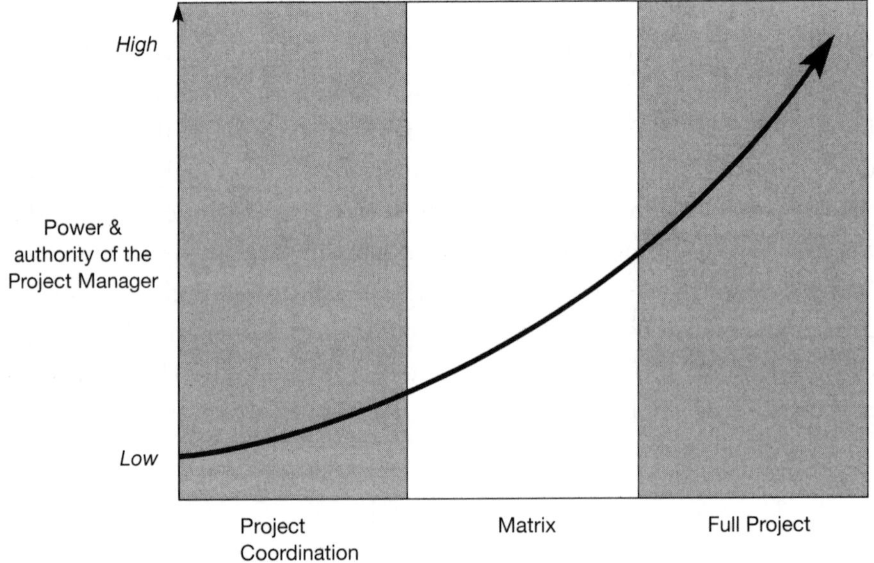

Figure 2.11 Project organizations
Companies can structure themselves with differing emphasis on line and project management authority. When the most power is invested in line management, project managers are reduced to a "coordination" role. In full project structures, the project manager has greater power than the line manager. The line manager is there to satisfy the resourcing needs of the projects and business as usual processes only. The mid-point between these extremes is the "matrix," where there is a balance of power which is derived from the role someone takes as well as their position in the line.

Some companies set up cross-functional groups to undertake particular tasks on an on-going basis. The most obvious are those groups which undertake the screening of proposals prior to entry to the project process. In this way the structures created match the process (rather than leading or following the process). This must also apply to any review or decision-making bodies which are created. The one most commonly found to be adrift is that relating to financial authorizations. Many companies have almost parallel financial processes shadowing their project processes, demanding similar but different justifications and descriptions of projects. This is usually found where finance functions have disproportionate power and act as controllers rather than in an assurance mode. The better companies ensured that there was little divergence between decisions required for finance and those relating to strategy. They make certain that financial expertise is built into the project in the same way as any other discipline, with finance people being included on the project team.

Projects are "temporary" and cease to exist once completed. Clear accountability for on-going management of the outputs in the line ensures that the right people are involved in the project and that the hand-over is clean and explicit. Career progression and continuity of employment for people involved in projects must be a top consideration. Projects are about change and about the future of your company. Good organizations ensure that the people who create these changes are retained and that projects are not seen as career limiting and the fast track to redundancy. You need your best people to create your future company, not the "leftovers" from running yesterday's company.

You need your best people to create your future company, not the "leftovers" from running yesterday's company.

Culture

Culture is probably the least reproducible facet of a company and the most intangible. It does, however, have a very significant impact on how projects are carried out and how project management is implemented.

For example, the corporate attitude to risk and the way a company behaves if high-risk projects have to be stopped will have far reaching effects on the quality of the outputs produced. In avionics the "least risk" approach is generally preferred to the "least cost" despite being within an industry in which accepting the lowest tender is a primary driver.

One company interviewed explicitly strives to make its own products obsolete as it clearly sees itself as a product leader. It is forever initiating new projects to build better products quicker and more frequently than the competition. This same company focusses its rewards on teams, not individuals, and takes great care to ensure its performance measurement systems avoid internal conflict. Another company admitted that its bonus schemes were all based on functional performance and not team performance despite 60 percent of the staff working cross-functionally. An example was given of a staff member who received no bonus for his year's work, but all his colleagues on the the same project (in a different department!) had large bonuses. This was not seen as "fair," and was the result of basing bonuses on something that could be counted easily rather than on something that actually counted!

Another company has no bonus scheme below senior management level but provides "Well Done" awards (financial) for individuals whom they consider merit them. These are given almost immediately after the event which prompted the award and are well appreciated. This same company also has 100 percent employee ownership and salesmen who are not commissioned.

Most of the companies interviewed encouraged direct access to decision makers as it improves the quality of decisions. Project roles, rather than "job descriptions" promote this. Functional hierarchies tend to have a greater "power distance" and decision makers become remote from the effects of their actions or the issues involved.

As a paradox, those companies which have the most comprehensive control systems (project accounting, resource management, time sheeting, etc.) are able to delegate decision making lower in the organization. Senior management do not lose sight of what is happening, and always know who is accountable.

A major producer of project scheduling software confided in me that when it came to managing its own internal business projects, all the good practice and advice the company advocated as essential to its customers was ignored. The culture of the company's management simply does not fit the product it sells. Companies can be very successful without any rational approach to business projects but are unlikely to remain successful for long.

WHAT HAPPENS TO PROJECT MANAGERS IN YOUR ORGANIZATION WHEN THE PROJECT IS FINISHED?

2.2

(a) They are kept on the payroll and assigned to a manager for "pay and rations" until a new project or suitable alternative work is found.

(b) They are put on a redeployment list and then made redundant if no suitable opening is found for them within x months.

(c) They leave the company straightaway if no suitable opening is found for them.

(d) They leave the company.

(e) I don't have this problem as they are all contracted in when needed.

If you answered (b) to (d) you are probably very functionally driven and projects tend to be difficult to undertake.

If you answered (e) you may be in a very fortunate position to be able to source such key people OR you are in the same situation as (b) to (d).

If you answered (a) you are probably in a good position to reap the rewards of project working or are already doing so!

Debate with your colleagues: what motivates your staff to work on projects?

If you answered (b) to (d), do you really expect to have your best people volunteering to work on projects?

Systems

A number of companies stated that the accounting systems must serve to integrate process, project and line management. Projects must not be seen as an "add-on."

Resource management and allocation was found to be a problem for many companies. Those which found least difficulty centrally managed their entire resource across all their departments so that the departments and the projects used the same core system; only the reporting emphasis was different.

Other companies had developed systems to cope with what they saw as their particular needs; for example, risk management or action tracking.

The American companies had also developed the practice of constantly validating their processes and systems through benchmarking.

Conclusion

The benchmarking study confirmed that:

- The staged framework is widely used for business change projects and is delivering better value than more traditional functionally based project processes. This is discussed further in Part Two of the book.
- A cross-functional, project management-based approach is essential. This is discussed further in Part Four of the book.

What is apparent is that the infrastructure which makes the projects work varies considerably, in particular the level of information that decision makers have to support them. For example, it is usually relatively easy to decide if a project in isolation is viable or not. However, if you are to decide which of a number of projects should go ahead based on relative benefits, answers to the following questions are needed:

- What overall business objectives is the project driving toward?
- On what other projects does this project depend?
- What other projects depend on this project?
- When will we have the capacity to undertake the project (in terms of people and other resources)?

- Can the business accept this change together with all the other changes being imposed? If so, when?
- Do we have enough cash to carry out the project?
- After what length of time will the project cease to be viable?
- How big is the overall risk of the full project portfolio with/without this project?

The challenge lies in having systems, structures, and a culture which address these, both at a working level and at the decision-making level. If this is not addressed it will result in:

- the wrong projects being undertaken;
- late delivery;
- failure to achieve expected benefits.

This will be in spite of having excellent processes and tools at an individual project level. These questions are discussed in Part Three of this book.

> In one company, it was not unusual to find directors reporting to graduates on projects. The directors are on the project teams to add their particular knowledge and skills and not to lead the project. This company saw nothing strange about this arrangement. The most appropriate people were being used in the most appropriate way.

Reorganizing isn't always the answer!

Quotation from Gaius Petronius Arbiter, AD66

ENEMIES WITHIN

Running a project is difficult enough, but we often make it more arduous than it need be by creating problems for ourselves. Here are a few examples:

Reorganizing – either the company or a part of it. Tinkering with your structure is usually NOT the solution to your problems, it just confuses people. The Romans realized this 2,000 years ago (see cartoon). If however you are a senior executive, this is a great way to hide non-delivery!

Functional thinking – not taking the helicopter, the company-wide view. This often happens when executives' or individuals' bonuses are based on targets which are at odds with the company's needs e.g. sales bonus rewarded on revenue, regardless of profit or contribution.

Having too many rules – the more rules you have, the more sinners you create and the less happy your people become. Have you ever met a happy bureaucrat?

Disappearing and changing sponsors – without a sponsor there should be no project. Continual changing of the "driver" will cause you to lose focus and forget WHY you are undertaking the project. Consider terminating such a project to see who really wants it!

Ignoring the risks – risks don't go away, so acknowledge them and manage them. If I said that a certain airplane is likely to crash, would you fly on it? And yet, every day executives approve projects when a simple risk analysis shows they are highly likely to fail.

Dash in and get on with it! – if a project is that important, you haven't the time NOT to plan your way ahead. High activity levels do not necessarily mean action or progress.

Analysis paralysis – you need to investigate, but only enough to gain the confidence to move on. This is the opposite to dash in and ignore the risks. It is also a ploy used to delay projects: ". . . I haven't quite enough information to make a decision, just do some more study work."

Untested assumptions – all assumptions are risks; treat them as such.

Forgetting what the project is for – if this happens terminate the project. If it is that useful, someone will scream and remember why it is being done.

Executive's "pet projects" – have no exceptions. If an executive's idea is really so good, it should stand up to the scrutiny that all the others go through. He or she may have a helicopter view, but he might also have his head in the clouds.

Part Two

A WALK THROUGH A PROJECT

"How narrow is the line which separates an adventure from an ordeal."

HAROLD NICHOLSON

In this part I will explain the management framework for a single project, taking it from being an idea through the various life cycle stages until benefits start being delivered to your business:

- **Make sure that your projects are driven by benefits which support your strategy.**
- **Manage your projects within a staged framework.**
- **Place high emphasis on the early stages.**
- **Treat gates as "entry" points to stages, not "exit" points.**
- **Address and revalidate the business aspects of the project throughout its life.**

How to use Part Two

Chapters 3 and 4 are for you to read and understand. The workouts are designed to help you place the project framework in the context of the projects you undertake in your business.

Chapters 5 to 11 comprise a skeleton project management framework. In these chapters, I explain what happens during each stage of a project and who is accountable. You can use these directly or adopt and adapt them to meet the particular needs and language you have in your company. Each chapter describes a set of "control documents" for that stage: the content for these is given on the CD-ROM. Each chapter concludes with a project workout in order to review any projects you currently have: choose the workout which matches most closely the life cycle stage of your project. Appendix C contains some ideas of how to construct your processes in practice.

In the final chapters (12 and 13) I take this basic framework and show how you can apply the principles of the staged approach to match diverse business situations.

How to use Part Two

The Project Framework
an Overview of its Gates and Stages

Projects as vehicles of change

Stages and gates

The project framework

Some key questions

How can I apply the framework?

Project management is still seen as a specialist discipline requiring special people who are difficult to find and to retain. While this is to a certain extent true, a scarcity of "project managers" should not be a barrier to any organization starting to develop a "projects" approach to managing its own future.

"The Golden Rule is that there is no golden rule."
GEORGE BERNARD SHAW

Projects as vehicles of change

"Projects" are rapidly becoming the way organizations should manage change, and this applies not only to traditional activities such as large construction projects, but also to any change initiative aimed at putting a part of your business strategy into action. Projects, in the modern sense, are strategic management tools and you ignore the newly reborn discipline of enterprise-wide project management at your peril. It is fast becoming a core competence which many organizations require their employees and leaders to have. It is no longer the preserve of specialists and the engineering sector, but an activity for everyone. The problem is that most people simply do not have the right skills. Project management is still seen as a specialist discipline requiring special people who are difficult to find and to retain. While this is to a certain extent true, a scarcity of "project managers" should not be a barrier to any organization starting to develop a "projects" approach to managing its future. Project management is simply applied common sense. All organizations say that their most important asset is their people (although the shareholders may be more interested in the balance sheet), but no company, however excellent, has a monopoly on "good people"; they are simply much better at getting "ordinary" people to perform in an extraordinary way and their few "extraordinary" people to perform beyond expectations. These companies provide an environment which enables this to happen. Add to this a few, well chosen project experts and you have a sound foundation for generating successful projects.

Projects, in the modern sense, are strategic management tools, and you ignore the newly reborn discipline of project management at your peril. It is fast becoming a core competence which many organizations require their employees and leaders to have. It is no longer the preserve of specialists and the engineering sector, but an activity for everyone.

Well managed projects will enable you to react and adapt speedily to meet the challenges of your competitive environment, ensuring you drive toward an attainable, visible, corporate goal. Most companies are never short of good ideas for improvement and your own is probably no exception. Ideas can come from anywhere within the company or even outside it: from competitors, customers, or suppliers. However, deciding which of all these good ideas you should actually spend time and money on is not easy. You must take care in choosing which projects you do, as:

- you probably don't have enough money, manpower, or management energy to pursue all of your ideas;
- undertaking projects which you cannot easily reconcile with your company's strategy will, almost certainly, create internal conflicts between projects, confuse the direction of the business, and, ultimately, reduce the return on your company's investment.

You should consider for selection only those projects which:

- deliver real benefits;
- meet defined business needs;
- are derived from gaps identified in business plans;
- have a firm root in your strategy (see p. 17).

Having created a shortlist of "possible projects" it is important you work on them in the right order, recognizing interdependencies, sharing scarce resources and bringing the benefits forward whenever possible.

Figure 3.1 shows this in a diagram. Selecting the right projects will help you achieve your business objectives by delivering benefits which support your strategy. Two key roles are associated with projects:

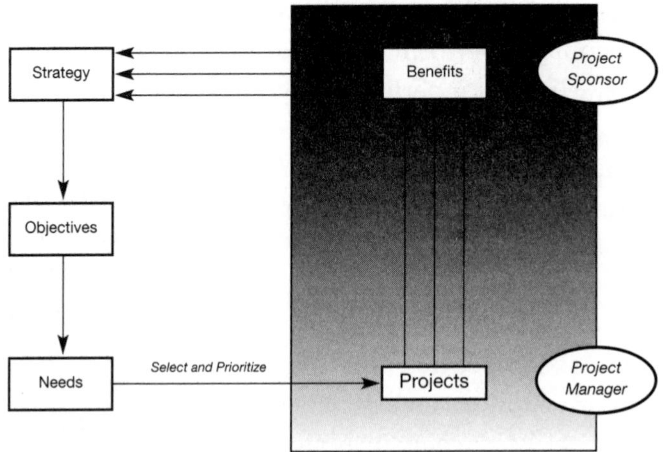

Figure 3.1 Select the right projects to support your strategy
Selecting the right projects will help you achieve your objectives by delivering benefits that will support your strategy. (Copyright © PA Consulting Group, London. Adapted with kind permission)

The project sponsor is the person who wants the benefits the project will provide.

The project manager is the person who manages the project on a day-to-day basis, ensuring that its deliverables are presented on time, at the right quality and to budget.

A simple illustration of these key project roles is that you may want to build an extension to your house that will give you a fully equipped den and/or home office. You want the benefits that will accrue. You and your family do not want all the dust, debris, and inconvenience that construction will entail, but you accept this is the price (together with the monetary cost) you are willing to pay in order to obtain the benefits you seek. By the same token, the architect is more interested in designing and seeing constructed an elegant and appropriate solution that will meet your needs. As project manager, he is not fundamentally interested in the benefits you seek, but rather in the benefits he receives for carrying out the work (his fee). He must, however, understand your needs fully so that he can deliver an appropriate solution. In a good partnership, sponsorship and management are mutually compatible. Thus:

- the **project sponsor** is "benefits focussed";
- the **project manager** is "action and delivery focussed."

The framework for managing business-led projects is aimed at making the results of projects more predictable by:

- being benefits focussed;
- building in quality;
- managing risks and exposure;
- exploiting the skill base of your company.

As a project proceeds over time, the amount of money invested in it increases. If none of this money is spent on reducing the risks associated with the project then it is poorly spent. Your objective is to ensure that risks are driven down as the project moves from being an idea to becoming a reality (see also pp. 18, 28).

Figure 3.2 demonstrates this. The investigative stages are crucial and you should hold back any development work until your investigations show you know what you are doing and have proved that the risks are acceptable.

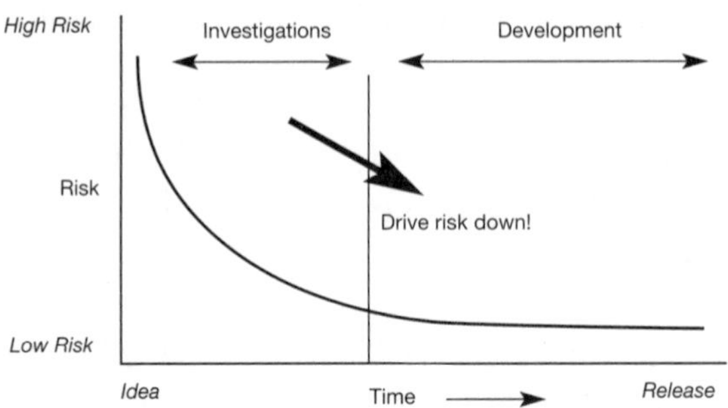

Figure 3.2 Managing the risk
The investigative stages are crucial and you should hold back any development work until your investigations show you know what you are doing and have proved that the risks are acceptable.

You do this by using a staged approach where each stage serves as a launch pad for the subsequent stage. In this book I have used five stages, but other models are equally acceptable if they suit the environment and culture of your company.

Stages and gates

Stages

Stages are specific periods during which work on the project takes place. These are when information is collected and outputs created.

For each stage in the project, you should carry out the full range of work covering the entire scope of functional inputs required (Figure 3.3). These functions should not work on the project in isolation but in a continuous dialog with each other, thus enabling the best overall solution to be developed. In this way your knowledge develops and increases on all fronts at a similar pace, and solutions are designed, built, and tested in an integrated way. No one area of work should advance ahead of the others. Your solution will not be what is merely optimal for one function alone but will be a pragmatic solution which is best for your company as a whole. This has the benefits of shortcutting the functional hierarchies, enabling the flat, lean structures we all seek to attain

Your solution will not be what is merely optimal for one function alone but will be a pragmatic solution which is best for your company as a whole.

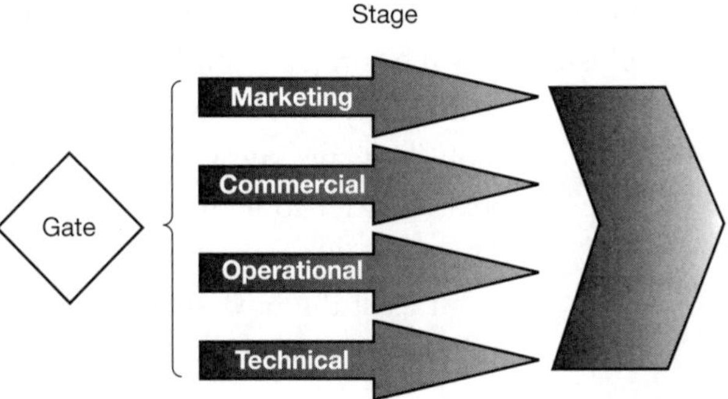

Figure 3.3 Address all aspects of the project in parallel
For each stage in the project, you should carry out the full range of work covering the entire scope of functional inputs required. In this way your knowledge develops and increases on all fronts at a similar pace and solutions are designed, built, and tested in an integrated way.

to work in practice as it forces people with different perspectives to work together, rather than apart. The business of the future, that is created and built using a cross-functional team, will find it much easier to run the all-encompassing cross-functional processes that business process re-engineers tell us is the way forward. Further, you should limit the work undertaken in any stage to that which is needed at the next gate: there is little point in spending effort and money until you need to.

RUNAWAY HORSES AND CATTLE DRIVES

A project is not a horse race, where the individual departments and functions are horses, each competing to see who can finish first. Projects are more like a cattle drive where all the cattle must complete the run to market in tip top condition. Some cattle will be faster and stronger (better resourced), other cattle are yoked together (by process and functional hierarchy). As drivers, we must ensure that some cattle do not get too far ahead and that others do not lag behind. We must also ensure that they aren't distracted by wolves (other projects) and scattered. But *please* don't take the analogy too far and start treating your people like cattle!

During each stage it is essential for the project manager to continuously forecast and reforecast the benefits, resources, and costs needed to complete the project. He/she should always keep the relevant functions informed, and check on behalf of the sponsor that the project still makes sound business sense. This is illustrated by the "project control cycle" in Figure 3.4.

Before you start work on any stage, you should always know what you are going to do next in order to increase your confidence and decrease risks.

Before you start work on any stage, you should always know what you are going to do next in order to increase your confidence and decrease risks; you should have a project plan for at least the next stage in detail and for the full project in summary.

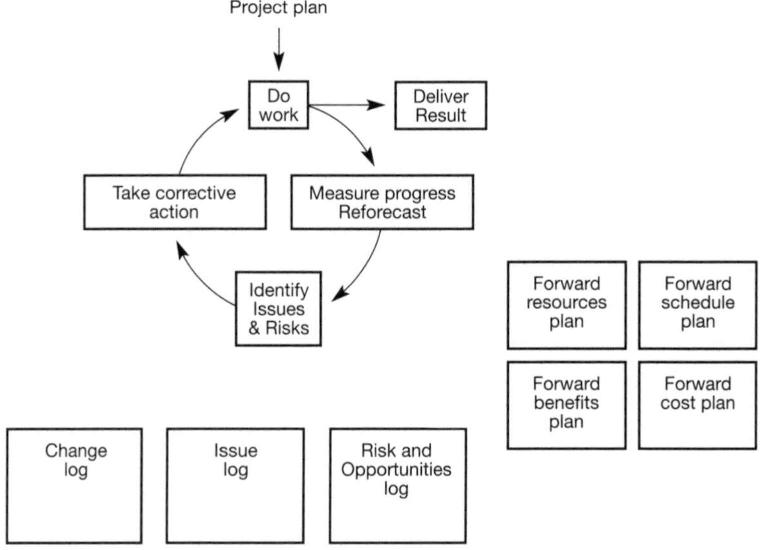

Figure 3.4 A typical stage

A stage may be represented by the project control cycle together with the key control tools you need to manage it (these are described in Part 4).

"An unwatched pot boils immediately."

H F ELLIS

Gates

Gates are the decision points which precede every stage. Unless specific criteria have been met, as evidenced by certain approved deliverables, the subsequent stage should not be started (see also p. 18). Gates serve as points to:

- check that the project is still required and the risks are acceptable;
- confirm its priority relative to other projects;
- agree the plans for the remainder of the project;
- make a go/no go decision regarding continuing the project.

You should not regard gates as "end of term exams," but rather the culmination of a period of continual assessment with the gates acting as formal review points.

Gate criteria are often repeated in consecutive gates to ensure that the same strands of the project are followed through as the project progresses. You should expect a greater level of confidence in the responses to the criteria, the further into the project you move.

At each gate you will need to answer three distinct questions (Figure 3.5):

- Is there a real need for this project and, in its own right, is it viable?
- What is its priority relative to other projects you wish to start?
- Do you have the funding to undertake the project?

It is convenient to think in terms of these questions because, in most organizations, discrete people or groups are needed to address each of them.

The first question concerns the viability of the project assuming no other constraints. Does it fit your strategy? Does it make business sense? Are the risks acceptable? You will see later on that this question is addressed by the "project sponsor."

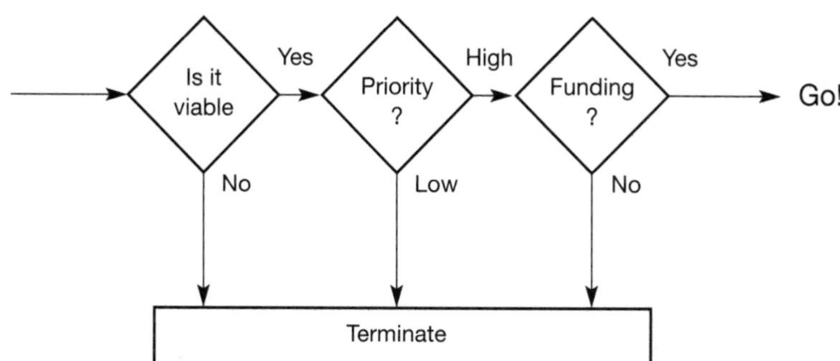

Figure 3.5 The three decisions required at each gate

The second question (priority) concerns the project in its context. It may be a very worthy project *but* how does it measure against all the other projects you want to do or are currently doing? Are there more worthwhile projects to address? Is it just "one more risk too far," bearing in mind what you are already committed to? This question is dealt with in Part Three where I will propose a basic method of managing such decisions.

The third question involves funding. Traditionally, businesses have discrete and very formal rules concerning the allocation of funds and which are generally managed by a finance function. So, you might have a viable project, it may be the best of those proposed BUT have you the working capital to finance it? This question is also dealt with in Part Three. If your finance function is less dominant, the funding question(s) come before the question of priority (2).

Gates – an end or a beginning?

Gates have traditionally been defined as end-points to the preceding stage. The logic is that the work in the stage culminates in a review (viz. end of stage assessment) where a check is done to ensure everything is complete before starting the next stage.

However, due to time pressures, it is often necessary to start the next stage before everything in the previous stage has been fully finalized. For example, in the typical framework in Figure 3.6, we see that it is sound sense to undertake a trial operation of our new output before all the process, training, and communication work is completed. What is essential is that we have sufficient work done to enable us to start the next stage with confidence. We are, therefore, left with the difficulty of having a traditional "rule" that common sense encourages us to break.

The solution to this dilemma is to treat gates as entry points to the next stage. In this way you can start the next stage (provided relevant criteria and checks have been done) as soon as you are ready, regardless of whether or not the full work scope of the previous stage has been completed. In this way, stages can overlap, reducing timescales, without increasing the risk associated with the project.

Treat gates as entry points to the next stage. In this way you can start as soon as you are ready, regardless of whether or not the previous stage has been completed.

This approach also opens another powerful characteristic of the staged framework. Gates are compulsory, stages are not. In other words, provided you have done the work needed to pass into a stage, how you arrived there is immaterial. This allows you to follow the strict principles of the staged process even if a stage is omitted. In Chapter 12, I will introduce the concept of "simple" projects and show how this principle enables them to be accommodated.

The project framework

As we have learned, projects draw on many resources from a wide range of functions within an organization. Ensuring these are focussed on achieving specific, identified benefits for the company is your key management challenge. You can increase the likelihood of success for your projects, and hence of your business, by following a project framework which:

- is benefit driven;
- is user and customer focussed;
- capitalizes on the skills and resources in the company;
- builds "quality" into the project deliverables;
- helps manage risk;
- allows many activities to proceed in parallel (hence greater velocity);
- is used by people across your whole organization.

As we have already seen in Part One (p. 17), sound approaches to tackling projects achieve all these objectives by breaking each project into series of generic stages and gates which form a framework within which every project in the organization can align itself.

This enables you to gain control of two key aspects of your business:

1 You know that each project is being undertaken in a rational way with the correct level of checks and balances at key points in its life.
2 You are able to view your entire portfolio of projects at a summary level and, by using the generic stage descriptions, know where each project is and the implication this has on risk and commitment.

The remainder of this part of the book concentrates on the "single" project (point 1) and takes you step by step through a framework you can use on your projects. Part Three will describe the management of portfolios of projects (point 2).

The project framework is shown in Figure 3.6 as a bar chart (see p. 58) and in Figure 3.7 as a diagrammatic overview. The stages are, briefly, as follows:

Identify the need – Proposal: a need is first formally recognized by describing it (i.e. say why you want to initiate a project). If known, you should also describe what you believe the project will produce (i.e. its output but don't jump to conclusions too soon).

Have a quick look – Initial Investigation Stage: the first stage in the project – a quick study of the proposal, to outline the scope and make a rough assessment of the possible ways of meeting the need, benefits, resources, and costs needed to complete it. At the end of this stage you should be sure of why you are doing it. You may also know what you are doing, although this may comprise a range of defined possibilities. You will know how to go about at least the next stage, if not the full project.

Have a closer look – Detailed Investigation Stage: a feasibility study, definition, and a full investment appraisal culminating in a decision to proceed with development work. At the end of this stage you will have high confidence in all aspects of the project and "What you wanted to do" becomes "What you are going to do!"

Do it! – Develop and Test Stage: the actual development and implementation work.

Try it – Trial Stage: a trial of all aspects of the development in the users' or customers' operational and working environment. What has been created may work very well under "test conditions," but does it work under normal operational conditions?

Use it – Release Stage: the last stage in the project when you unleash your creation on the world! This is when products are launched, new computer systems used, new manufacturing plant goes into production, new organization units start operating to the "new rules," new processes are invoked, acquisitions sealed, and disposals shed. The on-going operational aspects are embedded in the business and the project is formally recognized as complete.

About three to six months after completion, a check, known as a **Post-Implementation Review**, is done to see if the project is achieving its business objectives and its outputs are performing to the standards expected.

PORTFOLIOS, PROGRAMS, PHASES, STAGES, AND GATES

In this book I refer to STAGES and GATES as convenient descriptions for the periods when work is done and for the points in time when a check is made on the project prior to starting the next stage. Terminology often found in practice also includes:

For stage:	**For gate:**
Phase	Review
Step	Checkpoint
	Assessment

In this book, I reserve the use of the word **"phase"** to describe a project that is to be introduced or built with benefits designed to arrive in different time frames. For example, major roads projects are frequently introduced in phases so motorists can benefit from the first 20 miles built and do not have to wait for the full 80-mile stretch to be completed. Each phase is in fact a project in its own right and comprises a number of stages.

The word **"program"** is also problematic, much used and abused to the extent that it is often meaningless. For example I had a job title of "program manager," but I did not use it on my business cards as it did not tell anyone what I did; indeed it might even have misled them! I define a program as a tightly aligned but tightly coupled set of projects. Programs are discussed more fully in Chapter 13.

The word "program" is frequently used to bundle any projects together for the convenience of reporting, planning, or other management purpose. In this book I refer to these as a **"portfolio."** This is discussed further in Chapter 14.

In hierarchical terms the relationship is:

- the company project portfolio;
- program;
- project;
- phase;
- stage.

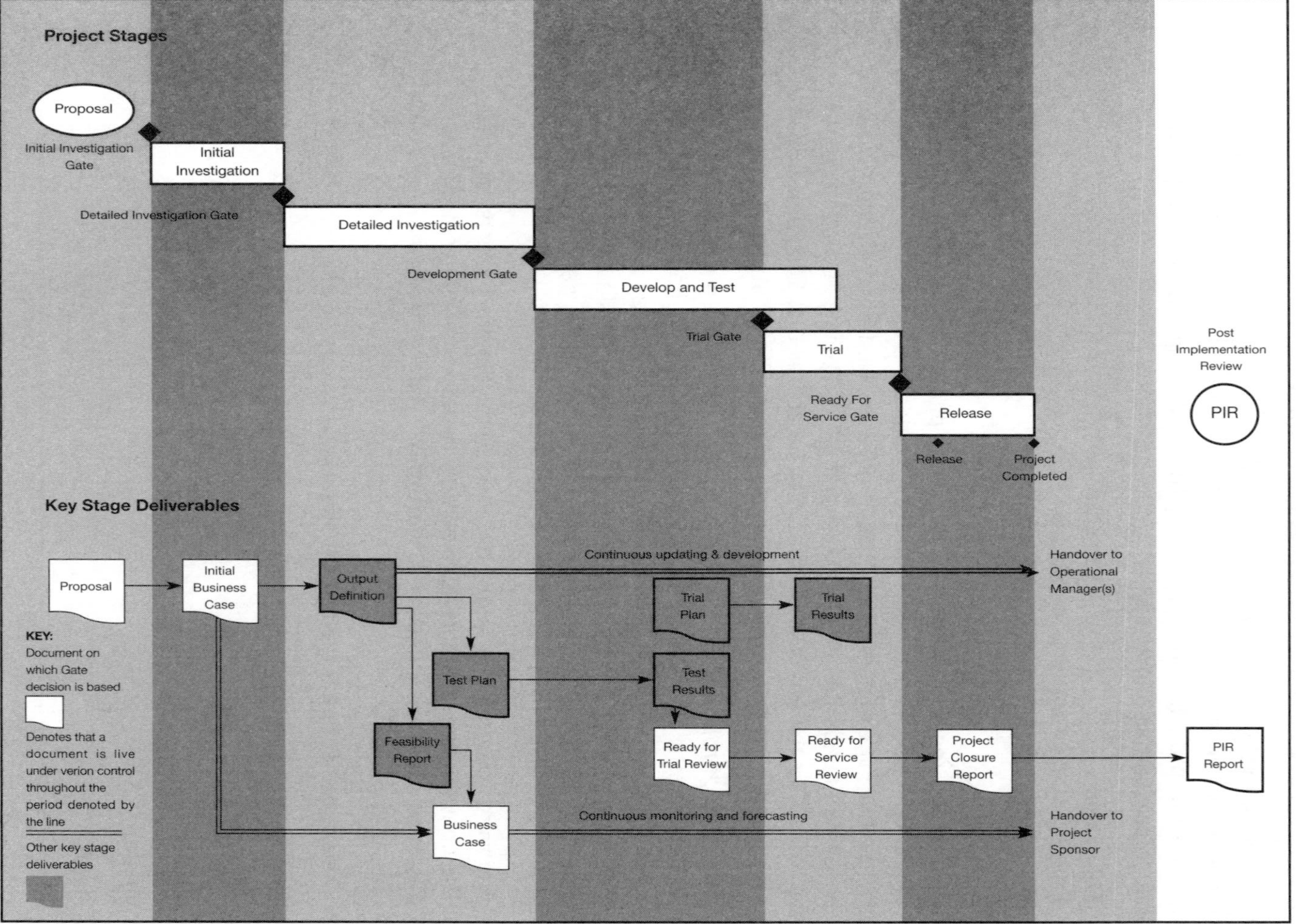

Figure 3.6 The project framework as a bar chart

The project framework is shown here in "bar chart format" at the top, with the project document deliverables for each stage shown below. These are described more fully in Chapters 5 to 11 ;see also Appendix B for more details on each document deliverable.

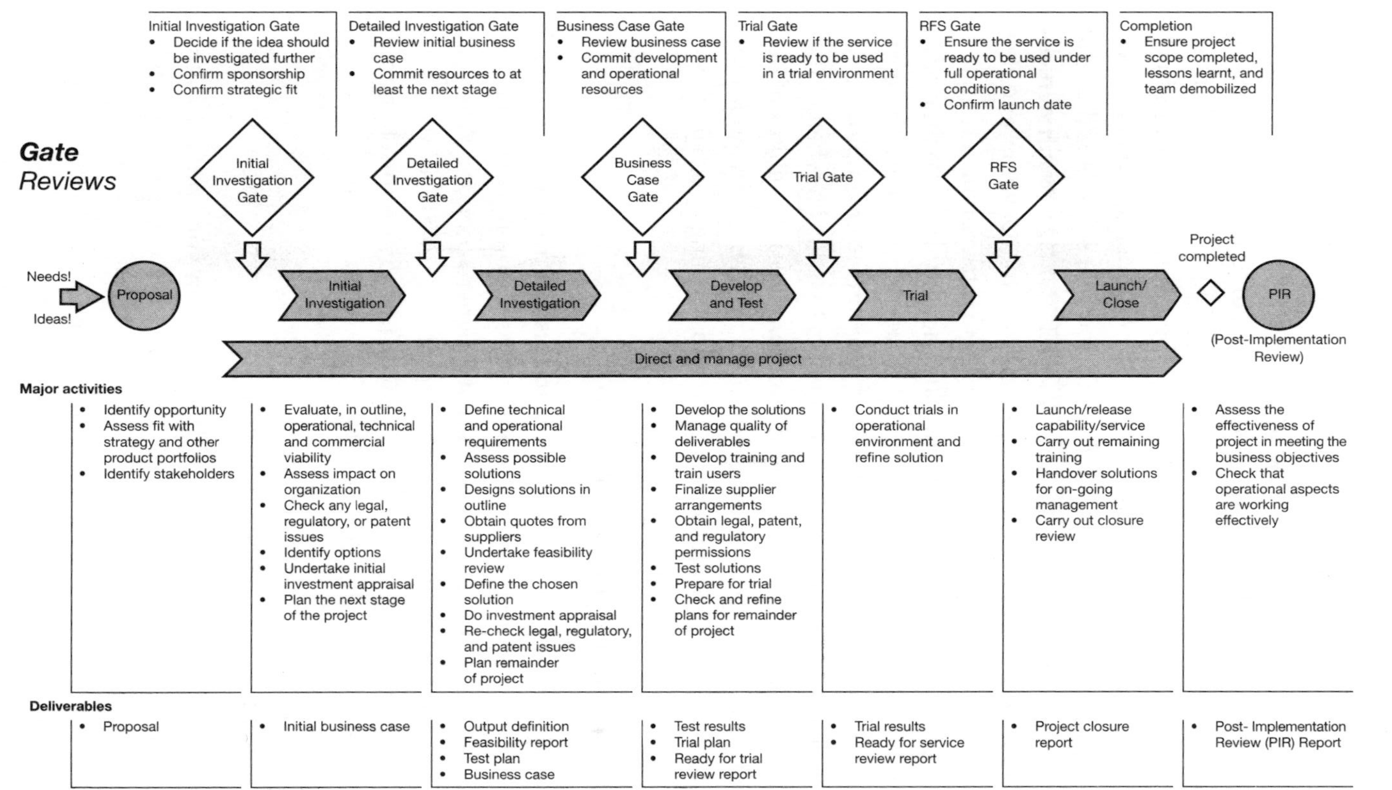

Figure 3.7 The project framework in diagrammatic form

The project framework is shown here in a format which clearly distinguishes between the gates and the stages. It also shows the activities and deliverables which relate to each stage.

Some key questions

How many stages should I have?

Consider the types of project you undertake in your business. Do they fit the generic stages described earlier? Are there some modifications you would like to make? Some organizations have only four stages, others six or more. Generally, the fewer the better, but they must be meaningful to you and fit every project you are likely to do. My experience is that five will fit most purposes, so if in doubt try five. Of the five stages used in this book, it is the Trial Stage which is often either left out (see "Is a trial really needed" later in this chapter) or merged in with the Develop and Test Stage. I prefer to have the trial as a distinct stage to differentiate it from testing. Testing is very much an internal, "private" activity. A trial on the other hand is "public" involving real users and customers. You are therefore open to poor press comment and to hostile reactions from employees. By making the trial a distinct stage you force people to focus on whether they really are ready. There have been enough high profile cases failures of beta tests on software and of premium automobiles receiving very poor press due to a poor state of market readiness to act as a warning to us all.

What should I call the stages and gates?

The stage and gate names I have chosen and used throughout this book have evolved over a number of years and are based on my experience of working in several companies on different business projects. What you choose to call them is up to you but that decision is not trivial. Words are emotive and hence can be both very powerful movers for change or inhibitors of change. In all companies there are words which:

- mean something particular to everyone;
- mean different things to different people.

You can build on the former by exploiting them in your project framework, provided the meaning is compatible with what you wish to achieve when using the words.

You should avoid the latter and choose different words, even making up new words if the dictionary cannot help you.

For example, working in one company I found the word "concept" problematic, despite its being very well defined and in the dictionary.

Stage names used in this book	*Possible alternatives*
Proposal "Identify the need"	Concept Initiation Ideation Idea generation
Initial Investigation "Have a quick look"	Pre-feasibility Initial assessment Preliminary investigation Evaluation Research
Detailed Investigation "Have a closer look"	Feasibility Definition Business case Evaluation Authorization
Develop and Test "Do it"	Implementation Execution Realization Develop Production Construction Build
Trial "Try it"	Beta test Validation Commissioning
Release "Use it"	Launch Completion Implementation Handover Acceptance
Post-Implementation Review	Business review Project audit Post Project review

"Concept" to some people was a high level statement of an idea (the meaning I wanted to convey), but to others it meant a detailed assessment of what has been decided should be done (this was not what I wanted). Rather than try to re-educate people in their everyday language, I found a word (proposal) which had no strong linkages to current use of language. There were similar problems with the word "implement": it had so many preconceived meanings that it was better not to use it at all! If you look at the list of possible names, you will notice that certain words appear in more than one place: this is a sure sign that they might be misunderstood.

The same issues apply to the naming of the gates. For these, however, it is often better to name each one according to the stage it precedes. This emphasizes the "gate as an entry point" concept. An alternative approach is to name the gate after the document which is used as the control on the gate. You will see I have mixed these. Again this is your choice, but make the same terminology apply across the whole organization.

Gate names used in this book	*Possible alternatives*
Initial Investigation Gate	Concept gate Proposal gate Initiation gate
Detailed Investigation Gate	Feasibility gate Evaluation gate
Development Gate	Business case gate Authorization gate Implementation gate Execution gate
Trial Gate	Beta gate Validation gate Commissioning gate
Ready for Service Gate	Operation gate Implementation gate Handover gate
Project completed	Closure gate Project end gate

How do I decide what work is done in the investigative stages?

The investigative stages exist in order to reduce risk (see Figure 3.2). Therefore everything you do should have that aim. If any proposed activity does not reduce risk, you should consider postponing it to a later stage.

Is a trial really needed?

"I have already tested this rigorously. Surely I don't really need to trial it all as well? Won't this just delay the benefits?"

This is a very valid question. The answer, as always, is "yes and no." Assume you have a choice of strategy from:

- product leadership;
- operational efficiency;
- customer intimacy.

(1) Under "product leadership" you are developing and delivering innovative, new products and services; you must be sure they really work as intended.

(2) Under "operational efficiency" you deliver what others deliver but more efficiently and at lower cost.

(3) Under "customer intimacy" you provide an experience for your customers such that they want to do business with you.

Thus, if your strategy is to have any practical meaning you must be sure that anything you do does not compromise it. The choice of "to trial or not to trial" comes down to risk. What is the likely impact on your business if this goes wrong? How confident are you that it won't go wrong? With this in mind, you may choose to subject certain aspects to a trial more rigorously than others – balancing the speed to benefits delivery with the risks.

Always assume that you need a trial. Omit it only if you have proved to yourself and your stakeholders that it will not add any value to your project. Never skip the trial because you are in a hurry! If in doubt, try it out.

Always assume that you need a trial. Omit it only if you have proved to yourself and your stakeholders that it will not add any value to your project.

If in doubt, try it out.

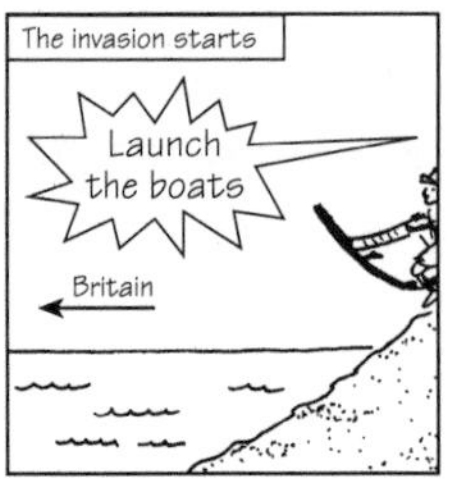

YOUR CURRENT BUSINESS PROJECTS

3.1

List the business projects you are undertaking at present in your organization. Based on the simple descriptions just given, state which stage of the project life cycle each project is at. If you find a project is in a number of stages, note which gate was most recently passed.

How can I apply the framework?

The staged approach is the framework for the management of any type of project, for any purpose. As such, it is flexible and provides project managers with the opportunity to tailor the process to suit the requirements of their individual projects. This ensures an optimum path through the generic project framework rather than one which is tied by bureaucracy. Any such tailoring of the project must, however, be recorded as part of the project definition (see p. 261).

Particular types of project require their own methodologies and steps but, provided you know how they match the overall high level framework, they can be used with confidence and in an environment where the business also knows what is happening. A common project framework will ensure alignment between different parts of the company with clearer communication and understanding. The following table shows how a range of different projects can fit into the framework.

Chapters 5 to 11 of this book describe the key actions, deliverables, and decisions for each stage and gate of the process. Chapter 12 looks at how you can apply this very simple framework to simple, complex, phased, rapid, and other types of project.

	Initial Investigation Stage	Detailed Investigation Stage	Develop and Test Stage	Trial Stage	Release Stage
Product development	Concept	Alternatives and feasibility	Develop and test	Market validation	Launch
Product withdrawal	Initial investigation	Detailed investigation	Develop and test	Pilot withdrawal	Close operations
Information systems	Analysis	Logical and outline physical design	Detailed design, build and test	Pilot	Cutover
Bid or tender	Receive request and evaluate	Prepare detailed tender	Develop, build, internal test	Commiss-ioning trials	Handover
Construction	Inception study	Feasibility study, tender design	Detailed design and construction	Commiss-ioning trials	Handover
Publishing	Proposal	Prepare manuscript	Edit, typeset	Final proof	Launch
IT	Requirements review	Analysis and design	Build	Beta test	Cutover

TALKING THE STAGES

A product marketing manager is accosted in the corridor by an engineer:

Engineer: I just heard from Bill that you've got plans to muck about with my installation. You ignore me as usual. Why on earth wasn't I told? It looks like a real big change!

Product Manager: But, Leigh, we only decided to start the initial investigation two days ago. I've told no one yet: the proposal goes out tomorrow.

Engineer: Sorry Bill. From what I heard, I assumed it was more advanced than that. I look forward to getting the proposal.

In this scenario, an interdepartmental conflict was diffused because, despite having totally different business backgrounds, they both understood the project framework for the company they worked in. If they had each talked in their own jargon (e.g. marketing concepts, pre-feasibility studies, inception reports) they would as likely as not have been none the wiser and continued their argument.

4

Who Does What?

The players

In simple terms a project needs a person: who comes up with the idea (the originator), who wants the project benefits (project sponsor), who manages the project (project manager), and who undertakes the work (the project team).

"Even emperors can't do it all by themselves."

BERTOLT BRECHT

Chapter 2 showed that a process is nothing without the culture, systems, and organization that support it (see pp. 15, 33). Project processes are no exception. Hence, to understand "projects" you need to have a firm grasp of who the players are and what is expected of them. The roles described as follows are relevant to a single project (see Figure 4.1). Roles required for running a portfolio of projects are described in Part Three.

In simple terms a project needs a person:

- who comes up with the idea – the originator;
- who wants the project benefits – project sponsor and project board;
- who manages the project – the project manager;
- who undertakes the work – the team managers and members.

Appendix C shows, in diagrammatic form, how these different accountabilities interact.

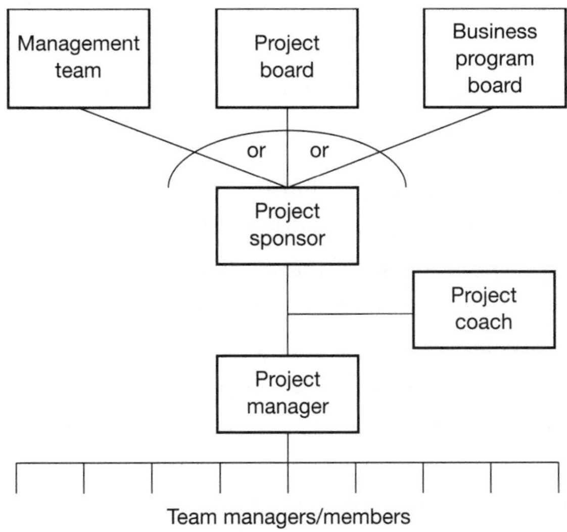

Figure 4.1 A typical project organization structure

The project sponsor who requires the benefits is supported either by a project board, management team, or business program board. The project manager reports to the project sponsor and is accountable for the day-to-day running of the project. A project coach supports these key roles. All team members report to the project manager.

The players

The originator

He/she is the person who identifies the "need" for a project and publishes it in the form of a proposal. This person can come from any function or level inside or outside the organization.

The project sponsor

The project sponsor is accountable for delivering the benefits to the organization. This is an active role and includes ensuring the project always makes sound business sense, involving all benefitting units (using a **project board** if appropriate), approving key deliverables and making decisions or recommendations at critical points in the project's life. There is only **one** project sponsor for each project and he/she should never take a narrow view based on his own line accountabilities. The project sponsor is usually a director, executive, or senior manager.

Project sponsor

The project sponsor is accountable for delivering the business benefits to the company. He/she will:

- ensure a real business need is being addressed by the project;
- ensure the project remains a viable business proposition;
- initiate project reviews (see Chapter 26);
- ensure the delivered solution matches the needs of the business;
- represent the business in key project decisions;
- sign off key project deliverables and project closure;
- resolve project issues that are outside the control of the project manager;
- chair the project board (if one is required);
- appoint the project manager and facilitate the appointment of team members.

The project sponsor is ultimately accountable to the chief executive/president via a project board (where required) or to an intermediate management team or board.

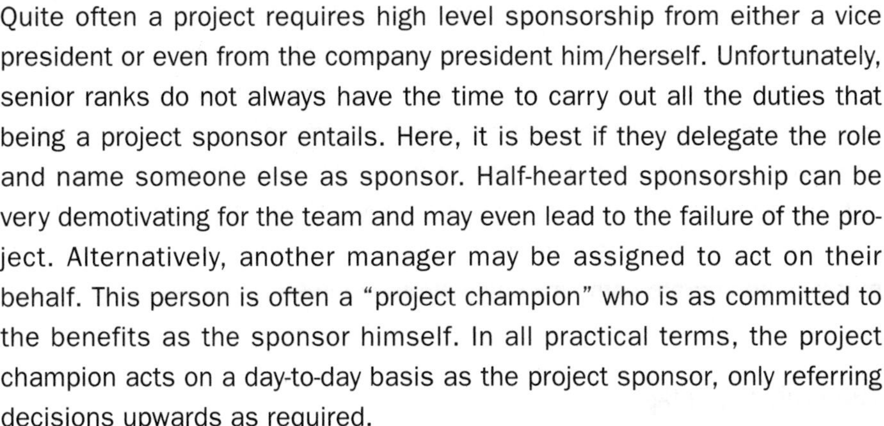

THE PROJECT SPONSOR'S TROOPER – THE PROJECT CHAMPION

Quite often a project requires high level sponsorship from either a vice president or even from the company president him/herself. Unfortunately, senior ranks do not always have the time to carry out all the duties that being a project sponsor entails. Here, it is best if they delegate the role and name someone else as sponsor. Half-hearted sponsorship can be very demotivating for the team and may even lead to the failure of the project. Alternatively, another manager may be assigned to act on their behalf. This person is often a "project champion" who is as committed to the benefits as the sponsor himself. In all practical terms, the project champion acts on a day-to-day basis as the project sponsor, only referring decisions upwards as required.

The project board

A project board is usually required for projects which span a number of functional boundaries and/or where the benefits are directed to more than one market segment or function. If no project board is required, the role can be undertaken by a program board or management team. A program board has accountability for a set of closely aligned projects. Programs are illustrated more fully Chapter 14. Unfortunately, bodies such as project boards are often ineffective, adding little value to the project. It is the project sponsor's responsibility as chair of the group to keep group members focussed on the key aspects of the project where their experience can be used to best effect.

The project board

The role of the project board (if required) is to enable the project sponsor to deliver the project benefits, and in particular:

- to monitor the project progress and ensure that the interests of your company are best served;
- to provide a forum for taking strategic, cross-functional decisions, removing obstacles, and for resolving issues.

A project board is often called a steering group, or steering board.

WHO'S RUNNING THIS ORGANIZATION?

Do you often find people in your organization hunting around for someone to "sponsor their project?" If so, who do you think is running the organization? Surely, it is the accountability of the business leaders (i.e. sponsors) to set the direction for the company and identify the needs that must be met. They should be the ones looking for people to manage their projects, not the other way round. Is your company led by its generals or by its troops? Is your project framework going to be a vehicle for change or merely an elaborate company suggestion scheme?

The project manager

He/she is accountable to the project sponsor for the day-to-day management of the project involving the project team across all necessary functions. Thus all project managers will need to be familiar with Parts Two and Four of this book. Depending on the size of the project, the project manager may be supported by a project administrator, or office support team.

Project manager

The project manager is accountable for managing the project on a day-to-day basis. He/she will:

- assemble the project team, with the agreement of appropriate line managers;
- prepare the project definition and detailed plans;
- define the responsibilities, work scope, and targets for each team member;
- monitor and manage project progress;
- monitor and manage risk and opportunities;
- manage the resolution of project issues;
- manage the scope of the project and control changes;
- forecast likely business benefits;
- deliver the project deliverables on time, to budget, at agreed quality;
- communicate with stakeholders;
- manage the closure of the project.

The team managers and members

The team managers and members are the "doers" who report to the project manager and are accountable for prescribed activities and deliverables. This may range from a complete subproject to a single deliverable. It is essential that the full experience of the team be brought to bear on any problems or solutions from the start. In the case of large projects, the project manager may choose to have a small core team, each member of which manages his or her own subsidiary teams either on work packages or subprojects. Project teams often comprise two parts:

The **core team** – those members who are full time on the project and report directly to the project manager. A core team size of six to ten people is about right.

The **extended team** – those members who report to the core team (team managers) and who may be part or full time.

It is essential that each member of staff working on your project has a clearly defined:

- role and reporting line to the project manager when working on the project (he/she may maintain their normal reporting line for other activities);
- scope of work and list of deliverables (both final and intermediate deliverables);
- level of authority (i.e. directions on what decisions he/she can and cannot take on behalf of his/her line function).

All groups of individuals associated with the project and which make up the team should be identified and listed with their role, scope, and accountabilities.

The team managers and members

Team managers and members are accountable to the project manager. The role of team members is to:

- be accountable for such deliverables as are delegated to them by the project manager, ensuring they are completed on time and to budget;
- liaise and work with other team managers and members in the carrying out of their work;
- contribute to and review key project documentation;
- monitor and manage progress on their delegated work scope;
- manage the resolution of issues, escalating any which they can not deal with to the project manager;
- monitor changes to their work scope, informing the project manager of any which require approval;
- monitor risk associated with their work scope;
- be responsible for advising the appropriate team member and/or project manager of potential issues, risks, or opportunities they have noticed.

In addition, a team manager:

- is accountable for directing and supervising the individual members of the team.

Project coach/facilitator

The project coach or facilitator is accountable for supporting the project manager, project sponsor and project board. This may be by pure coaching or by giving advice, facilitation, and guidance on project management. Both approaches will help project teams, both experienced and inexperienced, to perform beyond their own expectations. It is a role which is found infrequently but one which can prove extremely effective.

Remember in business-oriented projects, the participants are likely not to be fully trained and capable project managers. They need to have someone who can give them the confidence to work in a way which may be alien to them.

Remember, in many business-oriented projects, the participants are likely not to be fully trained and capable project managers. They may need to have someone who can give them the confidence to work in a way which may be alien to them.

THE POWER OF COACHING AND FACILITATION

A cross-functional team was put together with the aim of reducing the delivery time for a telecommunications product from ten days to less than two hours. The team comprised people drawn from line, operational roles who had little project management experience. A project coach was employed to facilitate the setup stages of the project and to provide ongoing guidance throughout the execution. Setup was hard work and many of the team complained that it was wasting valuable time which could be better spent doing "real work." Perseverance and a commitment on behalf of the coach to seeing the team succeed got the team through the early stages, and, once the development stage was underway, all of them understood the project fully. At the end, a marketing manager on the project commented to the coach, "I wondered what you were doing to us; I now see it was key to have the hassle at the start if we were to actually achieve our objectives." Things did go wrong on the project but, as all the core team members knew their own role and that of the others, changes could be more easily, speedily, and effectively implemented so that the overall objective was met. In fact the delivery time was reduced to an average of 20 minutes.

ROLES AND ACCOUNTABILITIES

This workout is best done with the project team, but may be done by the project manager or sponsor as an exercise in isolation.

1. Take any one of your key projects from Project Workout 3.1, and identify who (both individuals and teams) is involved in it. List them, one per Post-It Note. Place these on a flip chart.

2. Against each name, write in your own words what that person's needs or accountabilities are regarding the project.

3. On the left hand side of a separate flip chart, list the roles described in Chapter 4.

4. Match, as best you can, the names from step 2 to the key project roles described above.

5. For those names listed against "team member," divide them into "core team member" and "extended team member."

6. If you cannot allocate a person to one of the defined roles, put him/her in a separate cluster called "stakeholders."

Look at the role descriptions described in the chapter again. Do the individuals have the knowledge, skills, and competences to perform the roles?

You should have only one name against project sponsor and one against project manager. If not, your roles and accountabilities are likely to be confused. Further, it is not good practice if the sponsor and manager is the same person.

Project sponsor

- ☐ Can this person articulate the benefits the project will provide?

Project board

- ☐ As a group, does it have all the facets of the project covered?
- ☐ Have its members ever met as a group?
- ☐ Could they all describe the project and its current status consistently?

Core team members

- ☐ Do the core team members cover the required work scope between them?
- ☐ Do they ever meet with the project manager as a group?
- ☐ Could they all describe the project and its current status consistently?

Extended team members

- ☐ Do the extended team members know who they are accountable to on the project and what they have to deliver?
- ☐ Could they all describe the project and its current status consistently?

Stakeholders

- ☐ Your list of stakeholders may be extensive. They will be at all levels in the business, in diverse departments, they may be suppliers, they may be shareholders, the bank or even ... customers! Keep this list for use in Project Workout 19.5. (Stakeholders are discussed further on p. 282.)

ACTION

1. Review the roles and accountabilities on all key projects in your organization.
2. Build on the project list from Project Workout 3.1 and add the names of the project sponsor, project manager and project board.
3. Ask each project manager and project sponsor to agree a list of stakeholders.
4. Ask each project manager to list the team members and their role on the project.

5

The Proposal
Identify the Need!

Overview

Key deliverable

Process steps

The gate prior to the initial investigation is the first decision point when resources are committed to working on the proposal; it is also the point at which the potential project is first formally recognized. This gate is unique in that it is the only one in the project life cycle which does not require you to have a plan for how you undertake the work which follows.

"One of the greatest pains to human nature is the pain of a new idea."

WALTER BAGEHOT, 1826

Overview

The proposal describes the business need (i.e. it focusses on **why** you want a project) and, if known, what you want to do. You should document it formally and have it reviewed by potential stakeholders prior to a go/no go decision for starting an initial investigation. The proposal document is used as the key deliverable at the Initial Investigation Gate. This gate, just prior to the initial investigation, is the first decision point when resources are committed to working on the proposal; it is also the point at which the potential project is first formally recognized. The gate is unique in that it is the only one in the project life cycle which does not require you to have a plan for how you undertake the work which follows.

The proposal describes the business need (i.e. it focusses on why you want a project).

It is important for you to document the proposal as:

- it acts as the brief for the initial investigation stage.
- if you can't be bothered to write it down, why should you expect anyone to work on it?
- the mere fact of writing the proposal down serves to clarify thinking and ensure clear communication of your intentions.

Key deliverable

The Proposal is a short document (one to five pages) which outlines the need the project will meet, what it is intended to produce (if known), its benefits, and how it fits with current strategy. If known, the impact on the organization (market, technology, and operational), broad estimates of benefits and cost, and required time to completion are also included.

The CD-ROM contains a table of contents.

Deliverable	Prepared by	Reviewed by	Approved by
Proposal	Originator	Functions or business units likely to be impacted by or to benefit from the proposal	Sponsor

Process steps

1 The need (or idea!) for a project should result directly from your business strategies and plans. This is not always the case as, for example, commercial opportunities may be spotted as the result of technical innovation, operational experience, or from feedback from suppliers or customers.

2 The originator of the "idea" should identify a senior executive in the company who is likely to benefit most from the project. (If the project comes directly from the business plan, that person will be obvious, or may even be the originator!)

3 The senior executive first checks that a similar idea has not been proposed before. If it has, the "idea" should not be pursued further unless different circumstances now exist (market, technology, etc.). He/she should determine who else in the company has a stake in the idea in terms of benefit, impact, and/or contribution, and then appoint a potential project sponsor. In the case of large projects or small companies, the senior executive may become the project sponsor.

4 The potential project sponsor should write up the idea in the form of a proposal. The draft proposal is reviewed by the project sponsor, together with any other stakeholders identified in point 3. If necessary, it is amended. This review should look not only at the proposal in question but also at any other related proposals and projects. It is essential to screen out any proposal which does not form part of a coherent program of change related to the business's strategies and plans.

5 The potential project sponsor should identify a project manager who will be accountable for the Initial Investigation Stage.

6 The potential project sponsor should then complete the registration of the proposal and file a reference copy.

7 **Initial Investigation Gate**. This gate is the decision point concerning whether an initial investigation (business, technical, marketing, and operational) should be done and whether there are resources to do it. *If the proposal is accepted, the Initial Investigation Stage is started.*

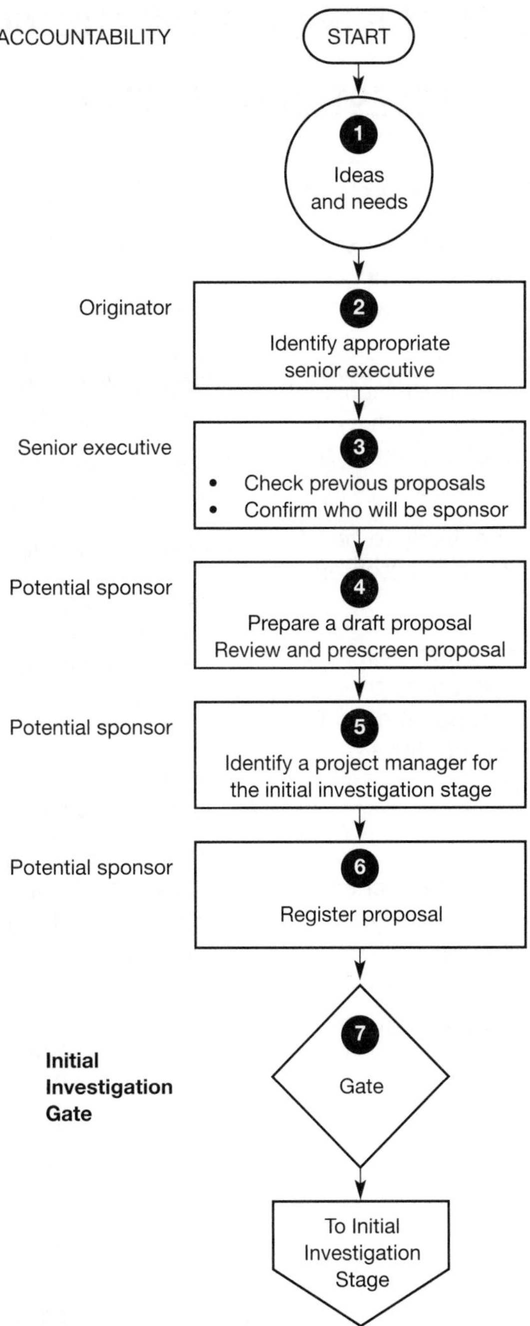

Figure 5.1 Steps prior to the Initial Investigation Stage

5.1

CHECKLIST FOR STARTING THE INITIAL INVESTIGATION STAGE

Business need and strategic fit

- ☐ Is it clear which business unit(s) or function(s) the proposal supports; does it fit the strategy?
- ☐ Is the opportunity attractive (size, share, cost saving, contribution, etc.) relative to alternative proposals?
- ☐ Is the proposal likely to be acceptable to the customers and users?
- ☐ Do any competitors have capabilities similar to this? If so, will this proposal provide us with any competitive advantage?

Health check!

- ☐ Has a project "health check" been done and been found acceptable (see p. 405)?

Accountabilities

- ☐ Has a project sponsor been identified for at least the Initial Investigation Stage?
- ☐ Has a project manager been identified for the Initial Investigation Stage?
- ☐ Can resources be committed to do the initial investigation?

Operational and technical

- ☐ Is the organization likely to be able to develop or acquire the required capabilities to support this proposal, if they don't yet exist?
- ☐ Is it technically feasible with current technology?
- ☐ Has the organization operational capability to support it? If not, can it acquire this?

Health check scores (from p. 405)

P	R	O	J	E	C	T	Total
☐	☐	☐	☐	☐	☐	☐	☐

Risk

☐ Low ☐ Medium ☐ High ☐ Impossible

Issues

Risk

Executive action

The Initial Investigation Stage

Have a Quick Look at It!

Overview

Key deliverables

Process steps

The goal of the Initial Investigation Stage is for you to examine the proposal as quickly as possible (say, within one to six weeks), and to evaluate it against the existing business plans of the company to determine if what is intended is likely to be viable in financial, operational, technical, and customer terms.

"To have begun is half the job: be bold and be sensible."

HORACE, 65–8 BC

Overview

The goal of the Initial Investigation Stage is for you to examine the proposal, as quickly as possible, (say, within one to six weeks), and to evaluate it against the existing business plans of the company. You need to determine if what is intended is likely to be viable in financial, operational, technical, and customer terms.

You will need to:

- make a preliminary assessment of the business opportunity, benefits, possible solutions, costs, technology needs, and the likely impact on the operational platforms and groups, infrastructure, and capabilities.
- check for overlap, synergy, or conflict with other projects in progress or capabilities in use.
- scope and plan the work content for the remaining stages of the project.

Key deliverables

The Initial Business Case document contains the business rationale for the project. It is the document which outlines WHY you need the project, WHAT options you intend to work on, HOW you will do it, and WHO is needed to make it happen. It also answers the question HOW MUCH? and hence is used to authorize the funding for at least the next stage of the project. The Initial Business Case does not comprise a full analysis, but only sufficient to enable you to decide if it is worthwhile continuing the project. The full Business Case will provide the definitive appraisal for the project and will be produced at the end of the next stage.

The Initial Business Case includes:

- a preliminary assessment of the financial aspects of the proposed development;
- an outline of the requirement in terms of customer/user "feel," technology, commercial, and market needs;
- a definition of the project which would be required to meet these (in detail for the next stage and in outline for the whole project).

It also evaluates the project against the existing strategies and goals of the company to confirm its fit and to determine if it is likely to be viable in both business, technical, operational, and customer terms. See the CD-ROM and p. 261 for more detail.

The Project Plan is a key appendix to the initial business case and defines the schedule, cost, and resource requirements for the project. This is defined in summary to completion of the project and in detail for the Detailed Investigation Stage.

Deliverable	*Prepared by*	*Review by*	*Approved, prior to gate, by*
Initial Business Case	Project manager	Impacted or benefitting functions and business units	Project sponsor
Project Plan	Project manager	Impacted or benefitting functions and business units	Project sponsor

Note: These are minimum roles and deliverables only. Each project should define its full set at the start of the stage. At the discretion of the project manager, a separate initial investigation report and/or output definition may also be produced.

Process steps

1 The appointed project manager engages the study team, registers the project, ensures a project account is opened, and informs all relevant stakeholders of stage entry (see Chapter 19).
2 The team, led by the project manager, undertakes the initial investigation and agrees the outcome with the project sponsor.
3 The team defines the project and prepares the project plans, in detail for the next stage and in outline beyond. The potential resource needs should be discussed and agreed with the relevant functions.
4 The project manager, with the team members, prepares and agrees the initial business case document.
5 The Initial Business Case, including the project plans, is reviewed by the project sponsor and any other relevant stakeholders. It is either accepted, rejected, deferred, or changes are requested.
6 **Detailed Investigation Gate**. This gate determines whether further resources should be invested in undertaking a detailed investigation.

If the initial business case is authorized, the Detailed Investigation Stage is started.

The Initial Business Case and Project Plans now come under formal version control. (Figure 6.1 shows the steps taken during the Initial Investigation Stage.)

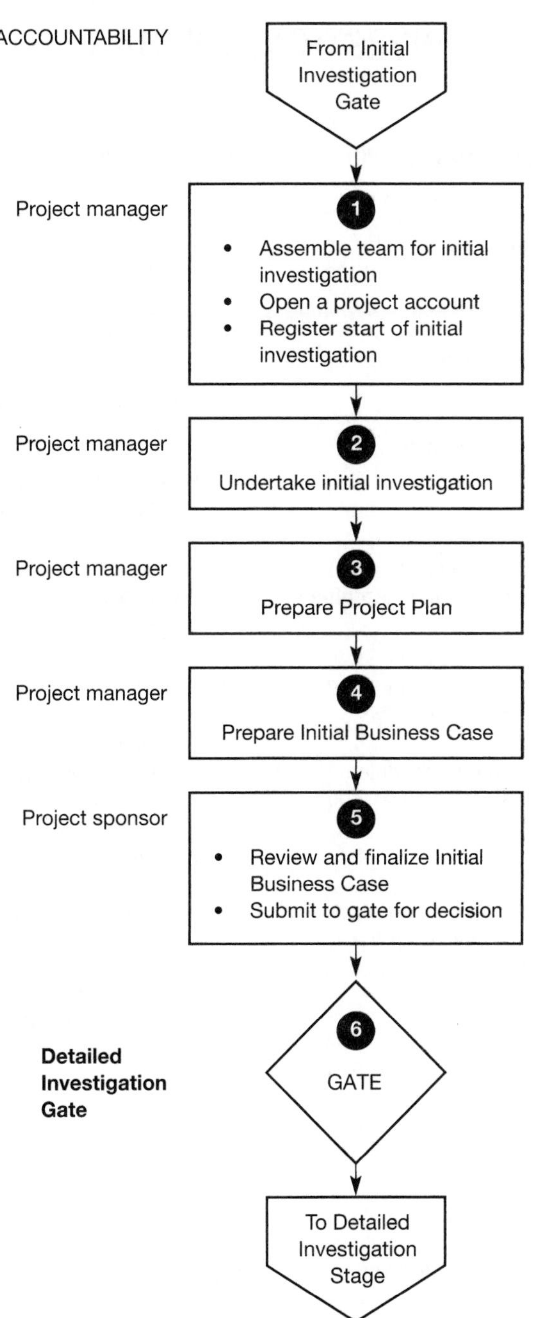

Figure 6.1 Steps in the Initial Investigation Stage

6.1

CHECKLIST FOR STARTING THE DETAILED INVESTIGATION STAGE

Business need and strategic fit

- ☐ Is it clear which business unit(s) or function(s) strategy and plan the project supports; does it fit the strategy?
- ☐ Is the business opportunity attractive?
- ☐ Are the risks acceptable?

Deliverables

- ☐ Is the Initial Business Case and investment appraisal acceptable?
- ☐ Is there a detailed schedule, resource, and cost plan for the Detailed Investigation Stage?
- ☐ Is there an outline schedule, resource, and cost plan for the full project?
- ☐ Have all the relevant business units and functions been involved in creating and reviewing the deliverables?

Health check!

Has a project "health check" been done and been found acceptable (see p. 405)?

Accountabilities

- ☐ Has a project sponsor been identified for the project?
- ☐ Has a project manager been identified for the project?
- ☐ Do you have the resources to undertake the Detailed Investigation Stage?

Operational and technical

- ☐ On current knowledge, is it technically feasible with current technology or is there a possible technical development path to provide the capability or service?
- ☐ Does the organization currently have the operational capability to support it? If not is it likely this can be put in place within the current/proposed process architecture?

Health check scores (from p. 405)

P	R	O	J	E	C	T	Total
☐	☐	☐	☐	☐	☐	☐	☐

Risk

☐ Low ☐ Medium ☐ High ☐ Impossible

Issues

Risk

Executive action

The Detailed Investigation Stage

Promising ... Let's have a Closer Look

Overview

Key deliverables

Process steps

"Understanding is the beginning of approving."

ANDRÉ GIDE, 1902

Overview

During the Detailed Investigation Stage you will identify and define the optimum solution and commercial proposition.

You will need to:

The next gate, for which this stage prepares you, is critical as it is the last point at which you can stop the project before substantial financial commitments are made.

- Evaluate possible options and identify a preferred solution.
- Ensure the preferred solution will meet the defined needs.
- Define process, technical, and operational requirements where appropriate.
- Test/research the concept with the target users and/or customers.
- Check any legal issues.
- Evaluate possible suppliers and partners.

The next gate, for which this stage prepares you, is critical as it is the last point at which you can stop the project before substantial financial commitments are made.

Key deliverables

The Output Definition is the fundamental source book describing the output of the project in terms of process, organization, systems, technology, and culture. It is the document which integrates all the individual system, process, and platform requirements. It also specifies how they will work together. The document will continue to develop as the project proceeds and will be handed over to the manager(s) of any operational parts before the project is completed.

The Feasibility Report builds on the Initial Business Case. It includes the recommendation for which option should be adopted as the solution (including processes), and compares it against rejected solutions in financial and non-financial terms (see the CD-ROM).

The Business Case contains the business rationale. It is the document on which the decision is made to authorize funding for the remainder of the project and the building in of costs and benefits to the business plan. The document is "live" and under strict version control for the remainder of the project (see the CD-ROM).

The Project Plan is an appendix to the business case and includes the detailed schedule, resource, and cost plans for the Develop and Test Stage with the remaining stages in summary.

The Test Plan is an attachment which documents the tests required to verify performance of any outputs from the project both in isolation and working as a complete system (see the CD-ROM).

Deliverable	*Prepared by*	*Review by*	*Approved, prior to gate, by*
Output definition	Project manager	Team members	Project sponsor
Feasibility Report	Project manager	Team members	Project sponsor
Business Case	Project manager	Team members and key functional managers	Project sponsor
Project Plan	Project manager	as above	Project sponsor
Test Plan	Project manager	as above	Proposed owners of deliverable

Note: These are minimum review roles and deliverables only. Each project should define its full set prior to the start of the stage.

Process steps

1 The project manager informs the stakeholders and key team members that approval and authority to start the stage has been given.
2 The project manager registers and sets up the project (see Chapter 19).
3 The detailed investigation work is carried out (within the project control cycle, see pp. 23, 52) to assess the possible solutions and a preferred option is recommended, bearing in mind the risks and the benefits. A feasibility report is prepared.
4 The feasibility report is reviewed, amended, if necessary, and agreed by the project sponsor who decides which option should be chosen and refined further.
5 Work on refining the chosen option is carried out. This may involve refining the **output definition**, the operational aspects, training plans, business processes, market plans, and system designs.

   The output definition now comes under formal version control.

6 The project manager, with the team (involving the stakeholders), prepares the detailed plan for the Develop and Test Stage and finalizes the business case document. These are reviewed with the team and amended, if necessary.
7 **Development Gate**. This gate determines whether the development and testing work should start.

If the business case is authorized, the Develop and Test Stage is started and the benefits, revenues and costs are built into the business plan.

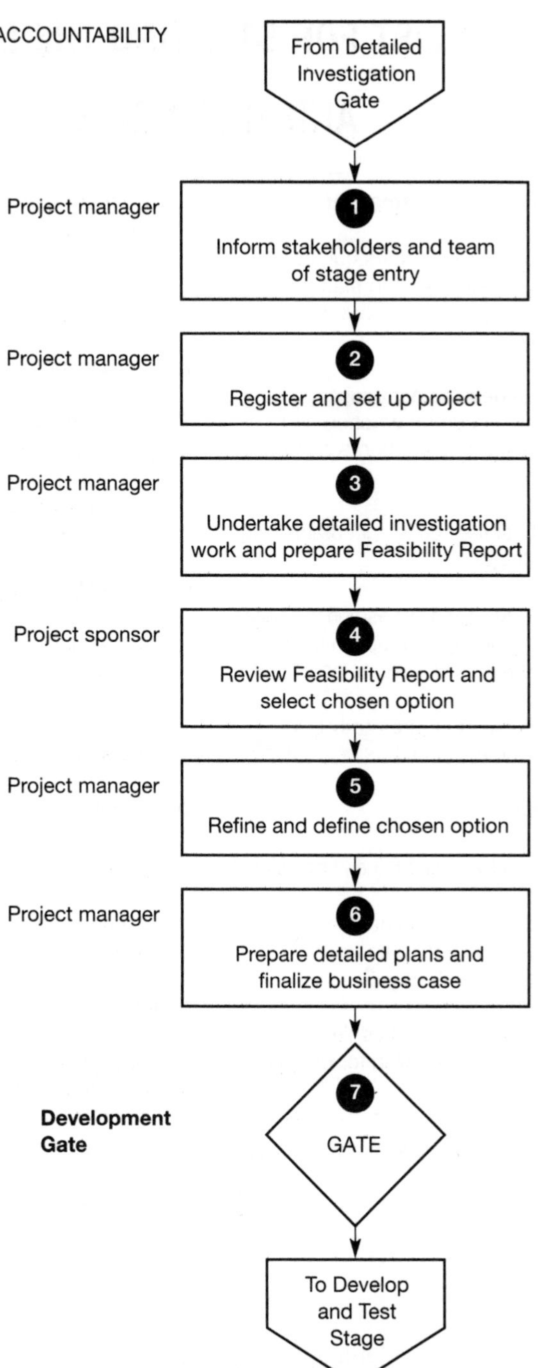

Figure 7.1 Steps in the Detailed Investigation Stage

7.1

CHECKLIST FOR STARTING THE DEVELOP AND TEST STAGE

Business need and strategic fit

- ☐ Is it clear which business unit(s) or function(s) strategy and plan the project supports; does it still fit the strategy?
- ☐ Have the development concepts (e.g. marketing) been researched and tested on target segments and the need reaffirmed?
- ☐ Is the business case acceptable and compelling?
- ☐ Have the key sensitivities and scenarios for the recommended option been checked and confirmed as acceptable?
- ☐ Is the Business Case ready to be built into the overall business plan?

Project plan

- ☐ Are the project plans full and complete?
- ☐ Is there a detailed schedule, resource, and cost plan for the develop and test stage?
- ☐ Is there an outline schedule, resource, and cost plan for the full project?
- ☐ Are there sufficient review points in the plan (see Ch. 26)?
- ☐ Has the project been designed to eliminate known high risks (see Ch. 23)?

Accountabilities

- ☐ Are there resources to undertake the Develop and Test Stage?
- ☐ Have formal commitments been made by the relevant line managers?

Operational and technical

- ☐ Is it technically feasible with current technology?
- ☐ Does the organization have the operational capability to support it?

Deliverables

- ☐ Is the output definition complete?
- ☐ Is it clear how the output will be tested?

Health check!

Has a project health check been done and been found acceptable (see p. 405)?

Health check scores (from p. 405)

P	R	O	J	E	C	T	Total
☐	☐	☐	☐	☐	☐	☐	☐

Risk

☐ Low ☐ Medium ☐ High ☐ Impossible

Issues

Risk

Executive action

The Develop and Test Stage

Do It!

Overview

Key deliverables

Process steps

The Develop and Test Stage is when you spend the bulk of the costs relating to the project.

"The world can only be grasped by action, not contemplation."
JACOB BRONOWSKI

Overview

The Develop and Test Stage is when you spend the bulk of the costs relating to the project. It comprises the outstanding design, development, creation, and building of the chosen solution and its supporting systems, manuals, business processes, and training. It concludes with a full test in a controlled environment. If this stage is of long duration (more than four months), it is essential that key review points are built into the plan to ensure its on-going viability is assessed (see "Reviews during a project", Chapter 26). It is also wise to have additional review points just prior to letting any major contracts relating to the project.

During this stage you will need to make a decision to start the Trial Stage. This decision can be taken prior to completion of the full work scope for the stage, as only activities required for the trial need be completed.

Key deliverables

The Test Results confirm that any testing has been completed in accordance with the test plans and acceptance criteria, prior to doing the ready for trial review. Any outstanding issues are noted (see the CD-ROM for table of contents).

The Ready for Trial Review Report is a short report which confirms that all deliverables, resources, and prerequisites across all functions required for starting the trial are in place (see the CD-ROM for table of contents).

The Project Plan: the schedule, resource, and cost plan for the Trial Stage should be fully detailed with the remainder of the project in outline. It will include the trial plan which documents the plan, conditions, environment, participants, tests, criteria, and results required for the pre-launch trial.

Deliverable	*Prepared by*	*Review by*	*Approval, prior to gate, by*
Test Results	Project manager	Team members	Project sponsor
Ready for Trial Review Teport	Project manager	Team members	Project sponsor
The Project Plan	Project manager	Team members	Project sponsor

Note: These are minimum review roles and deliverables only. Each project should define its full set prior to the start of the stage.

Process steps

1 The project manager informs the stakeholders and key team members that authorization to start development has been given.

2 The project manager assembles the team (including suppliers) and confirms the project controls, roles, and accountabilities for each individual. The plan (as produced at the end of the previous stage) should be reviewed to ensure it is still valid.

3 The work, as defined in the business case and laid out in the project plan, is carried out within the project control cycle (see pp. 23, 52). Work is done, progress is measured, issues and variances noted, corrections made. As deliverables are produced they are reviewed, amended, and finally accepted. These comprise those which are required prior to:

- starting testing;
- starting the Trial Stage;
- the Ready for Service Gate.

4 The tests are carried out, the results are reviewed and any modification and retesting done. The output definition may need to be amended in light of the tests.

5 While the testing is being carried out, other deliverables are being prepared. Finally, a review is done to check that all activities have been done and deliverables are ready for the trial to start.

6 All project documentation (including the project plan, output definition and business case) is updated.

7 **Trial Gate**. This gate determines whether you can start a trial of the proposed solution using real users or customers.

If the Ready for Trial Report is accepted, the Trial Stage is started (Figure 8.1).

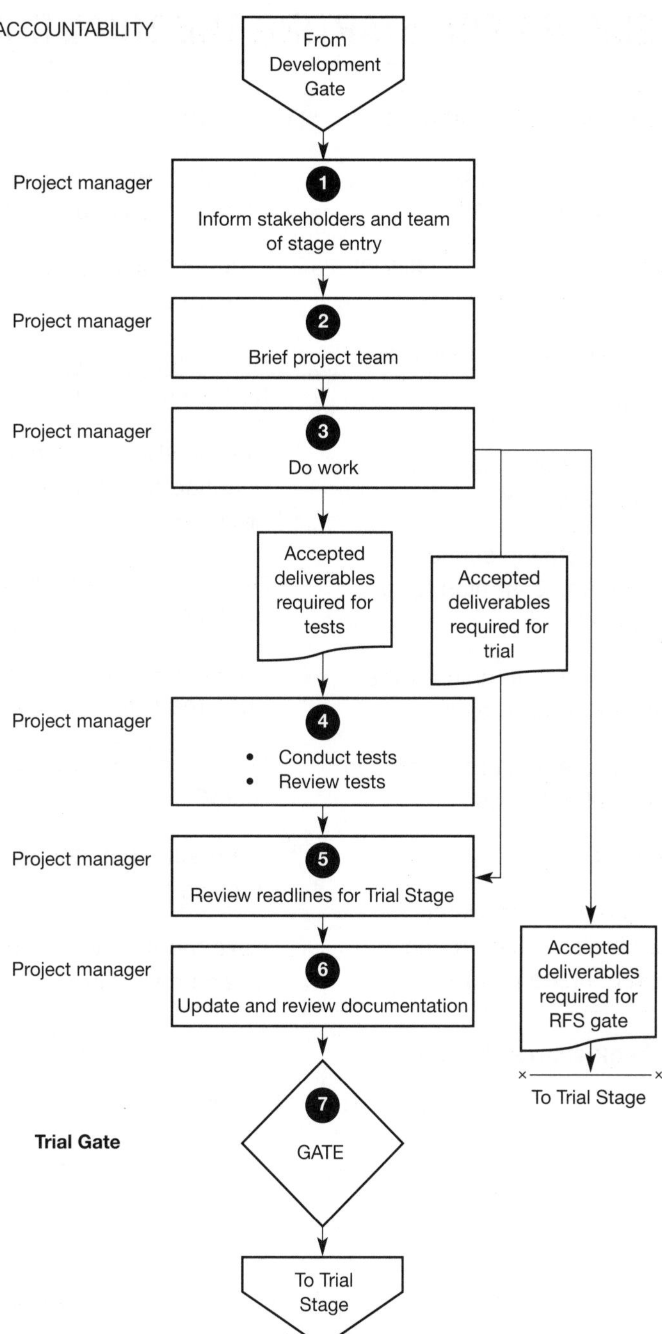

Figure 8.1 Steps in the Develop and Test Stage

8.1

CHECKLIST FOR STARTING THE TRIAL STAGE

Business need and strategic fit

- ☐ Is the project still a good business proposition?
- ☐ Is the project still correctly reflected in the overall business plan?
- ☐ Have all high risks been eliminated?

Project plan

- ☐ Is the project plan up to date, full, and complete?
- ☐ Is there a detailed schedule, resource, and cost plan for the Trial Stage?
- ☐ Is there an outline plan for the remainder of the project?
- ☐ Do we have sufficient resources to undertake the trial?

Health check!

- ☐ Has a project "health check" been done and been found acceptable (see p. 405)?

For the trial

- ☐ Have the tests been finished and the results accepted?
- ☐ Has the trial plan been prepared?
- ☐ Have checklists been prepared for the customers and users?
- ☐ Have customers/users been dentified and trial agreements drafted?
- ☐ Have the business processes been finalized?
- ☐ Are all relevant functions and units ready for the trial?
- ☐ Is the communications material ready?
- ☐ Are results monitoring systems in place?
- ☐ Have the trial acceptance criteria been agreed?

Health check scores (from p. 405)

P	R	O	J	E	C	T	Total
☐	☐	☐	☐	☐	☐	☐	☐

Risk

☐ Low ☐ Medium ☐ High ☐ Impossible

Issues

Risk

Executive action

The Trial Stage

Try It Out

Overview

Key deliverables

Process steps

The solution must be acceptable to the users, functionally correct, and highly likely to meet the organization's business objectives.

"The full area of ignorance is not yet mapped. We are at present only exploring the fringes."

J D BERNARD

Overview

During this stage, your partially proven solution is checked in the operational environment with live users and/or customers. The purpose is to validate:

- the solution is acceptable to the users and customers;
- all the capabilities work in a live environment, including all the business processes, and supporting infrastructure;
- the business objective is likely to be met.

In this respect, the solution must be acceptable to the users, functionally correct, and highly likely to meet the organization's business objectives (see also p. 63 if you are not sure if you need a trial).

Key deliverables

The Trial Results is a summary document which confirms that the trials have been completed in accordance with the plan and acceptance criteria and the developed solution is now ready to move to the Release Stage. Any outstanding issues are also noted (see the CD-ROM for table of contents).

The Ready For Service (RFS) review is a short report which confirms that all deliverables and prerequisite activities required before starting the Release Stage have been completed (see the CD-ROM for table of contents).

The Project Plan: the schedule, resource, and cost plan for the Release Stage should be fully detailed.

Deliverable	*Prepared by*	*Review by*	*Approved, prior to gate, by:*
Trial results	Project manager	Team members	Project sponsor
RFS review report	Project manager	Team members	Project sponsor
The project plan	Project manager	Team members	Project sponsor

Note: These above are minimum review roles and deliverables only. Each project should define its full set prior to the start of the stage.

Process steps

1. The project manager informs the relevant stakeholders and key team members that approval to start the Trial Stage has been given.
2. The project manager assembles the team and confirms the project controls, roles, and accountabilities for each individual. The plan (as produced at the end of the previous stage) should be reviewed to ensure it is still valid.
3. The work, as laid out in the project plan, is carried out within the project control cycle. Work is done, progress is measured, issues and variances noted, corrections made. As deliverables are produced they are reviewed, amended, and finally accepted.
4. The trial is carried out, the results are reviewed and any modification and retesting done:
   - prepare for trial;
   - conduct trial;
   - review trial performance.
5. While the trial is being carried out, other activities and deliverables (such as training) are being delivered from the Develop and Test Stage.
6. All project documentation (e.g. the project plan, output definition) is updated. The validity of the business case for the project must be checked.
7. Once work is completed, a review is done to check that all activities have been completed and deliverables produced to the extent that the organization is "ready for service." The project sponsor makes a recommendation to the decision makers for the gate.
8. **Ready for Service (RFS) Gate**. This gate determines whether you can start using the proposed solution in a full operational environment.

If the ready for service report is authorized, the Release Stage is started.

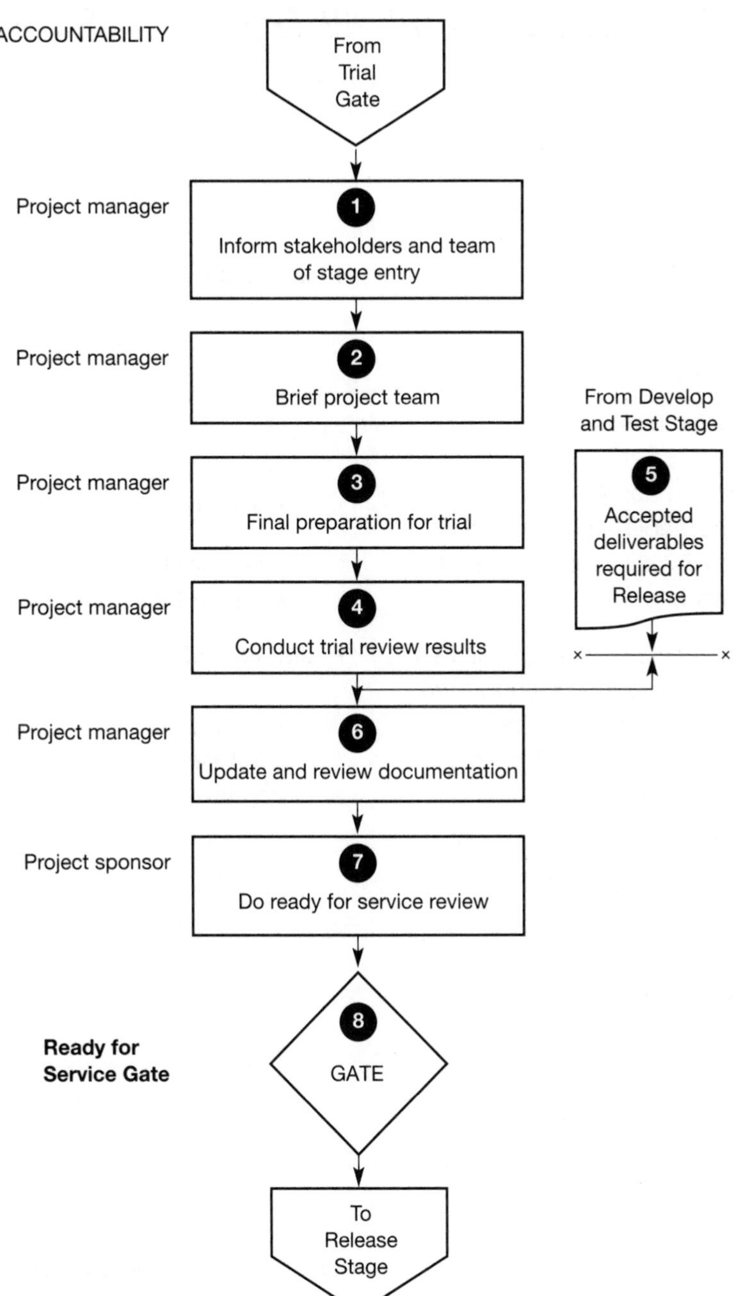

Figure 9.1 Steps in the Trial Stage

9.1

CHECKLIST FOR STARTING THE RELEASE STAGE

Business need and strategic fit

- ☐ Is the project still a good business proposition?
- ☐ Have all high and medium risks been eliminated from the project?

Ready for service

- ☐ Are you absolutely sure, beyond reasonable doubt, that it will work? (Your reputation is at stake!)
- ☐ Have process designs across the organization (and to third parties if needed) been accepted and is all training completed?
- ☐ Are benefits/results monitoring systems in place?
- ☐ Have the costs and benefits been reforecast against the business plan?

Project plan

- ☐ Is the project plan updated, full, and complete?
- ☐ Is there a detailed schedule, resource, and cost plan for the release stage?
- ☐ Do we have the resources to undertake the release stage?

Health check!

- ☐ Has a project "health check" been done and been found acceptable (see p. 405)?

Health check scores (from p. 405)

P	R	O	J	E	C	T	Total
☐	☐	☐	☐	☐	☐	☐	☐

Risk

☐ Low ☐ Medium ☐ High ☐ Impossible

Issues

Risk

Executive action

The Release Stage

Let's Get Going!

Overview

Key deliverable

Process steps

This is the stage when the "rubber hits the road."

"What we call the beginning is often the end.
And to make an end is to make a beginning."

T S ELIOT

Overview

This is the stage when "the rubber hits the road," you unleash your creation on the world and start to reap the benefits your project was set up to create. It involves:

- releasing the validated solution into its operational environment;
- the start of all operational support;
- the handover of the solution from the project manager to the functions and business units for on-going operation and assurance.

In addition, work is carried out post-release to ensure the environments left by the project are "clean."

It finishes with a project closure review, at which the project is formally shut down. The review takes the form of a "lessons learned" session. What worked well on the project? What didn't? Were all the controls effective and useful? What would we use again? What would we do differently next time? Closure is discussed in more detail in Chapter 27.

Key deliverable

The Project Closure Report contains the notes of solution handover and project closure, including "lessons learned" from the project in terms of how the processes, organization, systems, and team worked (i.e. the efficiency of the project). A terms of reference for the Post-Implementation Review is also included. A table of contents is included on the CD-ROM.

Deliverable	*Review by*	*Approval, prior to gate, by*
Project Closure Report	Involved key team members	Project sponsor

Note: These are minimum review roles and deliverables only. Each project should define its full set prior to the start of the stage.

Process steps

1 The project manager informs the stakeholders and key team members that approval to start the Release Stage has been given.
2 The project manager assembles the team and confirms the project controls, roles, and accountabilities for each individual. The plan (as produced at the end of the previous stage) should be reviewed to ensure it is still valid.
3 Final release activities and preparations are carried out (e.g. major print runs, manufacturing, final training).
4 The decision on the release date is confirmed and communicated to all who need to know. If there are any snags then release may be put "on hold" until they are sorted out.
5 The release takes place.
6 Preparations for project closure are made.
7 Any outstanding work to complete the scope of the project is carried out. This may include removing redundant data from systems, withdrawing old manuals, literature, or shutting down redundant capabilities.
8 The project closure review is held and the project sponsor declares the project formally closed:

- the project accounts are closed;
- the development(s) (with output definition(s)) is handed over to the line for on-going management;
- the terms of reference, accountabilities, and timing for the Post-Implementation Review are agreed (see pp. 119, 402);
- lessons on the efficacy of the project process are recorded and fed back to the process owner.

The project is now closed.

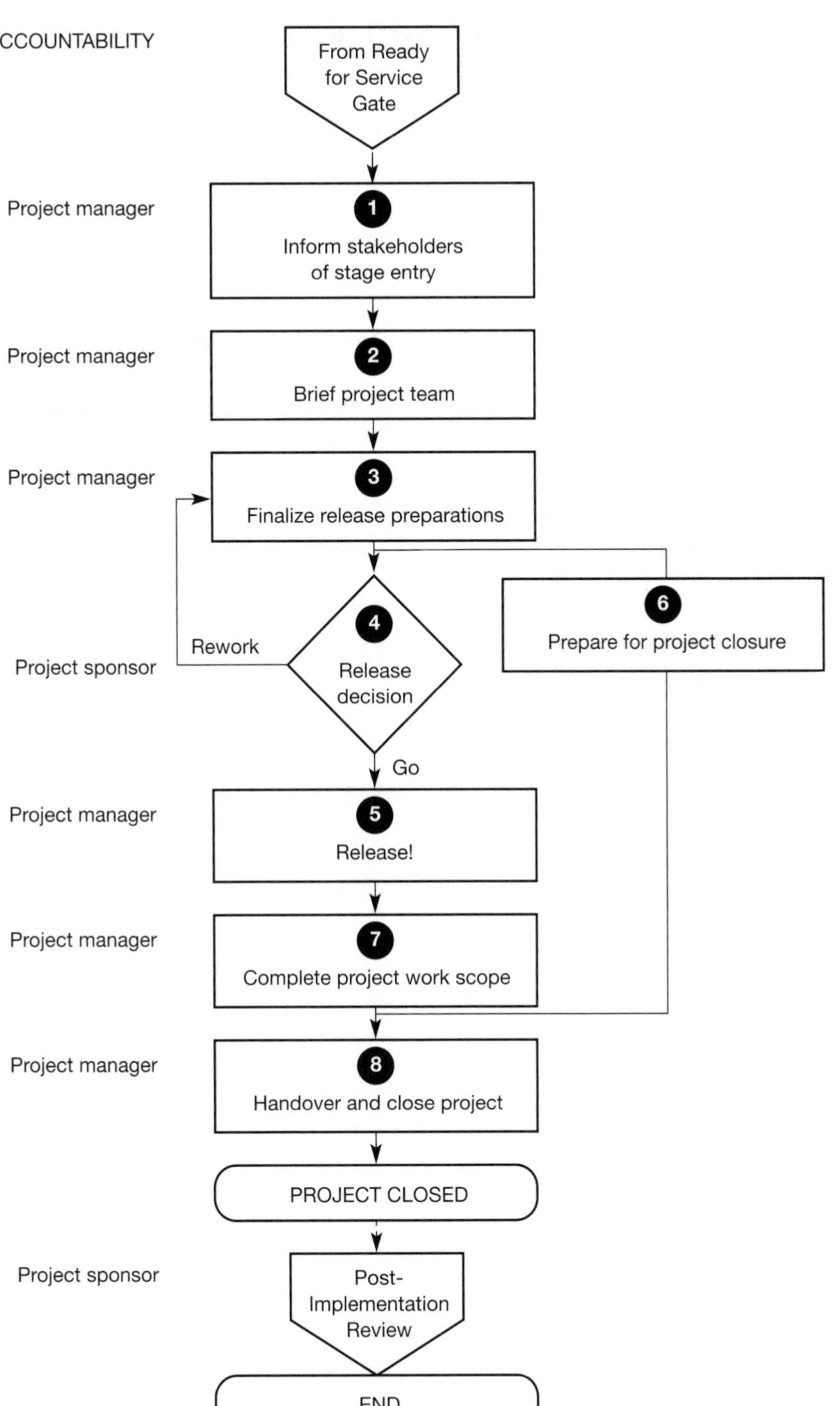

Figure 10.1 Steps in the release stage

10.1

CHECKLIST AT PROJECT CLOSURE

Business need and strategic fit

- ☐ Has the business forecast been updated to take into account the benefits arising from the project?
- ☐ Has someone agreed to be accountable for monitoring the benefits?
- ☐ Have review points and metrics for measuring the benefits been defined?
- ☐ Has the project account been closed so that no more costs can be incurred?

Risks and issues

- ☐ Have all issues been resolved?
- ☐ Has ownership of each outstanding risk and issue been accepted by a NAMED person in the line or in another project?

Post-Implementation Review (PIR)

- ☐ Have the timing, accountabilities, and terms of reference for the PIR been agreed?

Team/stakeholders

- ☐ Have all who need to know about the closure of the project been informed?
- ☐ Have team appraisals relating to the project been completed?
- ☐ Have those who deserve special thanks been acknowledged?

Lessons learned

- ☐ Have all lessons learned been recorded and communicated to the relevant process and documentation owners?

Handed over risks, issues and actions
Lessons learned
Executive action

The Post-Implementation Review

How Did We Do?

Overview

Key deliverable

To be effective, the review must not be used as a "witch hunt." If you use it in this way, you'll never have the truth presented to you again!

"You can do anything in this world if you are prepared to take the consequences."

W SOMERSET MAUGHAM

Overview

You should carry out a Post-implementation Review after sufficient time has elapsed for the benefits of the project to be assessable. The review cannot cover every aspect but it should establish whether:

- the predicted benefits were delivered;
- the most effective operational processes were designed;
- the solution really met the business needs, both for users and customers.

As the project sponsor is the one who wants the benefits and for whom the project is undertaken, it is in his/her interest to initiate the review. This review should result in action plans for improvement where necessary and hence help in the achievement of the benefits. For major projects this review may be carried out by an "audit" function, but in all cases it is better (although not essential) if it is conducted by someone independent from the project team. To be effective, the review must not be used as a "witch hunt." If you use it in this way, you'll never have the truth presented to you again! (See also Chapter 26 and p. 402.)

Key deliverable

The Post-Implementation Review (PIR) report assesses the success of the project against predefined criteria given in the business case and confirmed in the terms of reference for the PIR. It assesses how effective the project was in meeting its objectives and includes recommendations for improvements. The CD-ROM contains a table of contents.

Deliverable	*Review by*	*Approved by*
Post-implementation Review report	Independent reviewer or internal audit	Project sponsor

Note: Minimum review and approval criteria: the terms of reference should define all those who need to be involved.

11.1

CHECKLIST AT POST-IMPLEMENTATION REVIEW

Business need

- ☐ Are the benefits being delivered as expected?

Operational aspects

- ☐ Are all aspects of the solution working as envisaged?

Action

- ☐ Has a corrective action plan been put in place to address any shortfall in expected benefits?
- ☐ Has a corrective action plan been put in place to address any shortfall in operational aspects?
- ☐ Have all lessons learned been recorded and communicated to the relevant stakeholders?

Applying the Staged Framework

Four types of project

Fitting into the staged framework

Small stuff, or "simple" projects

Rapid projects

"Just do it" projects: loose cannons

Big stuff, or projects and subprojects

Work packages

*The staged process requires that, by the time you reach the Development Gate, you know, with a reasonable level of confidence, **what** you are going to do and **how** you are going to do it.*

"Through the unknown remembered gate."

T S ELIOT

The previous chapters have taken you through a project management framework you can use for each of your projects. This framework leads the project sponsor and project manager on a course which, if followed, will ensure that quality and purpose are built into your projects from the start and developed as you proceed to your end-point. It also ensures all projects undertaken in your company can be referenced to the same, defined, and known set of stages. How can this simple set of stages be applied to the different types of projects you have to do?

This framework leads the project sponsor and project manager on a course which, if followed, will ensure that quality and purpose are built into your projects from the start and developed as you proceed to your end-point.

Four types of project

In his book, *All Change, the Project Leader's Secret Handbook,* Eddie Obeng describes four types of projects, each of which deals with a different kind of change. I have shown these in Figure 12.1.

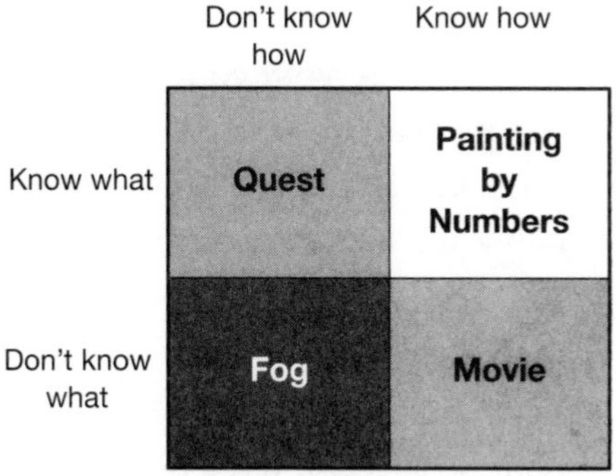

	Don't know how	Know how
Know what	**Quest**	**Painting by Numbers**
Don't know what	**Fog**	**Movie**

Figure 12.1 Different types of change project

If you know what you are doing and how you are going to do it, you have a "painting by numbers" project. If you know how but not what, you have a "movie." A "quest" is when you know what you want, but not how you will achieve it. Finally a "fog" is when you don't know what you want, nor how to achieve it.

Painting by numbers

Traditional projects tend to be of this kind. These projects have clear goals and a clearly defined set of activities to be carried out. You know *what* you want to achieve and *how* you will achieve it.

This project is often formally called a *closed project*.

Going on a quest

You are clear on *what* is to be done but clueless as to the means (*how*) to achieve it. It is named after the famous quest for the Holy Grail. The secret of this type of project is get your "knights" fired up to seek for solutions in different places at the same time and ensure that they all return to report progress and share their findings on a fixed date. You can then continue to send them out, again and again until you have sufficient visibility on how you can achieve your objectives.

Quests are invaluable as they give "permission" for your people to explore "out of the box" possibilities. However, they are notorious for overspending, being very late, or simply delivering nothing of benefit. You must keep very strict control over costs and timescales while allowing the scope free range.

This project is formally called a *semi-closed project*.

Making movies

In this type of project you are very sure of *how* you will do something but have no idea *what* to do. Typically your company has built up significant expertise and capability and you are looking for ways to apply it. There must be several people committed to the methods you will use.

This project is formally called a *semi-open project*.

Walking in the fog

This type of project is one where you have no idea *what* to do nor *how* to do it. It is often prompted as a reaction to a change in circumstances (e.g. political, competitive, social), although it can be set off proactively. You know you have to change and do something different; you simply can't stay still. You also may need to act with awesome velocity. This project needs, in some ways, to be managed like a quest. You need to have very tight control over costs and timescale; you need to investigate many options and possible solutions in parallel. Like a quest, these projects can end up in delivering nothing of benefit unless firmly controlled.

This project is formally called an *open project*.

Each of these project types has different characteristics and requires different leadership styles. They are also suited for different purposes.

Project type	*Type of change it helps create or man*	*Application*
Painting by numbers	Evolutionary	Improving your continuing business operations
Going on a quest	Revolutionary	Proactively exploring outside current operations and way of working (recipe)
Making a movie	Evolutionary	Leveraging existing capabilities
Lost in a fog	Revolutionary	Solve problem or explore area outside your current operations and way of working (recipe)

Source: Eddie Obeng *Putting Strategy to Work* (London: Pitman Publishing, 1996)

Fitting into the staged framework

The staged framework requires that, by the time you reach the Development Gate, you know, with a reasonable level of confidence, *what* you are going to do and *how* you are going to do it. That is to say, at the Development Gate you will have a painting by numbers project (see Figure 12.2). The investigative stages are there to give you the time, resources, and money to discover a solution to your problem. The Proposal will have settled *why* you need the project. However, your level of background knowledge will differ for each proposal you want to do.

This will have a considerable impact on the way you undertake the investigative stages and the level of risk associated with the project at the start. Painting by numbers projects tend to be less risky than others, but not always. Figure 12.3 shows this in a different way: a "normal" project (if there is such a thing!) can change from being a quest, movie, or fog to painting by numbers as it moves through the project life cycle. The clarity of your scope, timescale, costs, and benefits will improve as you gain more knowledge. In addition, as we learned earlier (p. 50), the level of risk should decrease as you progress through the project.

However, just to make your day, there are circumstances when you would allow a project to continue past the Development Gate as a fog, movie, or quest. The level of risk would be higher than under normal circumstances but that is your choice. The "game" of projects has principles but few rules. Directors have to direct and managers have to manage; that is your role. If an action makes common sense, do it and do it openly.

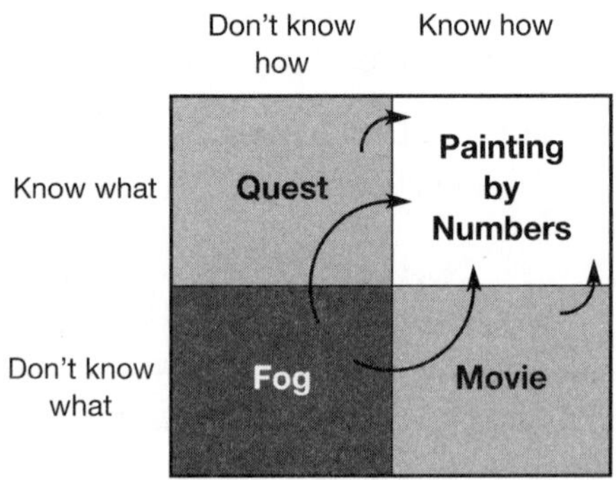

Figure 12.2 Creating a project you can implement

The staged framework requires, by the time you reach the Development Gate, that you know what you are going to do and how. That is to say, at the Development Gate, you will have a painting by numbers project. You may, however, start off as any of the project types – the investigative stages are the means by which you create the final project.

RULES AND EXCEPTIONS

Some companies tie themselves up in process rules bound neatly in files with quality assurance labels. These rules often go to great levels of detail covering every conceivable scenario.

I would argue that this is a fruitless exercise. It is far better to have a few basic principles and make sure your people understand why you need them and how they help them do their jobs. You can then handle the odd "exception" using "exception management," dealing with it on its own merits within the principles you have laid out. In other words, give the managers and supervisors the freedom to do their jobs and exercise the very skills you are paying them for.

If you write rules at a microlevel:

- you may get them wrong;
- you will spend a long time writing them thus diverting you from the real issues;
- people will look for "legitimate" ways round them;
- you will cause people to break them (perhaps through ignorance) and then risk making them feel bad about it;
- you risk employing an army of policemen to check that the rules are being adhered to.

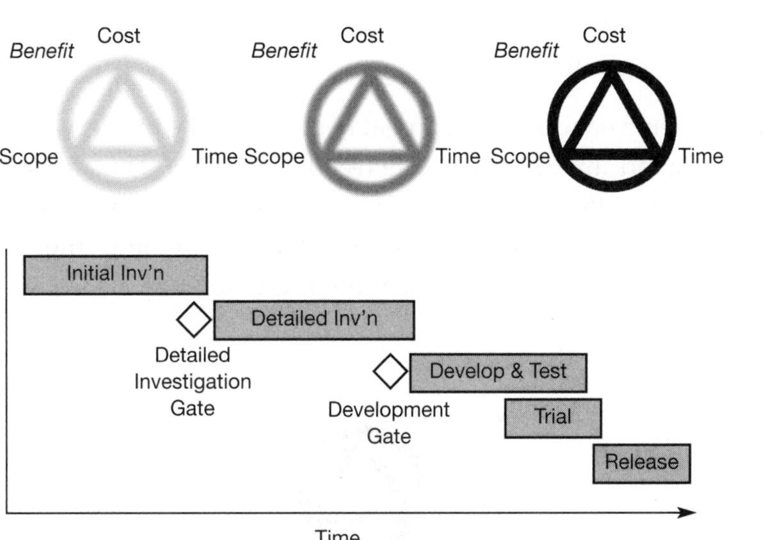

Figure 12.3 Getting to paint by numbers
A "normal" project can change from being a "quest," "movie," or "fog" to "painting by numbers" as it moves through the project life cycle. The clarity of your scope, timescale, costs, and benefits will improve as you gain more knowledge.

Small stuff, or "simple" projects

"I understand stages and gates," you may say, "but isn't it all a bit too much for smaller simple projects?" Let us take the example of how what I would term a "simple" project differs from the type of project normally associated with staged processes and how you can deal with them using the same management framework.

A normal project may start off as painting by numbers, a fog, a quest, or a movie. The investigative stages are worked through until you are confident (say, around 90–95 percent) the required benefits can be achieved. At the Detailed Investigation Gate you will have narrowed your options down and have approval and funding to complete the Detailed Investigation Stage. At the Development Gate you would have approval to complete the project as a whole – it has become a painting by numbers project.

With a simple project, you usually know a great deal about it before you even start. By the time you finish the Initial Investigation Stage you may have fully defined the project outputs and plan and your confidence level will be as high as it is normally for a larger project at the Development Gate (Figure 12.4).

In these circumstances, the Detailed Investigation Stage may either be:

- reduced in scope and time to become very small;
- or dispensed with altogether.

In these circumstances, full approval to complete the project can be given at the Detailed Investigation Gate (see Figure 12.5). This doesn't mean you can bypass the remaining gates, you still need to have reviews and checks to ensure on-going viability. So if you omit the Detailed Investigation Stage you must meet the full criteria of the Development Gate before you continue.

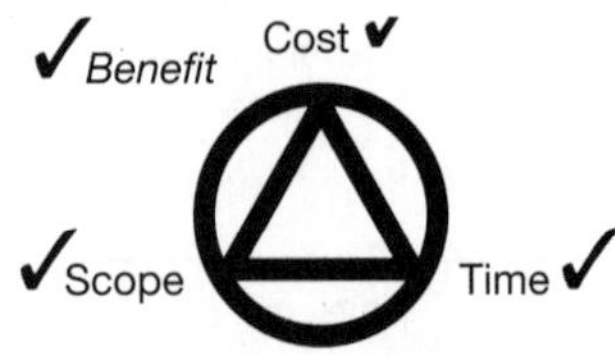

Figure 12.4 Simple project
A simple project can be defined very closely, in the Initial Investigation Stage.

In this way, you have used the principles of the framework, checking at every gate but you have avoided doing any unnecessary work. Making the key control documents, Initial Business Case, and Business Case identical enables this to happen without the need to duplicate any documentation. (See also p. 185 for a discussion of simple projects in relation to decision making.)

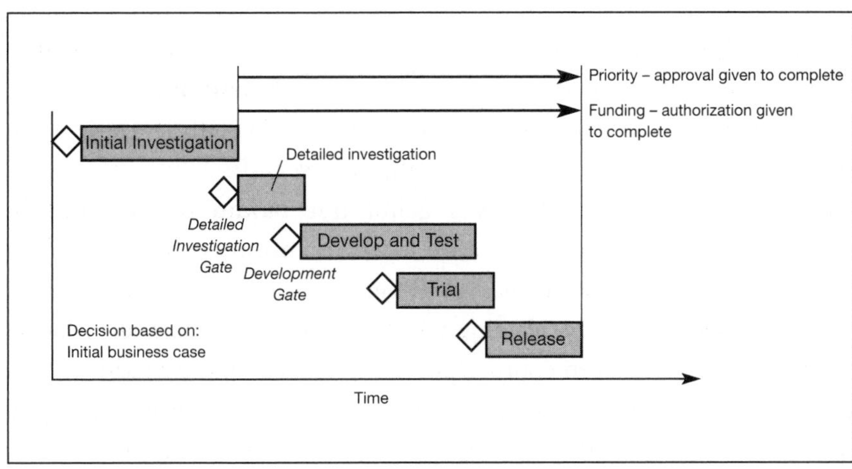

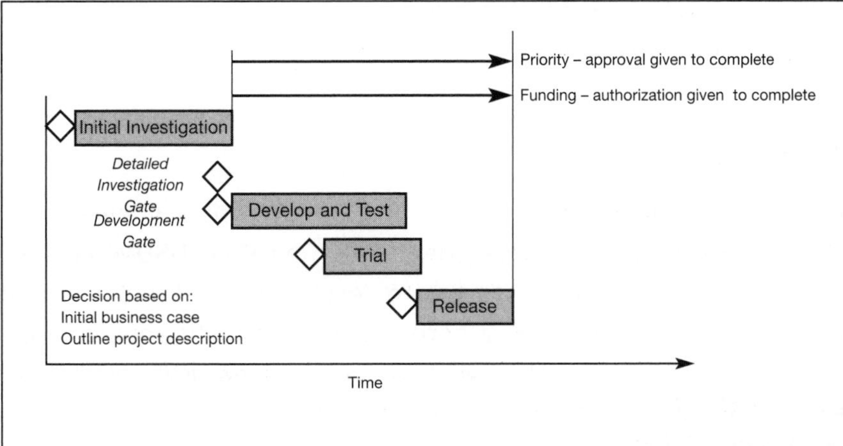

Figure 12.5 The stages for a simple project

The top diagram represents a project where some detailed investigation work still needs to be done. Nevertheless, the level of confidence is high enough to authorize and fund the project to completion.

The lower diagram represents an even simpler case where no further investigative work needs to be done. The project is checked against the criteria for the Development Gate and, if acceptable, moves straight into the Develop and Test Stage.

Rapid projects

Consider also the concept of "rapid development" or "dynamic system development" projects. These are particular development techniques or methods where a project is defined with a fixed budget and timescale but where the scope is varied to suit (see Figure 12.6). If the team runs out of time or money, the scope is reduced in order to meet the time/cost targets. Provided a predefined, minimum scope is delivered, the project will remain within its area of benefit viability. In many ways, it is like a "simple" project except that the scope is variable within known limits. You are, therefore, able to assign resources to it with confidence, knowing when they will become available for other projects.

Rapid techniques usually involve iterative requirements definition, design and delivery using either a prototype platform or the actual operational platform. Thus the Detailed Investigation Stage is often merged with the Develop and Test Stage. Having two stages running in parallel on closely knit work such as this can confuse people. The usual point made is "What stage do I book my time to on the time sheet?" This can be dealt with by dispensing with the detailed investigation altogether and moving straight from the Initial Investigation Stage to the Develop and Test Stage (similar to Figure 12.5, lower diagram).

RAPID OR RABID?

The lessons taught us that there is no "fast track" process. If there were, it would become the usual process (see p. 19). "Rapid" or "DSDM" are methods or techniques which enable you to develop your deliverables faster *within* the overall framework. A correctly designed and applied staged framework should not slow any projects down unless they need to be.

The lessons taught us that there is no "fast track" process. If there were, it would become the usual process.

Rapid application development techniques are used when they suit the particular circumstances of the project. If you use them merely because you are "in a hurry," you risk reducing your project to chaos, i.e. it will become "rabid" rather than rapid!

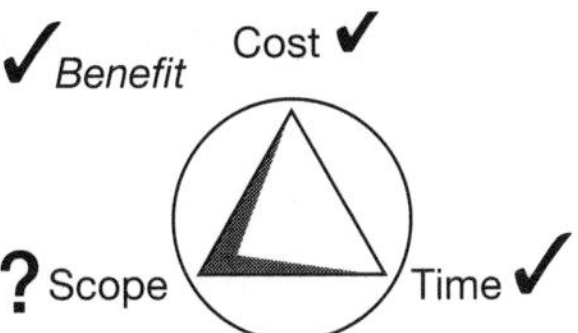

Figure 12.6 Rapid project
A project using rapid techniques has fixed timescale, cost, and minimum benefits. Scope varies to suit these constraints.

"Just do it" projects: loose cannons

There are cases when senior management will issue an edict to finish a project by a certain time whatever the cost. In certain circumstances this is a valid thing to do, especially when the survival of the company requires it. Such projects must be treated with extreme caution as often they come about as an executive's "pet project" and may have little proven foundation in business strategy. I would argue that there are very few instances in companies where something needs to be done regardless of the costs and consequences. These projects invariably start off being optimistic and end up bouncing around the organization with the demand that more and more resources are assigned to it without delay. Consequently, there can be considerable impact on day-to-day operations as well as significant delays to other projects, remembering delayed projects equate to delayed benefits. They also tend to be very stressful for those associated with them. The damage left in the wake of such projects can be awesome even if they appear to succeed!

Most organizations can cope with one of these kinds of projects – occasionally. Most organizations cope better if there aren't any. However, if you believe one is needed it should still be aligned into the project framework as closely as possible and managed as an "exception" (see also p. 186).

But before starting, consider:

- Why am I doing this?
- Is it really far more important than everything else in the company?
- Am I really sure what I am doing?

There must be very compelling reasons to allow a loose cannon project to start. Responding to a problem by panicking is not usually a good enough reason! Using the issue breakthrough technique is a better starting point.

You must be absolutely clear what other activities and projects it can be allowed to disrupt. You can create more problems, for yourself and for others, than you will solve. You must consider the real "cost/benefit" and take into consideration the inefficiencies and lost or delayed benefits from the disrupted projects. After all that, if you really must do it then:

1 Undertake an initial investigation first so you can make an informed decision;
2 Keep the project as short as possible (say, three months maximum). If you need longer, chunk the project up into smaller pieces.

- **No matter what project you want to undertake, always carry out an initial investigation so that you can decide, on an informed basis, the most appropriate way to take the project forward (e.g. normal, simple, rapid).**
- **Having decided your approach, record it in your initial business case in Section 2.10 on project approach (see p. 265).**

Big stuff, or projects and subprojects

Defining the scope and boundaries of a project is often problematic. The term "project," like its cousin "program," is used so loosely that it has very little meaning. In some cases, what one person calls a project, another will call a program. Similarly "subproject" and "project" can cause confusion. The relative structural relationship is identical:

Program	*is equivalent to*	Project
Project		Subproject

Nine times out of ten it doesn't really matter what you call things but, if you are to understand business projects fully, you need to be able to see the distinction.

If you are to have clarity of communication in your business, you must decide on the definitions which suit you best and stick to them (see p. 57).

A project, in a business environment, is:

- a finite piece of work (it has a beginning and an end);
- undertaken within defined cost and time constraints;
- *directed at achieving a stated business benefit.*

In other words, the key elements of benefit, scope, time, and cost are all present. The only place where all this is recorded is in the Business Case, which serves as the key review document for approving and authorizing the project in initial form at the Detailed Investigation Gate and in full at the Development Gate. As a working assumption, therefore, we can say a project is only a project if it has a Business Case. Business Cases are attached to business projects!

It, therefore, follows that . . . any piece of work, which is finite, time, and cost constrained but does not deliver business benefit, is not in fact a business project. It may be managed using project techniques or it may be a subproject or work package within a project. On its own, however, it has no direct value. Only when combined with other elements of work does it have any value.

Any piece of work, which is finite, time, and cost constrained but does not deliver business benefit, is not in fact a business project. It may be managed using project techniques or it may be a subproject or work package within a project.

Work packages

In any project, the project manager delegates accountability for parts of the work to members of the core team. This is done by breaking the project into work packages, usually centered around deliverables. Each work package has a person accountable for it. This work package can be decomposed again and again until you reach activity or task level. This structure is called a "work breakdown structure" (WBS) and is a fundamental control tool for a project.

The first level of breakdown is the project itself. The second level of breakdown comprises the life cycle stages (initial investigation, detailed investigation, etc.). Below this are the more detailed work packages.

The top diagram in Figure 12.7 shows this: the Develop and Test Stage comprises three work packages (XX, YY and ZZ). Of these, package YY is divided into three more (Y1, Y2, and Y3). The whole structure of the project flows logically from project to stage to work package. Each work package has its own defined time, cost, scope, and person accountable. It will *not* have its own discrete benefit. All things being equal, this is the way you should structure your projects. It provides good control as no part of the project can proceed into the next stage without all preconditions being present.

The bottom diagram in Figure 12.7 shows an alternative structure for exactly the same project. In this case, however, the project manager has chosen to treat work YY as a subproject. In other words, it has a single identifiable work package, which is itself divided into stages and then into the lower level work packages (Y1, Y2, and Y3). The remainder of the project is dealt with in the preferred way. There are risks in using this structure:

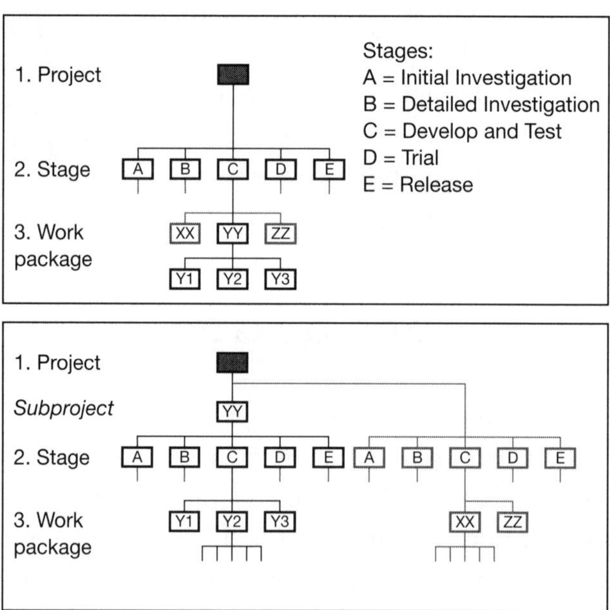

Figure 12.7 Explaining work packages and subprojects
The top diagram shows a project divided into the five stages of the project framework. Each stage can then be divided into a number of work packages (e.g. C is divided into XX, YY and ZZ). In the bottom diagram the same project has been restructured to have YY managed as a subproject.

- You may have a timing misalignment between subproject YY and the rest of the project as there are two separate life cycle stage sets.
- It is a more complex structure for the same work scope.

Both these require greater coordination by the project manager.

From this we are able to define subprojects more exactly.

Subprojects are tightly coupled and tightly aligned parts of a project.

The conditions under which you would choose to set up subprojects depend on the degree of delegation you want to effect – it is akin to subcontracting the work. You also find this type of structure happens as a result of systems and process limitations or reporting requirements. It may be more convenient to represent and report a completely delegated piece of work as a subproject as it may relate to work which has been let externally, under a contract or internally. Internally, many companies treat their software development in this way.

A Few Related Projects
Programs

Programs

Sharing projects: interdependencies

Some projects are simply too large to manage as a single entity.

"Adventure is the result of poor planning."
COL. BLASHFORD SNELL

Programs

We have seen that the staged project framework can be applied to any type of project for any purpose. It is a tool that you can adopt and adapt to suit your needs. Nevertheless, a simple string of activities, passing through five defined stages, may not give you the full flexibility you require. We saw in Figure 12.7 how we can manage the subparts of a project using the work break-down structure. This is how the project manager delegates work to the managers within the core team.

Programs

Some projects, however, are simply too large to manage as a single entity. It is often more convenient and effective to define the work in a series of closely related and linked projects, each of which is managed by a project manager, reporting to a program manager (Figure 13.1). The role of the program manager in this respect is identical to that of a project manager (as described in Chapter 4) except that detailed management of parts of the project is delegated, as is the associated administration. He or she will have a core team of project managers, rather than team managers.

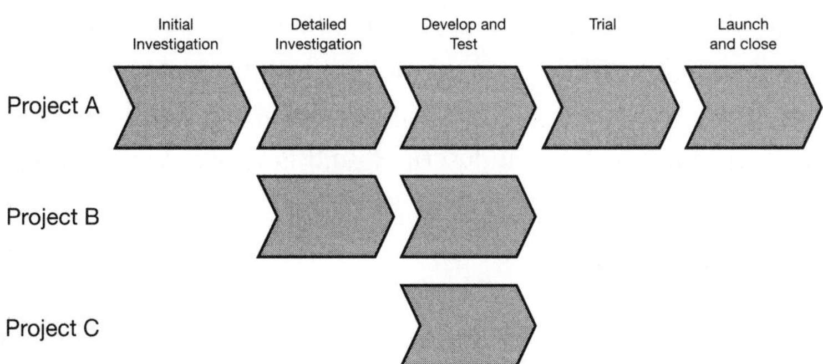

Figure 13.1 A program
A program where each constituent project is used to manage a substantial work scope.

Phased programs

Other projects are so extended in time it is beneficial to phase the development and delivery of the solutions. This ensures that the company starts benefitting as early as possible and also increases the likelihood of success (Figure 13.2). It also gives the company a "get-out" if the need the program was set up to fill either evaporates or if the chosen solution is not meeting it. The start-point for each new phase acts as just such a review point.

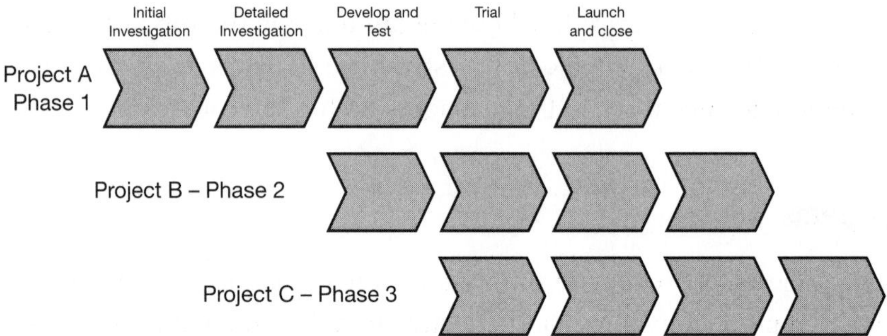

Figure 13.2 A phased program
A program comprising a number (in this case three) of phased deliverables, each managed as a project.

The permutations beyond this are endless. For example, you may have a phased program where each phase is itself a program such as that described in Figure 13.1. There are no rules, you just have to make it very clear what you are doing. The staged framework is very useful in this respect as it can give an overview of the program in terms of known stages such that any person in the organization can understand it. You should treat any program which is not described in this way as very suspicious.

Program organizations

Organization structures for programs are many and varied. However, in principle, they are very similar to those described in Chapter 4. The key difference is that instead of the structure comprising a project manager supported by team managers and members, it comprises a program manager supported by project managers, all of whom have their own teams.

This is shown in Figure 13.3. The accountabilities of a program manager in other respects is the same as that for a project manager. However the scale of most programs is such that the experience and skill set required to carry out the accountabilities are quite different.

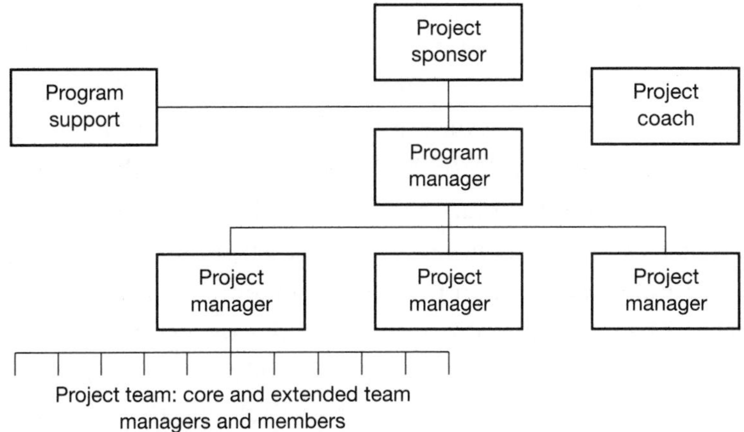

Figure 13.3 A typical program structure
A program structure comprises a program manager supported by Project managers. In addition, there is often a program support group to undertake the essential coordination, administration, and to implement common standards.

Sharing projects: interdependencies

A project comprises all the work required to ensure you put the changes in place to enable the benefits to be delivered. However, on occasions, the deliverable you require may be produced by another project, often within the same program, but not necessarily so. In this case your project is said to be *dependent* on the other project. Such interdependencies are noted in the business case in the "scope, impacts, and interdependencies" section (see also pp. 263, 311). Sharing of work between projects:

- adds to the efficient use of resources on your projects;
- ensures consistency between developments;
- reduces costs of projects for your business.

If this one software delivery is delayed by just a single problematic part of the development, relating to one project only, the whole bundle slips. In other words, the full set of interdependent projects is tied to the one with the greatest risk.

In all, it sounds like a "good thing." With most companies relying heavily on information systems to enable them to run the business, software development, whether in-house or out-sourced, is frequently required as part of business change and is "shared" between projects. From the point of view of the systems developer, it is preferable to batch requirements from new projects and deliver them as a new software release. It makes life easier for the development team for configuration management, for implementation, and for training. In many cases, this is in fact sound practice but it does need to be considered more widely than that. If you take this approach, a number of projects, serving different needs and under different programs, may be bundled together. If this one software delivery is delayed by just a single problematic part of the development, relating to one project only, the whole bundle slips. In other words, the full set of interdependent projects is tied to the one with the greatest risk. It is hardly surprising that software delivery is invariably "blamed" for making projects late. While I have made an example of software, the same principle applies to any deliverable which is shared between projects.

Don't build in risk from the start by bundling things that need not be bundled.

From a risk-management viewpoint it is often preferable to separate out the discrete developments and carry them out in discrete releases. Don't build in risk from the start by bundling things that need not be bundled. The loss of efficiency may be paid for many times over by the benefits flowing from having projects deliver on time.

PROGRAMS

Three different configurations of programs can be identified:

- **Portfolio**: a set of related projects aimed at meeting the business plan needs (or part of). These are dealt with in Part Three of this book as "business programs".
- **Goal directed**: a set of closely related projects aimed at creating a new capability (as described in this chapter). This is typically outside the usual routine of the organization. They are a way of effecting one-off, major change.
- **Heartbeat**: a set of activities managed around service delivery e.g. a large IT system.

These are shown below:

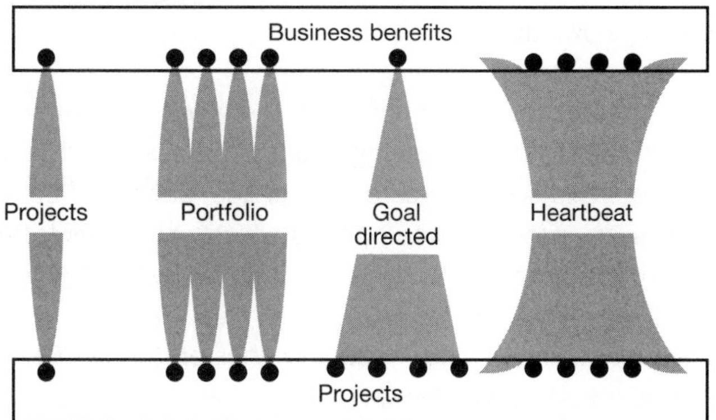

	Portfolio	*Goal directed*	*Heartbeat*
Program's control of projects	Co-ordinate to extract synergy benefits	Definition and direction of all projects within the program	Integration of identified changes into a cohesive program
Planning organization	Program overlays project roles: project sponsor and project manager retain strong relationship	Program acts as client for all projects	Program arbitrates between multiple client needs
Planning horizon	Indeterminate: as long as it adds value	Until the goal is achieved	Until the "system" is withdrawn
Program relationship with the line	Draws on line resources and complements line management with business leadership	Draws resources from line management	Takes on traditional line management role of functions (e.g. operational performance)

Source: Pellegrinelli, S. (1997) 'Programme management: organising project-based change', *International Journal of Project Management*.

13.1

QUESTIONING YOUR PROGRAMS

1. Choose any program in your company and identify the component projects.
2. Split each project into the five project stages, one stage per Post-It Note, using a different color for each project.
3. Prepare a large sheet of paper or a white board, indicating a timescale on the horizontal axis sufficient to include the entire program timescale. Draw a vertical "time now" line.
4. Place each project onto the board, with each stage aligned to the appropriate date. Can you actually do this? If not, question how you really know what is going on and how you can direct the program with any degree of confidence or knowledge.
5. Identify any interdependencies and mark them with a down arrow from the delivering project to the receiving project. Check for multiple two-way dependencies – this could indicate poor project scoping. Remember, interdependencies are potential weak points which can be forgotten or where accountability is abdicated.
6. Look for any very long stages – can you shorten these? Be very wary of any prolonged investigative stages.
7. Look for when benefits start to flow – can you redesign the program to achieve any benefits earlier than this?
8. Look at where your key review and decision points are (they should map onto your gates) – have you sufficient of these to ensure control? Be very wary if it has all been authorized in one lump.

Part Three

DEALING WITH MANY PROJECTS

"The certainties of one age are the problems of the next."

R H TAWNEY, 1926

In Part Two we looked at the framework for managing a single project, taking it from being an idea, through various life cycle stages until benefits are being delivered to your business. We also examined how the staged process could be used as a management framework for any type of project you might choose and/or bundles of related projects (programs).

In Part Three I will explain how you can keep track of all the projects and programs which together make up the set of initiatives aimed at changing your business to suit its future strategic direction. The different ways in which companies control the full portfolio of projects they are undertaking are as diverse and numerous as the companies themselves. It is here that the aspects of culture, structure, and systems come to the fore to influence what you actually do. There is no one "right" way, but there are many "wrong" ways!

- **Balance the risks across your project portfolio.**
- **Build the business case into your business plan as soon as the project has been approved.**
- **Make *informed* decisions on which projects you allow to continue.**
- **Prioritize *benefits*, not projects.**
- **Ensure that you have the freedom to change by having "white space" resources.**
- **Keep a list of the projects you are undertaking.**

How to use Part Three

Read Part Three with an open mind. Understand the principles. Note what needs to be taken into account. Consider how you can deal with these in your company with the particular constraints you have. Do not be too quick to discard the approaches given. Adapt them to meet your needs, within the constraints you have, but stick to the basic principles.

Portfolios of Projects

The Business Program

What's different about Business Program management

Managing the portfolio

Directing a "portfolio" of projects is a key management task, as it is this "bundle" of projects that will take you from where you are now to your, hopefully, better future.

"What shall become of us without the barbarians? Those people were a kind of solution."

CONSTANTINE CAVAFY, 1863–1933

The Business Program

In Chapters 12 and 13 we considered the following definitions:
A **project**, in a business environment, is:

- a piece of work with a beginning an end;
- undertaken within defined cost and time constraints;
- *directed at achieving a stated business benefit.*

Subprojects are tightly coupled and tightly aligned parts of a project.
Programs are a tightly coupled and tightly aligned grouping of projects.

We also saw how a project moves from being "undefined" to being "defined." This was then put into the context of four project types:

- painting by numbers;
- going on a quest;
- making movies;
- walking in a fog.

Once this is understood, you should be able to define a single project in terms of its life cycle stages. However, business is rarely so simple that a single project or even program can achieve all that is needed. The next step is to understand how bundles of programs and projects are used together with other business activities are used to further your aims. We will call these "Business Programs."

Business Programs comprise current benefit generating business activities together with a loosely coupled but tightly aligned portfolio of projects and programs, aimed at delivering the benefits of part of a business plan or strategy.

They are best explained by using a simple example.

You may have a business objective to increase your revenue from $10m to $15m in two years. You've chosen to do this by increasing your share of an under-exploited segment of your market. The alternative is to withdraw from that segment, milking whatever cash you can from it on the way. In order to achieve the required target revenue, you have found that you need to:

- Enhance your current product to include some new features. (Project 1 – enhance old product.)
- Develop a new product to exploit an unfulfilled need identified in the market. To do this quickly, you have decided to launch a basic version of the new product, as soon as practical, to start engaging the market. This would use existing manufacturing capability. (Project 2 – the basic new product.) The launch would be followed up four months later with an enhanced product which meets the full needs. (Project 3 – the enhanced new product.)
- Speed of delivery is a buying factor for your target market and current delivery channels are too slow. You need to decrease delivery time to protect revenues. If the speed of delivery can be greatly increased it will enhance revenues enabling you to win business off competitors. (Project 4 – decrease delivery time.)
- You also know there is a quality problem in manufacturing the current product. While the levels of faults have been acceptable to the target market in the past, this is not the case for the future. You need to reduce manufacturing faults and hence protect revenue. If faults stay at present levels, customers will choose alternative products. (Project 5 – reduce faults.)

You can see that the five projects are aligned to your overall strategy and that each provides a discrete business benefit. Most are independent. (Only Project 3 depends on Project 2 as you cannot enhance a product until you know what it is.)

Notice that the approach has been to split the new product development into two phases (Projects 2 and 3). This benefits you by gaining early revenue and having a foothold in the market. Traditionally, companies make their projects too big. Dividing projects into smaller pieces (chunks of change) makes success more likely and implementation easier.

Traditionally, companies make their projects too big. Dividing projects into smaller pieces makes success more likely and implementation easier.

Finally, you need to take account of the benefits you are expecting from the product as it currently is in the market. Your aim is to obtain a $15m revenue. The benefits from your current product and future projects and initiatives need to be sufficiently high to meet that target.

As a business manager, you are not particularly concerned with the individual performance of each project and product. Of more interest is the total benefit. Thus, if your current product starts to perform better than expected, a delay in a project may not be too significant. Only *you* can decide the relative importance of the projects within the business program.

How did the projects within the business program come about?

Keeping to the example, how did the managers derive their approach and end up with the five projects I described? The starting point was a problem for the directors of the company: they needed more revenue. They needed to look at their complete mix of products and markets and decide the most likely areas for gaining the extra revenue. (Perhaps they needed a new product and a new market!) One option identified by the review was that they either take a minimum prescribed market share of a particular segment or they withdraw from it completely. It was considered untenable to keep the status quo. This would lead to a decline in revenue to about $7 per year. This conversation is firmly within the domain of business strategy and planning. What is needed now is to take it to action.

The five projects could not, in fact, have come about directly as the result of a strategic review. The company simply would not have known enough to make that jump. At most, a required timescale and overall affordable budget annual cash flow could have been set (i.e. constraints applied by the business). However, a project could have been initiated to look at various options – a quest! The Initial Investigation Stage would spawn a set of possible projects. These may just have been:

- enhance the existing product (Project 1);
- develop a new product (Project 2);
- reduce faults (Project 5).

Each fulfills the definition of a business project by delivering discrete benefits. Each will further the aims of the company to attain more revenue.

However, the investigative stages of Project 2 came up with a constraint on manufacturing the new product. It was not possible to do it in the time available and hence a decision was made to create the product in two phases. We now have:

- enhance the existing product (Project 1);
- develop a new product (Project 2);
- enhance the new product (Project 3);
- reduce faults (Project 5).

Notice what has happened. Projects spawn projects! A simple business objective of "Get $15m revenue" has been translated into action in the form of five projects. When combined, these deliver the benefit which the business requires.

Again, the Detailed Investigation Stage of Project 2 found, as part of the market research, that delivery time was a more important buying factor than realized. If amendments to Project 2 were made to incorporate this, it would have slipped and the revenue targets would have been missed. Consequently, a separate project was started off to take this aspect into account (Project 4). (See Figure 14.1.)

Notice what has happened. Projects spawn projects! A clear business program objective of "Get $15m revenue" has been translated into action in the form of five projects. When combined, these deliver the benefit which the business requires. Note that each project is defined such that it delivers a slice of that benefit, either independently or, as in the case of Projects 2 and 3, in series. Also notice that the business solution has been broken into discrete pieces. This has the effect of making them easier to implement and also allows benefits to be delivered earlier than if the full scope were undertaken in a single project. You can also proceed with parts of the business program as soon as you're ready, while other parts are still in the fog!

Look at the projects that have resulted. Did they start off as fogs, quests, movies, or painting by numbers? Probably the mix is as follows:

Project 1 – enhance old product:	Painting by numbers
Project 2 – the basic new product:	Movie
Project 3 – the enhanced new product:	Quest or fog
Project 4 – decrease delivery time:	Quest
Project 5 – reduce faults:	Quest

Project 2 has to use existing manufacturing plant for producing the new product. Project 3 needs to be converted to a painting by numbers project if it is to succeed. Projects 4 and 5 are more open ended. You may spend a fortune looking at possibilities but still not achieve a breakthrough. This, on its own, gives you a feel for the risk you are facing. You are not likely to have too much confidence in the benefits for those projects which finish more than a year from now. So, to make sure that your business program is robust, you will need continually to reforecast your benefits. With a business program like that shown, a related business planning and forecasting cycle of three months would probably be about right.

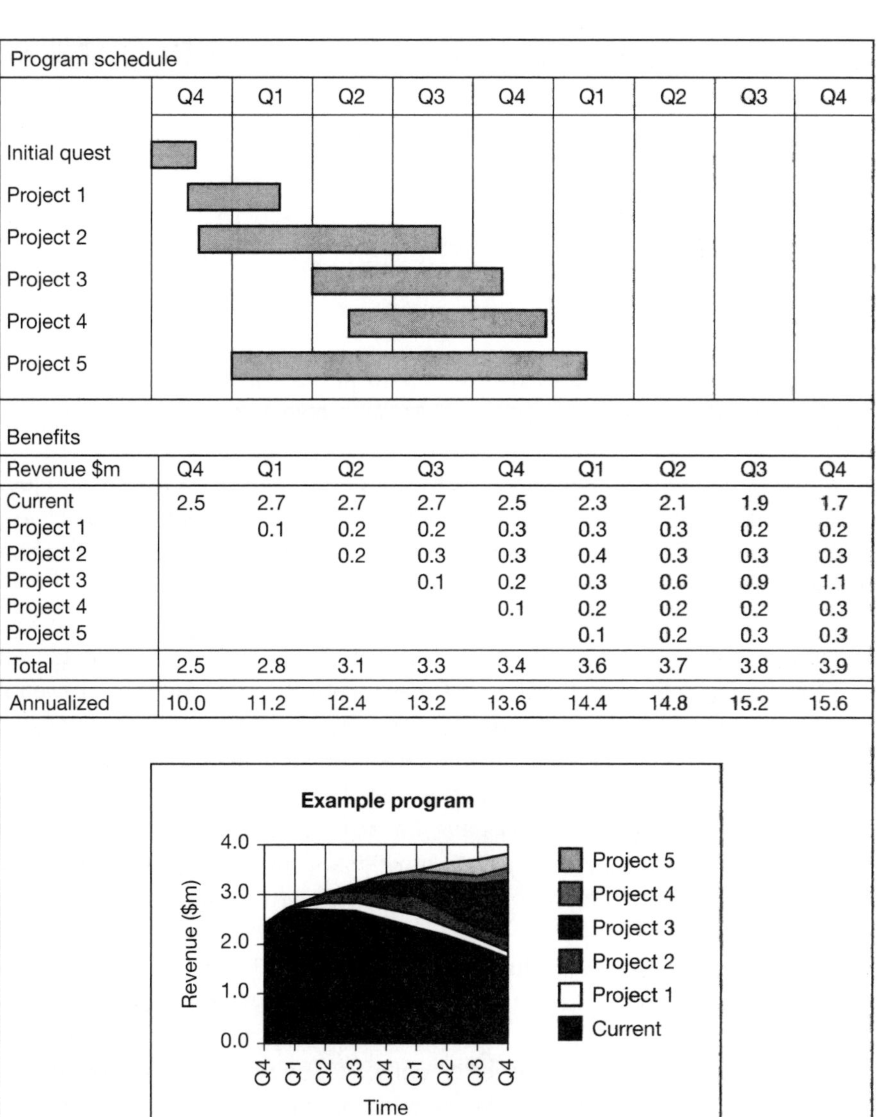

Revenue $m	Q4	Q1	Q2	Q3	Q4	Q1	Q2	Q3	Q4
Current	2.5	2.7	2.7	2.7	2.5	2.3	2.1	1.9	1.7
Project 1		0.1	0.2	0.2	0.3	0.3	0.3	0.2	0.2
Project 2			0.2	0.3	0.3	0.4	0.3	0.3	0.3
Project 3				0.1	0.2	0.3	0.6	0.9	1.1
Project 4					0.1	0.2	0.2	0.2	0.3
Project 5						0.1	0.2	0.3	0.3
Total	2.5	2.8	3.1	3.3	3.4	3.6	3.7	3.8	3.9
Annualized	10.0	11.2	12.4	13.2	13.6	14.4	14.8	15.2	15.6

Figure 14.1 Business Program schedule and expected revenue
The schedule for the projects within the Business Program is shown at the top; each bar represents a project. The middle part of the figure shows the slices of revenue expected as a result of each project coming to fruition layered on the revenues you expect from the current product. This is shown graphically below.

The example is necessarily simpler than most situations you will find in practice; nevertheless, it does demonstrate the key aspects of Business Programs.

14.1

STARTING TO BUILD YOUR BUSINESS PROGRAMS

1 Take the list of projects from Project Workout 3.1.

2 Write each one on a Post-It Note.

3 Start placing them on a wall or large white board in approximate chronological order.

4 Group together in bands across the board those which you believe are targeted at fulfilling the same primary business objective.

5 Identify any interdependencies between projects (i.e. where one project relies on the deliverable(s) from another in order to meet its objective). Draw an arrow from the project creating the deliverable to the one requiring the deliverable.

6 You may have a very complex picture by now! Try to simplify it. Projects with arrows going both ways between them are probably the same project even if you've defined them as separate. To test this, ask yourself if either one of the projects on its own produces any benefit to the business. If both projects are needed to deliver the benefit, they are the same project. Look for clusters of linked projects which have no arrows between them and other clusters. They may be your business programs. Look for projects which don't have significant benefits: mark them for possible termination (see p. 398).

7 Look at the complexity of the interdependencies. The more complex and interwoven, the more risky the portfolio becomes. Think of ways of rescoping projects to create a set of programs and projects which are relatively independent and deliver benefits early. Rescoping entails moving the accountability for producing a deliverable from one project to another.

Changes to projects

In some cases, it is necessary to include new scope in an on-going project. Proper management of changes to the project scope are required to ensure that only beneficial changes are made. Chapter 25 explains this more fully.

What's different about Business Program management?

Business Programs support business plans

Business Program management provides the framework and practical tool for managing multiple programs and projects in pursuit of defined strategic objectives. Business Program management complements project and program management but it takes a much broader, enterprise-wide view as it should also include benefits from current operations. Benefits from projects usually start after the project has been completed and the project team has been stood down. However, benefits from Business Programs start to flow as soon as the first project within the business program has been completed and its outputs incorporated into 'normal business'. The key focus for Business Program management is ensuring that current activities plus the programs and projects as a whole provide the benefit required overall, regardless of the performance of individual components. Other differences are highlighted in the table that follows.

The advantages of taking a "Business Program approach" is that you are able, as we have seen from the simple example, to break up the required changes into achievable pieces and manage the implementation in a coordinated way.

The advantages of taking a "Business Program approach" is that you are able, as we have seen from the simple example, to break up the required changes into achievable pieces and manage the implementation in a coordinated way. The change is therefore less likely to appear chaotic to the recipients (be they your own employees, your suppliers, or customers). You are also able to maintain a focus on the true objectives of the Business Program rather than be lost in the minutiae of delivery. This enables you to spot future gaps in benefits (either due to late projects or under-performance in benefit terms from ones already delivered) and take the necessary corrective action. You are also able to take a balanced view of the risks associated with a Business Program.

Business Program management	*Program and project management*
Broadly spread activity, concerned with overall strategic objectives as part of a business plan. It's a continuous activity, with no defined end-point	Intense, well defined and focused activity aimed at delivering a "slice" of benefit to the business program as defined in a business case. It is a discrete activity, with a defined end-point
Is suited to managing and balancing a large number of constituent programs and projects with complex and often changing interdependencies	Best suited to delivering achievable deliverables with a discrete objective
Is suited to managing the impact of and benefits from a number of aligned programs and projects in such a way as to ensure a smooth transition from the present to the new order	Is suited to delivering defined benefits within a given environment
Includes benefits from current operations and from the outcomes of current and future projects	Includes future benefits of the project or program itself
Is governed and constrained by company cash flow often seen as an annual budget	Is governed and constrained by a discrete project budget

Business Programs in small and large organizations

I have already mentioned the difficulties that certain words can create; "program" is just such a problematic word (see pp. 57, 143). No matter how hard you try there will always be someone, somewhere who takes a different view. Accept it and don't fight it. I expect there are many readers who say my definition of Business Program is their definition of program – neither of us is wrong. I just happen to look on a program as a BIG project. But in your organization, make sure your use you words consistently in all your written documents, especially management reports. If you use the language consistently, people will gradually pick it up. In this book I distinguish business program from program from project. In a small company the business program may represent the entire organization, in which case the term becomes redundant. In larger organizations, the business plan will need to be divided into a number of Business Programs each of which represents a part of the overall business plan.

Business Program accountabilities

If a Business Program is a chunk of the business plan, who is accountable for it and what are those accountabilities? For small organizations we have seen, from the last Point of Interest that "Business Program" may be a meaningless term – the company *is* the Business Program. It therefore follows that the role of the CEO or president and that of the senior team is relevant. In relation to projects, these roles are primarily about the leadership of change and this requires both sponsorship (benefit needs) and management (making it happen).

The Business Program Sponsor is accountable for ensuring that the portfolio of projects within his/her Business Program scope delivers the benefits the business requires.

The Business Program Manager is accountable to the business program sponsor for ensuring that the portfolio is planned and managed to ensure maximum focus and speed of benefit delivery.

A Business Program board, if required, would support the Business Program sponsor in his/her accountabilities.

Business Program Sponsor:

- Provides business direction to the Business Program in terms of decisions, initiating new projects, terminating unwanted projects and resolving issues.
- Delivers the combined benefits of the Business Program to the business.
- Ensures the scope of the Business Program covers the needs of the business.
- Assigns the project sponsor role for each project within the Business Program.
- Ensures the projects are progressed, by the project sponsor, through the authorization process.

Business Program Manager

- Identifies and plans for the underlying projects which form part of the Business Program.
- Identifies additional reserve for as yet unidentified projects.
- Prepares and maintains a plan of timescale, benefits and costs (budget) for the Business Program.
- Manages the portfolio of projects within the Business Program including interdependencies, to deliver the required benefits and ensuring the contributions of all parts of the organization are taken into account.
- Provides regular progress reports to the Business Program sponsor.

Business Programs and cross-company leadership

Test the business program roles. Replace the words **Business Program Sponsor** by **CEO** and **the business** by **shareholder**. Notice the fit? The implication is that the role is truly one of leadership and not one of functional management. Business Program Sponsors may be top directors or executives who have some functional accountability but in the world of projects, they need to take on a cross-company role as we know any single function can achieve very little on its own. (See also pp. 184, 200.)

CHUNKS OF CHANGE

14.2 Look at any one of your longer running projects, say over a six-month duration. Critically review it to decide if you could have implemented it in smaller pieces. What was the minimum that was needed to be done?

Look at projects you are starting off now. Can these be divided into more digestible pieces?

Forecasting cycles

How often do you do your business forecasting? Annually? Quarterly? Monthly? If you do it only annually, consider how you can have confidence in the forecasts. Do you really know so much about the future that you could forecast a year in advance? Is your company really in such a slow moving competitive environment?

Note: Forecasting is predicting what your management accounts and information systems will tell you in the future. Setting a target is not forecasting.

Managing the portfolio

In Chapter 1 we identified a number of commonly found deficiencies in how projects are managed. A key factor in the success of your company is the speed and effectiveness with which you can stay ahead of, or respond to, changing circumstances. Unless deficiencies in implementing the necessary changes are addressed, you will always be losing time and energy in fighting internal conflicts rather than addressing real external opportunities and threats.

No company, however, has just a single project, there are always several on the go and (as we have seen) "projects spawn projects" there will always be more to come, either as part of a program or as stand-alone initiatives. Directing this "portfolio" of projects is a key management task, as it is this "bundle" of projects that will take you from where you are now to your, hopefully, better future.

A portfolio is a range of investments held by a person or organization. A business program is a very special type of portfolio.

I also use the word portfolio to represent any bundle or grouping of projects which we may choose to select for the convenience of management, reporting, or analysis. After all, projects are investments of time and resources made by companies to achieve benefits. Thus, the full set of projects undertaken within a company is its company portfolio. The set of projects held by a project sponsor is a sponsorship portfolio. The set of projects project managed by a person or function is a management portfolio.

Like investments in the stock market, your portfolio of projects should be balanced with respect to risk. You should have some (but not too many!) projects which are risky, which will create a step change if they work or which are pushing forward the boundaries of your corporate thinking and capability.

At a company portfolio level, the actual performance of individual projects (or even programs) becomes less critical. You can accept some being terminated, some being late, some costing too much or simply delivering the wrong thing. What is more critical is that the whole portfolio performs well enough to move your business forward as effectively and efficiently as possible. Like investments in the stock market, your portfolio of projects should be balanced with respect to risk. You should have some (but not too many!) projects which are risky, which will create a step change if they work or which are pushing forward the boundaries of your corporate thinking and capability. Without these, you will be too rooted in today's paradigms and not reaching for new horizons.

Figure 14.2 illustrates the framework. Future benefits come from three sources in your company from:

- the operation of the company as currently set up;
- the changes created by projects you already have under way;
- proposals you have identified which need to be started.

Any change starts as a proposal, becomes part of the project portfolio and eventually its output is subsumed into "business as usual." The speed and reliability with which you can do this is a critical success factor for your organization.

So what are the prerequisites for managing a portfolio on a company-wide basis? The central "plank" to managing a portfolio is reliable management of the individual projects:

- **A staged approach**: you should use a simple staged framework for the management of your projects to enable key decisions to be made at known points (gates).
- **Good project control techniques**: you should ensure that a basic foundation knowledge of project management techniques is understood and practised.

To make these work, you must have an environment (Figure 14.2) for:

- **Strategic alignment**: ensuring you choose the "right" projects to turn your strategy into action.
- **Decision making**: you must make decisions which are respected, are the right ones and are made in the best interest of your company.
- **Resource management**: you must ensure that you have visibility of the availability and consumption of resources you need to undertake your projects and operate the outcomes.
- **Business planning**: you should make the management of your portfolio of projects a part of your business – it is not an optional extra. Projects **are** "business as usual".
- **Release management**: you need to know what projects you are doing, when, why, and who for.
- **Fund management**: you should ensure funding follows the projects you want to undertake.

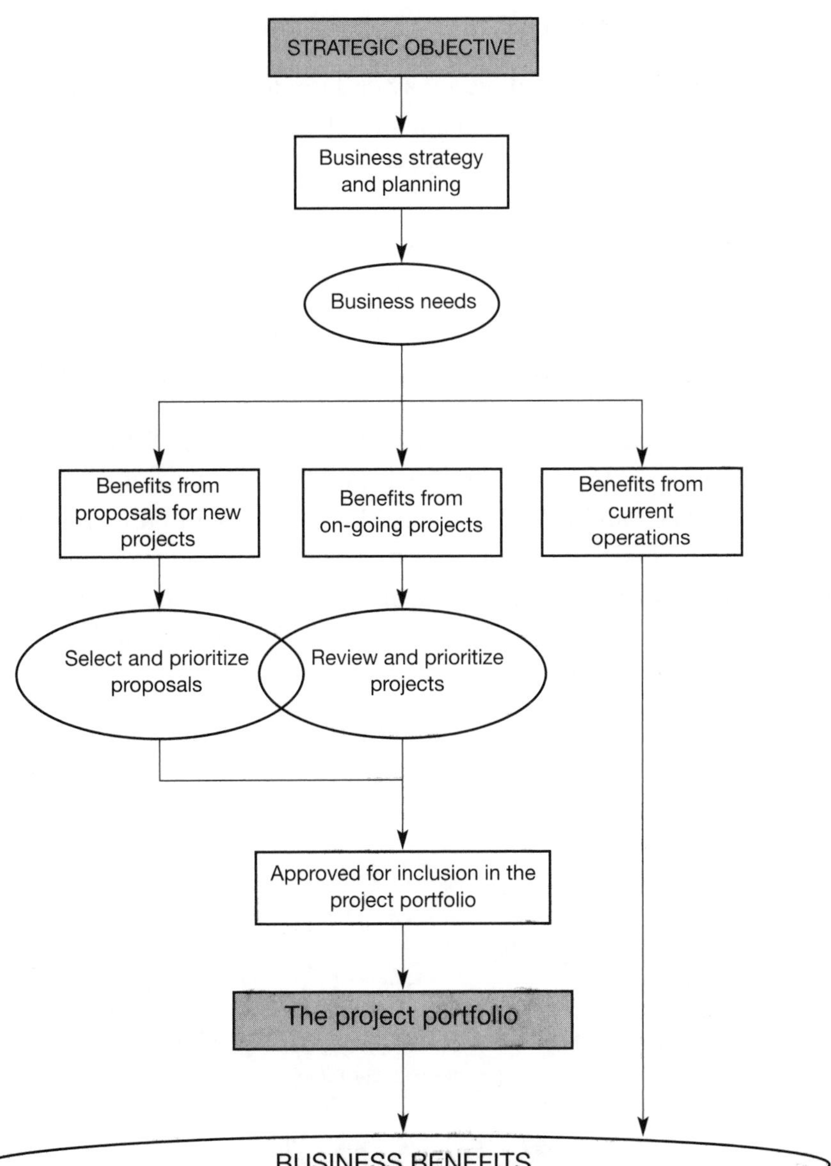

Figure 14.2 Proposals and projects in the context of strategy
Any change project you have starts as a proposal, becomes part of the project portfolio, and eventually its output is subsumed into "business as usual." The speed and reliability with which you can do this is a critical success factor for your organization. Compare the build-up of benefits in Figure 14.1 with this diagram to see how each part fits.

The lack of any of these capabilities has implications on your company:

- **Poor strategic alignment**: you may end up doing the wrong projects.
- **Poor decision making**: decisions made in one part of the company may be overturned by another part, decisions may take too long or too many projects may be initiated.
- **Poor resource management**: you don't know if you have sufficient resources to finish what you've started, let alone start anything new.
- **Poor business planning**: if you do not integrate the "future" as created by your projects into your business plan, how will the plan make any sense and how will you know if you have anyone to use the outcomes?
- **Poor release management**: if you have no method for listing and tracking the projects, they won't be visible and people are unlikely to know what has been authorized and what has not. You will not know which projects are interdependent.
- **Poor fund management**: you won't know if you have the funds to complete the projects you have started or be able to fund new ones. You will spend your money on the wrong things.

Business programs are a key tool which enable you to tackle three of these needs. Business programs are chunks of your strategy and your

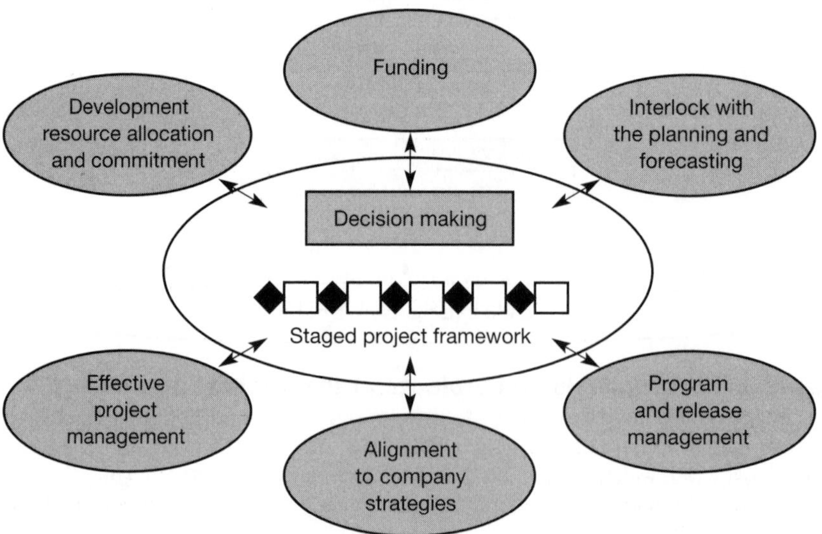

Figure 14.3 The environment for managing your portfolio of projects
The staged project framework is the central "plank" around which the key aspects of managing the portfolio revolve. While shown as separate "items" they in fact have a large degree of interdependence.

business plan. They are the link between what you do now and what you will do in the future. They therefore also form the most appropriate vehicle for dividing up your company's spending, with the highest priority business programs attracting the greatest investment.

THE PROJECT PROCESS ENVIRONMENT

The list of factors needed to control a project portfolio is long. In this workout you should assess your current "health" and use that as a prompt for discussion to help you decide which you need to concentrate on first.

Take each in turn and, with respect to projects and change initiatives in your company:

1 Assess, without any in-depth analysis, the effectiveness of each competence – 0 = no capability, 5 = excellent in your organization.

2 Discuss the implications on your organization of any lack of competence in each area and note them down.

Do not expect to be excellent in every area.

3 If you are basically satisfied with your assessment, consider whether the competencies you have actually work together as whole.

Competence	*Score*	*Implications*
Strategic alignment		
Decision making		
Resource management		
Business planning		
Release management		
Fund management		

There are Too Many Projects to Do!

Principles for selecting projects

Putting these principles into practice

Far too many projects!

By having a staged approach you do not need to make all the decisions at the same time. A staged framework enables you to make the necessary choices when you have adequate information to hand, rather than being forced into premature and ill conceived choices.

"When you choose anything, you reject everything else."
G K CHESTERTON

Principles for selecting projects

There are always far more ideas for projects to change a business than resources or money can support. To make matters worse, the less clear your strategy is, the more ideas there will be, thus compounding the problem.

How can you:

- make sure you undertake the projects you need to?
- limit the number of projects without stifling the good ideas?
- kill off the projects which have no place in your company?
- ensure that speed through the project stages is sustained?

The staged framework within which each project is managed, coupled with effective decision making and business planning, is the key to ensuring you can do all of this. By having a staged approach you do not need to make all the decisions at the same time. A staged framework enables you to make the necessary choices when you have adequate information to hand, rather than being forced into premature and ill conceived choices. Keeping to three basic principles will help you do this:

1. **Do not put a lid on the creation of new ideas for projects.**
2. **As soon as you can, make an informed decision on which projects to continue.**
3. **Having decided to do a project, do it, but stop if circumstances change.**

1. Do not put a lid on the creation of new ideas for projects

In Part 2 you saw that a project should not be started unless a person stands up as needing the benefits (the project sponsor). You should encourage the creation of as many ideas as possible, letting them originate in any part of the organization (see p. 81). Stifle creativity and you risk stifling the future growth of your company. The use of a targeted proposal template, such as that given in Appendix B, should ensure that enough information is collected about an idea (or need) to enable the company to review and approve or discount it on the grounds of strategic fit.

The decision to start a project is taken at the Initial Investigation Gate and is only concerned with the first of the three gate questions "Is there a real need for this project and, in its own right, is it viable?" (See p. 84.) Once the go ahead is given, the initial investigation should start.

A REMINDER OF THE KEY QUESTIONS

The decisions points prior to the commencement of each stage are called gates and answer three distinct questions:

1. Is there a real need for this project and, in its own right, is it viable?
2. What is its priority relative to other competing projects?
3. Do I have the funding to undertake the project?

If you are uncertain of your strategy, you will create more proposals than if you really understand the direction the company is to take. However, if a proposal passes this first gate, you know that at least one person (the project sponsor) believes the proposal does fit the strategy and should be evaluated. In this way you will benefit from knowing how your senior managers are converting their understanding of strategy into action. The aim of portfolio management is to make projects visible: the "outing of projects." If a manager is undertaking projects his colleagues consider to be outside the needs of the business, this will be exposed. Consider also what else such a manager may be doing which may be contrary to the direction of the business but which is invisible!

I cannot over-emphasize the impact that a clearly *communicated* strategy and business plan has on the effectiveness of selecting and managing your project portfolio. Part of this relates to the number of projects started and terminated. Three phases of corporate development can be observed, the ignorant, the enlightened and the leaders.

Phase 1 – The Ignorant. These companies do not realize the importance of the investigative stages and the power a staged project framework gives them. They spend little time on the early investigative stages but much effort is wasted in the later development stages. Their project success rate is low. These companies are inefficient and ineffective at implementing business projects.

Phase 2 – The Enlightened: These companies realize that a project framework is powerful. They spend a significant amount of time on the investigative stages and become excellent at terminating unwanted projects and doing thorough groundwork for those they wish to continue. Their project success rate is high. These companies are operating below "optimum" efficiency but are relatively effective at implementing business projects.

Phase 3 – The Leaders: These companies can run projects and portfolios of projects. They have a firm grasp on their strategy and what implementation looks like. Consequently, the proportion of time spent on investigative stages as a whole decreases as they are able to screen their proposals more effectively. (*Note*: The proportion of time spent on investigative stages on individual projects is still high.) Their project success rate is high. These companies are both efficient and effective at implementing business projects.

2. As soon as you can, make an informed decision on which projects to continue

The first gate enables you to start investigating the unknowns on the project. You should know *why* you are undertaking the project but, on some projects, you may not know *what* exactly you are going to have as an output or *how* you will go about it. For relatively simple projects you may know both these things. The objective of the initial investigation is to reduce this uncertainty. The output of the initial investigation should provide sufficient knowledge to:

- confirm strategic fit;
- understand the possible scope and implications;
- know what you are going to do next.

In other words, you will have the information to hand which will enable you to make an *informed* decision on whether the project should continue, rather than one based on your own "feel" and limited knowledge.

If you have only one project to do, its priority is easy to assess. It is PRIORITY ONE. If you have more than one project to review, the question of priority has no significance if you have the resources and funding to do them all when they are required. Priority only becomes an issue if you have insufficient resources to do everything you want to do, when you want to do it.

Priority only becomes an issue if you have insufficient resources to do everything you want to do, when you want to do it.

Assessing relative priority should be done on an informed basis and so cannot happen until you reach the Detailed Investigation Gate, after the output from the Initial Investigation Stage is available. Once the project sponsors have confirmed that they still need the benefits their projects will produce, you will need to concentrate on:

- the "doability" of the projects;
- their fit within the overall project portfolio.

Doability takes for granted the project sponsors' assessment of strategic fit and the soundness of each project on a stand-alone basis. It concentrates mainly on whether you have the resources and funding to undertake all the projects. If you do, a portfolio assessment is done.

The **portfolio assessment** looks at the balance of risk and opportunity for the proposed projects together with the current project portfolio. The aim is to assess whether this mix is in fact moving the company in the desired direction.

If you are unable to undertake all the desired new projects, you will need to make comparisons between them and choose which should continue. This implies that you need to *batch* your projects at the Detailed Investigation Gate to make this decision. In practice you will be deciding which projects should proceed as it is projects which lead to action but it is more powerful, from a decision-making viewpoint, to prioritize the *benefits* the projects produce rather than the activities the project comprises. After all, the benefits are what you need, not the projects. By prioritizing benefits you will:

It is more powerful, from a decision-making viewpoint, to prioritize the* benefits *the projects produce rather than the activities the project comprises.

- stay focussed on *why* you are doing the project;
- trap the projects, which actually have no real benefit!

It is best if the prioritization decision coincides with a review and reforecast of your business plan as a whole. You will be able to build whichever projects and benefits you need into the plan, while ensuring the totality of future benefits from "business as usual" and projects adds up to the figures you need (Figure 15.1).

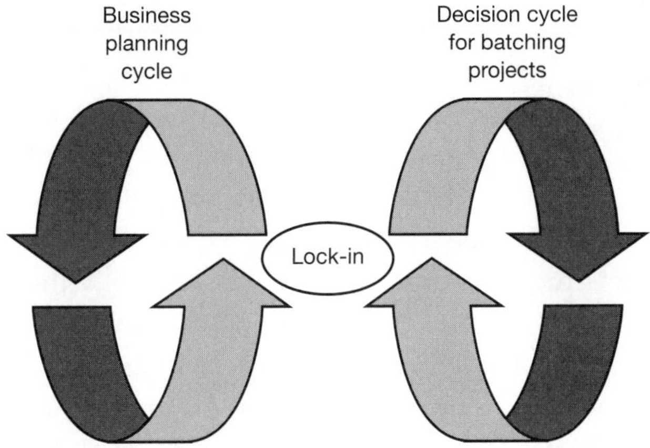

Figure 15.1 Matching the batching time frame to your business planning cycle

If the decision as to which projects should continue coincides with a review and reforecast of your business plan as a whole, you will be able to build whichever projects you need into the plan, while ensuring the totality of future benefits from "business as usual" and projects adds up to the figures you need.

ENOUGH INFORMATION?

You can always avoid making decisions by saying you haven't enough information. It's a very effective tactic for blocking anything you don't want done. You will never have enough information for decision making. You need to make an assessment of what you have at stake if your decision is wrong and balance this against what you stand to gain if your decision is right. If you have a staged approach to projects, coupled with good control techniques, you will be able to "de-risk" your decision making to the extent that you are answering the question, "Can I confidently continue with the next stage of this project?" You very rarely find you are making life and death choices for the company.

---

3. Having decided to do a project, do it – but stop it if circumstances change

Having decided to carry on with a project after the review at the Detailed Investigation Gate it is useful to presume it will continue. You, therefore, need only assess the relative merits of the new projects you wish to introduce to your project portfolio. This avoids going back over previous decisions and puts an end to the "stop–go" mentality that ineffective staged processes can result in. It is a strange phenomenon that today's "good ideas" tend to look more attractive than yesterday's! Consequently, the temptation is to ditch yesterday's partially completed projects in favor of new ones. The result is that nothing is actually finished!

> ***It is a strange phenomenon that today's "good ideas" tend to look more attractive than yesterday's! Consequently, the temptation is to ditch yesterday's partially completed projects in favor of new ones. The result is that nothing is actually finished!***

A presumption that on-going projects will continue does not mean that you should never stop a project that a project sponsor is relying on. For example, assume you have sufficient resources to do all except one new project and this cannot be done because a key, scarce resource is already occupied on an on-going project. In such circumstances you would usually presume the ongoing project continues and the new project is stopped or delayed. The new project, however, may have considerably more leverage, delivering greater benefit, in a shorter time, at less risk than the existing one. Hence you may take the view that it serves the overall interest of the company better to stop the existing project and start the new one. Such decisions should be very rare, as, if they are not:

- your portfolio will be unstable and you will run the risk of delivering nothing of value;
- it may be symptomatic of poor business planning and a lack of clearly understood strategy.

ABILITY TO CHANGE – DECISION MAKING

To what extent does the ability to devolve decision making influence how fast you can implement change? In the planning stages of a complex change program, the project managers identified each point which required either a board decision or the decision of one of the directors. In all, about 200 decisions were identified spanning nine key change projects. Figure 15.2 shows this. This begs some questions:

- Were the board members in fact capable of making that number of decisions in the timescales required, on top of all their "business as usual" decisions?
- Were there any decisions which could have been delegated to relieve them of the burden? If not, what impact would the decision overload have had on the program?

Notice the shapes of the two graphs. The board as a group has most of its decisions toward the front. As the projects get under way and alignment has been achieved, the bulk of the decisions is made by individual directors. The shape of the curve for the directors has both a front-end peak and peaks toward the back. This is because they not only approve the initial work, but also sign off completion of the key final deliverables toward the end of each project.

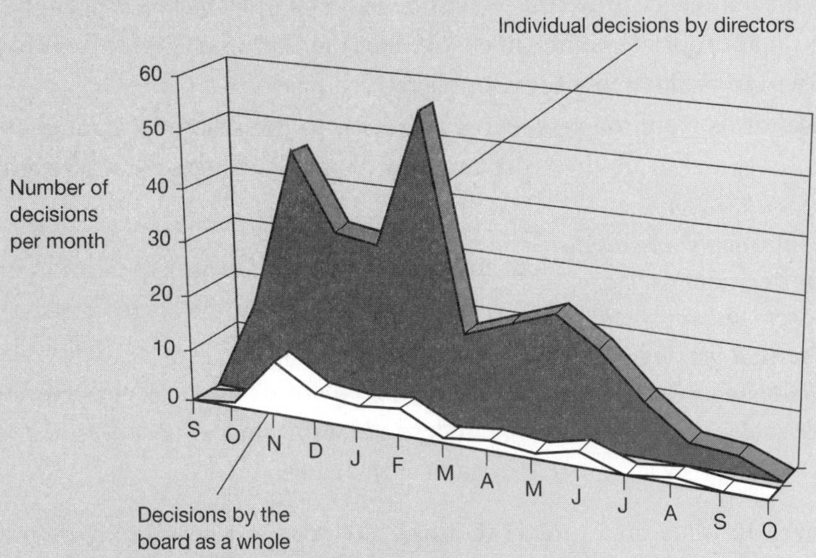

Figure 15.2 Decisions
In the planning stages of a complex change program, the project managers identified each point which required either a board decision or the decision of one on the directors. In all, about 200 decisions were identified, spanning nine key change projects.

Beware of trying to do too much.

Putting these principles into practice

Harnessing the staged framework

The management of the full project portfolio relies on the basic staged project framework being in place. Once established, this drives the interface to managing the full project portfolio. To ensure speed through the project stages you should minimize referral to any decision-making bodies outside the project team. Inefficient decision making at gates can double a project's timescale. Nevertheless, you must have sufficient referrals, at appropriate points, to ensure that the portfolio is under control, is stable and is likely to meet your needs.

Referrals from the project organization to the portfolio management organization usually happens at the gates (Figure 15.3). Thus:

To ensure speed through the project stages you should minimize referral to any decision-making bodies outside the project team. Inefficient decision making at gates can double a project's timescale.

- the management of a project is concerned with the work within the stages leading up to a gate decision;
- the management of the project portfolio is concerned with ensuring decisions are made at the gates.

Where an issue on a project requires a change, a referral may be made from the project management to the portfolio management during the course of a stage.

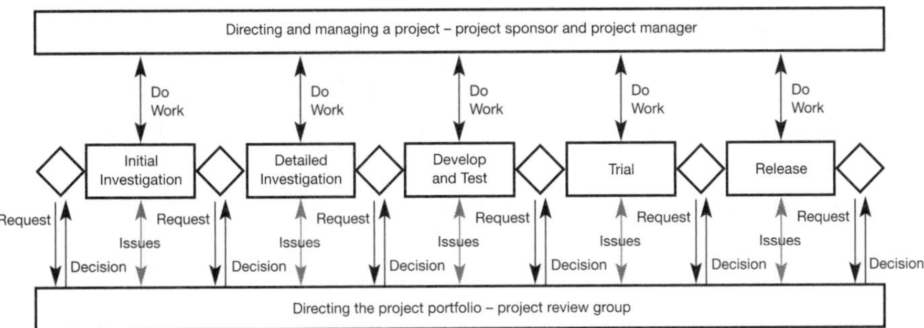

Figure 15.3 Interaction between managing a project and managing the portfolio

Referrals from the project organization to the portfolio organization happen primarily at the gates. Where a problem (issue) on a project requires a change, a referral may be made during the course of a stage. In this diagram, the project review group is shown as directing the portfolio; for large companies, a business programme board may take an intermediate role.

The choice of who contributes to the decisions is crucial. Earlier (pp. 53, 170) we saw that the decision is the culmination of three distinct questions. The roles relating to these are as follows:

- **The project sponsor** answers the gate question 1 – is there a real need for this project and, in its own right, is it viable? The project sponsor is the person who requires the benefits the project will deliver and who assesses its fit to strategy.
- **The project review group** answers the gate question 2 – what is the priority? It assesses the "doability" and integrity of the project portfolio as a whole. (The typical activities which this group undertake are given on p. 178.)
- **The investment review group** answers gate question 3 – do we have the funding? It ensures that the financial "rules" are applied, that the project makes sound business sense, and that funds are available to do it.

I have shown the roles of the investment review group and the project review group separately. In practice it is better, but not essential, if the roles are combined into a single body. Note that both these titles are used to illustrate a role required in the governance of projects; what you choose to call them is your choice – there are no commonly accepted terms. Also, you may choose to combine a number of roles in a single body.

1. ROLE OF PROJECT REVIEW GROUP

A cross-functional (or cross-process) group of decision makers for prioritization, issues escalation, and resource allocation. Its primary aim is to keep the pipeline of projects flowing. As such the project review group is the gate keeper for all the project framework gates.

The core group comprises the resource managers.

2. AIM OF PROJECT REVIEW GROUP

The project review group exists to manage and communicate the prioritization, planning, and pre-launch implementation planning for business change projects.

This includes ensuring that fully resourced and committed plans for projects are created and aligned within the company's rolling forecast.

3. ACCOUNTABILITIES

The accountabilities of the group are:

- to prioritize projects;
- to plan, at macrolevel, resources for projects;
- to plan, prior to launch, the required resources for on-going operation post-launch;
- to ensure that the project portfolio can be delivered within existing funding allocations by ensuring the company business plan reflects the project portfolio;
- to ensure each project is locked in and committed to by those required to develop it and operate the results post-release;
- to identify and provide recommendations on which development projects should proceed beyond the Detailed Investigation Gate;
- to identify options for resolution of issues involving resources and escalate to the board for resolution if appropriate;
- to manage the introduction of simple and emergency projects into the project portfolio between quarterly reviews;
- to ensure that functions have planned in "white space" resources to undertake initial investigations;
- to communicate/publish the current status of the project portfolio;
- to act as the change control point for the project portfolio.

Gate decisions

Assuming that the project, on its own, makes sound business sense, what else does the project review group need to know about a project before it can commit itself to it?

- What are the project's overall business objectives?
- On what projects does this project depend?
- What projects depend on this project?
- When will we have the resources to carry out the project (people and facilities)?
- Do we have enough cash to fund the project?
- Can the business accept this change on top of everything else we are doing?
- After what time will the project cease to be viable?
- How big is the overall risk of the portfolio with and without this project?

Each gate in the project framework is described, from the perspective of decision making, in the following sections.

Initial Investigation Gate

While all gates are held by the project review group, this first one is often delegated to a Business Program sponsor or manager. Any proposal which they believe is worthy of further study should pass into the

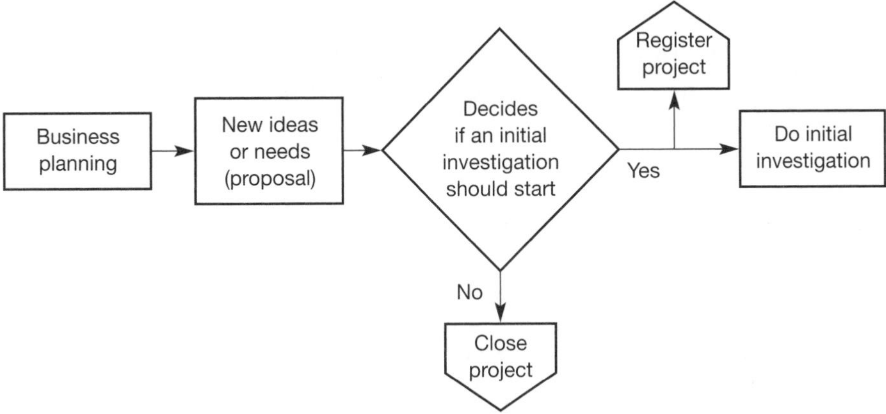

Figure 15.4 Decision process at the Initial Investigation Gate
Any idea that the project sponsor wishes to study further should be investigated without delay.

Initial Investigation Stage without undue delay (Figure 15.4). Some organizations have a special group to review proposals and take decisions on which should proceed. However, an effective business planning process should make such a group unnecessary. In most cases, except for extreme reactions to market or business conditions, the business plan should spawn the proposals, hence they will have effectively been "approved," at least in outline, through a business planning process.

Any proposal which the business program sponsor believes is worthy of further study should pass into the Initial Investigation Stage without undue delay.

Detailed Investigation Gate

Assuming each project has been approved by the project sponsor, the candidate projects are batched and an informed choice is made as to which should be authorized to proceed into detailed investigation (Figure 15.5). Two basic questions need to be asked by the project review group:

- Is it likely that all these projects can be completed?
- If we include them all, is the portfolio balanced?

If the answer to these questions is "yes," the full batch of projects proceeds into the Detailed Investigation Stage. If, however, all the projects cannot be done, then those in contention are compared and a decision is made as to which of them should proceed. Alternatively the constraint may be identified and, if possible, released (e.g. by delaying a project or applying new resources).

It should be your intention that any project which is allowed past this gate is going to move to completion *unless it loses its viability or*

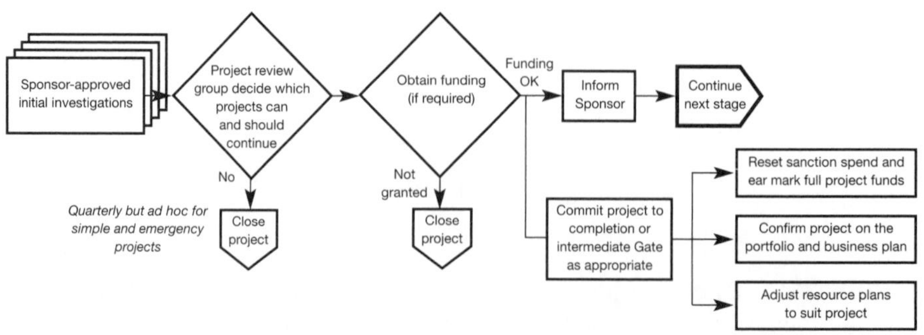

Figure 15.5 Decision process at the Detailed Investigation Gate

becomes unacceptably risky. For this reason you can think of this as the NO gate, i.e. where the business says "No, we will not consider that project further."

A project in which confidence to complete it is relatively high and which is committed to completion need not be referred back to the project review group unless it hits an issue which requires a reassessment of the project viability and resourcing. The "simple" projects referred to in Chapter 12 are an example of this. In other instances, however, the project review group will not have sufficient information to commit a project to completion. In which case, the project will be committed only as far as the Development Gate, when another assessment is done.

Once agreed by the project review group, the investment review group should provide funding to complete either the project or at least the Detailed Investigation Stage and the project costs, benefits, and resource needs should be locked into the business plan.

THE CAPACITY OF THE TOTAL SYSTEM IS THE CAPACITY OF THE BOTTLENECK

When the project review group assesses whether a project can be done, it must satisfy itself that ALL aspects can be done: operational, technical, marketing, process, etc. If one part is missing, then there is little point in doing any of the other work. Your ability to complete projects is, therefore, constrained by the bottlenecks imposed by scarce resources for a particular aspect of work. By undertaking a formal "doability" check, you will quickly identify any constraints and also be able to assess the cost to the company of missing or insufficient resource. This cost is the sum of the benefits from the projects you could not do because that resource was not available. This simple concept is the basis for what is called Critical Chain in Eli Goldratt's Theory of Constraints.

Development Gate

At the Development Gate, the project review group is only concerned with those projects it could not previously commit to completion. Again, the same questions are asked at the Detailed Investigation Gate. In principle, any project which has reached this gate is one which the business wants to continue. Forward planning should have earmarked the resources required to complete the project. As the presumption is to continue the project unless circumstances dictate otherwise, what is looked for here is confirmation that the project can continue. For this reason, the Development Gate should be considered as the YES gate. The investment review group provides funding to complete the project if this had not been given earlier. The business plan is amended to incorporate changes to costs, benefits, and resource needs resulting from the detailed investigation. The process is shown in Figure 15.6.

Trial Gate

The project sponsor is often delegated accountability for approving the move into trial. This is based on advice given by the project manager and team and is based on a ready for trial report. The project sponsor holds the decision as it is he/she who requires the benefits. Trials are often the first time a change is presented to the outside world and it is in the interests of the sponsor to ensure that a premature presentation does not compromise downstream benefits. The project review group needs to be consulted only if there are any prioritization issues. In such cases, the process in Figure 15.6 is followed.

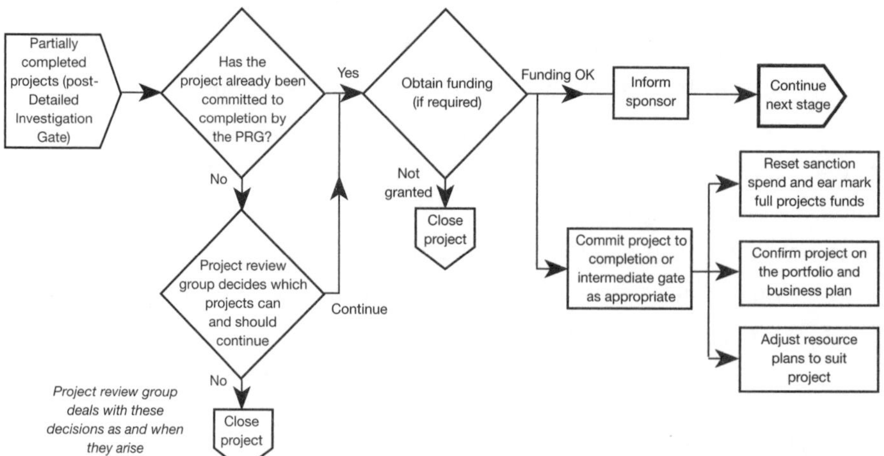

Figure 15.6 Decision process after the Detailed Investigation Gate
If the project has already been committed for completion and is still within the scope, timescale, and cost approved at the detailed Investigation Gate, no referral to the project review group is needed. The project just continues, obtaining extra funding, if not already allocated. For all other projects, the project review group needs to confirm it within the project portfolio.

Ready for Service Gate (RFS)

Again, this is primarily a project sponsor decision. As with a trial, the sponsor does not want the benefits jeopardized by releasing the project output before everything is ready. Alternatively, depending on the scale of the change, this decision could be made by a business program board, project board, or even a management board. The project review group only needs to be consulted if there are any prioritization or resource issues. In such cases, the process in Figure 15.6 is followed.

Summary of decision-making roles at each gate

The following table summarizes the decisions at the gates and who is involved. In the case of this table, a Business Program Board may delegate the decision to a Project Board or to the Project Sponsor. Consider this table as a starting point for you to assess the appropriate decision-making bodies and levels in your company. Remember, as the project definition document contains a list of deliverables and who has sign-off accountability (see p. 264), you are able to choose the most appropriate people or groups for each project on a case-by-case basis if your "usual rules" are not appropriate.

	Initial Investigation Gate	*Detailed Investigation Gate*	*Development Gate*	*Trial Gate*	*Ready for Service Gate*
Business program board	Decides if an initial investigation should start	Confirms the project should continue	Confirms the project should continue	Confirms the project should continue	Confirms the project should continue
Project review group	Not usually required	Decides if the detailed investigation should start	Decides if the project should be completed	No referral needed	No referral needed
Investment review group	Not usually required	Provides funding for the detailed investigation	Provides funding to complete the remainder of the project	No referral needed	No referral needed
Document on which gate decision is based	Proposal	Initial business case	Business case	Ready for trial report	Ready for service report
NOTES	Projects start as soon as practical	Projects batched for a comparative decision	Stage starts as soon as practical	Stage starts as soon as practical	Stage starts as soon as practical

GIVING UP SOME PERSONAL POWER?

Who has the authority to commit resources:

- in a department in your company?
- in a function within your company?
- anywhere within your company?
- in another, supplier company?

Treat the word "company" as independent operating division if you are in a global organization. The answers to these questions will probably be, respectively, the head of department, the head of function (often a director or vice president title), the CEO or chief operating officer and someone in that other company. In other words, the power to apply and commit resources usually lies within the functional or line management hierarchy. If this is the case, and companies need to draw on resources from anywhere to undertake projects, there is only one person (maybe two people) in the organization empowered to do this. The CEO and COO (if you have one). No person, no matter what their title is, has the authority to commit resources which are outside their domains. Unless a company organizes itself to have alternative structures to make cross-functional commitments, the top people will become overloaded with operational issues. Hence the need for a cross-company decision-making body such as a project review group. In effect, the owners of the resources are delegating part of their power to a cross-functional decision-making body and it therefore also holds that they should respect the decisions of that group and not unilaterally withdraw resources, for their own departmental or functional needs. If the lines of communication work and their person on the group plays their part, this should pose no problems.

Batching projects

Earlier (p. 172) I said that you would need to batch potential projects at the Detailed Investigation Gate so that you can make an informed decision regarding which should continue. If you do not have batching, prioritization can become meaningless. Projects are likely to be allocated resources on a first come, first served basis rather than on a "biggest win for the company" basis. Batching, however, begs two questions:

- How frequently should I do the batching?
- Won't this slow down the projects by introducing a pause?

As far as frequency is concerned, you need to select a time period which enables a reasonable number of initial business cases to be drawn up and to be compared with one another while not introducing too long a delay:

- Annual batching would be too infrequent. The business environment would have changed so much in that time that the exercise would be futile.
- Monthly may be too frequent. There may be an insufficient number of projects to allow meaningful decisions to be made.
- Quarterly is probably about right.

As for slowing projects down, the answer is no. Batching should not usually slow anything down. Unless there is spare resource available to undertake the project immediately, nothing can happen. Consider also that there is no point in rushing ahead with a project if it is the wrong one! Nevertheless, there will be cases where delaying a project to allow batching to occur is not in the best business interests. These cases are for:

- "simple" projects;
- emergencies;
- exceptions.

Simple projects were discussed in Part Two (p. 128). They are projects where you can see clearly to the end by the time you have completed the initial investigation. They also tend to consume few resources and little money. In such cases, the project review group allows the project to proceed into detailed investigation without delay, as the chances of the project compromising future "better projects" are very slim. A project may be thought of as "simple" by the project manager, but it is the project review group that actually decides this. I would also argue that defining, in quantitative terms, what constitutes "simple" may be a time-consuming and difficult exercise. Further, once you have defined it, you may find that project sponsors and managers massage their initial business cases to fall within your defined threshold and thus ensure their projects go through without delay. This is not the behavior you should encourage. It is more pragmatic to phrase the definition of "simple" in terms of principles and allow the project review group to exercise its own discretion.

After all it should be made up of responsible managers and not merely administrators of predefined "rules."

Emergencies are another exception to batching. I define an emergency as a project which, if delayed, would severely damage the company. An emergency is not a "panic" as a result of poor management in a particular part of the company. Unlike simple projects, emergencies may need to displace resources from on-going projects, thereby causing earlier commitments to be broken. If they aren't true emergencies, you will simply be moving the problem from one part of the company to another. As these projects can have a disruptive effect, the approval for them at the Detailed Investigation Gate should rest with top management (e.g. board), following a detailed impact assessment by the project review group.

Exceptions are any other type of project, other than emergency or simple project, that you wish to continue without going through a batching process. In other words, a pragmatic, but open and deliberate, decision, within the principles of business-led project management, which you deem to be in the company's interest. It is pointless to dream up possible scenarios and rules for these. It's a waste of time. Just deal with them as they arise. By definition, exceptions are "exceptional" and rare.

Beyond batching

The whole reason for batching is for you to decide, from among many contenders, which projects are the "right" ones to take on. By insisting on a named project sponsor, you are obtaining an unequivocal statement that at least one senior manager believes the project is the right project. By having a project review group, you are making a decision body accountable for ensuring the resource is available and that the mix of projects within the portfolio is the right mix. Poor business planning will make the jobs of the project sponsor and project review group more difficult. Conversely, good business planning will make it far easier. Add good information on the current and future commitment of resources and expected benefits and the project review group's task simplifies further. Good business planning will spawn the right proposals which in turn spawn the right projects. This being the case, batching may become less necessary. If you have a view of what is in the

The whole reason for batching is for you to decide, from among many contenders, which projects are the "right" ones to take on.

project pipeline, ready to arrive at the Detailed Investigation Gate, you will be able to allow more projects to proceed between batches without compromising future projects. Consultants and contractors do this all the time; can they wait and batch up which bids they would like to respond to? No, they have to take a view on their workload, assess the likelihood of success, the availability of resources, and the impact on them if they succeed. They then make a choice either to bid or not bid. (Remember which companies were found to have the best resource management systems? See Part One.)

Issues requiring a high level decision

Not all projects will go according to plan. There will be instances when changes to a project as defined and approved are desirable. Unless this is managed, scope, timescales, and costs will creep and the project "pipeline" will become blocked. There will be too much work to do and not enough people or cash to do it. Small changes can be dealt with either by the project manager or project sponsor. However, where a proposed change has an impact on other commitments the impact must be assessed and the approval of the project review group obtained. Chapter 25 describes the change process fully from a project manager's and sponsor's viewpoint. The process for handling escalated changes is very similar to that for the gate decisions described earlier. It is just that the need for the decision is driven by unexpected events rather than by reaching a predictable milestone (Figure 15.7).

The proposed change is reviewed by the project review group and, if it can be accommodated within the portfolio, approval is given to proceed. Authorization for any extra funding should also be given, if required. In some cases, the project review group may choose to alter the relative priorities of projects if there are resources or funding constraints. See Chapter 25 for a full treatment of "change."

Aids to decision making

Choosing how to decide between conflicting projects can cause a great deal of concern. Three methods commonly used are given in this section but no method is foolproof. You cannot make a process of decision making, you can only make a process of the information feeds required to make

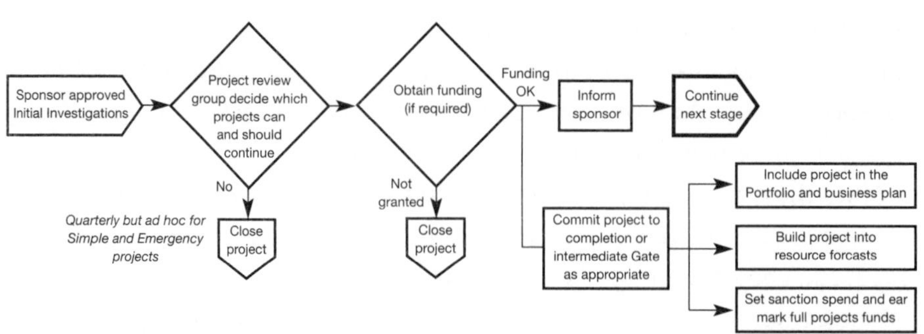

Figure 15.7 Decision process for an issue requiring a major change
The proposed change is reviewed by the project review group and, if it can be accommodated within the portfolio, approval is given to proceed. Authorization for any extra funding should also be given, if required.

You cannot make a process of decision making, you can only make a process of the information feeds required to make decisions. At the end of the day, decisions come down to a choice made by a person or group and not by a process or a clever business model.

decisions. At the end of the day, decisions come down to a choice made by a person or group and not by a process or a clever business model.

Executive decision

Just choose, based on the information you have to hand. This is a simple and often effective method especially if you do not have to justify your decisions! Sometimes, decisions are so marginal, it doesn't really matter what you decide!

The commercial director of an engineering company interrupted the chief executive asking him what color the new chauffeur cars should be. The chief executive picked up the phone and asked his personal assistant to come in.

"What color should our new cars be?" he asked.

"Red," the personal assistant replied.

"There, you have your answer," the commercial director was told. After the commercial director had left the room, the chief executive commented, "I like easy decisions which I can make quickly – it makes me feel good. But that was ridiculous!"

The cars were delivered in bright red, BUT the company's brand colors were blue and white!

Portfolio matrix techniques

Plot each project on a matrix with axes representing key decision-influencing factors, for example benefit versus risk, and choose those which are in the "less risky, most benefit" quartile (Figure 15.8). The limitations of this method are that you can only have two dimensions: to use more, you have to invent creative formulae for weighting a collection of factors into a single one. It is, however, relatively simple and can help you analyze a potentially complex set of projects. Its output can, by the same token, be very misleading and, as a minimum, basic management sense should be used to verify the model. In addition, it may tend to favor short-term projects over strategic projects or vice versa and this can lead to an unbalanced portfolio.

Benefit modeling

Many consultants now have program optimization models. In these, the business objectives are stated in quantitative terms, usually a mix between financial figures and quality of service indicators. The candidate projects are fed into the model together with constraints, such as capital and resources, and the computer program derives an "optimum" project mix. In addition "essential projects" and dependencies are also incorporated. The output from such models can be very enlightening and stimulate some extremely productive discussion. This, on its own, can improve the quality of the final decision. Of interest, the model I saw also had a constraint called "chief executive's project." This allowed any project to be forced into the program. It is more informative than the matrix method but does require specialized knowledge to construct and faith in the comparative business cases and performance indicators between the constituent projects.

A company found that its pipeline of development projects was blocked. There were too many projects (about 120) being undertaken and very few were actually being completed. The company set up an exercise to get these on-going projects under control. First, each project was aligned to a staged framework (similar to that in Part Two) and then ranked on a matrix, based on difficulty versus benefit (Figure 15.8). The objective was to include the least difficult projects which gave the most benefit and which were almost complete into the portfolio. The remainder would be stopped. The exercise was not without difficulties but it did result in a smaller and more focussed portfolio of projects. The matrix selection method used was known to be imperfect as it favored short-term revenue-generating projects over longer term strategic projects. However, it was considered adequate for the task required of it but something better would be needed later, when they would be adding new projects to the portfolio.

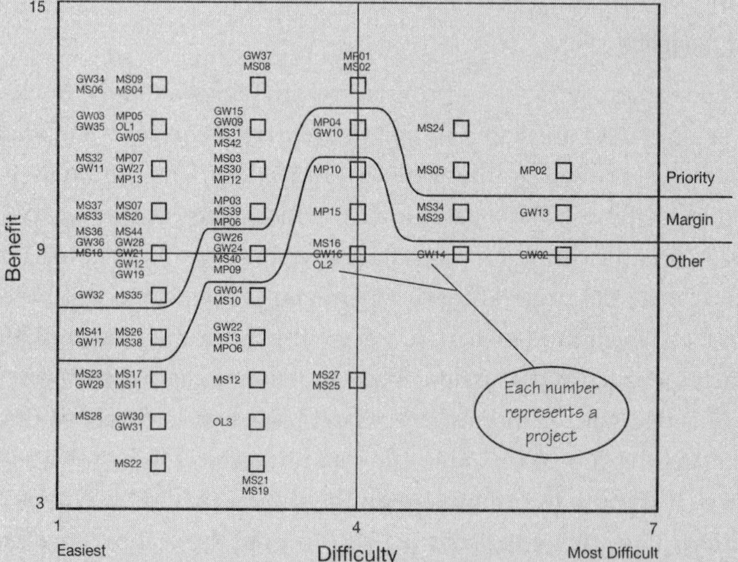

Fig 15.8 Example of using a matrix to aid the selection of projects
Each project is plotted on a matrix with axes representing key decision-influencing factors; in the example shown, this is benefit versus risk. Those projects which are in the "less risky, most benefit" quartile (top left) were chosen for priority review.

They agonized over the type of tool they would use when the next batch of projects needed to be prioritized. As it turned out, they did not need to prioritize for six months. The project managers, during the initial investigations, had already identified potential blockages and changed the approach and scope of their projects to circumvent them. The project review group was able to let all new projects continue. Twelve months on and no tool had yet been devised. However, the portfolio was still under control and projects were being completed at the rate of two to three a week.

DECISION-MAKING BODIES

This workout is for you investigate who contributes to and makes decisions regarding your business projects and when.

1 Identify all the individuals or groups in your company that contribute to and make decisions regarding your company's projects. List them on the left of a flip chart or white board.

2 Show what decisions these each make, e.g., I have shown the decision-making bodies proposed in this chapter.

3 Consider and discuss:

- Are all three questions (p. 170) represented in your company?
- Are the accountabilities on p. 178 covered?
- Has each individual or body the authority to make the decisions?
- Is sufficient information available to those involved?
- Is question 2 considered "cross-functionally"? If not, consider what effect this has on projects which require resources from a number of different functions.

4 Finally, decide who is accountable. Remember, accountability cannot be shared (see p. 250).

Individual or group	*Question 1: Soundness of individual project*	*Question 2: Priority versus other projects*	*Question 3: Funding*	*Remit*
Project sponsor	X			Ensure project is viable
Business program	X	X in own portfolio		Ensure business program is viable
Project review group		X across the company	available	Ensure company portfolio is viable and resources are
Investment review group			X	Ensure investment criteria are met

Far too many projects!

So far I have concentrated on decision making on projects where the resources are the limiting factor. This is not always the case. It may be that decision making itself becomes more critical. I have already explained how a project review group can work to ensure that you commit only those projects you have the capacity and capability to implement. There may, however, be too many of these for a single group to deal with, so, while you may have the capacity to implement them, you may lack the capacity to decide! The first case study in this Chapter is an example of this.

In the benchmarking study we noted that companies have some resource which is shared and some which is separate (see p. 26). The former led to greater flexibility, while the latter led to easier, more discrete decision making. If you have separate resources, you can have a dedicated project review group. You will need to rely on business planning to check that the level of resource applied is in line with strategy as it will not be easy to reallocate these people. Where there is shared resource, you have greater difficulty. How can you divide the project review group into a number of subsidiary parts, capable of handling the volume of projects you have? The options for this include:

- by business area (function);
- by target market plus "corporate";
- by driver.

If you choose to make decisions based on function, you will fall straight back into the trap of encouraging function-based projects, working in isolation. This is not a rational choice if you want a benefits-driven, cross-functional approach.

You could choose to have the project review groups based on your target markets. This has the advantage that you align projects to your customers' needs. Further, if there is little sharing of projects between segments, a logical division would be apparent. You would need to have a "corporate" project review group to deal with those projects which did not sit within any particular segment.

Another way is by driver. You categorize your projects by those which are directly related to:

- the service or products you offer;
- increasing your capacity to offer more of the same service or product;
- increasing the efficiency of your operations;
- building new overall capability or infrastructures.

This has the advantage that you are quite clear as to what the reason is for the project being undertaken.

Regardless of which way you choose to cut up your project review group, you will find that:

- decisions from two or more groups will come into conflict at some time. It is vital that you have an escalation route to settle these;
- it will sometimes be difficult to categorize a project. This does not really matter, as all projects should be following the same staged framework which itself leads to more informed decision making regardless of how you label the project.

Finally, when it comes down to making choices between projects, you will need to make sure that the number of projects proposed and undertaken is in line with corporate strategy. You can encourage this by linking the funding of projects to decision making. Two examples of this conclude the chapter.

Example 1
If project review groups are based on market segments you could decide, based on your strategy, which is the most critical and which the least important and ration project funds accordingly. Thus, if the strategy in segment A is to "milk cash and withdraw" you would have no funding for new capabilities or operational improvements unless they can also be applied to other segments. You would allocate the major share of the development funds to the most important emerging segment.

Example 2
If project review groups are based on drivers, you decide, from your strategy, what relative importance you need to put to each driver. For example, if you see a need to increase operation efficiency, you would have more funds for the "efficiency" budget than for the others.

Have I Got the Resources?

Obtaining resources and holding on to them can be very problematic, especially in functionally oriented companies, where the balance of power is firmly held by line-management. In these circumstances, resources are often committed to projects on the basis of good intention, rather than on good information.

"You've got a goal, I've got a goal. Now all we need is a football team."

GROUCHO MARX

Conditions for total resource planning

In 1993 the University of Southern California analyzed 165 teams in a number of successful organizations to assess the effectiveness of teamwork. Two reasons for teams failing to deliver were found:

- Project objectives were unclear.
- The right people were not working on the project at the right time.

In looking for solutions to these two issues, they found that using a "projects approach" gave significant benefits in clarifying objectives (which is just as well or it would conflict with the message in this book!). On the question of resources, they found that having visibility of available resources and obtaining commitment of the required resources was key. In other words, if you haven't got the right people you can't expect to complete your project.

Obtaining resources and holding on to them can be very problematic, especially in functionally oriented companies, where the balance of power is firmly held by line management. In these circumstances, resources are often committed to projects on the basis of good intention, rather than on good information. Consequently, they can be withdrawn, at whim, by the owning department if it believes that its own need is greater than that of the project. The result is that resource and skill shortages do not become apparent until they are a problem. An effective method of resource allocation and commitment is, therefore, needed which meets three conditions:

- **Condition 1**: you have a clear view of how resources are being consumed on a project by project basis.
- **Condition 2**: you have visibility of the resources available, or soon to be available, within the forecasting horizon of your company.
- **Condition 3**: commitment of resources should be based on clear information and forms the basis of an "agreement" between the departments providing the resources and the projects consuming the resource.

Meeting these conditions will enable you to anticipate potential resource conflicts before they become a problem.

Many of the problems that companies face in trying to allocate their resources efficiently come about as a result of some misconceptions regarding projects and resources. These misconceptions are:

- people work only on projects and do nothing else;
- resources are allocated to projects;
- a project manager can choose who she wants to work for them.

In practice you will find that:

- In most organizations, much of the work is not done on projects, but as part of running the business on a day-to-day basis (for example, in my own department (product management), 25 percent is spent on development projects, 15 percent on general management and administration, 40 percent on product management and 20 percent being sick, trained, and on paid leave).
- Work is given to people. Your core employees are there all the time and being paid. You pay them regardless of whether they are working or on paid leave. There are some people you can turn on and off like a tap (temporary or agency staff), but I doubt if these are your key people.
- A project manager will state what he needs for the project and the line manager will allocate the most appropriate (or convenient) people. The line managers should know their people and their capabilities. They should also be competent in the field of work they are accountable for and hence be best placed to decide who will fit a given role on a project.

The companies who were best at managing and committing their resources were the consultancies. Their systems and processes were well tuned for this. Tight margins require that they have their staff on fee-paying work for as much of the working year as possible. They also need to continually form and reform teams from across the company to address the assignments.

In the benchmarking study, I found that the companies that were best at managing and committing their resources were the consultancies. Their systems and processes were well tuned for this. Tight margins require that they have their staff on fee-paying work for as much of the working year as possible. They also need continually to form and reform teams from across the company to address the assignments. Further, they are never quite sure when a client is going to require their services but when a client does, they have to respond fast.

They, therefore, have a conflict that:

- their employees should be gainfully engaged on fee paying work, i.e. they need to drive staff utilization up;
- they need to have enough slack in the allocation of resources to enable them to respond to new requests quickly, i.e. don't drive utilization up too high.

(Compare this with the need on business projects to do an initial investigation of a proposal as soon as possible while trying to do as many of the required projects – it's very similar.) Rather than talk theoretically, I will explain a basic, but very effective resource management method from one of these types of companies.

The company is an engineering consultancy with about 1,200 employees in various locations worldwide. Traditionally, margins in these companies were very high and, as long as the people were working on assignments (projects), good profits were made. Management systems did not need to be sophisticated. However, the company did have a time-recording capability for all its employees so that time could be booked to assignment accounts and charged on to clients. Time for non-assignment work was also captured, either as process activities (marketing, sales, etc.) or as overheads (training, paid leave, sickness), i.e. the company met **condition 1** for resource management.

The competitive environment changed and the company found itself very rapidly being drawn into a lower margin industry. It was essential to "commercialize" the management systems of the company fast if they were to retain control. The first attempt was to collect three sets of data from assignment managers, each required by different central functions:

- The invoicing department wanted a forecast of the invoices which would be sent out so that they could ensure they were staffed up to make sure invoices went out quickly.
- The financial controller wanted a forecast of cash due, so that he could manage the working capital required and manage the payment of bills.
- The operations director wanted to know who was allocated to assignments and who was coming free so he knew what work he could accept (resource management).

Needless to say, the assignment managers did not look on these three sets of "new demands" kindly. Nevertheless, they did their best.

The future role of functions

If what people do counts more than the function or department they belong to and if you are to use people to best effect anywhere in your organization, what is the role of the functions? You now know that few changes can be made within a single function in your company. You generally require people from a number of areas contributing to the processes, activities and projects you are undertaking.

In the traditional hierarchy, each head of function decides not only the strategic direction of their function, but also what each and every one of his/her employees will do and how it will be done. The danger, if functions are too dominant, is that they will drive the business as they see fit from their own perspective. This may not be in line with the drivers that the company leadership wants to effect. The outcome is that the company becomes out of balance. For example, efficiency is often seen as a good goal. So also is responsiveness to customer needs. However, the latter may require you to carry excess capacity in order to meet customer needs at short notice. If one function is driving "efficiency" up by reducing capacity while another is creating a proposition around responsiveness there is likely to be a mismatch and dissatisfied customers.

The projects approach, like the current move toward cross-business processes, aligns all the required skills and capabilities around the attainment of a business objective. In the case of a process, the objective is better operations. In the case of a project, the objective is change for the better. Thus, the functions are not leaders in driving the business, but rather suppliers of people and expertise to projects and processes. The accountability of a head of function is to ensure that the right people are available in the right numbers to service the business needs. They will be accountable for pay, employee satisfaction, and personal development. Other key roles will start to become apparent. There will need to be those, expert at particular disciplines, who will create strategy, develop and maintain technical architecture, manage projects, or manage people. However, they will not do this just in the context of a single function, but rather in the context of the complete company, working wherever needed across functional boundaries to achieve the business objectives.

It also draws into question the role of a company director or executive. Many of these people hold titles which are really "mega-head" of department (e.g., marketing director), however, with the concept of business programs and cross-functional working, such traditional titles start to become meaningless. Our top people should be leaders of the business; (*all* the business) and their incentives should be tied to cross-business achievement, not just potentially suboptimal improvements in their own areas.

When looked at together, the three discrete sets of information proved very interesting. The forecast of work, in hours, could be multiplied by a factor to give a good approximation of the invoice values. The cash received should be the same as that invoiced (forgetting bad debts). The only difference between the three sets of figures should be timing:

- the time from doing the work to invoicing represents work-in-progress days;
- the time between invoicing and cash received represents debtor days.

However, even taking account of the timing difference, the three sets of figures could not be reconciled. The forecast was unreliable and inconsistent.

The solution they implemented to deal with this divergence was very simple. They asked for the same data, but had them collected at the same time on two linked data sheets:

- a manpower sheet;
- a financial sheet.

The **manpower sheet**: each assignment manager listed the people (by name, or by grade/discipline) required on the project. Against each, he forecast the number of hours each would book in a given month. There was a cap on the maximum hours each month to provide for unexpected work and "down time." (Look ahead to Figure 16.2 for an example.)

The **financial sheet**: the hours from the manpower sheet were then costed at actual salary rates and entered into a second financial sheet as time costs (cost of labor). To this sheet, the assignment manager added the forecast of non-labor costs. He also added, at the top of the sheet, the forecast of invoices required to be sent out, with a line below showing when the cash would be received. In short, they ensured that all necessary data were collected at the same time, using the same form. The whole forecast was input to a computer, added, and sorted so that summary reports and analyses could be obtained. The result was consistent data giving consistent forecast reports. No matter who needed the information, they knew it was compatible with that used by others for different purposes. It was so good that the marketing department was able to provide a full analysis of the business on a segmented basis every month, both historic and future. Previously, such an analysis used to take three months to complete.

One of the reports produced from this system was for the heads of function: they each received a listing of all the people within their department, together with a list of which assignments they were committed to and for how many hours each month. The company, therefore, had visibility of its future resource needs, i.e. the company met **condition 2**, visibility, for resource management. (Look ahead to Figure 16.3 for an example.)

The first few months of operation were problematic as people adjusted the forecasts to take account of what they had learned. However, after a short time it stabilized and became a reliable source of management information. From thereon, whenever the company had a request for work from a client or was invited to tender for work, it could assess whether it was likely to have the resources available to meet the need, and/or design the bid to fit around its known commitments. Also, as the requesting project completed the resource forecast, this became the "agreement" between the project manager and the supplying department. i.e. they fulfilled **condition 3** for resource management.

The frequency of reforecasting was set at quarterly intervals as it was expected that the effort of constructing the forecast would be too onerous on a monthly basis. The assignment managers were given the option to do it monthly if they wanted to. In practice they all chose to do a monthly forecast as it was easier to maintain and amend on this more frequent basis rather than start at a lower level of knowledge on a quarterly basis.

In practice they all chose to do a monthly forecast as it was easier to maintain and amend on this more frequent basis rather than start at a lower level of knowledge on a quarterly basis.

This company:

- knew what each project and activity in the company consumed by way of resources (condition 1);
- had clear visibility, at a high level, of its resource availability (condition 2);
- made future commitments on the basis of knowing what was currently committed and who was available without compromising previously made commitments (condition 3).

In short, it had achieved a level of knowledge about the application of company resources that many companies can only dream of. Did this process provide reasonable figures? The financial controller predicted the year-end results, six months in advance, to within an accuracy of 2 percent, excepting extraordinary accounting items. While individual assignments within the portfolio exhibited a degree of instability in forecasting, the population, as a whole, was very stable.

This example dealt with a consultancy company, where it is crucial to have a tight hold on resources. When one moves into the manufacturing or the service sector, the management of resources becomes less visible and is often hidden within functional hierarchies. Certain parts may be exceptionally well managed (such as individual manufacturing units, warehousing, telephone response call centers) but these are usually contained within a given function and deal with day-to-day business rather than change. Business projects frequently draw on resources from across an organization, not just from one function. If just one part is unable to deliver its contribution to a project, the entire venture is at risk. Few companies have, or yet see the need for, the capability to manage their entire employee workforce as a block of resources that can be used anywhere, at any time, just as in a consultancy organization. However, as in consultancy organizations, managers should make sure that their people are being applied to productive work, rather than merely playing a numbers game with head count and departmental budgets, this just leads to suboptimization which may be of no benefit at all (see Chapter 20).

Managers should make sure that their people are being applied to productive work, rather than merely playing a numbers game with head count and departmental budgets.

You need all your resources in place to succeed.

White Space – the freedom to change

The gap between what your resources are committed to and the total resource you have available is what I term **"white space."** It is the resources that you have not yet committed to a given activity or project. If you fulfill conditions 2 and 3, you will know your white space:

White space = resources available – resources already committed

In the very short term this should be small. It will grow as you look further into the future.

White space is fundamental to a company's on-going health. If you haven't any in the short to medium term, you are paralyzed. You have no one available to change the business to meet new threats or exploit new opportunities unless you withdraw them from previously committed work. White space gives you the resources to effect change in the future. "We are in a fast moving environment" is the common cry nowadays. If this is truly the case, then you need to ensure that you have "white space" resources ready to meet future needs. You know the people will be required but you are not yet sure exactly what for. If you have no people to change things, things won't change

White space must cater for two distinct needs:

- First, it must cover the need to undertake initial investigations resulting from new proposals. These people must be available at very short notice, and must be highly knowledgeable if the investigations are to have any value.
- Second, you need the resources to undertake the projects themselves, following approval at the Detailed Investigation Gate.

White space gives you the resources to effect change in the future. "We are in a fast moving environment" is the common cry nowadays. If this is truly the case, then you need to ensure that you have "white space" resources ready to meet the future needs.

Compare the former to a company putting a bid together – if this is done by inappropriate people, the bid may be lost or the company may have committed itself to a financial disaster. Just because business projects are "internal" it does not mean you should not apply the same rigor as you would with external matters. It's your company's future in both cases.

Figure 16.1 represents "white space" in graph form. The figure could apply to a complete company, a division, a function, or whatever. However, unless you can build this picture you will be taking risks every time you need to set off another initiative.

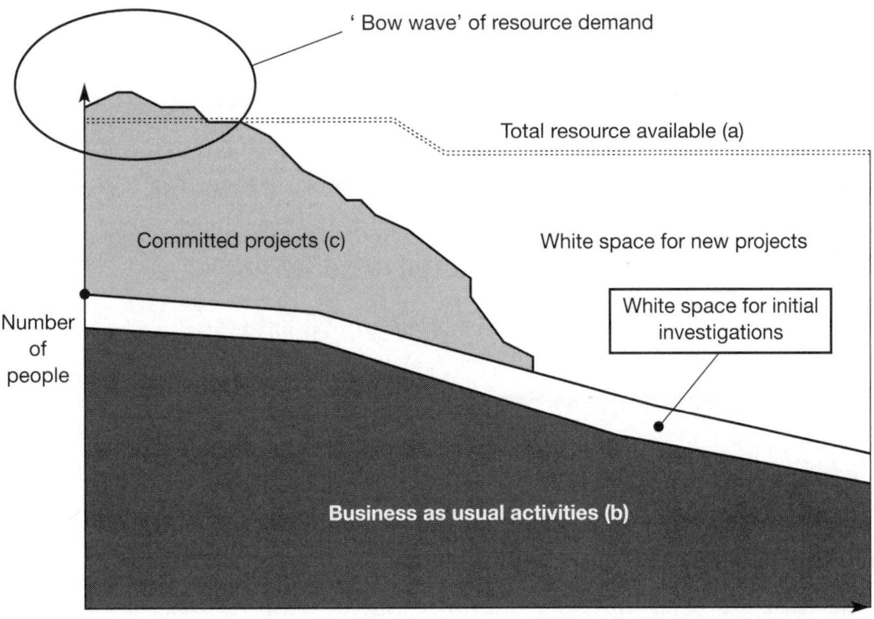

Figure 16.1 White space
White space is the gap between the resources you have (a) and those already committed (b + c). In the very short term this should be small. It will grow as you look further into the future. Notice the short-term bow wave which results from optimistic demands to the immediate needs.

How can I meet the three conditions?

The extent you need to employ formal systems to collate the past and future use of your resources depends on your company. At one extreme, you will need time recording to know what people have been working on, at the other you can rely on the line managers filling that gap.

Time recording

Those companies which require time recording for other business critical needs will, like as not, already have it. Few companies who don't, won't. It is an emotive system to implement. It can look and feel like bureaucracy gone mad. Some people are so against it they will leave a company rather than fill in a time sheet. It is often bound up in emotive words such as "trust." "If you can't trust me to work on the right thing, I don't want to work for you." Few finance or marketing functions are on time recording. However, it is very common in engineering and technical departments. Despite this, time recording can be a key to making a flat structure work. It allows people to be accountable for activities and projects which range far beyond their functional patch. It can enable job enrichment. It also enables you to delegate more without losing visibility and control. If implementing time recording, you need to balance the cost of doing it with the information gained. Consider:

- what the reports provided by the system will tell you;
- how they are structured;
- who has access to them.

If you don't have some kind of time recording, you won't know how much your projects are costing. Consequently, you will rely on line management reports for controlling costs which in turn keeps the balance of power firmly in the line management camp rather than shifting it toward the project view of life.

Also consider the timing for implementing a time-recording system. The only reason you have the system is for the reports – if they don't help you meet your overall needs at the moment, don't do it yet. If the basic understanding and acceptance of their use is not in place you will have an uphill struggle to make them work. Preferably, you should wait until those within your company (project sponsors, project managers, functional resource managers) have identified the need themselves.

Finally, remember that if you don't have some kind of time recording, you won't know how much your projects are costing. Consequently, you will rely on line management reports for controlling costs which in turn keeps the balance of power firmly in the line management camp rather than shifting it toward the project view of life. Time recording, if properly implemented with appropriate reporting, will give you an extra degree of freedom to manage your business.

Manpower forecasting

Manpower forecasting is a natural follow-on from time recording. It is merely a prediction of how many hours will be booked by whom against a particular activity or project. Forecasts can be created by one of three different roles.

Forecast made by	*Comment*
Each individual forecasts his/her own time input based on what he/she has already been briefed on and is committed to doing	In most cases, individuals will not have sufficient visibility of the work needed. They will only forecast the work they have been told to do, not what their managers know needs to be done, but for which no briefing has as yet been given. Forecasts on this basis will be very short term and hence of limited use
The resource manager forecasts the people required to meet commitments already made	This lets the "supply" side drive the forecast. This means that the estimates are likely to be good BUT unless well coordinated with every project manager, the timing may be very wrong. The total of such forecasts may show no deficit of resources, but the functions may have made choices regarding the project priorities, which are not rightfully their decisions to make
Each project manager forecasts the people who he/she expects and requires to work on the project based on the project plan (see Figure 16.2)	This lets the "demand" side drive the forecast. Estimates will match the plan timescales and should be agreed with the individuals on the project team. The total of these forecasts may show that certain resources are allocated beyond their capacity. This is good to highlight, then a business decision can be made to decide how to deal with the conflicts (see Figure 16.3)

On the whole, the third method is more likely to serve the needs of the business than the other two. It allows the projects which are driving the change to set their demands in accordance with their business objectives. It highlights any conflicts and allows a business decision to be made, rather than one being made by the limiting function. Further, it allows the project manager to increase or decrease the demand for resources openly.

In Chapter 15 the principle was: "Having decided to do a project, do it. But stop if circumstances change." In other words, the project manager continues to flex his forecast of resources to complete the project, based on current knowledge. If the manpower forecast is costed and tied into financial forecasts you can be sure that the project will be reviewed if its cost exceeds the sanctioned amount. The business managers (e.g. project review group) can then make an assessment of whether the project should continue. It is their decision, not that of the functions supplying resource.

A major pitfall of putting in systems to enable you to have visibility of your resources is that they can be made too complicated. Take the following scenario:

1 The project schedule and scope drive resource needs.
2 You can assign resources in project plans using project-planning software and obtain a profile of who is required, and when.
3 This can be downloaded into a central database and analyzed for the company as a whole.
4 Resource conflicts are spotted by the "system," which, based on priority rules, automatically levels the conflicting resources by moving lower priority activities back in time.
5 The output from the global resource analysis is fed back to the individual project plans, which show the resultant slippage.

There is software that can handle all this in an integrated way, so, no doubt there are companies who manage it this way. However, this level of integration and automation is neither always necessary nor, in a company environment (as opposed to program environment), always desirable. For example, it would mean that every project would need to use the same or closely compatible, planning software and be fully resourced at activity level. On its own, this has dubious value, when all you need is "visibility" of resources such that you can make decisions on overall resource availability. Detail is not necessarily needed.

Provided that you use the same high level work breakdown structures and projects as the basis for the forecasts, the resources can be held in a separate, simpler database. You use this to analyze and report on those resources where demand looks as if it will exceed capacity – this in turn tells you which projects may come into conflict. The project managers and the resource managers of the contentious projects and resources can then discuss and agree how the conflict should be handled. If they cannot agree, the issue should be escalated to the project review group.

There is no need for sophisticated analysis and resource levelling ı managers can manage it.

When you add up the total of resources required you will observe a "bow wave." That is to say, over the short term, the demand for resources exceeds availability (see Figure 16.1). In systems I have seen this always happens. Project managers are optimistic about the work they believe will be done in the next month and not enough account is taken generally of the reactive work that people have to do in addition to their project duties.

Placing a "cap" on the maximum hours forecast per person is a simple and effective way of dealing with the "bow wave." Assume that a month has four weeks, each of 36 hours, i.e. 144 hours. It is highly unlikely that anyone will actually book 144 hours against a single project on his/her time sheet. It is even less likely that a large population would all book 144 hours; some would be sick, be assigned to urgent work elsewhere, go on training courses, attend a presentation to a key customer, or whatever. By making a simple rule that if a person is full time on a project, you forecast only 85 percent of 144 hours (122 hours) and build in an allowance for this.

By depressing the maximum forecasting capacity, you allow a contingency (white space) which allows you to do other reactive work or overrun current work without compromising the plan. Experience with forecasting will tell you the right percentage for your company.

Figures 16.2 and 16.3 show a typical manpower forecast for a project and a typical report on resource demand for a function.

Project: YT2Z/Triton 2000
Detailed Investigation Stage

MANPOWER - ROLLING FORECAST (HOURLY)

Period: 4 wks to 28 Sept 1997

Assume $ 10 per hour

Resources	F'cast Month	ACTUAL TO DATE Month	Year	Life	FORECAST Oct	Nov	Dec 97	Jan 98	Feb	Mar	Apr	May	Ju				Q3	Q4	Q5	Q6	Beyond	F'cast Outturn
					134	**134**	**157**	**127**	**134**	**172**	**119**	**119**	**172**	**134**	**127**	**172**	**432**	**425**	**425**	**432**		
Category 1	70	70	280	560	56	70	70	70	84	112	28											1050
Category 2	75	75	300	600	60	75	75	75	90	120	30											1125
Category 3	30	30	120	240	24	30	30	30	36	48	12											450
Category 4	95	95	380	760	76	95	95	95	114	152	38											1425
Mann. J P	130	130	520	1040	104	130	130	130	156	208	52											1950
Fuller, W	100	100	400	800	80	100	100	100	120	160	40											1500
TOTAL HOURS	500	500	2000	4000	400	500	500	500	600	800	200											7500
CUMULATIVE					4400	4900	5400	5900	6500	7300	7500	7500	7500	7500	7500	7500	7500	7500	7500	7500	7500	

This is the guide to the maximum hours per month

Forecast may be by resource category or by individual

This number of hours are forecast by the Project Manager to complete this stage

Figure 16.2 Manpower – rolling forecast by project

This is a typical report on which manpower needs can be forecast. In this case, the figure shows the forecast for the detailed investigation stage of a project. It shows, on the left, the actual hours already booked to the stage and, on the right, the forecast hours and total. The guide for the maximum hours is shown below the date line. If this report is costed it provides the data required for the time cost line in the financial forecast (see Figure 21.4). (Adapted by kind permission of Professional Applications Ltd, UK)

Development Function KLO
Function Manager: Perry, TM

MANPOWER - ROLLING FORECAST BY FUNCTION (HOURLY)

Period: 4 wks to 28 Sept 1997

Name/ Number	DETAILS Gd	Disc	ASSIGNED TO Project Code	Managed by:	FORECAST Oct	Nov	Dec 97	Jan 98	Feb	Mar	Apr	May	Jun	Jul	Aug	Sep	Q3	Q4	Q5	Q6
					134	**134**	**157**	**127**	**134**	**172**	**119**	**119**	**172**	**134**	**127**	**172**	**432**	**425**	**425**	**432**
Brown, HJ/00345	B	KT	Y4RT	KLO	120	100	70	50	20	10	20	60	60	20	5					
			Y5FT	KLO	4	25	25	50	50	60	50	20	20							
			Zf5H	HNY	23	9	20	20	8	16	5									
			Total		147	134	115	120	78	86	75	80	80	20	5					
			% available		-10%		27%	6%	42%	50%	37%	33%	53%	85%	96%	100%	100%	100%	100%	100%
Green, HJ/00346	C	KT	Y4RT	KLO	20	10		10	20	10	10	5								
			HJUI	HNY	110	80	20		10											
			Total		130	90	20	10	30	10	10	5								
			% available		3%	33%	87%	92%	78%	94%	92%	96%	100%	100%	100%	100%	100%	100%	100%	100%
Unassigned	D	KT	Y4RT	KLO			70	50	5	5	5	5								
			YTDD	FE	9	20	20	20	30	30	20									
			KRG	HNY	120	45														
			Total		129					35	25	5								
			% available		4%					80%	79%	96%	100%	100%	100%	100%	100%	100%	100%	100%
TOTAL HOURS COMMITTED					4603	4987	4976	3426	3467	3479	2156	1087	432	210	25					
TOTAL % AVAILABLE					-1%	-9%	7%	21%	24%	41%	47%	73%	93%	95%	99%	100%	100%	100%	100%	100%

Each person or employee category in the function is listed here

Grade

Discipline

The projects the person is assigned to are shown against their name. The cost centre with management accountability is also given

Hours committed

% availability

The total committed hours for the function is shown here. The availability is White Space.

Figure 16.3 Manpower – rolling forecast by function

Once all the project manpower forecasts have been collated, they can be sorted to give each line manager a listing of the people in his/her department or function, stating to which projects each is committed. (Adapted by kind permission of Professional Applications Ltd, UK)

How detailed does resource forecasting need to be?

High level forecasting vesus detail

The objective of resource management, in the context of portfolios of projects, is to have sufficient visibility of the use and availability of your resources to enable you to commit, with confidence, to starting new projects without compromising the completion of existing projects. It follows then that the forecast does not need to be fully detailed. In fact, as all forecasts are, crudely, a range of very good to very poor guesses, the likely deviations in elements which make up the forecast can be very significant while not affecting the total figure much at all.

Forecasts can be on two levels:

- high – this is equivalent in manufacturing of a master production schedule;
- detailed – this is equivalent in manufacturing to a shop schedule.

It is the high level forecast that you should be concerned with in managing portfolios of projects. The detailed forecast is the accountability of the line and project managers; they decide when the work is actually done and by whom. You should not try to combine the two! In the example I used to explain resource management, the company used the following for its high level forecasting:

- forecast, by person or skill group/grade in hours;
- per month, for the next 12 months;
- per quarter, for the following year.

This was in the context that at the start of any financial year this company had 50 percent of its resources for the year already committed. The reason they used hours was simply because that is the basis on which they charged their clients and hence how their time sheets were completed and actuals were reported. Their forcasting frequency was monthly; weekly forecasts would have given little, if any, extra value. However, their manpower (or time sheet) frequency and reporting was weekly. Monthly was too infrequent as deviations from plans would be spotted too late for corrective action to be taken.

In contrast to this, another company, at the start of the financial year only had 25 percent of its resources for the year already committed. They, therefore, used to forecast by person only, in days per week. They used "days" as their measurement unit as, again, that was how they charged their clients and hence how their time-recording system captured and reported the data. Their frequency for forecasting was weekly for manpower and monthly for other costs.

Sales pipelines are very difficult to estimate especially in industries where the buying pattern is a few large purchases rather than the mass market consumer pattern. An industrial engineering company had a pipeline of about 350 prospects, totalling potential revenue of £300m which after factoring in the probability of the customer wanting to proceed and the probability of the bid being won, totaled £50m. Despite this being made up of inputs from six different people, in six different divisions on three continents, one third of the prospects churning every quarter and potential sales and win probabilities changing frequently, this pipeline stayed very consistent in total displaying little major shift month on month.

Avoiding micro planning – a solution by applying constraints theory

The primary constraint for project is the resource that can be applied. No resource equals no progress. We also know that microplanning every activity for every person on every one of maybe 50–500 projects is likely to be a fruitless exercise. Reality changes too fast and estimating is not that reliable. So how can we find a way through this such that our estimates and our commitments to undertake the work are realistic?

Every system, process, or organization has a constraint which limits how much it can achieve (its throughput). In corporate, multiproject environments, there is a single department or work group which is the **constraint**. In very complex organizations it may be very difficult to identify who this is; however, most people intuitively feel where the problems lie. You hear it in their language, "Oh, it's those people in IT," or "we'd better design this so Technology don't need to be involved". Some people actually argue that you could assume there is no resource constraint at all; we just spend our time flitting from task to task in a complex round, wasting energy. They say if we organized better, there would be plenty of resources to do what we really need to do. Others say there are many constraints, not just one, each one sheltering behind the other. Whatever your view, be you a purist "there is only one constraint" person or a realist saying "it's all a constraint!," the problem remains and needs to be addressed.

A solution lies in the practical application of the Theory of Constraints. If it is so difficult to find the bottleneck, simply choose a department to be the appointed constraint. Then plan the workflow through this single department to ensure maximum throughput. This means ensuring:

- they receive early warning of work;
- they receive the work as soon as it is ready (no hand-off delays);
- they work only on this (or a defined minimum number) and clear it as soon as possible (that is to say, they avoid bad multi-tasking).

We also need to ensure that delays on one project do not have a knock-on effect on all subsequent projects. We do this by ensuring that between each project, the resource has sufficient safety margin built in to absorb the routine, "unexpected" delays. This is called a **capacity buffer**.

By protecting the constraint in this way, we stagger the flow of projects in the company. We only need to schedule this one resource fully. The constraint becomes in effect a drumbeat to which all other departments march. We can plan projects independently of each other but, by tying them to the "drum", we are able to stagger them in a rational way. The safety (or buffers) provided around the drum resource also provide safety time for work in other departments. Figure 16.4 illustrates this.

- Planning is used to resolve as many problems as possible as early.
- Monitoring during execution is done by managing the buffers.
- There would need to be a strong hold on when projects are released for work; this would be the accountability of the project review group (see page 184).

If applying this method, individual projects should also be planned in such a way as to increase the reliability of delivery. This is discussed in more detail in Chapter 21 and is the subject of Eli Goldratt's *Critical Chain* (1997).

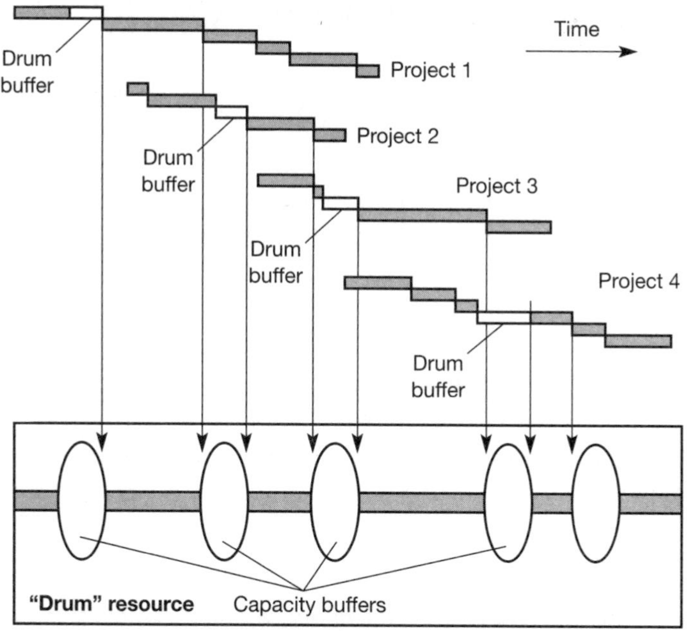

Figure 16.4 Building project timescales around the drum department
The projects are scheduled so that work required in the "drum" department is done in logical sequence without bad multi-tasking. A drum buffer in each project protects the resource from delays within each project. A capacity buffer protects the knock-on effects of delays in one project on all downstream projects.

WHO IS RESPONSIBLE?

This critical chain solution is not simplistic and is not an easy one to put in place. It requires some fundamental changes in behavior:

Senior executives will have to stagger the release of new projects and new project stages. (Most havoc in multiproject environments is wrought by top managers wanting "just one more . . . NOW!")

Resource managers will have to reduce bad multi-tasking in their departments (perhaps no more favors!).

Team managers and members will have to undertake their work as fast as possible, ensuring a smooth handover.

. . . and companies in cash-rich industries will find this more difficult because there is little financial imperative to change behavior.

16.1

WHAT'S YOUR "WHITE SPACE?"

This workout is for you to use as a discussion point or to identify the capacity your company has available to change itself. Assume that any projects to change your current way of working need to be managed and staffed from within your current head count. Try to construct a picture, like the one in Figure 16.1. As a start, look 12 months ahead only.

Hints
Break up the problem by function if this helps.

Use the list of projects you derived from Workout 3.1 – number each project.

Try to cluster similar groups of people together and build the picture in the following order:

1. total head count (a);

2. people (either grouped or as individuals) running the current operations (processes) (b);

3. people (either grouped or as individuals) working on projects which are currently in progress (c).

Your percentage of white space is (a – (b + c)) / a%

Consider how fast your business and competitive environment is moving and in this context discuss the following points:

1. Will the amount of white space you have allow you to develop enough new products and sufficiently improve your operational and management systems and processes to maintain or enhance your position in the market?

2. How far into the future does white space become available? If you had a requirement NOW, how long would you have to wait before you could start working on it without displacing any of your current projects or activities?

3. Is there hidden capacity in your business? How do you know?

4. Do you have any people who can be deployed quickly onto new projects and who probably do not know what they will be doing next week (i.e. resources for initial investigations)?

5. Have you ever started off a set of change projects or initiatives which people say they are keen on but which fail to deliver because insufficient time is made available for them? If so, what does this tell you?

An Environment for Managing Your Portfolio

New structures for old

The tools to help it work: systems

Lists: keeping tabs on your projects

What would such a system look like?

Management accounting systems

Putting your systems together

Some companies are well on their way to managing themselves "out of their functional boxes." Most are not.

"I've got a little list. I've got a little list."

W S GILBERT

In this chapter I will look at the type of environment you need to have in place around your projects and throughout your company if a projects approach is to succeed. You should now have a feel for the way a project progresses through its life cycle (Part Two) and how the wider decision-making framework can be organized to help you choose the right projects and not overcommit your resources.

In Chapter 2 we saw how any process does not sit in isolation but in the context of the structures, culture, and systems you choose to wrap it in. In this chapter we will look at structures very briefly and then at the systems.

New structures for old

The whole approach for projects is to enable you to deploy the people you need anywhere in the company where they can, due to their mix of skills and competences, add the greatest value. The objective is to break through functional and departmental barriers to the extent that the word "cross-functional" becomes unnecessary. In effect, your functional structure – which was so important in the "old days" – becomes secondary to the key business processes and change projects which work across it. In such an environment, reorganization, as a means of responding to problems, becomes less necessary (now what are the new executives going to do to prove they've arrived?). See also cartoon on page 39.

The power bases of the new companies will be more associated with the roles of people and groups. Consequently, the important structures will be those associated with project sponsorship and decision-making bodies; these are the people and groups which will carve out the future shape of the company.

The power base of the old functions was that they held the people, the budgets, and any decisions within their domain. Often these were decisions which should have been taken on a company-wide basis. The power bases of the new companies will be more associated with the roles of people and groups. Consequently, the important structures will be those associated with project sponsorship and decision-making bodies; these are the people and groups which will carve out the future shape of the company. They will be more associated with directing and coaching than managing. In fact, one could conceive of an organization where the traditional "director at the top of a function" is no longer deemed to be a sensible arrangement. When it comes to "direction," we should be directing whole companies and not just parts of it. Of course, every function needs a "man at the top" to ensure that the work undertaken is of the highest standard, that people are happy, and the "architectures" are robust. However, just because someone is an exceptional people manager or gifted technical expert, it does not mean he or she has the breadth of knowledge, skills, or competence to direct a corporation. Or even that he or she wants to be a director! The corporate world is full of people promoted beyond their levels of competence, through no fault of their own.

Some companies are well on their way to managing themselves "out of their functional boxes." Most are not. The decrease in importance of functional hierarchy is not going to happen by someone merely decreeing it. It has its place, and its uses. Much of the day-to-day work in many companies is ideally suited to departments provided the hand-offs and process flows are efficient and uninterrupted. It's when it comes to change that the problems and limitations become apparent. Before you let go of the reins of traditional cost center management, you need to build alternative communication channels, management frameworks and systems. You cannot "fly blind." Once in place, they will be so useful that the old hierarchies will naturally decay, fall into disuse, and become less irrelevant.

A company ran itself on a full matrix. It knew all its costs both by cost center and by project and activity. It had had a stabilized structure for many years but finally decided that the emergence of new disciplines and a more unified approach to the market required a reorganization of departments. This took about three months to put in place. However, financial reporting and work continued as usual as mostly everyone was working to a set of roles relating to prescribed accountabilities. The fact that there were no departments for a while made little difference to day-to-day work or reporting. They were already used to crossing boundaries.

DISCUSSION: REORGANIZATION

17.1

If you dismantle the functional structure of your company, in whole or in part, would you be able to maintain full management control and reporting during the change period?

The tools to help it work: systems

"The most useful thing I have is a list of what I'm meant to be working on," said a senior manager from an information systems function.

He was pointing out that, previously, the people in his function were asked to work on the systems parts of numerous projects spanning marketing information, financial, billing and customer service processes among many others. He had learned that it was impossible for his function on its own, to prioritize this workload, decide what needed to be done, when and what should not be done. The outputs they produced were valueless unless they were combined with the other component parts of the project. By having a company-agreed "list" of projects, he is now very clear which projects the company wants done and that no others should be worked on. In addition, the staged framework ensures that any particular part of the project does not proceed ahead of the others and that full checks on resource availability have been carried out.

The conclusion is that the key control tool to help you manage your project portfolio and ensure that work around the company is aligned is the publication and maintainenance of a "list of projects."

The conclusion is that the key control tool to help you manage your project portfolio and ensure that work around the company is aligned is the publication and maintainenance of a "list of projects."

What does the project "list" look like?

Once people start talking about lists, the words "computers, "spreadsheets," and "databases" spring easily to mind. These are the tools that make managing the "list" easier. All too often, however, these systems can be made too complicated and have a tendency to be taken over by the technical people who create them – they can be fun. You need to keep in perspective that they are only tools, which help the company achieve its objectives and so must be suited to the processes, systems, and culture they serve. Reporting is a key part of the tools. It does not matter how good the data you put in are, if you can't get useful information out, they prove an empty shell at best and totally misleading at worst. (You will find that if you can't get the information out, people will not bother to put anything in, no matter how much you plague them!)

SYSTEMS AS A DRIVER FOR CULTURAL SHIFT

Good systems can help support the drive to move culture in a particular direction. If, for example, you want to favor a projects environment where personal accountability is key, then having real people's names attached to accountabilities can be powerful. This is especially so if the system that holds that data is easily accessible to those named people and to those who depend on them.

Systems needs

Your "list" systems need to be designed such that users, with differing requirements, can access the same data to obtain the information they need, in a format which is convenient for them. They need to be able to:

- **select** the data they want to view;
- **sort** the data in an order that suits them;
- **report** in a format or template which serves their needs.

Information systems for keeping track of portfolios of projects generally center around three sets of data:

- resources;
- non-financial data;
- financial data.

I dealt with resources in Chapter 16. The other two sets are dealt with in the following sections. Finance functions tend to have focussed accounting systems dealing with the "money matters." These systems are not primarily designed for holding the non-financial data which you will find useful. Systems are available which can do both, but they are mostly in their infancy and not mature enough to deal with the wide range of ways people want to manage their businesses.

An investment review sign-off process in a major company required that all the departmental managers impacted by the project had to sign the front sheet in ink. The result was a sheet with anything up to 25 signatures on it. Somewhere in that forest of names was a decision maker.

The new process still requires the impacted functions to review and commit to the project, however, no signatures are required. The only signatures are those of the decision makers:

- the project sponsor;
- the director of the department with overall project management accountability;
- the director with the budget which will fund the project.

It is quite clear who is accountable for the decision: he who wants it, he who does it, and he who pays for it.

"No snowflake in an avalanche ever feels responsible."

STANISLAV LEE

Lists: keeping tabs on your projects

If you are keep a track on your projects you will need to have a definitive list of the requests for new proposals and the projects currently in progress. The following should give you a feel for the basic requirements.

Capturing the new proposals

A proposal needs to be logged with a unique reference number from the moment a sponsor wishes to declare its existence. This MUST be prior to the Initial Investigation Gate. It may be as early as when a strategy or plan document is created and flags up the need for a potential project and hence earmarking of funds. A proposal document need not be created before a request is logged, however, sufficient information must be available to describe the possible objectives, output definition, and benefits of the potential project.

A proposal is converted, via the Initial Investigation Gate to a project as an initial investigation and on into the staged framework.

It should be possible to track back from any project which is in progress to find where the original request/proposal came from. In addition, if a request/proposal is converted to a project, it should be possible to see whether the project was in fact completed or terminated early. "Key word searches" are useful to analyze the population of activities based on any of the header or other data for each proposal (e.g. rejected, terminated, etc.).

Projects list

There is a need for a central "database" which can be used as a passive information system/reporting tool for individual projects and portfolios of projects. This system(s) should contain all projects being undertaken in the company. The database should be available to, and provides information in support of, gate decision makers, resource managers, business planners, and project sponsors.

The requirements are for you to have:

- project header data (name, accountabilities, etc.);
- interdependencies with other projects;
- milestone data;
- cost data;
- progress information;
- useful and targeted reporting.

Project header data

The following data should be held for each project:

- project number, project name, business objectives, project framework stage, project sponsor, sponsoring business area, project manager, managing business area; this will be in the business case (see p. 257);
- which "Business Program" the project belongs to (if any);
- which program the project is part of (if any);
- whether the project is "standard," "simple," or "emergency," as defined in Part Two;
- the platforms, systems, processes, and products impacted by the project;

- specific header data which are relevant to specific categories or type of project, e.g., project review group.

Project interdependencies

The project definition of each project includes its interdependencies. A dependency is defined as a deliverable produced by one project, which is needed by another project in order to achieve its targeted benefits (see also pp. 263, 311). It is essential that this is known, defined and maintained. It must be possible to enquire:

- which project(s) depend on this project;
- which project(s) this project depends on.

A simple listing of projects and those which it depends on may be sufficient for your needs, but if the database is to be used as a decision support tool to enable portfolios of projects to be analyzed and the business impacts seen, you may need to include more detail. This could comprise the planned and forecast dates for the transfer of each key dependent deliverable from one project to the other.

If the database is to be used as a decision-support tool to enable portfolios of projects to be analyzed and the business impacts seen, you may need to include more detail. This could comprise the planned and forecast dates for the transfer of each key dependent deliverable from one project to the other.

Milestone data

The system should hold:

- milestone schedule data as original baseline (with date set), current baseline (with date set), achieved date (if completed), forecast date (for uncompleted milestones);
- the milestones in the staged framework (Detailed Investigation Gate, Development Gate, Trial Gate, RFS Gate, Release, project completed);
- project manager-defined milestones in addition to those already stated.

Cost data

If project costs are held in a separate financial system, it is useful to import them into a central management information system to enable you to report on mixes of financial and non-financial information. The system should hold:

- actual costs to date for the project by project stage;

- forecast costs to completion by project stage;
- costs in two categories:
  — manpower (time costs);
  — external purchases.

Benefits forecasting data

The system should hold the "benefits" forecast for each project both in "plan" form (i.e. as per the authorized business case), and as a forecast (i.e. the best guess outcome at the current point in time). This may also be in the form of 'conditions of satisfaction' (see p. 292).

Progress information

The system should be able to be used as a corporate reporting repository, capable of producing a standard report (see p. 276) for each project containing:

- key header data;
- business objectives;
- progress summary and outlook;
- financial summary;
- milestones;
- issues and risks;
- changes (via formal change management).

Reporting generally

The requirement is to provide a range of user roles with targeted, selected, and sorted reports to meet their needs. Users will require either:

- detailed reports on individual projects, or
- a summary reports for portfolios of projects as selected, sorted using any of the other data field criteria.

So users:

- **select** which projects they are interested in (based on the data stored in the information system;
- **sort** the data in the order they need (at least three levels of sort criteria);
- **choose a report** from a set of prescribed templates at a full, summary, and/or analysis level.

The standard reports should be either:

- qualitative (i.e. non-numerical);
- or quantitative (cost-based, benefit based, timescale), with subtotals and totals.

Examples

1 A project sponsor may select a portfolio report showing all the projects he is sponsoring.
2 A head of function or director may select a portfolio report of all the projects being sponsored by himself and anyone else in the function.
3 Or he may select a report of all the projects which will benefit his function.
4 A line manager may select a portfolio report of all the projects which are being managed by his/her staff.

ACTIVE AND PASSIVE REPORTING

You should always distinguish between active and passive reporting. If you want stakeholders to know something, you should tell them. You should not expect them to consult a projects database to find out if anything of interest has happened which is critical for them to know. Project databases are passive and you cannot assume that anyone will look at them.

What would such a system look like?

The following figures show a typical computer-based project "list." Figure 17.1 shows the appearance of the screen. The user has selected to view the project portfolio, sorted by project sponsor. A window then appears which lists all the project sponsors in alphabetical order, with the "status" shown below. Phillipa Brixham has projects she is sponsoring which are currently in progress. It is then possible to "drill down" to see a list of those projects with key data against them (Figure 17.2). Finally, the full data for each project can be displayed on a form such as in Figure 17.3.

Figure 17.2 shows the typical detail you need to show in a project database at summary level. The example includes all the key data such as project number, name, accountabilities, and analysis fields. This is followed by a statement on the progress status of the project. The RAG status is used to indicate the general level of confidence the project manager has in completing the project. Green means everything is going along fine; amber means there are a few issues but they are under control, and red means "Help! Something needs fixing." (Figure 17.4 shows the financial data for project 644). Additional data which could be shown include project costs, benefits, and interdependent projects.

Figure 17.3 shows a listing targeted at a project sponsor, Phillipa Brixham. It lists the projects she is sponsoring, the stage of development, the project manager's name, RAG status (see Figure 17.2) and the dates for a key milestone on which she wishes to focus. Similar listings should be produced, selecting and sorting from any of the data which are held in the database.

RAG STATUS

If using critical chain project scheduling (see p. 329), the RAG status would indicate the degree to which the project buffer had been used.

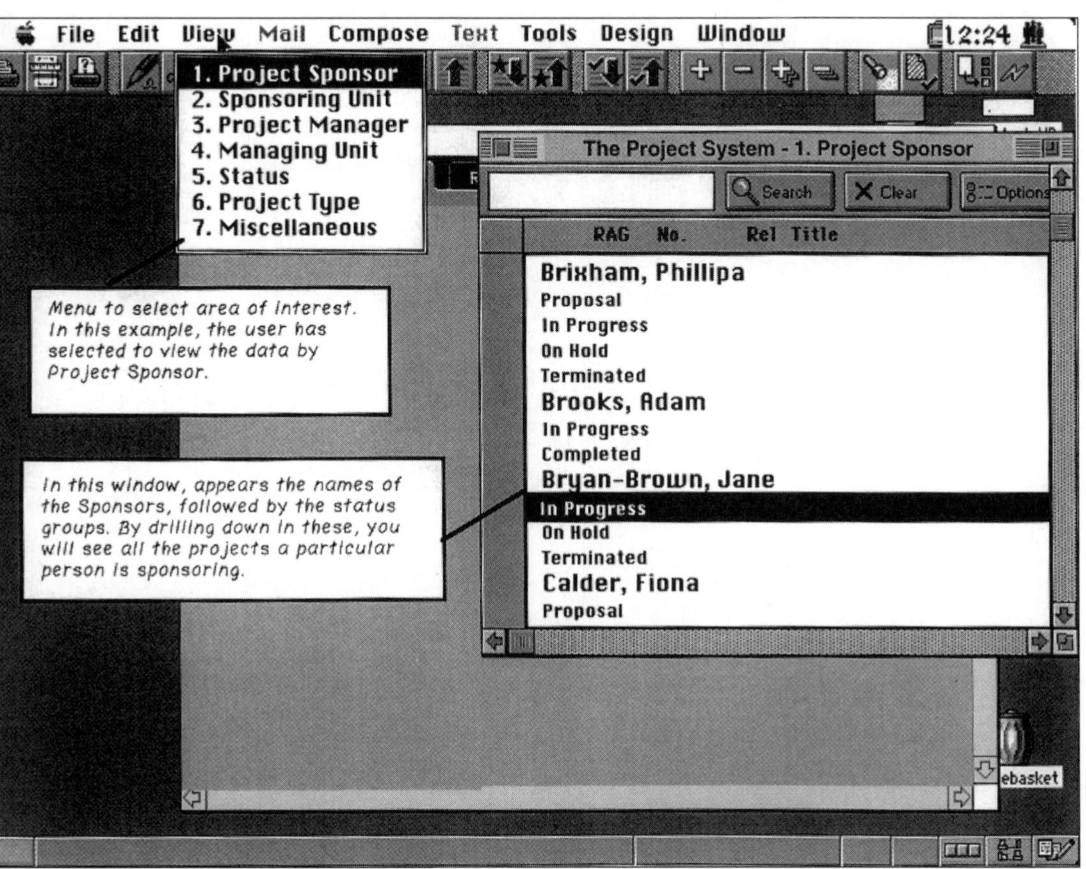

igure 17.1 Screen image of a project list (menu, sponsors' names)

/hen using a system, the user should be able to select the way they wish to view the data and the report ›rmat required. In this example, Phillipa Brixham wants to see her sponsorship portfolio. She has some rojects in progress, some proposals, some projects terminated, and some on hold. The listing in Figure 7.2 shows what they are.

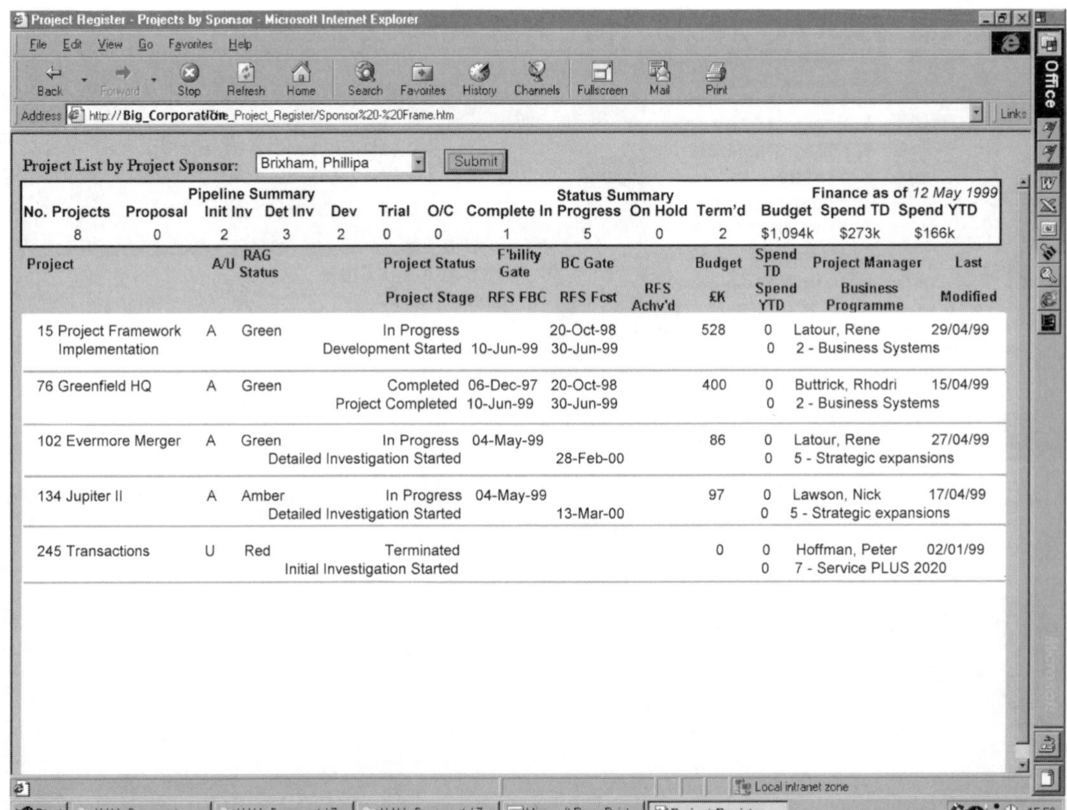

Figure 17.2 Screen image of typical detail from a project list

In this example the database is web based and is filtered and sorted to show a sponsorship portfolio. At the top is a summary of the portfolio pipeline, showing how many projects are in each stage and the status of each. There is also a financial summary. Below this, is a section for each project showing the key data: its RAG status, stage, status (in progress, terminated etc.), who the project manager is and the business program it forms a part of.

Project tracking

Project No.: 644
Title: Transaction 800
Status: In progress
Stage: Ready for service

Project Type 1	Project Type 2	Status
Service Efficiency Capacity Infrastructure	**New** Enhancement Fix Withdrawal	**In progress** On hold Terminated Completed

Sponsorship	Management
Sponsoring unit: Treasury management **Committed units:** Treasury management **Project sponsor:** Bryan-Brown, Jane	**Managing department:** Special projects dept **Project manager:** Bell, Peter **Last updated By:** Fuller, Jane **Last update Date:** 1 Dec 2005

1. Business objectives
To put in place a new infrastructure to expedite cash flow from the Dentrix product family and enable a decrease in working capital of $300k.

2. Summary, status and outlook	RAG status
2a Summary (120 characters max) RFS ACHIEVED 30 Oct 2005. Delay in launch expected **2b Status and outlook** **ISSUE:** A delay in putting the new capability into service is expected due to the failure of a previously delivered and tested item of equipment. The supplier has agreed to replace the faulty unit one has been dispatched by air freight.	Red **Amber** Green

3. Key milestones					
	Original baseline date	*Current baseline date*	*Current forecast date*	*Date achieved*	*Confidence H/M/L*
Initial Investigation Gate	31 Jul 2005	31 Jul 2005	31 Jul 2005	31 Jul 2005	
Detailed Investigation Gate	01 Sep 2005	01 Sep 2005	01 Sep 2005	01 Sep 2005	
Development Gate	14 Sep 2005	14 Sep 2005	14 Sep 2005	14 Sep 2005	
Trial Gate	01 Oct 2005	24 Oct 2005	26 Oct 2005	28 Oct 2005	
Ready for Service Gate	30 Sep 2005	31 Oct 2005	31 Oct 2005	15 Nov 2005	
Launched	01 Nov 2005	01 Dec 2005	05 Dec 2005		High
Project completed	Jan 2006	Jan 2006	Jan 2006		High
Optional user-defined milestones					
Receive PYS software from project 469	14 Sep 2005	14 Sep 2005	14 Sep 2005	14 Sep 2005	

Figure 17.3 Typical report from a project database

A typical presentation of the key facts relating to a project can be presented concisely as a report. Try to follow your normal reporting style (see p. 277).

Management accounting systems

The missing dimension

"What we do is more important than where we sit in the organization." This may be what we feel but it is not what many of our company management accounting systems measure or report. Currently many companies count only two dimensions:

- a cost center code (from which cost center's money is spent);
- an analysis code (what it is spent on).

They do not say **how** the money is applied, i.e. what is actually done with it.

Sometimes they try to do this in part by using a cost center code or an analysis code to capture the essence of where money is applied. For example, a cost center is opened to capture costs for a particular project. While this may be pragmatic, it does not serve the full management accounting needs of the businesses of the future.

A third dimension of accounting is needed to cover the application of our funds regardless of what they are spent on and regardless of which cost centers "fund" or resource them. I call it an "application code."

In essence, this is a "source and application of internal funds" which is useful at a grass roots management level as well as at senior management level.

So the three dimensions are:

- **cost center code** – where money/resources come from;
- **analysis code** – what it is spent on;
- **application code** – to what it is applied.

The sum of each will always equal the same number as they are just different ways of looking at the money used in the business. It is essential this balance is made or we will encourage "leakage" of funds or "cheating."

The application code

What does an "application code" look like? There should be three mutually exclusive application code types:

- **P type** – this is about creating change; taking us from what we do now to what we do tomorrow, i.e. projects.

- **A type** – this is doing "business as usual" processes. In the steady state, e.g., retaining and acquiring customers, doing management tasks (business processes).
- **X type** – this is down time such as sickness, leave, training.

Typically X type is about 20 percent of total "people" expenditure. But who really knows how much we spend on running our existing business (A type) as opposed to changing it (P type)? Do we even have a feel for what this should be?

A P, A, and X type of management accounting system would give us the knowledge to sharpen our focus and ensure that we only do those things which are important to our meeting our strategic objectives, rather than merely keeping track of who spends the money.

Consider the picture of the business when using the traditional cost center code with the new application code:

	Total spend
Cost center 1	20
Cost center 2	30
Cost center 3	40
Cost center 4	10
Total company	**100**

We know the costs in each cost center (the shaded part) (cost center 1 = 20, cost center 2 = 30, etc.) but we have no idea how the money and people are applied. This is revealed when the third dimension is added, giving us a richer picture of our business:

	Down time	Process activities			Projects		Total
	X	A1	A2	A3	P1	P2	
Cost center 1	4	10	4	—	2	—	20
Cost center 2	7	5	10	—	3	5	30
Cost center 3	10	10	—	—	20	—	40
Cost center 4	2	—	—	8	—	—	10
Total company	**23**	**25**	**14**	**8**	**25**	**5**	**100**

For the first time we will be able to run our businesses based on "what counts," i.e. where we apply our efforts rather than "what we can count," i.e. the cost center.

In this environment, cost centers will become "homes" where "pay and rations" are sourced and experience and expertise fostered. Many cost centers will be focused on particular activities but that is not a prerequisite. The application code will say what they are doing:

- away on paid leave?
- being trained?
- performing as part of the "business as usual" task?
- contributing to a project?

By introducing the third dimension on all of our costs (people included), we will know what we are applying ourselves to.

The advantage of this is that the balance of power will move away from cost centers as the "fund-holding barons" of the old hierarchical organization toward the flat structured "what we do is important" new corporation. AND ... our key management tool (the management accounting system) will support this.

Management by accountability will thrive, as accountabilities will be tied to application codes which operate across the whole company, regardless of the cost center to which the person holding the accountability belongs. In this way, any person can sponsor or work on any project or activity anywhere in the company without you losing control of the finances or the head count. For example, Figure 17.4 shows a typical financial report for a project sponsor. It shows the person is sponsoring five projects, one of which is terminated, one on hold and three in progress. This person is accountable for over $1m spend across the company.

As the three dimensions must balance, there is little scope or benefit for "cheating." If a project is running over budget, there is no point in hiding its cost within another project or activity even if the owner would accept it! It would merely rob Peter to pay Paul and different performance indicators would move in opposite directions accordingly.

It would stop the racket of "head count." It would no longer matter how many people you had in a cost center as you would be concentrating more on what they did. There need be no pushing people out of the "home" cost center to do a "project" only to fill their position with another (net effect equals one more head).

BOOKKEEPING!

You should distinguish between the management of costs from a management accounting perspective and from a financial perspective The latter relates to "bookkeeping" and where the transactions appear in the formal chart of accounts. In the management of projects, this is of little or no use. Managing the actual spend and cash flow provides far greater control.

This may sound a radical approach, but it is within the capability of many companies. It would require "time sheeting for all," but we all do it now (e.g. we all fill in sickness notes, paid leave forms, etc.) In addition, as the bulk of employees only do one A type application and some X types, time sheets could be generated by default with only the exceptions requiring input. This would give you the freedom to deploy anyone anywhere, not "lose them," and know what their input is being applied to. Thus "doing projects" will stop being dangerous; no longer will they be the fast track to redundancy!

Further, we are in a rapidly moving business world. By adopting the management approach given here, reorganizations of departments will become less important and can be done at any time in the financial

We are in a rapidly moving business world. By adopting the management approach given here, reorganizations of departments will become less important and can be done at any time in the financial year.

year. P, A, and X will be the way we will run our businesses!

The requirements for such a system, incorporating project costing, would be that each application code should:

- have a unique reference number;
- have costs captured against a work breakdown structure, representing, as a minimum, the stages of the project framework;
- have forecasts set;
- be viewed with or without absorbed overheads;
- have the staged authorization of funds;
- have three status for transaction postings:
  - — open for forecast only;
  - — open for cost and forecast;
  - — closed.

Reporting should be flexible to reflect the life of a project, the current financial year, and the future, enabling interest groups (such as project sponsors) to see their own projects as a portfolio.

Figure 17.4 is an example, which follows on from Figure 17.3 and shows the costs associated with Phillipa Brixham's sponsorship portfolio. If your management accounting system is linked to your project database, these data could also appear at the foot of the report shown in Figure 17.2. Similar reports should be produced, selecting and sorting from any of the data which are held in the accounting system, with the ability to summarize at any level of the project work breakdown structure.

This report is for a particular sponsor

PROJECT SPONSOR PORTFOLIO REPORT

Project Sponsor: Brixham, Phillipa

Period: 4 wks to 28 Sept 1997

$ 000s	A	B	C	D	E	F	G	H	J	K	L	M	N	P
No PROJECTS	MONTH	LIFE							FINANCIAL YEAR		FORECAST TO COMPLETION			
	Actual	Actual to Date	Previous to Date	F'cast Outturn	Revised Budget	Variance	Commited	Original Budget	Actual to Date	F'cast Outturn	This FY	Next FY	Beyond	Total to Complete
In progress														
755 Inventory free warehouse Phase 1	12	56	44	214	220	6	43	200	56	182	126	32		158
828 International acquisition B	14	72	58	167	150	-17	12	150	60	120	60	30	5	95
627 Logistics Management System IV	23	567	544	590	600	10	34	600	234	257	23			23
On hold														
832 Automated HR Appraisals		124	124	156	160	4		150	32	64	32			32
Terminated														
721 Improve Customer Support		12	12	24	24			110	12	24	12			12
TOTAL PORTFOLIO	49	831	782	1151	1154	3	89	1210	394	647	253	62	5	320

The total line shows the sum of the projects that the person is sponsoring

Figure 17.4 Typical financial summary

This report shows the financial summary of Phillipa Brixham's sponsorship portfolio. It matches the non-financial data given in Figure 17.2. This report shows that she is accountable for $1.15m authorized spend on five projects, one of which has been terminated, and another put on hold. Only one of her projects, 828, is forecast to overspend.

Putting your systems together

In the previous sections, we looked at the three primary information needs (resources, non-financial, and financial) and have seen how they could be handled in our information systems. We have also seen how resource management relates to project cost forecasting, and how this in turn builds into the business plan. Each system is targeted at a particular need; however, they are all related. Figure 17.5 shows the relationship in diagrammatic form. Actual expenditure on your projects is captured by the accounting system (the shaded boxes). These costs can be handled on both a project-focused basis and on a more traditional, cost center basis. Forecast of manpower (person hours) is costed and then combined with the forecast of purchases to produce an overall cost forecast for the projects.

At the point marked "A" the manpower forecasts are taken off and collated to give an early view of resource needs for line managers and the company as a whole. Once the actual costs and forecast costs have been collected they can be combined to produce the project financial accounts and summary reports. They can also be fed into the project database and combined with other, non-financial data, to produce an overall reporting capability. Where you keep your data, and how the reports are produced, will depend very much on the systems you have in your company. But, regardless of this, the overall logic and flow should be very similar to that examined here. It won't be easy to put in place, but if you have a vision of the future of your business system's strategy, you will gradually be able to build the full set. You will also find that having simple, separate systems may be the most pragmatic way forward, even if it means some temporary duplication of data and the risks that entails. It is better than not having a view of your project portfolio at all.

Web technologies are ideally suited to providing, quick, simple, and effective reports from disparate systems. They also have the advantage that user training is minimal if your organization already has a desktop strategy rolled out. Web technologies can also be used for data capture. For example, the Lotus Notes example in Figure 17.1 could easily be substituted by a web front-end interfacing to any modern database system such as Microsoft Access or Oracle as in Figure 17.2.

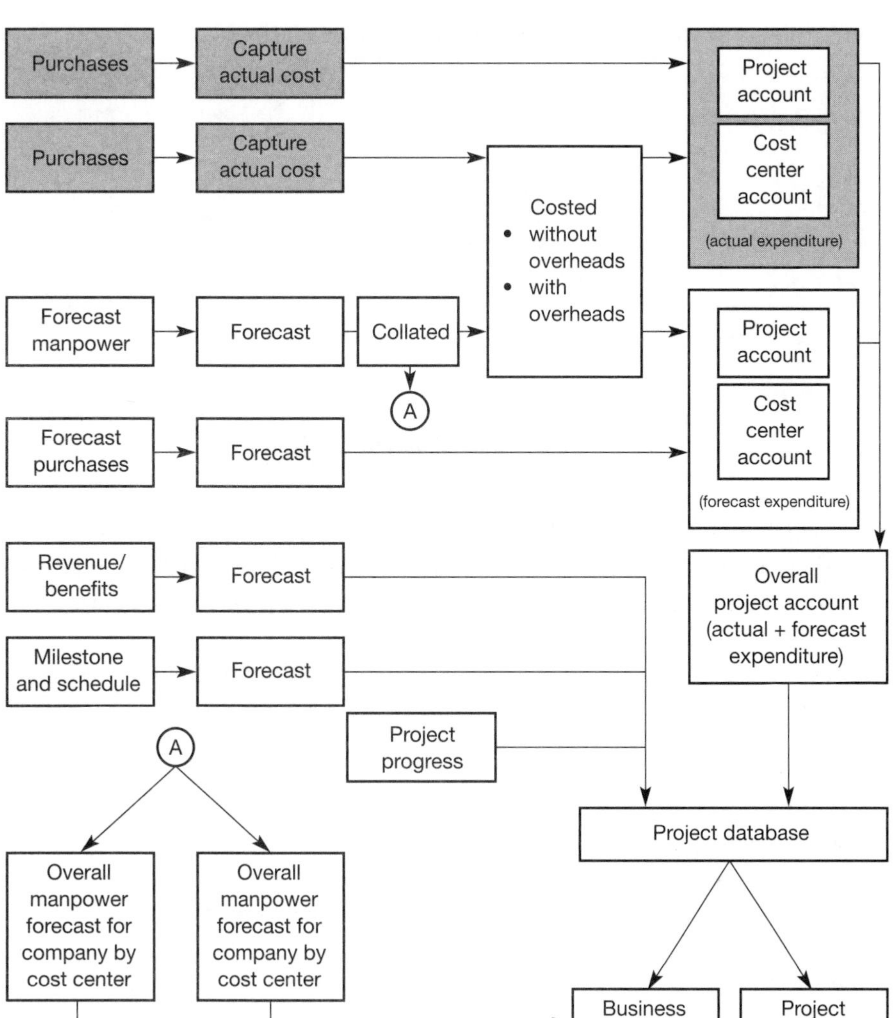

Figure 17.5 The complete system

The links between resources, costs, benefits, and other project systems. The outputs include both project reporting and the necessary inputs required for business planning (see also Figure 14.3).

Don't think a systems solution is always the best solution.

17.2

YOUR OWN SYSTEMS

1. Make an enlarged copy of Figure 17.5. Mark it up with highlighter pens, indicating the elements you currently have in place (shade in yellow) and those parts which you already plan to put in place (shade in another colour).

2. Are the elements you have shaded designed to be compatible with each other?

3. On a flip chart:

   - list elements which are missing;
   - list the data which would be contained within these elements;
   - list the information are you lacking as a result.

4. Consider, based on what you have in place, what actions you could take to fill any gaps you have identified in the systems environment supporting your projects framework.

Part Four

MAKING PROJECTS WORK FOR YOU

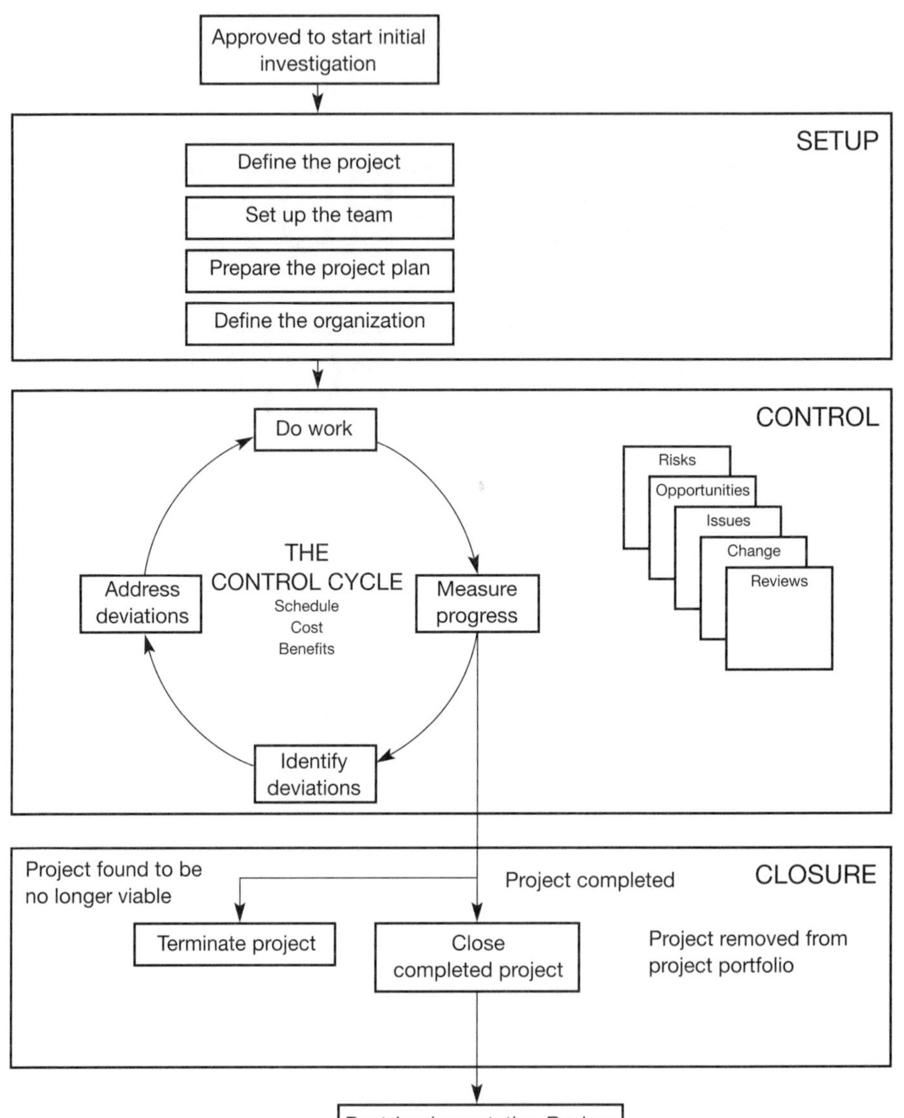

Figure 18.1 The full project control environment

The project control environment can be represented in three sections, starting with "setup" and ending in "closure." Between these are the tools and techniques for monitoring and controlling the project. These controls apply throughout the life of the project.

"People love chopping wood. In this activity one immediately sees results."

ALBERT EINSTEIN

In Part Two, I explained the management framework for a single project, taking it from being an idea through the various life cycle stages until benefits are being delivered to your business.

In Part Three, I showed how you could manage a number of projects, which together make up the portfolio of initiatives which are changing your business to suit its future strategic direction.

In this part, I return to the single project and explain the tools and techniques you can apply to ensure that projects are kept under control and are likely to deliver the promised benefits. Figure 18.1 shows the full project control environment, starting with "setup" and ending in "closure." Between these are the techniques for monitoring progress and handling risks, issues, opportunities, and reviews. At the heart is the project control cycle. These factors apply throughout the life of the project, regardless of which stage you are currently working within:

- **Encourage team work and commitment.**
- **Practice single point accountability.**
- **Break down functional barriers by using a cross-functional team.**
- **Manage your stakeholders' expectations.**
- **Build excellence in project management techniques and controls across your company.**
- **Ensure success by planning for it.**
- **Monitor and control against the agreed plan.**
- **Manage changes to the plan actively.**
- **Close the project formally.**

How to use Part Four

The sections in Part Four are written as working guides for you either to apply directly or to adapt to include in your own control framework. Many of the chapters include workouts to help you apply the guides in practice.

Project Teams and Style

Culture: the way we do things around here

Project teams and style

I thought you were doing that!: accountability

An environment in which energy is expended on blame and fault finding, rather than looking for solutions to problems, will damage morale and hinder the performance of any team.

"I must follow them. I am their leader!"

ANDREW BONAR LAW

- **Encourage team work and commitment.**
- **Practice single point accountability.**
- **Break down functional barriers by using a cross-functional team.**

Culture: the way we do things around here

Culture has two fundamental elements:

- the norms and behaviors of a group;
- unconscious programming of the mind leading to a set of similar collective habits, behaviors and mind sets.

(*Source*: Eddie Obeng *Putting Strategy to Work*, Pitman Publishing, 1996)

While this book is not primarily aimed at culture, interpersonal skills, and the often named "soft" aspects of project management, it would be remiss not to summarize the key aspects which have been shown to encourage success in a projects environment.

As Obeng has pointed out, "People create change and people constrain change," and culture is what people are about. Let us remind ourselves of the fundamental differences between working in a project, as opposed to in a line environment.

Line management is about maintaining the existing processes. It is performed in a relatively stable environment. It often abhors change as it affects the ever increasing drive for efficiency. People work in defined jobs and have defined work to carry out. It is often (but not always!) predictable.

Project management is about change. Projects are one-off activities, carried out over a finite time period. They often break new ground and step into the unknown. They require management that can adapt to conflicting pressures, changing requirements, and unfamiliar situations. Projects are often staffed by groups of people from disparate functions and locations.

The managers of these environments do not necessarily share the same skills and competences, nevertheless, a company environment must be set up such that the two aspects of management (steady state and change) can coexist.

Project teams and style

In line management, the manager or the supervisor has the power and authority to instruct a person in his/her duties. In many companies however, the project managers have little authority of this nature. Most likely, they should have this authority, but that is not always the reality. They have to deliver the project using a more subtle power base which is more rooted in the shared commitment of the team than in directives. No matter how good a project proposal is or how thoroughly the investigative stages have been undertaken, the bottom line is that success is rarely achieved by a poorly led, ill-motivated group of individuals. (Notice I have not used the word "team.") It is widely recognized that team work and team spirit in line roles leads to better results than sticks and sanctions. In projects, team working is even more crucial. A project team has a short time to form, normalize its behaviors and start performing. In addition:

Success is rarely achieved by a poorly led, ill-motivated group of individuals.

- a team may be dispersed geographically.
- its members may have other duties to attend to.
- the most appropriate people may not be available.

This can place demands on individuals, particularly those new to projects, as it can set the stage for conflicts of loyalties, which the project manager and others must recognize and try to avoid. The project manager must be the leading player in creating and fostering a team spirit and enrolling the commitment of those associated with the project. The project sponsor and line managers of the project team members have a similar responsibility. Their behavior and actions can derail a project just as drastically, or even more so, than any by the project manager. Clear reporting lines, good information flow, realistic work plans, and defined project roles will also help "ease" the pathway.

Leadership style and team values are also important. An open, even handed approach which encourages good communication and gives those in the project the confidence to raise potential problems tends to be the most effective. An environment in which energy is expended on blame and fault finding, rather than looking for solutions to problems, will damage morale and hinder the performance of any team. This approach must be present in fact as well as theory. For example, most project-scheduling software shows which activities are late. What's the point of reporting on them if you can't do anything about it? What is important is knowing which ones count and which are likely to be late.

When dealing with your team, or indeed any other stakeholders, assume they will act to avoid pain and seek pleasure. Assume they won't really care about anything else. If you concentrate on inconsequential trivia and absolute adherence to process, so will they. Publicly reward the behaviors you want to encourage. Success depends on the commitment and willingness of each team member to succeed.

> ***Publicly reward the behaviors you want to encourage.***

> *"He that complies against his will*
> *Is of his own opinion still."*
>
> SAMUEL BUTLER

ENCOURAGING OPEN COMMUNICATION

A team progress meeting had just finished and the participants were talking as they left the room. One was overheard by the project manager saying to a colleague that a deliverable he is accountable for was going to be nine months late. This had major implications on the project and yet had not been stated at the progress meeting. The project manager was understandably annoyed. Which was more important to him, the fact that the delay had not been reported or that there was a delay at all? He took the view that he needed to know about delays in sufficient time to deal with them. He therefore made a point of encouraging the reporting of bad news, being careful not to harangue the messenger for delays or whatever. This did not mean he was soft on people not delivering to plan but rather showed his focus on recognizing problems and achieving the objectives in spite of them.

I thought you were doing that!: accountability

How many times have you been in a meeting, with your colleagues and the following has happened:

Chairman: Right. That's agreed then. Bob and Dave, you sort that one out and let us know next week.

Next week . . .

Chairman: Bob, what happened?

Bob: I don't know. I thought Dave was doing something on this.

Dave: Oh! I was waiting for you to phone me.

Some clarity on who was actually accountable was needed. Bob and Dave might both have been necessary, as skilled, knowledgeable resources, to carry out the action, but only one of them should have been accountable. This is called "single point accountability."

The person who is accountable is not necessarily the person who does the work, but the one who sees that it is done. This is not only useful in a meeting environment but also in planning projects. We have already introduced the accountabilities of the project sponsor and project manager. The project manager is accountable for managing the work on a day-to-day basis, ensuring the deliverables are in place at the required time, quality, and cost. He or she cannot do it all, or in many cases manage it all. We have also seen how a project is decomposed into life cycle stages (see p. 135). This decomposition can be followed through with major packages of work being made the accountability of a particular, named, core team member. These work packages may be divided into smaller packages and ultimately into individual activities and tasks. This decomposition is called a work breakdown structure (see p. 133).

In practice, single point accountability means every work package at any level in the work breakdown structure has a person named as accountable for it.

In practice, single point accountability means every task, activity, and work package at any level in the work breakdown structure has a person named as accountable for it. This has four advantages:

- It is clear what is expected of each person.
- Overlaps should be eliminated as no deliverable can be created by two different work packages.
- If a gap in accountability appears (due to loss of a team member, for example), the next person up the tree is accountable to fix it.
- If scope, cost, or time proves to be inadequate to create the deliverables, it is clear who is accountable for raising these issues.

In practice, accountability is shown in the way that project plans (bar charts) are designed. The examples given in Chapter 21 clearly show accountability.

"The business of everybody is the business of nobody."
LORD MCCAULAY

Encourage an open, even-handed style to encourage communications.

Project Setup

How to go about it

Set up the project team

Prepare a project definition

Prepare the project plan

Define your project organization

Engage your stakeholders

This chapter explains the steps you need to take during the Initial Investigation Stage to set up a project and ensure that control is established from the very start.

"Mix a little foolishness with your serious plans; it's lovely to be silly at the right moment."

HORACE, 65–8 BC

- **Understand the driving business need.**
- **Define the scope and boundaries for the project.**
- **Use your team to define and plan the project.**
- **Harness your stakeholders' influence.**

This chapter explains the steps you need to take during the Initial Investigation Stage to set up a project and ensure that control is established from the very start. For clarity these steps are described sequentially, but in practice you will find that you need to do them in parallel, as each step may influence any of the other steps.

How to go about it

There are five key steps for you to follow when setting up a project:

1. Set up the project team.
2. Prepare a project definition.
3. Prepare a project plan.
4. Define your project organization.
5. Engage your stakeholders.

The purpose of formally setting up the project is for you to state explicitly the *business drivers*, *scope*, and *objectives* for the project, that is:

- *why* you are doing it;
- *what* you will produce;
- *when* you will produce it;
- *how* you will approach the project;
- *who* will be involved;
- *how* much it will cost and benefit you.

This information is gathered in a document (the Initial Business Case) and together with the associated plans, provides you with the starting point (baseline) on which all subsequent project decisions will be taken and against which you can measure project performance.

The headings under which you should define your project follow. I have chosen to structure the document in three parts, each serving a different interest group. It is important for you to avoid having to write up your project in many differing ways to meet differing needs. For example, it is not unusual for finance functions to want a "special" document on which to base the authorization of funds for the project. However, good design of a key document, such as that outlined here, can avoid such duplication and thus reduce your workload and the discrepancies which can appear if separate documents are required for different interest groups.

WHAT A WASTE OF TIME!

"But why do I need to write it all up? Isn't it just a waste of time?"

Writing up your project in a structured and thorough way helps you to ensure that all the important aspects are covered. The template is, in itself, a checklist for building quality into your projects.

Unless you are the only person involved in the project, you will need to communicate your intentions. *You* may know everything about the project, but if the others who need to be involved don't understand what you are trying to achieve, the project will fail. The document is your explicit form of communication.

Keep the document brief. Put in the minimum content to communicate the bare essentials. Ironically, the simpler the project, the more people tend to write, as they know so much about it. Larger, more complex projects are frequently ill defined and too brief.

Headings to define your project

The three parts of the business case are:

Part 1 – Finance, which is primarily aimed at the finance function. They will be interested in this section as a priority and then Section 2.1 to 2.4.

The project sponsor will also be interested in this as it sets out the financial criteria to be met.

Part 2 – Project Definition is of interest to the project sponsor, stakeholders, and project team. It is the meat of the document.

Part 3 – Project Organization is of most interest to the project manager and team as it sets our how they have organized themselves.

These comprise:

Section	*Section heading*	*Question answered*
1	FINANCE	
1.1	Financial appraisal	HOW MUCH?
1.2	Sensitivity analysis	HOW MUCH?
2	PROJECT DEFINITION	
2.1	Background	WHY?
2.2	Business objectives	WHY?
2.3	Benefits	WHY?
2.4	Output definition	WHAT?
2.5	Scope, impacts, and interdependencies	WHAT?
2.6	Deliverables	WHAT?
2.7	Timescales	WHEN?
2.8	Risks and opportunities	CONTEXT?
2.9	Prerequisites, assumptions, and constraints	CONTEXT?
2.10	Project approach	HOW?
2.11	Analysis of options	HOW?
3	PROJECT ORGANIZATION	
3.1	Review and appraisal points	HOW?
3.2	Change control	HOW?
3.3	Progress reporting	HOW?
3.4	Project team and stakeholders	WHO?

The content of Part 2 is described in detail later in this chapter.

Set up the project team

The typical "project structure" was described in Chapter 4 and is shown again in Figure 19.1.

Project teams are:

- short term, being established only for the duration of the project;
- cross-functional, to provide the necessary skill mix;
- frequently part time, with team members fulfilling line and project tasks.

Bearing this in mind, it is essential that you agree the project roles from the start (e.g. project sponsor, project manager and project board membership) with the individuals concerned and their line managers (if appropriate). As many of the team members are likely to be part time and have other daily duties to attend to, it is essential that you agree with their line managers what their commitments are and how you should handle changes to this. The line managers may also have a quality assurance role to undertake, if so this must be agreed. If necessary, write and agree a role description, defining the individual's accountabilities. Even

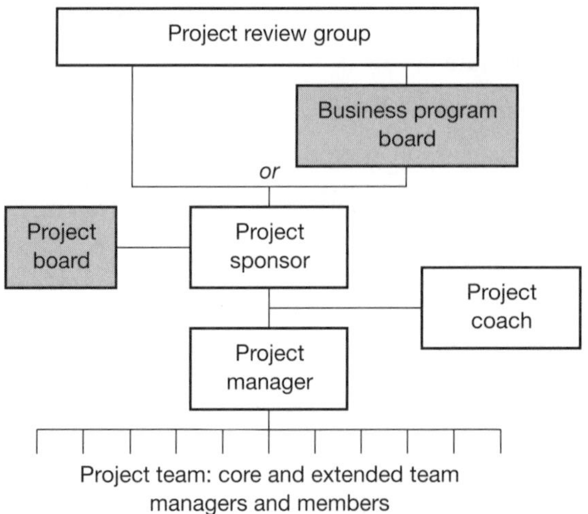

Figure 19.1 A typical project organization structure
The project sponsor requires the benefits, possibly supported by a project board, and reports to the project review group or to a business program board. The project manager reports to the project sponsor and is accountable for the day-to-day running of the project. A project coach supports these key roles. All team managers and members report to the project manager.

if these descriptions are never referred to again, the act of creating them with the individual, and agreeing them, will clarify that person's role and ensure there are no misunderstandings. Finally, do ensure that accountability for any activity or work package on the project rests with a single person only. Shared accountabilties do not work; they lead to omission, duplication, and confusion (see also p. 250).

You should summarize the key members' roles in Section 3.4 of the initial and full business case documents.

You should create, with the team, a set of values for the project to share and an agreed way of working together. Project Workout 19.1 provides some ideas for this. Fostering team spirit is the responsibility of all on the team, led by the project manager. The sooner the team can settle down to work together in an environment of openness and trust, the better it will be for the project. Project setup is the ideal time to do this. Even if *you* know what to do on the project, sparing the time for the team to contribute will lead to greater commitment and better results. Preferably the early days of the project should be spent as much as possible as a group working in a creative environment. Project planning is an ideal vehicle for forming the team as well as being of vital importance to achieving results. Projects that are designed solely by one person usually lack the vitality and level of involvement necessary for achieving extraordinary results.

Projects which are designed solely by one person usually lack the vitality and level of involvement necessary for achieving extraordinary results.

Accountability: what you can count on a person to do. That person and only that person can be called to account if something he/she has accountability for is not done.

Responsibility: what a person is, or feels, responsible for. It assumes commitment on the part of that person, beyond his/her own accountabilities, to act responsibly to ensure that the project objectives are met.

You may be *accountable* for ensuring a computer system functions correctly. I would be acting *responsibly* if I told you of any defects I observed.

In projects it is essential that accountabilities are clearly stated and are unambiguous so everyone knows who is called to account. Similarly, team commitment should be fostered which promotes responsible and open behavior by all team members.

19.1

THE FIRST TEAM MEETING

This is best done in a relaxed atmosphere without any tables acting as barriers between people. The "board room" arrangement is not recommended. Team meetings are best in rooms with space to move around and wall room for flip charts. Confined rooms confine thinking.

The first time team members gather is very important and can set the tone for the rest of the project. Some individuals may know each other (and you) well. Others may know no one. Some may have worked together before on other projects. Even if some have not met before, they may have preconceived ideas of others on the team based on gossip and rumor from other colleagues. It is you, as project manager, who must bond this disparate group into a committed team. One way of doing this is to:

- bring the group members to respect each other;
- create a set of team rules!

Respect each other

1 Ask all present to introduce themselves and say a little about their interests outside work. Ask them to tell the others something about themselves that none of the others knows.

2 Ask each person to say what his/her commitments are to the project, why he/she would like to see it succeed, and what that person will do to help success become a reality.

3 When the individual has finished, each of other team members should build on what that individual has said about him/herself by saying what skills and competencies they know or feel the person has which they respect. Keep to positive and strong points only.

On receiving this acknowledgment, the individual should not be embarrassed. "Thank you" is all he or she needs to say.

4 Steps 1 to 3 should be gone through for every person in the group.

This may sound contrived, but it does work if treated seriously. It can remove or dispel rumor. It brings people onto a personal footing.

Team values

Creating a set of "rules" that the team agrees to live by and uphold is also a powerful way of bonding:

1 Brainstorm a set of values or rules for the team to live by. Put these on a flip chart.

2 The team should then select those which it wants to live by.

3 Display the values prominently in the team's workroom and at every team meeting.

During the brainstorm, individuals will often shout out things that annoy them. For example, if someone really gets heated if meetings start late, he may want the rule/value "All meetings start on time." The brainstorm list, therefore, becomes a set of potential "hot buttons" which can turn each person from a likeable, rational soul into an angry unreasonable one. It's good to know what these are at the start! Some of the most powerful values can also appear very shallow. One senior team had "chocolate" as a value. At every meeting someone was accountable for bringing one or two bars of chocolate. It became a symbol of "looking after each other" and something to joke about to lighten the tension when business issues were weighing heavily and the team could not agree a way forward.

Prepare a Project Definition

Part 2, the project definition section of the initial business case document, defines your project – why you are doing it, what you will produce, and how you will go about it. The details for each section are as follows:

2 Project Definition

2.1 Background

Describe, briefly, the background to the project:

- Explain why the project has come about (e.g. as a result of a strategy study, as a result of findings from another project).
- Refer to any other associated projects or initiatives, business plans, or conclusions from previous studies.

2.2 Business objectives

You should describe why you are doing the project. Explain:

- the business objectives the project will satisfy;
- the needs the project fills;
- how the project supports your business strategy.

2.3 Benefits

You should describe the benefits you hope to achieve from the project (see also Chapter 20). These may be in two forms:

- *Financial* – these should be stated in "money" terms (e.g. increased revenue, cost savings, etc.).
- *Non-financial* – changes in operational and key performance indicators should be quantified. If you are unable to quantify a particular benefit, describe it as best you can – just because you can't count it, doesn't mean to say it does not count.

Include a statement on what else the project will accomplish, for example, say what new possibilities will be created operationally, commercially, or for new projects.

In addition you should outline:

- the minimum conditions of satisfaction required in order to declare the project a success (e.g. achievement of a specific market share, revenue, cost saving);
- the method for measuring and confirming the achievement of each benefit;
- any possible events which, if they occur, will lead you to consider terminating the project.

Answering the question "Why?" is very important. There are four basic reasons why you should want a project:

- to earn more revenue;
- to save costs;
- to reduce working capital;
- to enable you to remain in business.

All programs (related projects) will ultimately be aiming for one or more of these. However, in a program, individual projects may focus on other benefits, for example, improving performance and service quality. Other projects are created as vehicles to learn about new markets, technologies, or approaches. Be honest when stating the business objective. If you pretend a "learning" project is a revenue generator, don't be surprised if it is cut in favor of projects which generate greater revenue.

2.4 Output definition

You should describe, in one paragraph, what the project is going to produce overall. This may be a new product, a new culture, process, manufacturing line, computer system, etc. Section 2.6 will list the key deliverables and these need not be stated here. The output definition document will contain the detail.

2.5 Scope, impacts and interdependencies

Define the work necessary to meet the business objectives outlined in Section 2.2 and to create the output described in Section 2.4. Include:

- the work needed to be undertaken;
- the boundaries of the project;
- any aspects which are specifically excluded from the project;
- key interdependencies with other projects (see p. 311).

You should also state, in broad terms:

- the impact the project will have on current operations and existing projects;
- the functions or departments in your company which will be affected.

Interdependency. If Project B requires a deliverable from Project A in order to achieve its objective, Project B is dependent on Project A, i.e., a deliverable is passed from one project to another.

For example, Project A builds a computer platform as one of its deliverables. Project B uses this platform to run software it has built as one of its deliverables. If Project A failed, Project B will fail as it is dependent on it. A deliverable can be created by one project only. It may, however, be used by many subsequent projects.

A deliverable can be created by one project only. It may, however, be used by many subsequent projects.

SCOPE

The project scope must comprise everything which is needed to ensure that the benefits can be delivered. There should be no assumptions that "others" are providing a key part. If other projects are providing deliverables, this must be stated explicitly and not assumed.

2.6 Deliverables

List the major deliverables from your project and which are needed to create the output described in Section 2.4. Deliverables may take two forms:

- *Final deliverables* – which are to be handed over by the project team to the users at the end of the project (e.g., hardware, software systems, brochures, product specifications, tariffs, business processes, advertising campaigns).
- *Temporary deliverables* – which are to be produced during the course of the project for review and sign-off (e.g., feasibility report, business case).

For each deliverable, specify:

- the format and content in which it is to be produced (e.g. a written report, TV advertisement);
- the named individual accountable for its production;
- the named individual(s) accountable for reviewing and/or signing it off.

If the list is extensive, you should detail them in an appendix and list the only key ones in the main body of the document (see p. 326).

2.7 Timescales

Outline the overall project timescales by stating the target completion dates for key milestones. Include all the staged framework milestones:

Development Gate, Trial Gate, RFS Gate, launch, project complete (see p. 325). Add any other significant milestones or events such as the letting of a major contract.

2.8 Risks and opportunities

This section should contain:

- a list of the significant risks and opportunities that may potentially jeopardize or enhance the success of the project;
- actions that will be taken at the outset to reduce the likelihood of each risk identified;
- actions or contingency plans that may be implemented, should any risk or opportunity happen.

You may conveniently present this in the form of a risk and opportunities log. (See Chapter 23 for a full discussion of risks and opportunities.)

2.9 Prerequisites, assumptions, and constraints

Include:

- any circumstances outside your control which must be in place if your project is to be successful;
- all assumptions that have been made about the environment (e.g., economic factors, competitors, systems, people) in which your project is to be conducted;
- any constraints which have been imposed on your project which may affect the outcome.

It is important that you list all assumptions and constraints, even if they appear obvious to you; they may not be so obvious to others associated with the project.

It is important that you list all assumptions and constraints, even if they appear obvious to you; they may not be so obvious to others associated with the project.

2.10 Project approach

Describe how the project will be undertaken and explain why you have chosen this particular approach. Include:

- a work breakdown structure (e.g. phases, stages, subprojects, work packages) with justification;
- key interdependencies between subproject elements and with suppliers.

Where subprojects are complex, you should consider having each one formally defined by the sub project manager using Parts 2 and 3 of this document.

2.11 Analysis of options

Summarize the key points from the investigative studies, stating which options have been rejected and which have been carried forward for further analysis. Give your reasons for any choices made.

19.2

DEFINING A PROJECT

Take any new project that you are associated with. With the project sponsor, project manager and key team members, create, on flip charts in a workshop environment, the project definition part of the business case document. Base it on the template given in the section above.

Ensure you answer every section fully – it all counts.

Note where there are gaps in the answers, and be honest. You will fool no one but yourself in the long term.

Work with the team to fill the gaps identified in this workout:

- If you don't know *why* you are doing the project, consider terminating it.
- If you don't know *what* you are delivering, regard your costs and timescales as unstable and your risk high.
- If you don't know *when* it will be done, carry out more investigations until you do know.
- If you don't know *how* you will approach the project, regard risk as high and investigate further.

PROJECT DEFINITION CHECKLIST

Use this checklist to review any projects currently in progress.

Criteria

- ☐ Has a project definition been written, reviewed by the stakeholders, and approved by the project sponsor?
- ☐ Do the scope and objectives of the project meet the needs of the business?
- ☐ Have the benefits been fully assessed and quantified wherever possible?
- ☐ Do the benefits match the needs?
- ☐ Have all the risks been identified and categorized?
- ☐ Has a comprehensive and satisfactory work breakdown been developed?
- ☐ Does the work breakdown reflect the deliverables to be produced?
- ☐ Are all key logical relationships between projects and activities clear?
- ☐ Has the plan been developed to minimize or offset the risks?

The only way a project can be delivered is by its deliverables. For each deliverable check:

- ☐ Are the project deliverables relevant and are they feasible both to produce and implement?
- ☐ Have quality criteria been established?
- ☐ Is it clear who is accountable for preparing each deliverable?
- ☐ Is it clear who will review the deliverable prior to signing off acceptance of each deliverable?
- ☐ Is it clear who will sign off each deliverable?
- ☐ Has sufficient time been allowed for reviewing/amending each deliverable?

PROJECT DEFINITIONS

A major food manufacturer was undertaking a radical reorganization of its processes and working methods. This involved warehousing, distribution, manufacturing, marketing, human resources, and sales. In all, there were seven projects within the complex change program. A considerable amount of study work had been completed and some of the projects had actually started. The managing director asked his management team, each member of which was sponsoring one or more projects, to write up each project in a form similar to that given in this book. When asked how long it would take, they all said a week. The managing director gave them two weeks.

Seven weeks later the last project definition arrived. "What took you so long?" the managing director asked. One director said that as he was writing his, it dawned on him he wasn't really sure what he was doing. Further, when they read each others' documents they were surprised and often perturbed at what they were doing. The extra time was to work on the gaps and to check that they all formed a coherent program.

TESTING IF PEOPLE ARE REALLY WORKING ON THEIR DEFINITIONS OR MERELY PAYING LIP SERVICE

With the projects in the case study, I designed a front cover with a space for the name and signature of the project sponsor and project manager, No one was asked to sign anything. Of the seven documents, four came back, unprompted, with both signatures and the other three with only that of the project manager.

Guess which projects proceeded more smoothly and with fewer misunderstandings!

I do not advocate inky signatures on every piece of paper. It looks too much like bureaucracy. However, it can be used as a device to test commitment in a culture where a signature has value.

Prepare the project plan

Preparing a project plan enables you to control the project by:

- **defining the scope** – specify the activities which need to be performed to complete the project scope and the target dates for their completion;
- **assigning accountability** – identify an owner for each activity who will be accountable for its completion;
- **monitoring progress** – provide the baseline against which progress will be measured.

The content and format of the schedule plan are described in the following sections. While these deal with schedule plans, the approach is also valid for the related resource and cost plans which should always use the same work breakdown structure.

Earlier in this chapter we discovered that "Projects which are designed solely by one person usually lack the quality and level of involvement necessary for achieving extraordinary results." I was illustrating the vital team-building benefits of working together at the start of the project. However, the benefits are far more practical and tangible than that. If a team develops an approach to the project and plans it together, there will be debate and argument based on the differing perspectives of each team member. As a result of such discussions, each member will come to understand the needs and viewpoints of the others. Building a good plan is hard work, however, once done, all the reasons for it being as it is are embedded in the minds of those who created it. Each individual is less likely to make independent decisions on his/her work scope which will have adverse effects on the work of others. Similarly, when things go wrong (as they probably will), the team will know more instinctively the correct way to handle it. Team members will be more likely to concur on the method of resolution: they will have already cleared away all the interfunctional blockages in their minds when they created the original plan.

If you have no plan, all roads lead there.

The project was one which comprised a number of related software changes to four interrelated systems. The owners of each system had planned their part of the project, BUT no one had as yet put them all together. They spent two full days locked in a room listing what each needed from the others and eventually built a plan which showed how the whole project fitted together. They had it on large sheets of paper with Post-It Notes joined by arrows. It was hard work. They didn't understand each other. Everyone else was unreasonable. They didn't know why the "others" had to do their work in such an inconvenient way (a way inconvenient to them).

Once completed, the plan looked obvious. The approach was clear and the team members were happy with each other. They had even agreed who would be accountable for end-to-end testing across the systems (previously missing from the plan). When the inevitable happened and one team member's part went wrong, there was no blame apportioned, only solutions offered. They didn't even need to consult the plan; they knew it well enough as it was theirs.

The project was completed successfully.

"Planning is everything – the plan is nothing."

EISENHOWER

Content of the project plan

A good project plan should include the following:

- **Stages** – these represent the natural high level break points in the project life cycle (e.g., initial investigation, detailed investigation, develop and test, trial, release).
- **Work packages** – these represent the clusters of work within each stage, usually focussed on a key deliverable.
- **Activities** – these are the individual components of work within the work packages that must be undertaken to complete the project. Each activity should be defined in terms of its start and end dates and the name of the individual accountable for its completion.
- **Milestones** – these are the significant events (often representing the start of a stage) which should be used to monitor progress at a summary level.
- **Deliverables** – each of the key deliverables defined in the project definition should be shown in the plan. Use milestones to represent their completion.
- **Reviews** – include reviews at key points throughout the project when progress and performance will be critically evaluated;
- **Interdependencies** – define all inputs from (and outputs to) other projects. These should include all those defined in the project definition.

You will very rarely be able to plan a project in full at the very start but you should always be able to plan the next stage in detail, with an outline plan for the remainder.

Format of the project plan

Project plans are most conveniently presented as bar charts, two forms of which are illustrated on the following pages:

- In detail – (Figure 19.2) a progress bar chart, used by the project manager and the team members to control their day-to-day work. This contains all the elements defined in the previous section.
- In summary – (Figure 19.3) a management summary used to present overall progress of the project to the project sponsor, project board, and other interested parties. This should show the stages, milestones, and other important activities necessary to give an overview of the project. (See Chapter 20 for a fuller treatment of schedule planning.)

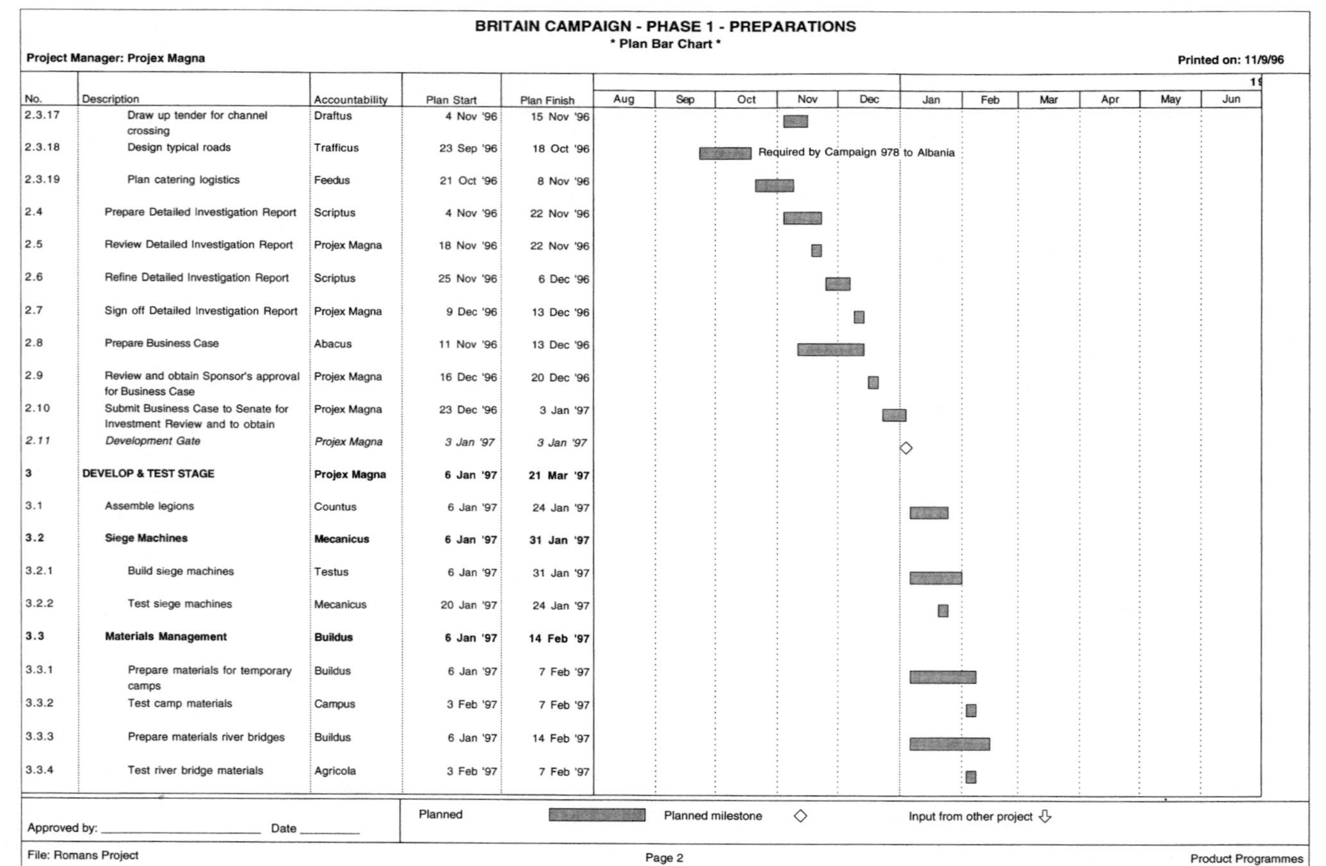

No.	Description	Accountability	Plan Start	Plan Finish
2.3.17	Draw up tender for channel crossing	Draftus	4 Nov '96	15 Nov '96
2.3.18	Design typical roads	Trafficus	23 Sep '96	18 Oct '96
2.3.19	Plan catering logistics	Feedus	21 Oct '96	8 Nov '96
2.4	Prepare Detailed Investigation Report	Scriptus	4 Nov '96	22 Nov '96
2.5	Review Detailed Investigation Report	Projex Magna	18 Nov '96	22 Nov '96
2.6	Refine Detailed Investigation Report	Scriptus	25 Nov '96	6 Dec '96
2.7	Sign off Detailed Investigation Report	Projex Magna	9 Dec '96	13 Dec '96
2.8	Prepare Business Case	Abacus	11 Nov '96	13 Dec '96
2.9	Review and obtain Sponsor's approval for Business Case	Projex Magna	16 Dec '96	20 Dec '96
2.10	Submit Business Case to Senate for Investment Review and to obtain	Projex Magna	23 Dec '96	3 Jan '97
2.11	*Development Gate*	*Projex Magna*	*3 Jan '97*	*3 Jan '97*
3	**DEVELOP & TEST STAGE**	**Projex Magna**	**6 Jan '97**	**21 Mar '97**
3.1	Assemble legions	Countus	6 Jan '97	24 Jan '97
3.2	**Siege Machines**	**Mecanicus**	**6 Jan '97**	**31 Jan '97**
3.2.1	Build siege machines	Testus	6 Jan '97	31 Jan '97
3.2.2	Test siege machines	Mecanicus	20 Jan '97	24 Jan '97
3.3	**Materials Management**	**Buildus**	**6 Jan '97**	**14 Feb '97**
3.3.1	Prepare materials for temporary camps	Buildus	6 Jan '97	7 Feb '97
3.3.2	Test camp materials	Campus	3 Feb '97	7 Feb '97
3.3.3	Prepare materials river bridges	Buildus	6 Jan '97	14 Feb '97
3.3.4	Test river bridge materials	Agricola	3 Feb '97	7 Feb '97

Figure 19.2 A typical detailed project plan

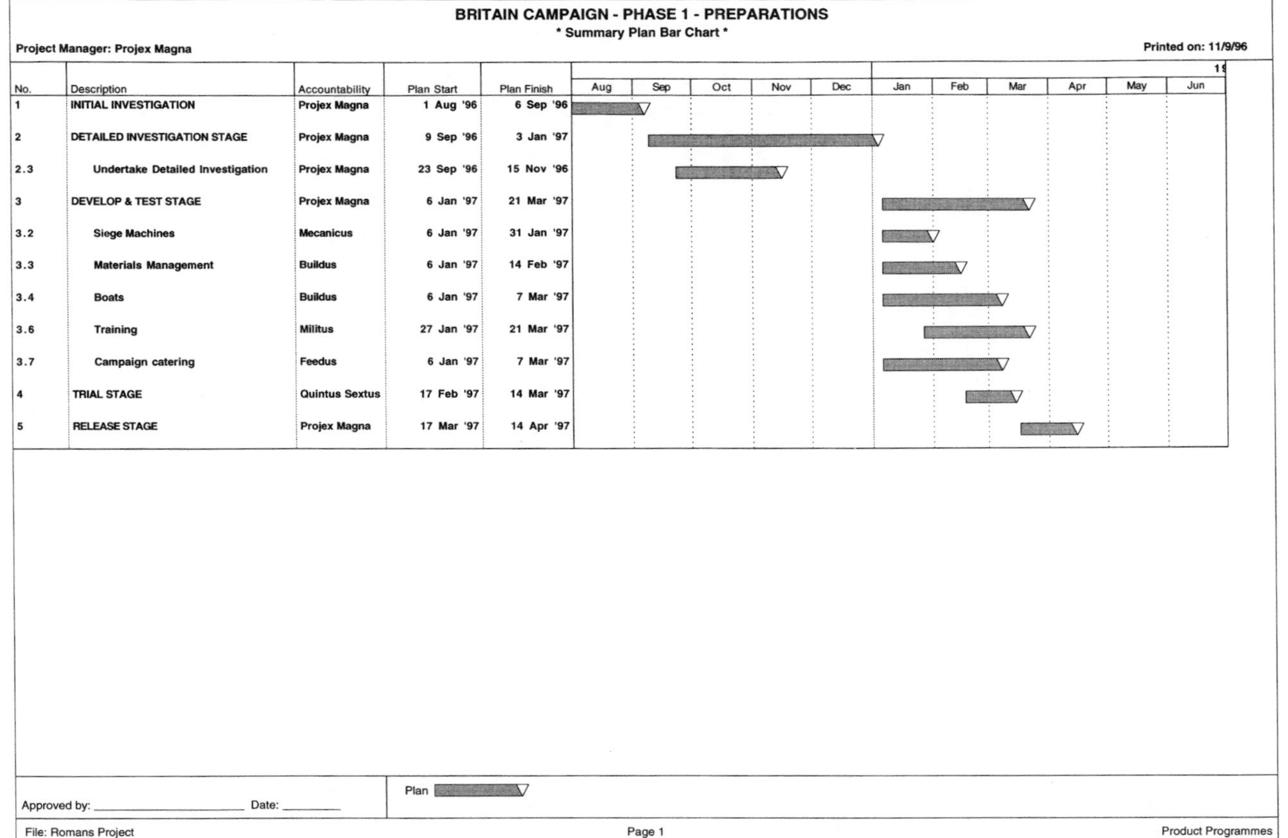

BRITAIN CAMPAIGN - PHASE 1 - PREPARATIONS

* Summary Plan Bar Chart *

Project Manager: Projex Magna

Printed on: 11/9/96

No.	Description	Accountability	Plan Start	Plan Finish
1	INITIAL INVESTIGATION	Projex Magna	1 Aug '96	6 Sep '96
2	DETAILED INVESTIGATION STAGE	Projex Magna	9 Sep '96	3 Jan '97
2.3	Undertake Detailed Investigation	Projex Magna	23 Sep '96	15 Nov '96
3	DEVELOP & TEST STAGE	Projex Magna	6 Jan '97	21 Mar '97
3.2	Siege Machines	Mecanicus	6 Jan '97	31 Jan '97
3.3	Materials Management	Buildus	6 Jan '97	14 Feb '97
3.4	Boats	Buildus	6 Jan '97	7 Mar '97
3.6	Training	Militus	27 Jan '97	21 Mar '97
3.7	Campaign catering	Feedus	6 Jan '97	7 Mar '97
4	TRIAL STAGE	Quintus Sextus	17 Feb '97	14 Mar '97
5	RELEASE STAGE	Projex Magna	17 Mar '97	14 Apr '97

Approved by: ______________ Date: ________

File: Romans Project | Page 1 | Product Programmes

Figure 19.3 A typical summary project plan

Define your project organization

Once you have your project defined and planned out you should make sure that other organizational aspects of the project are addressed, including defining:

- project administration needs (filing);
- project progress reporting needs;
- who can authorize changes to the project;
- what formal review points are required.

The last three points are documented in Sections 3.1 to 3.3 of the initial business case.

Project administration

Projects can generate a considerable volume of information, correspondence, and reports, most of which needs to be accessible and some of which needs to be archived. It is essential that the project manager sets up the administration of the project as soon as practical and that he/she makes sure that all team members and support staff understand what is required and available. The format and media for storing such documentation can vary from being paper based to a full electronic "groupware" platform accessed via an intranet. In many cases, different sections will be held in different formats thus harnessing the capabilities of any support tools and avoiding duplication. Regardless of how you choose to store the information, its content will be similar. The following comprises a structure on which to base your own project filing requirements. Benchmarking shows that many companies have a prescribed framework, such as the following, to ensure that records are kept in a consistent way, thus enabling newcomers to the project to know where to start looking for the information they require.

Contents of a project file

1. ***Project summary details***

This should comprise a short description of the project and the names of those holding the key accountabilities. The summary, as held on a project-tracking system, should fulfill the needs of this section (see p. 231).

2. *Contact list*

A list of all the team members, their roles and how they can be contacted.

3. *Project log*

A chronological record, owned by the project manager, of significant meetings, events, and commitments. This should refer to detail in other sections of the file where appropriate.

4. *Business case and change log*

This section contains the fundamental definition of and case for your project. The change log is an amendment record, listing any changes to the business case which are under consideration or which have already been approved or authorized. By having a change log as a supplement to the Business Case, you avoid the need for updating the main document for every change. You need only reissue it when the number of changes becomes too unwieldy to keep in separate documents.

5. *Progress reports*

All regular and special progress reports should be retained. If a number of different reports are to be prepared for particular audiences, this section should be subdivided accordingly.

6. *Project logs*

- Issues log.
- Risk log.
- Opportunity log.
- Lessons learned.

7. *Schedule*

This section contains a copy of the most recent schedule showing achievement and forecast against the agreed plan.

8. *Finances*

This section contains a copy of the most recent cost and benefit position showing achievement and forecast against the agreed plan.

9. *Meetings*

All meetings should either be minuted or notes should be produced to promote clear communication. This should include:

- agreements: record any agreements made (even agreements to disagree!);
- actions: be clear who has the accountability for any actions, when they have to be done by, and who are the recipients for outputs from those actions.

10. ***Key control deliverables***
This section comprises a listing of the key control deliverables (with accountabilities for preparation, review, and sign-off). Copies of the documents themselves must be held for team use and archive purposes.

For Gate Decisions	Other deliverables
Proposal Ready for Trial Report Ready for Service Report Project Closure Report Post-Implementation Review Report	Output Description Feasibility Report Test Plan Test Results Trial Plan Trial Results

PLUS any others that are required, as defined in the project definition section of the Business Case, such as detailed specifications, requirements, documents, tender documents, etc.

11. ***Correspondence***
Record of all incoming and outgoing correspondence.

12. ***Reviews***
Copies of any additional project reviews, other than the mandatory gate reviews (held in Section 10), should be kept.

For complex projects, individual subprojects and work packages should follow a similar structure to that held for the overall project.

Progress reporting

If you are the project manager, you are accountable for controlling the project and taking the necessary actions to ensure that it delivers the expected outputs. You therefore need to be clear what is actually happening.

You should gather your team together on a regular basis (preferably physically) and check what progress has been made and what progress is forecast. You should also assess the issues which have arisen and the risks which are looming on the horizon.

Progress should be recorded by updating the project schedule and cost forecasts to show:

- activities completed and milestones achieved;
- forecasts of completion dates for activities in progress (or not yet started) where these are known to differ from the agreed plan (e.g., slippage);
- costs spent to date;
- forecasts of costs to complete the current stage of the project and for completing the project in full.

Additionally you should prepare, for the project sponsor and other key stakeholders, a concise written progress report which includes the following information:

1 **Business objectives.**
2 **Progress summary and outlook.**
3 **Financials.**
4 **Milestones.**
5 **Issues.**
6 **Risks and opportunities.**
7 **Changes.**

A description of the content of each of these sections follows. Progress reporting should be active, with you telling the stakeholders what they need to know in as concise a form as possible. If your company has a single defined format for the report then that is excellent. It helps make sure the reports are full and complete and aids the reader by providing a familiar, consistent format. So, if you have a reporting system, use the same headings (see p. 231).

Make sure your reports:

- are honest and open, without undermining confidence;
- are focussed on key issues;
- balance the good and the bad news;
- acknowledge the achievements of the team.

UNDER A BUSHEL

Don't be modest; if you don't acknowledge the achievements made by you and your team on the project, don't be surprised if the stakeholders don't either. It has been said that the definition of an easy project is one which is successful. If it wasn't easy, it would have failed. The project managers and teams of successful projects are, therefore, in danger of becoming "invisible" or having their achievements undervalued even if it was their own hard work, excellent planning, and adherence to best practice which got them there. DON'T BE INVISIBLE!

Contents of progress report

1. *Business objectives*

As many stakeholders will not be familiar with your project from its number or title, you should summarize:

- the business objectives the project will satisfy;
- how the project supports your business strategy.

This is taken from Section 2.2 of the initial or full business case (see p. 262).

2. *Progress summary and outlook*

Briefly describe the progress of the project both in terms of achievements to date and expected future performance. For any significant schedule slippage or cost variance give:

- the reason;
- its impact;
- any corrective action being taken.

3. *Financials*

Provide a summary of the project finances in terms of expected benefits, spend to date and total expected spend compared to that planned.

4. *Milestones*

List the major milestones. These should at least be the gate milestones as defined in Part Two. For each give:

- original and current baseline date;
- forecast date or actual date achieved.

5. ***Key issues***

Describe the key issues which require escalating beyond the project manager for resolution. For each give:

- the nature and impact of the issue;
- action being taken to resolve the issue and who is accountable.

£000	Actual spend this month	Actual to date	Previous to date	Estimate to completion	Forecast at completion	Budget
Time costs	20	920	900	370	1290	1180
Purchases	20	480	460	150	630	520
Scope reserve				0	0	100
Contingency				70	70	200
TOTAL	40	1400	1360	590	1990	2000

	Original date	Current baseline date	Current forecast date	Date achieved	Confidence H/M/L
Initial Investigation Gate	31 Jul 2005	31 Jul 2005	31 Jul 2005	31 Jul 2005	
Detailed Investigation Gate	01 Sep 2005	01 Sep 2005	01 Sep 2005	01 Sep 2005	
Development Gate	01 Oct 2005	01 Oct 2005	0 Oct 2005	01 Oct 2005	
Trial Gate	24 Oct 2005	24 Oct 2005	24 Oct 2005	24 Oct 2005	
Ready for Service Gate	31 Oct 2005	31 Oct 2005	31 Oct 2005	31 Oct 2005	
Release	01 Dec 2005	01 Dec 2005	18 Dec 2005		High
Project completed	02 Jan 2006	15 Jan 2006	08 Feb 2006		High

6. ***Key risks and opportunities***

Summarize the high risks and major opportunities which have arisen. For each give:

- the nature and impact of the risk or opportunity;
- action being taken to manage the risk or opportunity and who is accountable.

7. ***Changes***

List all outstanding changes which are beyond the project manager's authority to authorize. For each give:

- the reason for the change;
- impact of the change;
- who is accountable for authorizing the change.

8. ***Attachments***

It may be convenient to attach, for detailed reference:

- cost report;
- progress bar chart;
- issues log;
- risks log;
- opportunities log;
- change log.

Change control

Once the project has been authorized, its scope, cost, benefits and timescale are baselined and used as the basis on which to monitor progress. Under certain circumstances it is, however, legitimate (and often desirable and/or unavoidable) to change these baselines. Who authorizes such changes depends very much on the impact. It is, therefore, essential that the extent of the authority given to the project manager and project sponsor is defined. (Chapter 25 describes this more fully.)

Document who has accountability for authorizing changes in Section 3.2 of the initial or full business case.

Review points

The management framework comprises a staged approach to projects with the "gates" defining the key points when a formal project review is undertaken. However, the time lapse in some stages can be very long, particularly in the Develop and Test Stage. It is, therefore, essential that a sufficient number of additional review points are built into the plan to check that:

As a guide, a project should have a formal review every three months or when a major commitment is to be made. The occurrence of such reviews should be formally documented, as they comprise an essential part in managing the risks on a company-wide basis.

- the project still meets a real business need and is achievable;
- the quality of the deliverables is adequate;
- the plans are in place;
- the project organization is working.

As a guide, a project should have a formal review every three months or when a major commitment is to be made. The occurrence of such reviews should be formally documented as they comprise an essential part in managing the risks on a company-wide basis.

Reviews are often regarded as taking up valuable time and hampering progress on the project. However, it is in the project sponsor's interest that reviews take place with accountability to make sure they happen. (Chapter 26 discusses reviews more fully.)

Document the additional reviews in Section 3.1 of the Initial or full Business Case.

19.4

PROJECT ORGANIZATION CHECKLIST

Use this checklist to audit any projects currently in progress.

Criteria

- ☐ Have progress reporting formats been set up?
- ☐ Have progress reporting lines been set up?
- ☐ Has a system for capturing and managing risks and opportunities been set up?
- ☐ Has a system for capturing and managing issues been set up?
- ☐ Has a system for recording and approving changes been set up?

Engage your stakeholders

Stakeholders are those affected by the project. All those involved in the project are, therefore, stakeholders. However, there are also those who take no direct part in the project as team members, but whose activities will in some way be changed as a result. These could be users of new systems, people in new departments resulting from reorganizations (or those made redundant), those taking roles in new processes as managers, supervisors, and workers. Often the project is of little importance to them but they are of great consequence to the project if their consent is critical to success. It is essential to identify them because it is critical to enroll them at an early stage in the project to ensure their power does not cause the project to fail later. Never underestimate stakeholders' ability to ruin your best laid plans!

Never underestimate stakeholders' ability to ruin your best laid plans!

It is both the project manager's and project sponsor's role to ensure that all stakeholders are adequately briefed on the project. Too much communication will drown them – they won't read it. Not enough will mean your project will be lower down their priority list than you want it to be.

Engaging stakeholders and keeping them enrolled is a taxing but essential task. It is accomplished both by a formal communication plan and by "enrolling behavior" on behalf of all the project team on both a planned and opportunistic basis.

STAKEHOLDER INFLUENCE MAPPING

To be done in project team mode.

1 Brainstorm who your stakeholders are. Write each on a Post-It Note and stick them onto a white board or flip chart. Stakeholders may be individuals or groups.

2 Cluster the stakeholders into groups based on similar need or impact from the project. Rationalize the stakeholder list if possible, but don't worry if you can't.

3 Define the role of each stakeholder (Figure 19.4). Stakeholder roles are defined as:

- **Decision maker** – this stakeholder is required to make a decision regarding the project.
- **Influencer** – this stakeholder has influence over the project and/or over the decision makers.
- **Player** – this stakeholder is required to play a part in the project, perhaps providing resources, facilities, or review time.
- **Consent** – the consent of this stakeholder is required if the project is to be a success (e.g., computer system users, customers).

Take each stakeholder in turn and, using one flip chart per stakeholder, answer the following questions:

- What is this person or group's stake in the project?
  - — Are they needed to resource it?
  - — Are they directly affected by it?
  - — Are they indirectly affected by it?
  - — Are they unaffected, but still have the power to influence it should they choose to do so?

- What is their role?
- Have they a positive, neutral, or negative towards the project?

4 Write "ME" in a bubble in the center of a white board. Write those stakeholders you have direct access to around "ME" and join them to "ME" with a line. Use a single line for a weak link and a double line for a strong link. Use + or –, or 0, to indicate if they are positive, negative, or neutral to the project. Use ? if you don't know. This map indicates the stakeholders you have direct access to.

5 Write the remainder of the stakeholders in boxes around the edges of the white board. Using + , – , 0, to indicate if they are positive, negative, or neutral to the project. Use ? if you don't know.

6 Write on the white board the names of others you have access to but who also have access to one or more of your stakeholders.

You now have a "stakeholder influence diagram." You can use this to decide how best to enroll a particular stakeholder. You may do it yourself or it may be more effective to have others do it on your behalf.

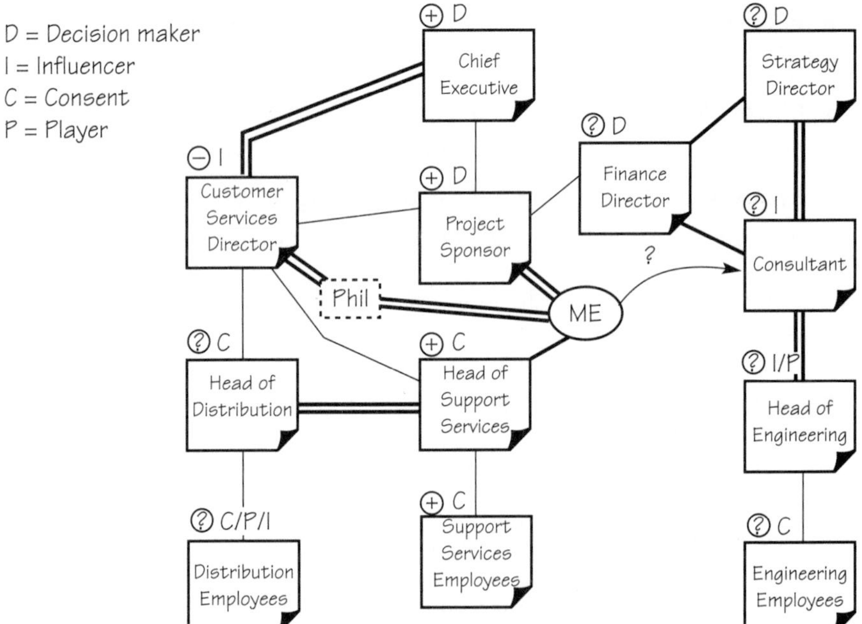

Figure 19.4 A typical stakeholder influence map

- Regarding stakeholders who are negative or neutral. You need to address them.
- For those stakeholders where the line of influence is missing or very long. You must aim to shorten it to gain access to that person.
- As for those whose attitudes are unknown, you must find out what they are.

19.6

STAKEHOLDER COMMUNICATION PLANNING AND TRACKING

Work with your project team using the output from Workout 19.5.

Planning

1 On a flip chart, brainstorm the following for each stakeholder:

- the messages you need them to receive;
- possible methods/media or people you could use to communicate with them;
- frequency of communication.

Consider, if you were them, what you would want to know and when? Aim to see things from their perspective. If possible, ask them!

2 On a large sheet of paper or a white board, list each stakeholder along the top.

3 Decide who should receive the standard regular progress report. Put an asterisk over the relevant stakeholder to indicate this.

4 Brainstorm the possible communications which you may wish to send out to the stakeholders. Write each on a Post-It Note. Place these on the chart on the left-hand side, in chronological order.

5 On smaller Post-It Notes, add a tick to show which stakeholder(s) is "hit" with each particular communication.

6 Review how frequently each stakeholder will receive a message. Is it too often? Is it not frequently enough? Rearrange the Post-It Notes until you create a plan that the team is comfortable with (Figure 19.5).

7 Transfer the key communications to your schedule plan and "fix" the plan onto your white board by rewriting directly onto it rather than onto Post-It Notes.

Do not be concerned that you cannot see very far into the future. The objective is to make sure you consider who you need to communicate with, when, and how.

Tracking

Using the same white board output, simply write the communication made and the date on the left hand side, ticking the relevant stakeholder columns.

You will thus build a listing from which you will easily see who you have missed. You can then work both from your formal plan and add extra communications when you see these as desirable. Also you will be confident that they look rational and consecutive to the recipients.

	Date	Sponsor	Chief executive	Strategy director	Finance director	Heads of units
Start-up brief	1/3/97	✓	✓	✓		
Team brief	12/3/97	✓				
Memo A	14/3/97		✓	✓	✓	✓
Memo B	21/4/97		✓	✓		
Presentation	4/4/97	✓				✓

Figure 19.5 Stakeholder communications
An example of a chart to keep track of communications to key stakeholders.

Managing Benefits

Benefits and drivers

Forecasting benefits

Timing of benefits

In short, benefits are about making more money, about using existing resources and assets more efficiently, and about staying in business.

"What is a man profited, if he shall gain the whole world, and lose his own soul?"

ST MATTHEW 16:26

- **Always measure benefits against a known baseline.**
- **Make benefits tangible, where ever possible.**
- **Place benefits in the wider business context.**
- **Look out for unwanted side effects from your project.**

Benefits and drivers

Obtaining benefits is the sole reason for undertaking a project. If there are no benefits, there should be no project. It is for this reason that the role of project sponsor is vital. He or she is the person in the organization who requires the benefits to fill a particular need, in pursuit of a stated business objective.

To be "legitimate," a project must achieve at least one of the following conditions:

1 maintain or increase profitable revenue to the business, now or in the future;
2 maintain or reduce the operating costs of the business, now or in the future;
3. maintain or reduce the amount of money tied up within the business, now or in the future;
4 support or provide a solution to a necessary or externally imposed constraint (e.g., a legal or regulatory requirement).

In short, benefits are about making more money, about using existing resources and assets more efficiently, and about staying in business. Drivers are frequently defined by words such as "growth," "efficiency," "protection," "demand" which reflect a company's focus at any point in time.

The first three conditions relate to the net cash flow into the business. Money is the company's key measure of commercial performance. It includes measurement of revenue, investments, and the costs of running the business.

The fourth condition is often referred to as a "must do" project. It is nevertheless essential that such projects are fully costed in order to determine the least cost, highest value approach to fulfilling the need. This cost can then be placed in the context of the business as a whole in order to determine whether the company, or the impacted part of the company, can afford the change and remain a viable commercial concern.

BEWARE OF EFFICIENCY "SAVINGS"

When looking for efficiencies, be very careful not to waste time and energy suboptimizing aspects of your business. What counts is the **throughput** of your business, not the individual efficiencies or asset utilization of the different parts. Partially finished goods are not the aim, finished goods are. The trap people fall into is assuming that by increasing the efficiency of every part of a business, the whole business will become more efficient. This is not the case, as efficiencies are not additive. This can be very simply demonstrated.

Consider a factory with a five-step process, machines A, B, C, D and E, with a required throughput of 100 units/day. In an ideal world each machine would be sized for 100 units/day. But we live in a world of breakdowns and unexpected events. If each machine operated with 90 percent reliability, the chances of you actually obtaining 100 units/day are only 60 percent. You therefore need to oversize your machines to protect your throughput and you deal with breakdowns by ensuring that each machine has a stockpile in front of it to protect against a break down further up the chain. However, much of the time individual machines won't break down and if you are aiming for each machine to operate as near as possible to its limit (i.e., peak efficiency) you will find that stockpiles of partially finished goods will swamp the downstream machines. The net effect will be **decreased** efficiency downstream because it simply cannot cope with corresponding increase in throughput.

Eli Goldratt likens this to a chain in his Theory of Constraints. A chain's strength is determined by the weakest link and you cannot strengthen the chain by adding weight to any other link. In fact, you only weaken the chain, as the weak link now has an even greater load to bear.

Tangible and intangible benefits

Benefits can be:

- **tangible** – those which can be stated in quantitative terms;
- **intangible** – those which should be described as far as is possible.

Wherever possible, benefits should be tangible and clearly articulated. Tangible benefits may be measured either in financial or non-financial terms. **Financial benefits** describe the business objectives in terms of:

- revenue;
- contribution;
- profit enhancement;
- savings in operating costs or working capital.

Non-financial benefits describe the value added to a business that is directly attributable to the project but which cannot be described in financial terms. Again, these benefits should be tangible and measurable, such as:

- operational performance measures;
- process performance measures;
- customer satisfactions measures;
- key performance indicators (KPI).

Care should be taken however, to query why we should spend money addressing any particular measure or indicator; if it doesn't eventually help you achieve any of the four conditions given at the start of this chapter, you should seriously consider terminating the project. You may argue that increasing service quality could help you to retain customers, or attract new customers, in which case a financial benefit should result. Also, increasing service quality may enable you to remain in business. You should be able to justify any such assumptions even if the calculation of financial effect is somewhat tenuous.

Difficulties with measurement

All the quantitative benefits above can be measured at corporate level, however, they cannot always be measured directly for an individual project. You may need to take alternative approaches as illustrated in the following examples.

Example 1 – using a surrogate measure, it is not always possible to measure profit for products. In such cases, an alternative measure should be chosen which can be measured and which has a known relationship to profit. Revenue and margin may be such measures. You may also use measures such as numbers of customers, churn, percentage utilisation.

Example 2 – measuring at a higher level, it is not always possible to relate an increase in demand for a service directly to a recent enhancement to that service; it might be the result of other dynamics in the market. In such cases, the project should be tied to a higher level program or business program, where the benefits can be measured. For example, an enhancement to a service may be bundled with the overall service which is tracked at product level rather than by the individual projects and initiatives which make up the product plan.

Conditions of satisfaction

Despite difficulties with measurement, every project should have a recognizable method for knowing whether it has been a success. Conditions of satisfaction are used to supplement benefits measurements. They are the conditions which, if met, enable you to declare the project a success. They need to be chosen such that they are indicative of meeting the benefits and may relate to a reduction in faults, increase in customers or such like, measured at a particular, defined point in time.

Conditions of satisfaction are the conditions which, if met, enable you to declare the project a success.

NET BENEFITS

When talking of benefit always think in terms of **net benefits**, that is to say, what's left after you've counted the cost.

Forecasting benefits

An initial estimate of the benefits and costs must be prepared during the Initial Investigation Stage. During the Detailed Investigation Stage the estimates must be turned into firm forecasts and be agreed by the project sponsor.

Forecasts serve two purposes:

- first, they enable evaluation of the project;
- second, they provide information against which the post launch performance of the project can be measured.

There are four guiding principles for forecasting revenues and benefits:

1 Forecasts must be realistic.
2 Benefits must be matched by the costs of achieving the benefits.
3 Benefits (prices, sales volume, etc.) and costs must be based on the same assumptions.
4 Costs and benefits must be forecast for the worst, best, and most likely outcome (scenarios).

Revenue forecasting needs to take account of three factors:

1 Volume/demand.
2 Pricing.
3 Costs.

The overall financial benefit to the company is the product of demand and price less costs. This is the basis for justifying any number of projects whether they are for a new product, a campaign or for increasing efficiency. It is important to keep the total picture in mind to make sure that projects are not created which merely suboptimize a part of the business, creating little overall benefit. For example, there is little point in installing a highly efficient new platform for a service for which demand is decreasing and the volumes required to achieve the efficiency will never be realized.

Keep the total picture in mind to make sure that projects are not created which merely suboptimize a part of the business, creating little overall benefit.

Timing of benefits

When looking at benefits always consider the timing. The earlier you can obtain benefits, the better it is for your business and the quicker you will recover your investment. Discounted cash flow calculations are designed to ensure that the time value of money is taken into consideration when comparing different projects and when deciding whether to invest. This is also why you need to look for opportunities to design your projects to ensure early benefits delivery.

Just as early benefits are a good thing, so delayed benefits are bad. The cost of delays can far outweigh any investment costs and turn a viable project into a financial embarrassment.

Figure 20.1 shows the cash flow for a project over a four-year period. The company is looking for a 30 percent return on investment and this meets it adequately. If this project were to slip two quarters, the benefits would also slip, reducing the present value of the project by about 30 percent. It would actually be worth overspending by 50 percent in order to prevent this delay in benefits and regain some of the potential loss. This is not to say that project overspends should be encouraged, especially in a situation when you cannot be sure that injecting money will actually improve anything. It all comes down to risk. What is important is to understand how sensitive a particular project is to slippage and plan accordingly. (Sensitivity analysis is dealt with in Chapter 23.)

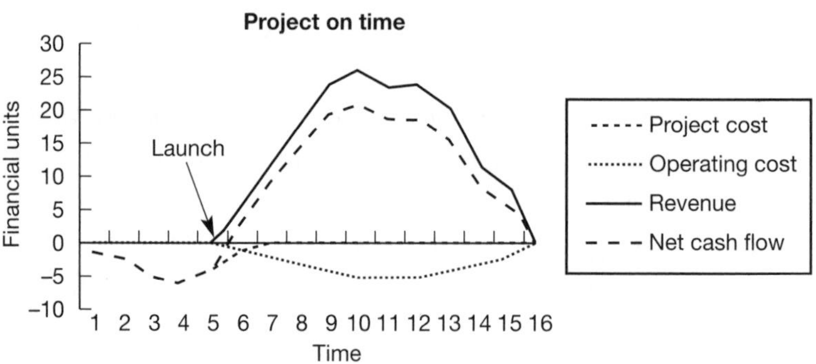

Figure 20.1 Cash flow for a project "on time"
A two-quarter delay to this project would turn it from being a good investment to a financial embarrassment.

Timing is often critical to success

20.1

WHY ARE YOU DOING THIS PROJECT NOW?

Write your list of projects from Workout 3.1 on a flip chart. Against each write:

- why you are undertaking the project;
- why it is being done now, rather than later.

Link your answers back to your business plan or business strategy. For internal projects, consider whether you have the right portfolio. For external projects (i.e. those for customers/clients), test whether that work is targetted at a chosen market segment.

Managing the Schedule

The project schedule

Summary and detailed schedule plan

Tracking progress toward your objectives

Schedule reports

Reports used when drafting a plan

Report used to update the forecast

Reports used for progress reporting

So why are we nearly always late?

The management of the project schedule is one of the most important and fundamental of project management techniques. So much so that many people (wrongly) think that schedule management is project management.

"There can't be a crisis next week. My schedule is full."

HENRY KISSINGER

- **Plan in outline for the full project.**
- **Break the project down into manageable pieces (work packages).**
- **Plan in detail before you start any work.**
- **Once a plan is agreed, baseline it.**
- **Measure progress against the baseline.**
- **Keep your eye on the future – forecast, forecast, forecast.**

The project schedule

You will find the management of the project schedule is one of the most important and fundamental of project management techniques. So much so that many people (wrongly) think that schedule management is project management. At a simple level, the schedule tells you how long the project, or any part of it, will take. In addition to giving dates, a well produced project schedule also tells you:

- who is accountable for every aspect of the project;
- the approach being undertaken;
- the major deliverables from the project;
- the timing of key review points.

SCHEDULE OR PROGRAM?

I have used the word "schedule" to mean the management of project time-scales. I use this word rather than the common alternative "program" as the latter has come to mean many different things including:

- a very large project;
- a set of interrelated projects;
- a sequence of phased projects;
- a portfolio of projects bundled for management reporting;
- a portfolio of projects bundled by management accountability.

In this book "program" is defined as a tightly aligned and tightly coupled set of projects. (See also page 57).

The schedule is also the basis on which cost and resource plans are constructed. However, unlike costs and resources, which are seen by only a few people observing a project, key dates are very visible. A well publicized delivery date for a project is, when missed, very hard to hide. While "time" may not be the most important aspect for you on some of your projects, an observer may develop their own perception of "success" or "failure" purely from the performance of your project against the publicized target dates.

The ability to build and manage the schedule plan is one of the essential skills that all project managers should have. Planning is far too important for you to delegate to junior team members, especially in the early stages of the project when the overall strategy and approach are being developed. The plan sets the course for the remainder of the project. Once agreed and set (at the Development Gate) it is very difficult to change or improve on. All the decisions which have the most leverage on time, costs, and benefits will have already been made.

Planning is far too important for you to delegate to junior team members, especially in the early stages of the project when the overall strategy and approach are being developed.

Done effectively, the project plan will benefit you and the team by providing:

- a baseline against which to measure progress (without a plan, words such as "early" or "late" have no meaning);
- a common understanding of the approach you are taking to achieve your objectives;
- a breakdown of the project workload into manageable pieces (work packages) based on the deliverables/outputs wherever possible;
- a clear way of showing interdependencies between activities and work packages within the project and to/from other external projects;
- a listing of accountabilities for different activities and work packages;
- a tool for evaluating when corrective action is needed.

Further, as already discussed in Chapter 19, the actual activity of creating a project plan by using the full team serves to forge a team spirit and a high level of common commitment.

All projects are undertaken within an environment of risk. Good planning is done in the full knowledge of those risks. You should therefore:

- avoid avoidable risks by planning the project in a different way;
- contingency plan for the unavoidable risks.

> *"The only way to be sure of catching a train is to miss the one before it."*
>
> G K CHESTERTON

Summary and detailed schedule plan

You need to consider your plan on two levels:

- summary;
- detail.

The former is used to map out the entire project, while the latter is used to show the detail for the current stage. For work packages done by others (for example, by a contractor), the person or group doing the work will prepare the detail. However, you need to be satisfied that the plan is workable and includes sufficient checkpoints for you to monitor progress. Developing a schedule plan is an evolutionary process which starts with a statement of key objectives, deliverables, and scope, followed by the preparation of a summary plan (Figure 21.1). This will comprise:

- the approach to be adopted (or alternatives from which the preferred option will be chosen during the detailed investigation);
- the breakdown of the project into stages and work packages relating to project deliverables (note these same packages should also be used for resource and cost management);
- the key dates, milestones, and time constraints relating to the project;
- review or decision points;
- interdependencies with other projects.

From this you should be able to estimate:

- the resources required;
- the cost of the project.

Before you start work on any stage of the project, you should ensure that detailed plans are prepared. The criteria for all the entry gates in the staged framework from the Detailed Investigation Gate onward

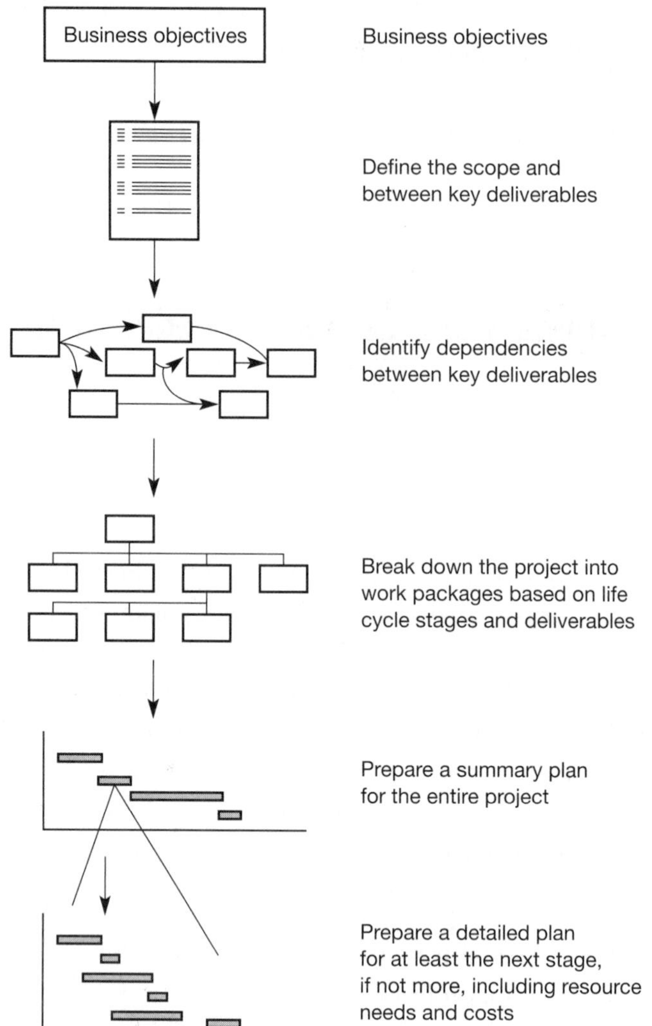

Figure 21.1 Project planning

Project planning starts with the business objectives and ends with detail plans, including schedules, resources and costs.

include a detailed plan as a prerequisite. Detailed planning will involve work undertaken within your own organization and checking that third parties (such as contractors and suppliers) have planned in sufficient detail with adequate checkpoints for control purposes. The detailed planning process is similar to the outline process except that you will be be working in more detail, on perhaps one aspect of the project at a time. This includes:

- breaking down each work package into activities to represent the work content for each project deliverable;
- identifying dependencies between activities;
- agreeing completion dates for each activity with those accountable;
- checking that key milestones and the overall project completion date can still be achieved;
- ensuring that there are appropriate check and review points;
- ensuring that time and resources are allocated for planning the next stage.

STARTING THE PLAN OFF

Introducing Post-It Note Planning from the future!

21.1

I said earlier that planning is too important to delegate to junior team members. "But," argue many people, "I do not know how to use these sophisticated planning packages we have on our PCs," or "I haven't any planning software on my PC," or even "I haven't got a PC!"

Such excuses do not make sense. Projects have been with us for centuries and certainly since well before computers became commonplace. All you need to start planning is:

- your brain;
- your team;
- a set of Post-It Notes;
- flip chart markers;
- a very big wall covered in paper or a large white board to which onto which to stick your Post-It Notes.

You should do this exercise as quickly as possible. In the early stages of a project it is more important to start getting the feel of the task ahead of you than to worry about "correctness" and detail.

Take the output from Project Workout 19.1 and with the same team in workshop format, using flip charts, white boards and Post-It Notes:

1 Display the flip charts from the previous workout on the walls so that the team can see the project objectives, description, and deliverables.

2 Take your set of Post-It Notes and write the name of each deliverable down, one per sticker. Write a "D" in the top left hand corner to denote deliverables. Put them on the left of the board.

3 On other Post-It Notes write:

- Development Gate.
- Trial Gate.
- Ready for Service (RFS) Gate.
- Release.
- Complete.

Draw a diamond on the top left hand corner to denote key milestones. Put them on the left of the board.

4 Take the "Complete" note and put in at the far right of the board. Then add the "Release" note and the "RFS" note thus:

5 Pointing at the RFS note ask the question: "What must I have done before I have RFS?" If the answer is some of the deliverables, add them to the board to the left of RFS, with an arrow leading to the RFS note. For example:

6 Take each deliverable in turn and ask the same question as 5: "What must I have done before I have xyz deliverable?" This will be either:

- more deliverables from the left of the board;
- new deliverables not previously identified;
- activities you need to do which you want to capture.

If you "invent" an activity, label it with "A" in the top left. Add Post-It Notes to the board to the left of xyz deliverable with an arrow leading to it.

7 Continue as per step 6, on the activities, milestones and deliverables until you have used up all the deliverables from the left hand side and you are satisfied that you have identified the starting point for the project. Don't be worried if you do not know what order some deliverables are put in or do not know the sequence of activities in all areas. If you did know this, your project would be relatively simple. Make a note of the "problem areas" as they are issues which must be planned into your work schedule as problems to investigate and solve. Once you have finished, stand back and look at the pattern. Relocate some stickers to simplify if necessary.

8 Look at the plan again and make broad estimates of how long each activity will take. Don't worry if you are wrong. Note down those for which you have very little confidence in your estimate on your list of "problems to solve later."

9 You should notice several tranches of notes, each of which leads to a key deliverable. There may, for example, be work and deliverables relating to a computer system, a publicity event, the installation of a new item of plant. These are clues to your work breakdown structure (WBS), the key packages of work within each life stage of your project. Where possible choose your WBS with as few interdependencies between work packages as possible.

Relocate some of the Post-It Notes to simplify the appearance if necessary. Rationalize any long sequences if it does not seem that showing them adds value to the overall plan. (Remember this is a summary plan only.)

10 Consider alternative ways of approaching the project, perhaps by brainstorming or discussion. Start again using an alternative approach.

11 You should have created one or two summary plans. You will have discussed differing options, identified areas of uncertainty or ignorance, and have started coming to a common understanding. You should also have been able to add some flesh to the bones of your project definition.

This may be sufficient at this stage or you may need more sessions. Assuming you have made as much progress as you can, the work packages should be allocated to key team members to start working on as part of the initial investigation.

USE OF PROJECT MANAGEMENT PLANNING SOFTWARE PACKAGES

There are many commercially available software packages for schedule management, all of which also have the capability for handling resources and costs. Using planning packages can be of great assistance to project managers in their work, particularly for projects with more than 50 to 100 activities. The point at which using a software package is effective depends on how well a person can use it. More experienced users will find project-planning packages more beneficial for smaller projects than those who are less able. The examples shown in this book were prepared using Microsoft Project but similar layouts and reports can be prepared using other software packages (PMW, Artemis, Open Plan, etc.).

Remember, planning software is a tool for you to use and not an end in its own right. It is not magic and will only give you a short cut to calculating and reporting on schedules. It cannot tell you if your fundamental approach is wrong or a major task is missing.

One danger of planning software is that a "planner" works in isolation to construct a plan for the team. Computer screens are small and do not make good work sheets for teams. The Post-It Notes method in Workout 21.1 will test your basic approach and will ensure your team are agreed and aligned. When that has been done, by all means, "computerize it."

I was given the task of looking at a project plan which had been created for a complex change project for a manufacturing company. I was told that there were six projects and about 400 activities. The complexity was due to over 50 interdependencies between the projects.

I printed out a network chart of the project (the equivalent of the Post-It Note plan) and laid it out on the factory floor like a carpet. A half day of study and marking up resulted in a much simpler program. There were still six projects, but now only five interdependencies. The original project scopes had been defined largely on departmental lines. By focussing on deliverables, I was able create relatively independent projects so that each project manager had greater degrees of freedom to manage his or her projects without the need to involve the others.

Good planning pays dividends.

Tracking progress toward your objectives

"Nothing is inevitable until it happens."

A J P TAYLOR

Tracking progress toward your objective is essential. If you don't do it you simply won't know when you are going to arrive. The control cycle is shown in Figure 21.2: once a plan has been agreed, it is necessary to measure progress against the plan, reforecast to the end, note any variances and take steps to bring the project back on schedule if need be.

There are many ways to measure progress, the commonest being:

- assessing percentage complete;
- assessing the remaining duration for an activity;
- estimating the date when a task will be completed.

Many people use the "percentage complete" method. However, this method has potential problems if a realistic estimate of percentage complete cannot be determined (such as measuring hours worked); it is not unusual to find an activity is 90 percent complete for 90 percent of its duration! A simpler method is to estimate the date when a task will be completed.

It is not unusual to find an activity is 90 percent complete for 90 percent of its duration!

An activity is either:

- completed (i.e. 100 percent complete);
- not started (i.e. 0 percent complete);
- or started, but not complete.

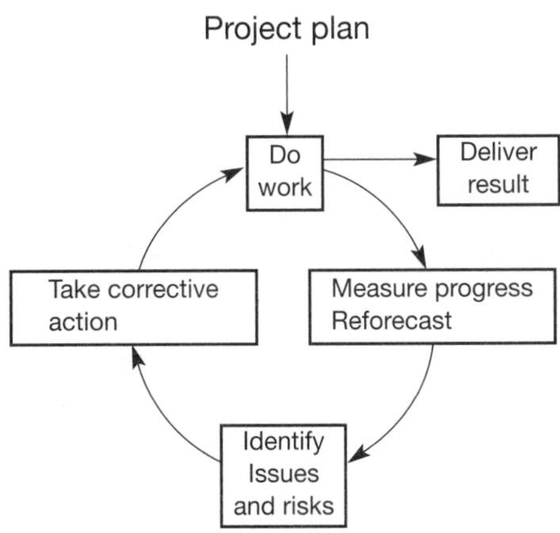

Figure 21.2 Schedule control cycle

Activities which are started, but not finished, are assumed to be 0 percent complete, but a current best estimate of the expected finish date is made. A special form (Figure 21.8) can be designed to record this information.

The schedule should be updated at least monthly, but for faster moving projects, weekly or fortnightly would be more appropriate. This update cycle should tie in with the regular progress reporting on the project as it is the most concise method of showing what has been achieved and what is to happen next. Summary reports should be used for reporting upward, and detailed reports should be used for reporting to the project team.

Do not concentrate only on what has been completed. Look at what is coming up next. Consider, based on your experience to date, whether the timescales allocated are adequate; if they aren't, you may need to take corrective action. Anticipating problems is good practice and gives you more time to find solutions. If problems are ignored they don't go away, they grow. Keep in mind your main focus: to reach the RFS Gate, when benefits start to flow. You do not need to have every activity completed on time. Every duration in your plan is basically a guess. Some will be good, some will be appalling, others will be the unfortunate victims of Murphy's Law. As a project manager too much concentration on the wrong detail will divert your attention from the real issues.

Keep in mind your main focus: to reach the RFS Gate, when benefits start to flow. You do not need to have every activity completed on time.

Reforecasting the schedule is not a change to the plan. It is an assessment of how the project is proceeding compared to the plan.

PLAN INSTABILITY

Quite often you will find that when starting work and monitoring against a plan you have difficulty assessing progress. This may happen because the work is in fact being undertaken in a different way from that planned. In most cases this is not a problem if the key milestones, dates, and interdependencies are not affected. It can be symptomatic of "microplanning," i.e., planning done at too detailed a level.

At other times it is simply because the plan has not been fully thought through. In which case it needs to be changed to reflect the actual work to be done (using the change management guidelines, of course). Changes of this nature often occur in the early part of a project as a result of uncertainty. The plan should become stabilized quite soon if you apply yourself and your team to it. You may also find that a particular work package is unstable. This could indicate that the manager in question has not planned it properly and is not in control, or that it is inherently risky. Both reasons need your management attention.

Schedule reports

Consistent format and layout

You must have a clear and consistent legend for the family of reports you will produce. Figure 21.3 is a typical example.

Bar charts can be confusing to the uninitiated and difficult to read. So it is good practice to use consistent formats and styles. The following points should be noted:

- The numbering used for activities clearly shows their level in the project hierarchy. The list is ordered such that each activity is shown within its relevant work package within the relevant life cycle stage.
- Activities are best described using an active verb, e.g., "Prepare data." Milestones or targets are activities of zero duration and are best described using a passive verb, e.g. "Phase 1 completed." The dates on the activity list should be updated to reflect progress and current expectations of finish dates.
- The accountability column has the name of the single point of accountability for every activity at every level.
- Show both the plan and the actual/forecast on the graphical section of the chart. In this way progress is very obvious.

When reading any of the project reports, it must be clear where the report came from and what it refers to. It is, therefore, good practice to have "quality" headers and footers on each page so that the reader is absolutely certain of the source and status of the report being read.

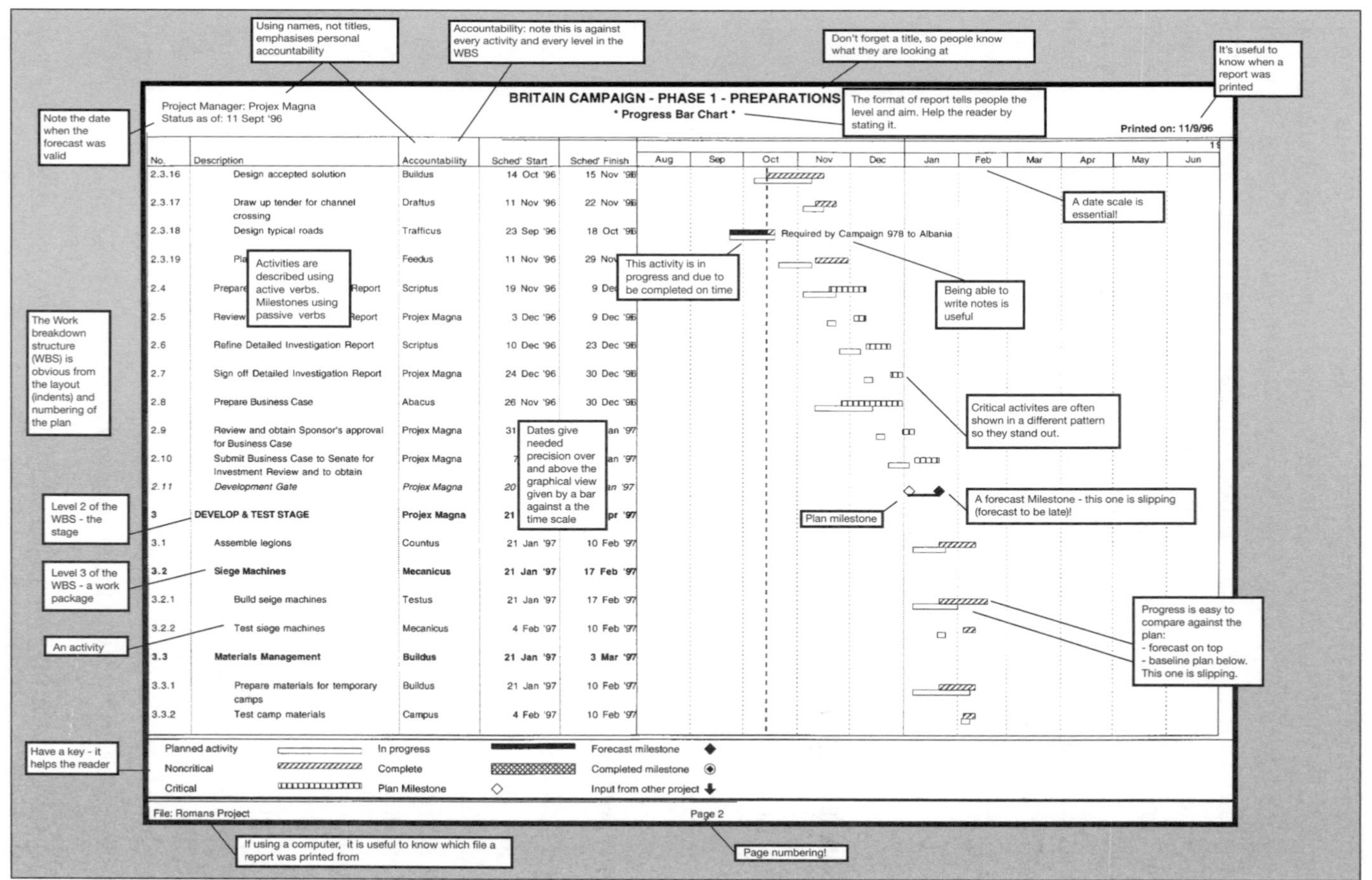

Figure 21.3 Schedule report

Inter-project dependencies

Many projects require deliverables from other projects as a prerequisite to completion. For example, a software project may require another project to deliver a particular hardware configuration before it can be tested.

The plan for a project should show only those activities for which the project manager is accountable. Activities done by others in other projects should not be shown in detail. Such linkages should, however, be explicit.

It is very important to ensure that the scope of each project is well defined, particularly when different departments in a company are involved. If the full scope of each project is not clear, then accountability for delivery becomes vague and this will threaten project success. It will often be found that senior management and line management who are not intimately involved in a project or series of projects will have different perceptions of the scope of a project and may even view a package within a project as a "project" in its own right.

The breakdown of a project into discrete work packages related to specific deliverables is essential if confusion is to be avoided. The plan for a project should show only those activities for which the project manager is accountable. Activities done by others in other projects should not be shown in detail. Such linkages should, however, be explicit and the example reports shown later in this chapter have been designed with this in mind. The reports show a **down arrow** on the date when the deliverable is due to be completed and is ready for use by the receiving project.

When considering dependencies between projects, the following question should be asked: *"What do I (in Project A) require from other projects in order that I may complete the defined scope of work?"*

This may result in a list of one or more specific deliverables which should be identified in the other project plan(s). The project manager(s) of the other project(s) should be aware of what you require and by when. Two projects cannot be accountable for delivering the same deliverable!

Two projects can not be accountable for delivering the same deliverable!

Report formats

The following section contain examples of schedule reports and are presented in the order in which they will normally be used (Figure 21.4).

The examples were prepared using Microsoft Project, but similar layouts can be prepared using other packages. They are all derived from the same basic data; they are simply different ways of viewing those data.

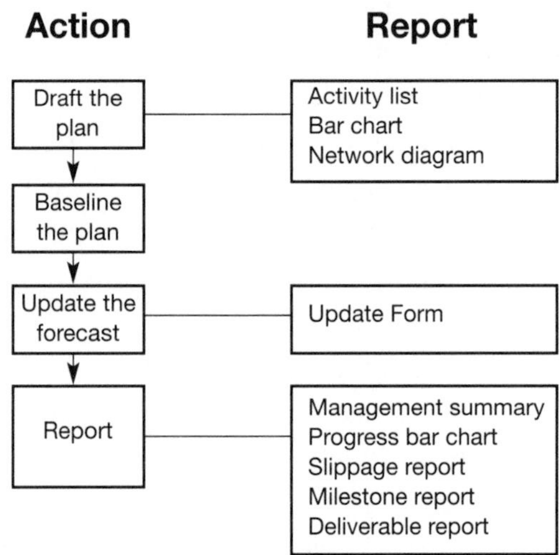

Figure 21.4 Schedule report formats

Reports used when drafting a plan

Activity list

Purpose: the activity list records all activities associated with the project, i.e., what needs to be done, who is accountable, how long it will take, and by when it should be completed. The list is used to identify activities and milestones and to give information on outline plans (Figure 21.5).

When to use it: the activity list is best used when drawing up a plan, to aid thinking through the key activities, milestones, and their dependencies. It is a simple and useful way of communicating a plan if bar charts or other graphic presentations cannot be prepared.

ACTIVITY LIST BRITAIN CAMPAIGN

WBS	Description	Accountable	Dur'	Plan start	Plan finish	Sched' Start	Sched' Finish	Number	Preceded by?	Summary?	Comment	Sign-off?
1	INITIAL INVESTIGATION	Projex Magna	27d	1 Aug '96	6 Sep '96	1 Aug '96	6 Sep '96	1		Yes		
2	DETAILED INVESTIGATION STAGE	Projex Magna	96d	9 Sep '96	3 Jan '97	9 Sep '96	20 Jan '97	12	11	Yes		
2.1	Assemble Team	Projex Magna	10d	9 Sep '96	20 Sep '96	9 Sep '96	20 Sep '96	13		No		
2.2	Prepare Development Definition	Publius	16d	23 Sep '96	25 Oct '96	23 Sep '96	14 Oct '96	14	13	No		Sponsus
2.3	Undertake Detailed Investigation	Projex Magna	51d	23 Sep '96	15 Nov '96	20 Sep '96	29 Nov '96	15	13	No		
2.3.1	Locate mapping of Gaul	Surveyus	10d	23 Sep '96	4 Oct '96	23 Sep '96	4 Oct '96	16		No		
2.3.2	Maps of Gaul available	Surveyus	0d	4 Oct '96	4 Oct '96	4 Oct '96	4 Oct '96	17	16	Yes		Cartus
2.3.3	Do reconnaisance	Surveyus	20d	23 Sep '96	18 Oct '96	14 Oct '96	8 Nov '96	18	16FS-10d	No		
2.3.4	Estimate enemy troop numbers	Countus	15d	7 Oct '96	25 Oct '96	28 Oct '96	15 Nov '96	19	18FS-10d	No		
2.3.5	Define number of legions required	Countus	10d	14 Oct '96	25 Oct '96	4 Nov '96	15 Nov '96	20	19FS-10d	No		
2.3.6	Prepare recruitment plan	Countus	5d	28 Oct '96	1 Nov '96	18 Nov '96	22 Nov '96	21	20	No		Claudius
2.3.7	Investigate possible routes	Surveyus	20d	7 Oct '96	1 Nov '96	7 Oct '96	1 Nov '96	22	16	No		
2.3.8	Design siege machines	Mechanicus	30d	23 Sep '96	1 Nov '96	20 Sep '96	31 Oct '96	23		No		Marcus
2.3.9	Draw up tender for siege machines	Draftus	10d	4 Nov '96	15 Nov '96	1 Nov '96	14 Nov '96	24	23	No		
2.3.10	Design temporary camps	Buildus	30d	23 Sep '96	1 Nov '96	26 Sep '96	6 Nov '96	25		No		Hadrian
2.3.11	Draw up tender for siege machines	Draftus	10d	4 Nov '96	15 Nov '96	7 Nov '96	20 Nov '96	26	25	No		
2.3.12	Design river bridges	Buildus	25d	23 Sep '96	1 Nov '96	14 Oct '96	15 Nov '96	27	16FS-20d	No		Neptune
2.3.13	Draw up tender for river bridge parts	Draftus	10d	4 Nov '96	15 Nov '96	18 Nov '96	29 Nov '96	28	27	No		
2.3.14	Receive tunnel designs	Buildus	0d	23 Sep '96	23 Sep '96	14 Oct '96	14 Oct '96	29		Yes	From Campaign 321 - Gibralter	Orpheus
2.3.15	Decide how to cross English Channel	Buildus	10d	23 Sep '96	4 Oct '96	23 Sep '96	4 Oct '96	30		No		
2.3.16	Design accepted solution	Buildus	25d	7 Oct '96	8 Nov '96	14 Oct '96	15 Nov '96	31	30	No		
2.3.17	Draw up tender for channel crossing	Draftus	10d	4 Nov '96	15 Nov '96	11 Nov '96	22 Nov '96	32	31FS-5d	No		
2.3.18	Design typical roads	Trafficus	20d	23 Sep '96	18 Oct '96	23 Sep '96	18 Oct '96	33		No	Required by Campaign 978 to Alb	Mercury
2.3.19	Plan catering logistics	Feedus	15d	21 Oct '96	8 Nov '96	11 Nov '96	29 Nov '96	34	18	No		
2.4	Prepare Detailed Investigation Report	Scriptus	15d	4 Nov '96	22 Nov '96	19 Nov '96	9 Dec '96	35	15FS-10d	No		
2.5	Review Detailed Investigation Report	Projex Magna	5d	18 Nov '96	22 Nov '96	3 Dec '96	9 Dec '96	36	35FS-5d	No		
2.6	Refine Detailed Investigation Report	Scriptus	10d	25 Nov '96	6 Dec '96	10 Dec '96	23 Dec '96	37	36	No		
2.7	Sign off Detailed Investigation Report	Projex Magna	5d	9 Dec '96	13 Dec '96	24 Dec '96	30 Dec '96	38	37	No		Sponsus
2.8	Prepare Business Case	Abacus	25d	11 Nov '96	13 Dec '96	26 Nov '96	30 Dec '96	39	35FS-10d	No		
2.9	Review and obtain Sponsor's approval for	Projex Magna	5d	16 Dec '96	20 Dec '96	31 Dec '96	6 Jan '97	40	39,38	No		Sponsus
2.1	Submit Business Case to Senate for Inves	Projex Magna	10d	23 Dec '96	3 Jan '97	7 Jan '97	20 Jan '97	41	40	No		
2.11	Development Gate	Projex Magna	0d	3 Jan '97	3 Jan '97	20 Jan '97	20 Jan '97	42	41	Yes		

Figure 21.5 A typical activity list

Bar chart

Purpose

The bar chart (or Gantt chart) is a representation of the schedule plan in graph form. It shows the duration of activities against a timescale. It also defines who is accountable for each activity and work package, and the place of each activity in the work breakdown structure (Figure 21.6).

When to use

The bar chart is probably the most effective way of communicating a schedule. For this reason it is highly recommended for inclusion in the project plan and for use in communicating plans whenever possible.

Completion

Bar charts can be produced manually or by using computer software, at summary and detailed levels. They are produced from the activity list once the start and end dates of each activity have been calculated. The left hand portion contains a reference number, description, duration, the name of the person accountable, and the start and finish dates. The right hand part shows a bar against a timescale which spans from the start to the finish of the activity. Milestones (dates for key events) are shown as diamonds. Dependencies from outside the project are shown as down arrows.

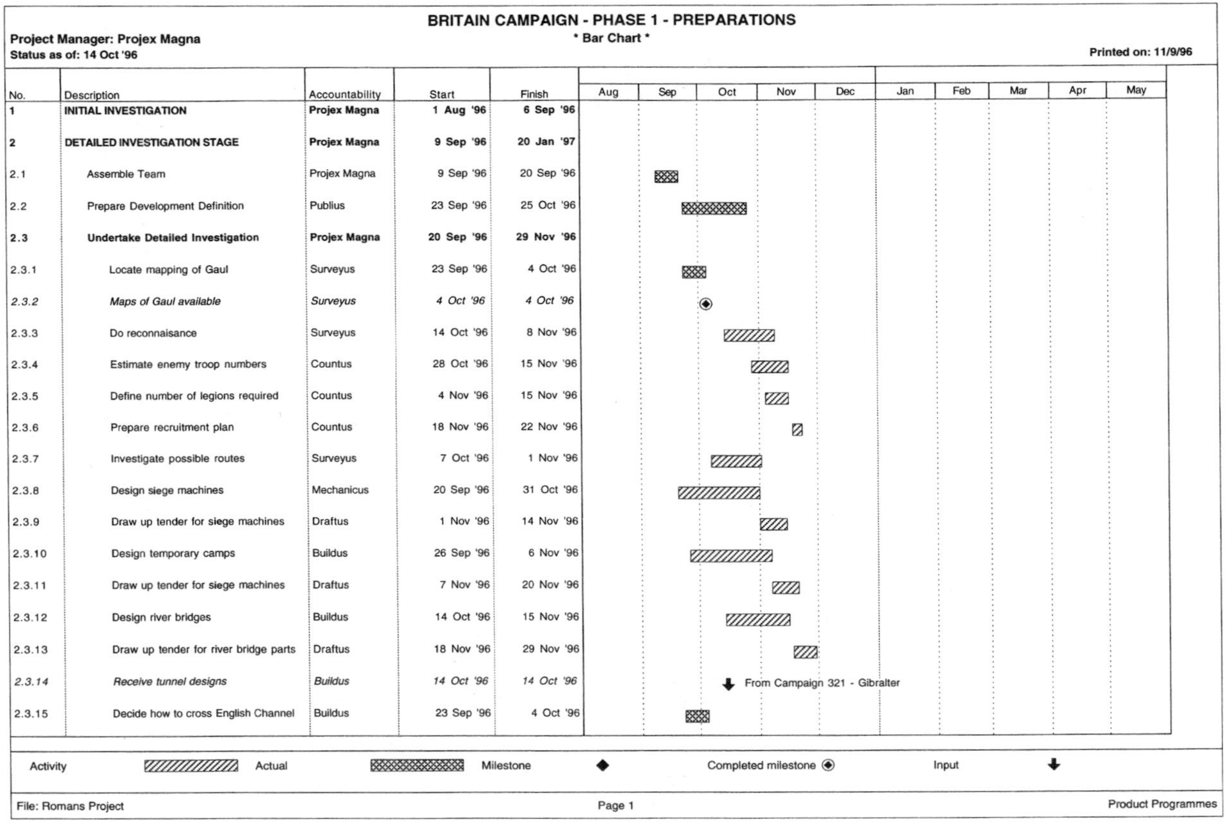

BRITAIN CAMPAIGN - PHASE 1 - PREPARATIONS

* Bar Chart *

Project Manager: Projex Magna

Status as of: 14 Oct '96

Printed on: 11/9/96

No.	Description	Accountability	Start	Finish
1	**INITIAL INVESTIGATION**	**Projex Magna**	**1 Aug '96**	**6 Sep '96**
2	**DETAILED INVESTIGATION STAGE**	**Projex Magna**	**9 Sep '96**	**20 Jan '97**
2.1	Assemble Team	Projex Magna	9 Sep '96	20 Sep '96
2.2	Prepare Development Definition	Publius	23 Sep '96	25 Oct '96
2.3	**Undertake Detailed Investigation**	**Projex Magna**	**20 Sep '96**	**29 Nov '96**
2.3.1	Locate mapping of Gaul	Surveyus	23 Sep '96	4 Oct '96
2.3.2	*Maps of Gaul available*	*Surveyus*	*4 Oct '96*	*4 Oct '96*
2.3.3	Do reconnaisance	Surveyus	14 Oct '96	8 Nov '96
2.3.4	Estimate enemy troop numbers	Countus	28 Oct '96	15 Nov '96
2.3.5	Define number of legions required	Countus	4 Nov '96	15 Nov '96
2.3.6	Prepare recruitment plan	Countus	18 Nov '96	22 Nov '96
2.3.7	Investigate possible routes	Surveyus	7 Oct '96	1 Nov '96
2.3.8	Design siege machines	Mechanicus	20 Sep '96	31 Oct '96
2.3.9	Draw up tender for siege machines	Draftus	1 Nov '96	14 Nov '96
2.3.10	Design temporary camps	Buildus	26 Sep '96	6 Nov '96
2.3.11	Draw up tender for siege machines	Draftus	7 Nov '96	20 Nov '96
2.3.12	Design river bridges	Buildus	14 Oct '96	15 Nov '96
2.3.13	Draw up tender for river bridge parts	Draftus	18 Nov '96	29 Nov '96
2.3.14	*Receive tunnel designs*	*Buildus*	*14 Oct '96*	*14 Oct '96*
2.3.15	Decide how to cross English Channel	Buildus	23 Sep '96	4 Oct '96

Aug Sep Oct Nov Dec Jan Feb Mar Apr May

From Campaign 321 - Gibralter

Activity | Actual | Milestone | Completed milestone | Input

File: Romans Project | Page 1 | Product Programmes

Figure 21.6 A typical bar chart

Network diagram

Purpose

The network diagram is probably the most useful and most under-used way of depicting a project. It is used to show the logical relationship (dependencies) between different activities, work packages, or projects. It is needed when the logic is complicated enough to require special attention. Network diagrams can be used for identifying natural checkpoints in the project as the network will show where various strands come together. They are invaluable for calculating project float and determining the critical path (Figure 21.7).

When to use

The network should be used whenever a complex sequence of events needs to be shown clearly. This is particularly useful when first drawing up a plan, as it is not always obvious what the logical dependencies are. It is also a useful format to use at planning workshops, for determining dependencies between activities, before any idea of timescale/duration has been gained.

The network diagram is probably the most useful and most under-used way of depicting a project.

Completion

The plan is developed by mapping out those activities which can be performed in parallel and those which must be carried out sequentially. Activities or milestones are represented in boxes and their relationships with preceding and succeeding activities are shown using arrows. An activity may not start until its predecessor has been finished. This is called a "precedence network" and is the most versatile method for depicting the logical sequence of the project. For complex projects they are best prepared using project planning software.

For planning workshops the activities, milestones, and deliverables would be written on "Post-It Notes." Then, starting at the end of the project with the final deliverable, you need to ask yourself: "What would I need to have in place in order to achieve this?"

This sequence is repeated until the start point in the project is reached (see Project Workout 21.1 on p. 303).

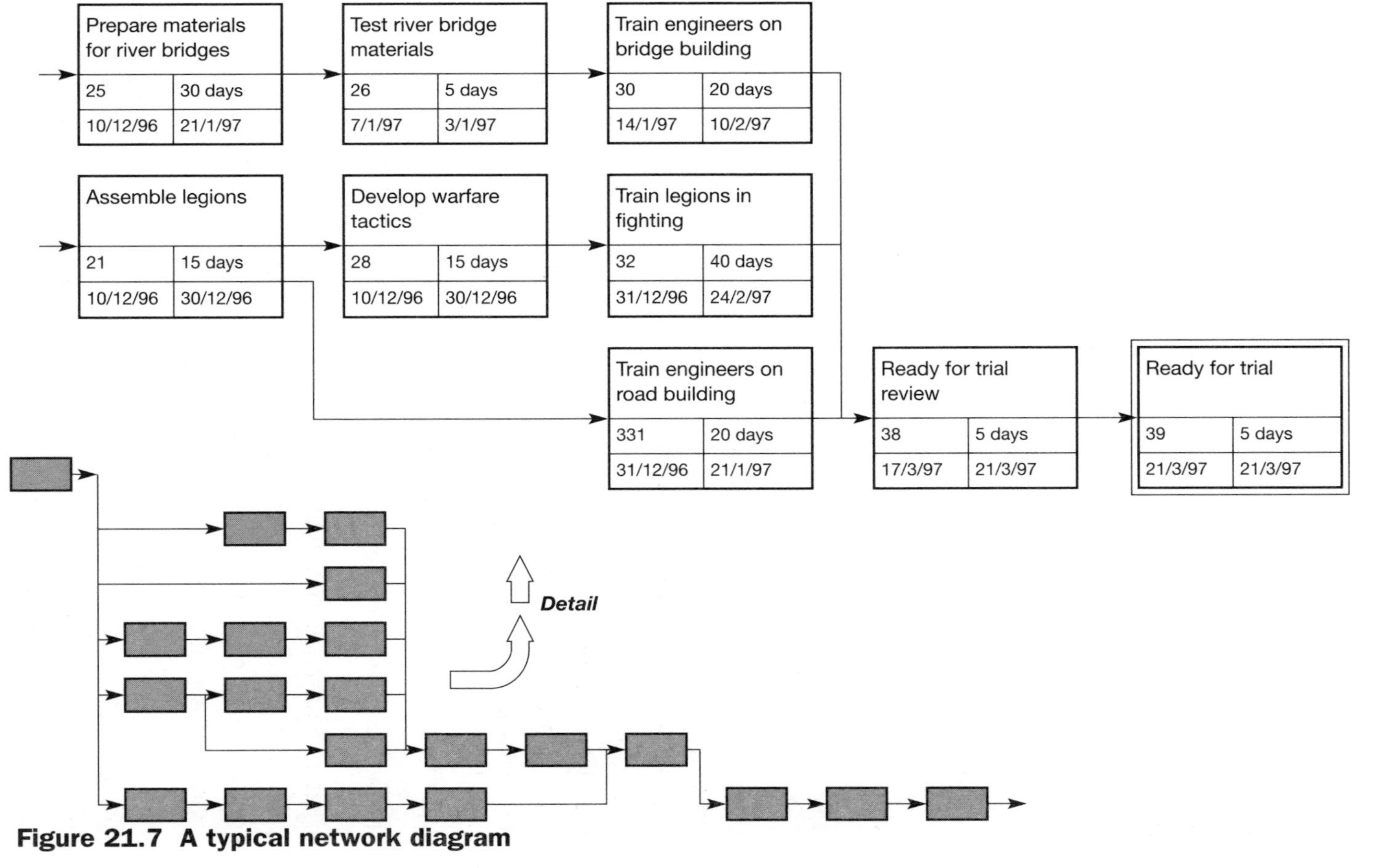

Figure 21.7 A typical network diagram

Report used to update the forecast

Update form

Purpose:

The update form is used to collect data for tracking progress on the project (Figure 21.8).

When to use

The form is used every time the project manager wishes to check on progress. This should be at least monthly, at month-end, but for many projects it is desirable to update the project weekly or fortnightly.

Completion

The form comprises a filtered selection of unstarted and incomplete activities within a given date range. It has the following columns:

- the reference number of each activity;
- activity description;
- C column (complete) and S column (started);
- the actual start and finish dates;
- the expected finish date (for started activities);
- the forecast start and finish dates calculated last time the project was updated;
- the baseline planned finish date (as a reminder);
- a comment column to record pertinent notes.

The person responsible for reporting progress:

- enters S for all started activities in the "S" column and the actual start date and expected finish date in the relevant columns;
- enters C for all completed activities in the "C" column, giving actual start and actual finish dates.

If it is apparent that forecast dates for future activities are wrong, sufficient information should be given to allow these to be replanned. Those activities which should have started, but have not, should be slipped forward to start on the update date – their finish date will also slip unless the duration is changed.

BRITAIN CAMPAIGN - PHASE 1 - PREPARATIONS

*** Update Form ***

Project Manager: Projex Magna

Status as of: 14 Oct '96

Printed on: 30/1/97

No.	Description	Accountability	C or S	Dur	Actual Start	Actual Finish	Expected Finish	F'cast Start	F'cast Finish	Plan Finish	Comments
2	**DETAILED INVESTIGATION STAGE**	**Projex Magna**		**96d**	**9 Sep '96**	**NA**	**NA**	**9 Sep '96**	**20 Jan '97**	**3 Jan '97**	
2.3	**Undertake Detailed Investigation**	**Projex Magna**		**51d**	**20 Sep '96**	**NA**	**NA**	**20 Sep '96**	**29 Nov '96**	**15 Nov '96**	
2.3.3	Do reconnaissance	Surveyus		20d	NA	NA	NA	14 Oct '96	8 Nov '96	18 Oct '96	
2.3.4	Estimate enemy troop numbers	Countus		15d	NA	NA	NA	28 Oct '96	15 Nov '96	25 Oct '96	
2.3.5	Define number of legions required	Countus		10d	NA	NA	NA	4 Nov '96	15 Nov '96	25 Oct '96	
2.3.7	Investigate possible routes	Surveyus	S	20d	7 Oct '96	NA	NA	7 Oct '96	1 Nov '96	1 Nov '96	
2.3.8	Design siege machines	Mechanicus	S	30d	20 Sep '96	NA	NA	20 Sep '96	31 Oct '96	1 Nov '96	
2.3.9	Draw up tender for siege machines	Draftus		10d	NA	NA	NA	1 Nov '96	14 Nov '96	15 Nov '96	
2.3.10	Design temporary camps	Buildus	S	30d	26 Sep '96	NA	NA	26 Sep '96	6 Nov '96	1 Nov '96	
2.3.11	Draw up tender for siege machines	Draftus		10d	NA	NA	NA	7 Nov '96	20 Nov '96	15 Nov '96	
2.3.12	Design river bridges	Buildus		25d	NA	NA	NA	14 Oct '96	15 Nov '96	1 Nov '96	
2.3.14	Receive tunnel designs	Buildus		0d	NA	NA	NA	14 Oct '96	14 Oct '96	23 Sep '96	From Campaign 321 - Gibralter
2.3.16	Design accepted solution	Buildus		25d	NA	NA	NA	14 Oct '96	15 Nov '96	8 Nov '96	
2.3.17	Draw up tender for channel crossing	Draftus		10d	NA	NA	NA	11 Nov '96	22 Nov '96	15 Nov '96	
2.3.18	Design typical roads	Trafficus	S	20d	23 Sep '96	NA	NA	23 Sep '96	18 Oct '96	18 Oct '96	Required by Campaign 978 to Albania
2.3.19	Plan catering logistics	Feedus		15d	NA	NA	NA	11 Nov '96	29 Nov '96	8 Nov '96	

File: Romans Project | Page 1 | Product Programmes

Figure 21.8 A typical update form

Reports used for progress reporting

Management summary

Purpose

The management summary is a concise presentation of the progress bar chart (Figure 21.9) aimed at providing a summary report on project progress.

When to use

This format is best used for reporting to project boards, project sponsors, and other stakeholders.

Completion

The report contains only the specific lines of information (summary, detail, or milestone) that you wish to present. The report should be kept as short as possible, concentrating on the project life cycle stages, key work packages, and milestones.

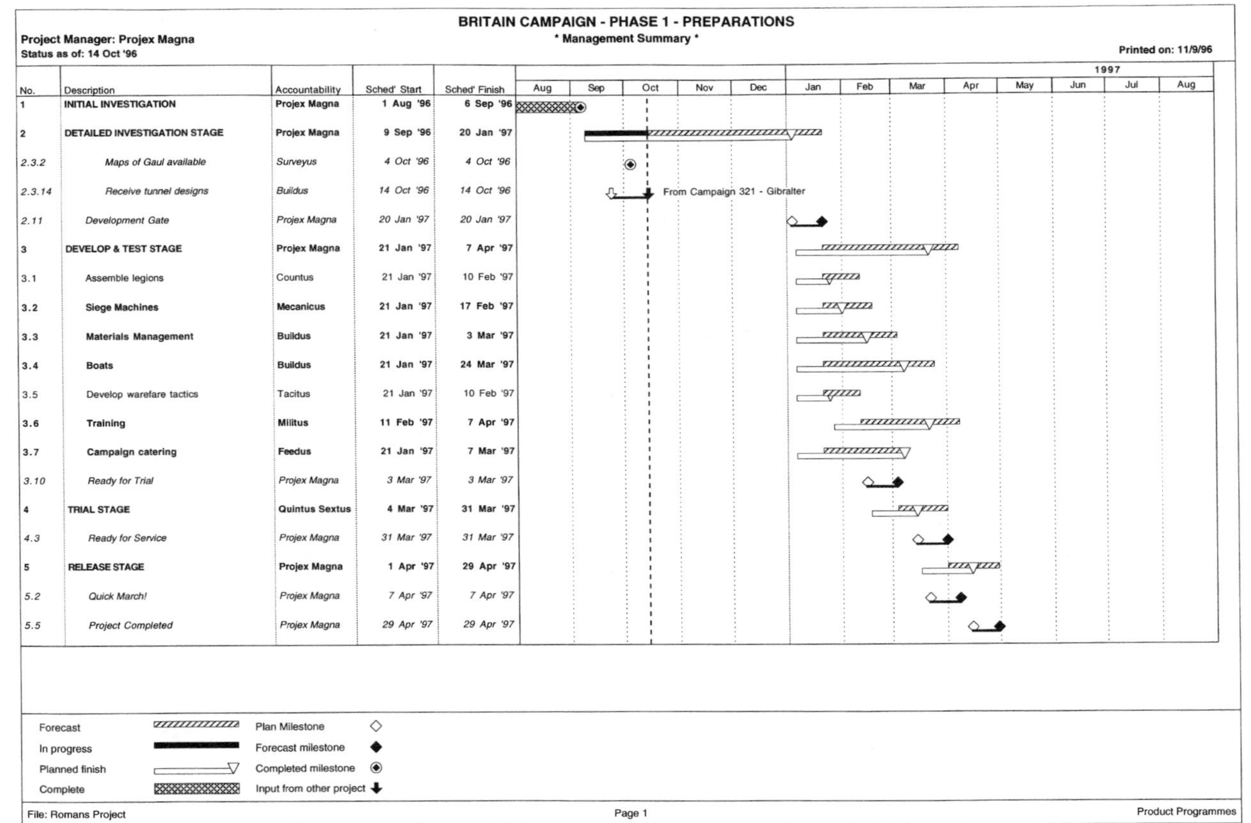

BRITAIN CAMPAIGN - PHASE 1 - PREPARATIONS
* Management Summary *

Project Manager: Projex Magna
Status as of: 14 Oct '96

Printed on: 11/9/96

No.	Description	Accountability	Sched' Start	Sched' Finish
1	**INITIAL INVESTIGATION**	**Projex Magna**	**1 Aug '96**	**6 Sep '96**
2	**DETAILED INVESTIGATION STAGE**	**Projex Magna**	**9 Sep '96**	**20 Jan '97**
2.3.2	*Maps of Gaul available*	*Surveyus*	*4 Oct '96*	*4 Oct '96*
2.3.14	*Receive tunnel designs*	*Buildus*	*14 Oct '96*	*14 Oct '96*
2.11	*Development Gate*	*Projex Magna*	*20 Jan '97*	*20 Jan '97*
3	**DEVELOP & TEST STAGE**	**Projex Magna**	**21 Jan '97**	**7 Apr '97**
3.1	Assemble legions	Countus	21 Jan '97	10 Feb '97
3.2	**Siege Machines**	**Mecanicus**	**21 Jan '97**	**17 Feb '97**
3.3	**Materials Management**	**Buildus**	**21 Jan '97**	**3 Mar '97**
3.4	**Boats**	**Buildus**	**21 Jan '97**	**24 Mar '97**
3.5	Develop warefare tactics	Tacitus	21 Jan '97	10 Feb '97
3.6	**Training**	**Militus**	**11 Feb '97**	**7 Apr '97**
3.7	**Campaign catering**	**Feedus**	**21 Jan '97**	**7 Mar '97**
3.10	*Ready for Trial*	*Projex Magna*	*3 Mar '97*	*3 Mar '97*
4	**TRIAL STAGE**	**Quintus Sextus**	**4 Mar '97**	**31 Mar '97**
4.3	*Ready for Service*	*Projex Magna*	*31 Mar '97*	*31 Mar '97*
5	**RELEASE STAGE**	**Projex Magna**	**1 Apr '97**	**29 Apr '97**
5.2	*Quick March!*	*Projex Magna*	*7 Apr '97*	*7 Apr '97*
5.5	*Project Completed*	*Projex Magna*	*29 Apr '97*	*29 Apr '97*

Figure 21.9 A typical management summary

Progress bar chart

Purpose

The progress bar chart is a more complex version of Figure 21.6 which is used to compare forecasts against the agreed plan and hence highlight variances (Figure 21.10).

The progress bar chart shows the current forecast dates for each activity and milestone compared with the baseline plan. The dates given are the actual or current forecast dates. Comments from the progress "update form" (see Figure 21.8) may be included against any item.

When to use

The bar chart is probably the most effective way of communicating a schedule plan. Progress reports may be made more concise if a bar chart is used to detail progress rather than progress being described in text.

Completion

Bar charts can be produced manually or by using computer software at summary/outline, and detailed levels. They are produced from the activity list once the start and end times of each activity have been calculated. The left hand portion contains a reference number, description, duration, the initials of the person accountable, and the start and finish dates. The right hand part shows a bar against a timescale which spans from the start to the finish of the activity. Milestones (dates for key events) are shown as diamonds. The plan dates are shown as a line below the current forecast so that a visual appreciation of slippage is readily apparent. Figure 21.3 on p. 310 describes how to read the bar chart.

More complex but informative versions of the progress bar chart can be developed which show the "float" available for each activity and dependencies between activities.

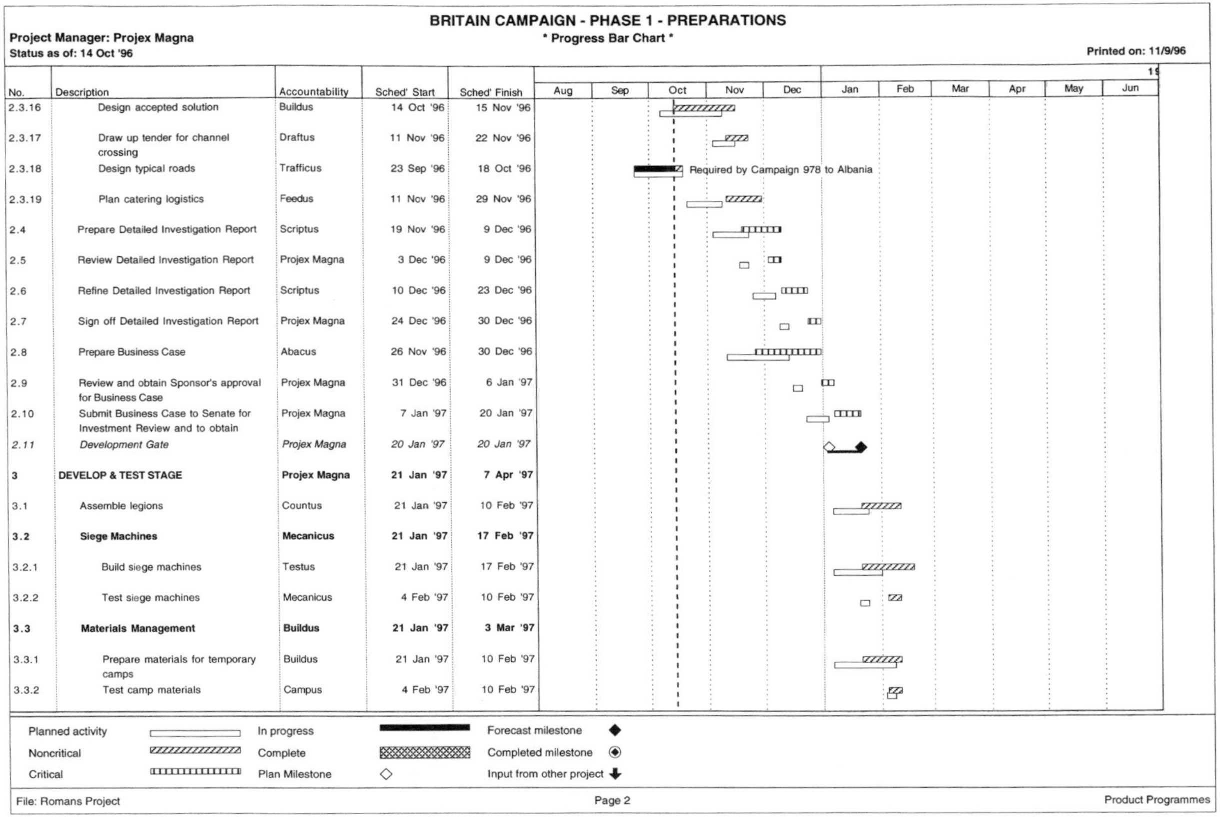

BRITAIN CAMPAIGN - PHASE 1 - PREPARATIONS
* Progress Bar Chart *
Project Manager: Projex Magna
Status as of: 14 Oct '96
Printed on: 11/9/96
No. | Description | Accountability | Sched' Start | Sched' Finish
Aug Sep Oct Nov Dec Jan Feb Mar Apr May Jun
2.3.16 Design accepted solution | Buildus | 14 Oct '96 | 15 Nov '96
2.3.17 Draw up tender for channel crossing | Draftus | 11 Nov '96 | 22 Nov '96
2.3.18 Design typical roads | Trafficus | 23 Sep '96 | 18 Oct '96
Required by Campaign 978 to Albania
2.3.19 Plan catering logistics | Feedus | 11 Nov '96 | 29 Nov '96
2.4 Prepare Detailed Investigation Report | Scriptus | 19 Nov '96 | 9 Dec '96
2.5 Review Detailed Investigation Report | Projex Magna | 3 Dec '96 | 9 Dec '96
2.6 Refine Detailed Investigation Report | Scriptus | 10 Dec '96 | 23 Dec '96
2.7 Sign off Detailed Investigation Report | Projex Magna | 24 Dec '96 | 30 Dec '96
2.8 Prepare Business Case | Abacus | 26 Nov '96 | 30 Dec '96
2.9 Review and obtain Sponsor's approval for Business Case | Projex Magna | 31 Dec '96 | 6 Jan '97
2.10 Submit Business Case to Senate for Investment Review and to obtain | Projex Magna | 7 Jan '97 | 20 Jan '97
2.11 Development Gate | Projex Magna | 20 Jan '97 | 20 Jan '97
3 DEVELOP & TEST STAGE | Projex Magna | 21 Jan '97 | 7 Apr '97
3.1 Assemble legions | Countus | 21 Jan '97 | 10 Feb '97
3.2 Siege Machines | Mecanicus | 21 Jan '97 | 17 Feb '97
3.2.1 Build siege machines | Testus | 21 Jan '97 | 17 Feb '97
3.2.2 Test siege machines | Mecanicus | 4 Feb '97 | 10 Feb '97
3.3 Materials Management | Buildus | 21 Jan '97 | 3 Mar '97
3.3.1 Prepare materials for temporary camps | Buildus | 21 Jan '97 | 10 Feb '97
3.3.2 Test camp materials | Campus | 4 Feb '97 | 10 Feb '97
Planned activity
Noncritical
Critical
In progress
Complete
Plan Milestone
Forecast milestone
Completed milestone
Input from other project
File: Romans Project
Page 2
Product Programmes

Figure 21.10 A typical progress bar chart

Slippage report

Purpose

This report is used to focus attention on activities which are likely to be late. This enables the project manager to take whatever action is necessary to bring the project back on schedule. The objective is not to use the report as a tool to "punish" those accountable for slippage, but rather to focus attention on putting things right. With this in mind, the slippage report details only incomplete activities (Figure 21.11).

When to use

This report is useful for identifying those current and future activities which are forecast as slipping and hence focus his attention on remedying the situation. It is best used for plans of more than 50 activities when a software package can extract the "offending" activities automatically. If you are using critical chain schedule management this report will be replaced by a buffer report (see Figure 21.16).

Completion

The report is compiled by extracting the late (and unfinished) activities from the updated activity list. Most computer project-planning packages have routines for preparing this type of report.

BRITAIN CAMPAIGN - PHASE 1 - PREPARATIONS

Project Manager: Projex Magna *** Milestone Report ***

Status as of: 14 Oct '96 **Printed on: 11/9/96**

WBS	Description	Planned Finish	Forecast Finish	Actual Finish	Slippage	Comment
2	**DETAILED INVESTIGATION STAGE**	**3 Jan '97**	**20 Jan '97**	**NA**	**11d**	
2.3	**Undertake Detailed Investigation**	**15 Nov '96**	**29 Nov '96**	**NA**	**10d**	
2.3.2	Maps of Gaul available	4 Oct '96	4 Oct '96	4 Oct '96	0d	
2.3.14	Receive tunnel designs	23 Sep '96	14 Oct '96	NA	15d	From Campaign 321 - Gibralter
2.11	Development Gate	3 Jan '97	20 Jan '97	NA	11d	
3	**DEVELOP & TEST STAGE**	**21 Mar '97**	**7 Apr '97**	**NA**	**11d**	
3.3	**Materials Management**	**14 Feb '97**	**3 Mar '97**	**NA**	**11d**	
3.3.5	Material test certificates ready	7 Feb '97	24 Feb '97	NA	11d	
3.7	**Campaign catering**	**7 Mar '97**	**7 Mar '97**	**NA**	**0d**	
3.7.3	Place contract for food supplies	17 Jan '97	3 Feb '97	NA	11d	
3.10	Ready for Trial	14 Feb '97	3 Mar '97	NA	11d	
4	**TRIAL STAGE**	**14 Mar '97**	**31 Mar '97**	**NA**	**11d**	
4.3	Ready for Service	14 Mar '97	31 Mar '97	NA	11d	
5	**RELEASE STAGE**	**14 Apr '97**	**29 Apr '97**	**NA**	**11d**	
5.2	Quick March!	21 Mar '97	7 Apr '97	NA	11d	
5.5	Project Completed	14 Apr '97	29 Apr '97	NA	11d	

File: Romans Project Page 1 Product Programmes

Figure 21.11 A typical slippage report

Milestone report

Purpose

The milestone report shows progress against the key targets for the project. These are items which should be specifically mentioned in the project documentation (Figure 21.12).

When to use

This format is an excellent, non-graphical way for communicating progress and expectations on the timing of key milestones such as the delivery dates for products, or interface dates with other projects.

Completion

The report is presented in tabular form showing the milestone description, the planned date, the current forecast of the date, and the actual date achieved. The final column indicates the slippage (how late) of a milestone compared to the plan. The report is made up of all those activities of zero duration from the activity list which the project manager wishes to highlight. Most computer project-planning packages have routines for preparing this type of report.

BRITAIN CAMPAIGN - PHASE 1 - PREPARATIONS

Project Manager: Projex Magna *** Milestone Report ***

Status as of: 14 Oct '96 **Printed on: 30/1/97**

WBS	Description	Planned Finish	Forecast Finish	Actual Finish	Slippage	Comment
2	**DETAILED INVESTIGATION STAGE**	3 Jan '97	20 Jan '97	NA	11d	
2.3	**Undertake Detailed Investigation**	15 Nov '96	29 Nov '96	NA	10d	
2.3.2	Maps of Gaul available	4 Oct '96	4 Oct '96	4 Oct '96	0d	
2.3.14	Receive tunnel designs	23 Sep '96	14 Oct '96	NA	15d	From Campaign 321 - Gibralter
2.11	Development Gate	3 Jan '97	20 Jan '97	NA	11d	
3	**DEVELOP & TEST STAGE**	21 Mar '97	7 Apr '97	NA	11d	
3.3	**Materials Management**	14 Feb '97	3 Mar '97	NA	11d	
3.3.5	Material test certificates ready	7 Feb '97	24 Feb '97	NA	11d	
3.7	**Campaign catering**	7 Mar '97	7 Mar '97	NA	0d	
3.7.3	Place contract for food supplies	17 Jan '97	3 Feb '97	NA	11d	
3.10	Ready for Trial	14 Feb '97	3 Mar '97	NA	11d	
4	**TRIAL STAGE**	14 Mar '97	31 Mar '97	NA	11d	
4.3	Ready for Service	14 Mar '97	31 Mar '97	NA	11d	
5	**RELEASE STAGE**	14 Apr '97	29 Apr '97	NA	11d	
5.2	Quick March!	21 Mar '97	7 Apr '97	NA	11d	
5.5	Project Completed	14 Apr '97	29 Apr '97	NA	11d	

File: Romans Project Page 1 Product Programmes

Figure 21.12 A typical milestone report

Deliverable report

Purpose

The deliverable report lists all the key deliverables from the project stating who is accountable for preparing them, reviewing them, and finally signing them off. These are items which should be specifically mentioned in the project documentation (Figure 21.13).

When to use

This format is used when the project manager wants to focus on the deliverables and be explicit about who is accountable for the quality aspects for each.

Unless we know who is to review a deliverable and sign it off, we cannot be certain that what is being produced is really fit for purpose.

Completion

The report is an extract from the full project plan with those activities and milestones relating to deliverables filtered out to produce a listing. Most computer software packages can be customized to do this.

BRITAIN CAMPAIGN - PHASE 1 - PREPARATIONS

Project Manager: Projex Magna

*** Deliverable Report ***

Status as of: 11 Sep '96

Printed on: 11/9/96

WBS	Description	Accountable	Planned Finish	Forecast Finish	Review by:	Sign off by:	Comment
2	**DETAILED INVESTIGATION STAGE**	**Projex Magna**	**3 Jan '97**	**20 Jan '97**			
2.2	Prepare Development Definition	Publius	25 Oct '96	14 Oct '96	Project Team	Sponsus	
2.3	**Undertake Detailed Investigation**	**Projex Magna**	**15 Nov '96**	**29 Nov '96**			
2.3.2	Maps of Gaul available	Surveyus	4 Oct '96	4 Oct '96	Vercingetorix, Flavius, Antonio	Cartus	
2.3.6	Prepare recruitment plan	Countus	1 Nov '96	22 Nov '96	Lucretia, Vespasian	Claudius	
2.3.8	Design siege machines	Mechanicus	1 Nov '96	31 Oct '96	Hannibal Minor, Romulus	Marcus	
2.3.10	Design temporary camps	Buildus	1 Nov '96	6 Nov '96	Flavia, Sextus	Hadrian	
2.3.12	Design river bridges	Buildus	1 Nov '96	15 Nov '96	Hannibal Minor, Romulus	Neptune	
2.3.14	Receive tunnel designs	Buildus	23 Sep '96	14 Oct '96	Vercingetorix, Flavius, Antonio	Orpheus	From Campaign 321 - Gibralter
2.3.18	Design typical roads	Trafficus	18 Oct '96	18 Oct '96	Vercingetorix, Flavius, Antonio	Mercury	Required by Campaign 978 to Albania
2.7	Sign off Detailed Investigation Report	Projex Magna	13 Dec '96	30 Dec '96	Project Team	Sponsus	
2.9	Review and obtain Sponsor's approval for Business Case	Projex Magna	20 Dec '96	6 Jan '97	Project Team, the Senate, Abacus	Sponsus	
3	**DEVELOP & TEST STAGE**	**Projex Magna**	**21 Mar '97**	**7 Apr '97**			
3.2	**Siege Machines**	**Mecanicus**	**31 Jan '97**	**17 Feb '97**			
3.2.1	Build siege machines	Testus	31 Jan '97	17 Feb '97	Hannibal Minor, Romulus	Marcus	
3.3	**Materials Management**	**Buildus**	**14 Feb '97**	**3 Mar '97**			
3.3.5	Material test certificates ready	Buildus	7 Feb '97	24 Feb '97	Hannibal Minor, Romulus	Neptune	
3.4	**Boats**	**Buildus**	**7 Mar '97**	**24 Mar '97**			
3.4.1	Build boats	Floata	7 Mar '97	24 Mar '97	Hannibal Minor, Romulus	Neptune	
3.5	Develop warfare tactics	Tacitus	24 Jan '97	10 Feb '97	Mark Anthony, Octavian	Julius Caesar (retired)	
3.7	**Campaign catering**	**Feedus**	**7 Mar '97**	**7 Mar '97**			
3.7.4	Obtain for food for troops	Feedus	7 Mar '97	7 Mar '97	Hannibal, Quintus, Septimus	Remus	
3.9	Ready for Trial Review	Projex Magna	14 Feb '97	3 Mar '97	Project Team	Sponsus	
4	**TRIAL STAGE**	**Quintus Sextus**	**14 Mar '97**	**31 Mar '97**			

File: Romans Project | Page 1 | Product Programmes

Figure 21.13 A typical deliverable report

So why are we nearly always late?

"How does a project get to be late? ... one day at a time."
F BROOKS

Despite decades of project management experience, backed up by ever more sophisticated technology, projects still deliver late. Unless, of course, the timescales set were so generous that even a donkey could have brought it in on time. That, however, is hardly a situation most business managers will find themselves in. When really questioned about project timescales most people will admit that speed is not necessarily the most important aspect but *predictability* is. If you are developing a new product, most marketing and sales people would rather have it in four months' time, if promised in four months' time (and working) than have it in three months' time when promised it in two. Once you have achieved predictability, you can concentrate on reducing the overall time taken.

We have seen that a project's duration is basically the sum of the guesses of the durations of those activities on the critical path. This is the definition of critical path. We decide the project approach using network planning and we guess (some guesses are very sophisticated) how long each activity will take, bearing in mind the resources needed to work on it. It's all very logical. From here on, human behavior takes over. If I am a project team member, what should I ask the project manager to put in the plan:

- a short duration I am unlikely to meet;
- a medium duration I might meet if I'm lucky;
- a prudent (longer) duration I'll probably meet.

Most people will choose the last of these – they like to be considered reliable. What then happens is they:

- start work on the activity as late as possible as more "urgent work" is needed first (it's just as well they put in a prudent estimate);
- work on other projects at the same time, juggling between the frantic exhortations of the different project managers and their line manager;
- have a meeting cancelled and so actually start work and finish it EARLY. But they don't tell anyone, just in case they are expected to be so fortunate next time, i.e., late hand-offs.

In short this one activity is protected by a safety margin which the team member's experience shows is needed. In fact, all activities have their in-built safety. The major drawback is, from a company viewpoint, it doesn't matter whether a particular activity is late or not. What matters is when the project as a whole delivers and benefits start to flow. Conceivably a project could be 95 percent on time and grossly late. Safety is not additive if it is wasted. Statistically, projects plans built this way are more likely to be late than on time. They will hardly ever be early!

It doesn't matter whether a particular activity is late or not. What matters is when the project as a whole delivers and benefits start to flow.

The critical chain – a solution?

In his book *Critical Chain*, Eli Goldratt proposes a solution to this problem. Rather than add safety into each activity, as described here, add it in a single lump at the end of the project (Figure 21.14). In practical terms he says:

- cut the durations given by the team in half;
- at the end of the project, add a safety time equal to half the sum of the safety times you trimmed.

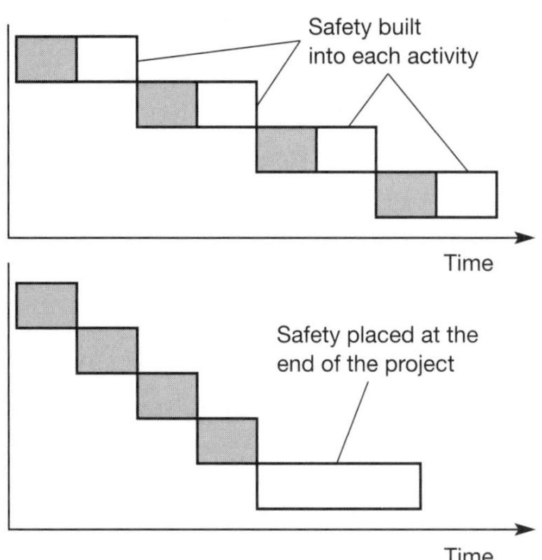

Figure 21.14 Putting safety where it counts
Removing the safety from each activity and placing it at the end of the project enables you to use it when you need to rather have it wasted by the student syndrome, multi-tasking, or late hand-offs.

In this way you can place the safety in a position where it really counts, at the end of the project, where you can use it.

In this way you can place the safety in a position where it really counts, at the end of the project, where you can use it.

However, you will have a number of challenges:

- Why should anyone accept you trimming their time estimates? Be very clear that you are adding half of it back at the end of the project.
- You'll need to be very used to activities being "late." In fact, "late" may no longer be a useful word and this may have implications on reporting.
- You will need to become used to tracking projects by measuring how much safety is consumed rather than by activity completion alone.
- You will need to resist senior managers cutting the safety from the end and thus dooming you to certain failure.

You will also need to encourage three behaviors (i.e. doing work at the last minute):

- Stop the student syndrome (i.e. doing work at the last minute).
- End multi-tasking.
- Hand over as soon as you have finished the activity.

END OF THE PROJECT?

The safety should not actually be put at the end of the project. It should be placed prior to the point in the project when you start earning benefits. For most projects following the project framework in Part Two, this is at the RFS Gate. The work beyond this, while essential, is not critical to immediate benefit realization.

This method relies on you producing a good network diagram and resourcing the schedule in a similar way to traditional critical path methods. It differs, however, in:

- choosing a critical route through the project which includes activities which are either on the critical path or which form a constraint due to resource contention;
- the choice made for activity duration and where any safety is placed.

As we have seen, safety is placed towards the end of the project. This is called a **project buffer**. However, if a project has a network with several feeders, you will need to protect the critical chain from delays in incoming activities. **Feeder buffers** are used for this. A project buffer protects the entire project from any delay in the critical chain activities. The feeder buffers protect the critical chain from delays on non-critical chain activities (Figure 21.15). The project manager uses a buffer report as the key monitoring tool (Figure 21.16).

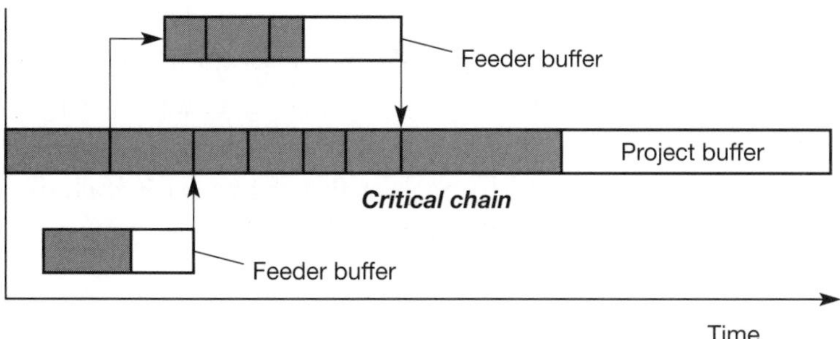

Figure 21.15 Project and feeder buffers
A project buffer protects the entire project from any delay in the critical chain activities. The feeder buffers protect the critical chain from delays on non-critical chain activities.

Triathlon project
Buffer report

Ref	Buffer name	Buffer end	Buffer length	% Buffer used	RAG
56	FB| Training agreed	2 Feb 2001	6 days	100%	Red
62	FB| Unit test 5	27 Feb 2001	8 days	73%	Red
109	PB| Ready for Service	21 May 2001	22 days	36%	Amber
87	FB| Acceptance	24 Apr 2001	12 days	31	Green
48	FB| Roll out hardware	15 Jan 2001	6 days	0%	Green
91	FB| Integration test	13 Mar 2001	10 days	0%	Green

Figure 21.16 A typical report using critical chain schedule management
Rather than concentrate on activity dates, the report shows each buffer by type (FB = feeder buffer; PB= project buffer), its length and how much has been used. From this, the project manager can pinpoint the parts of the schedule which require attention. A simple RAG status helps summarize the status e.g. Green more than 66% of buffer remaining; Red less than 33% of buffer remaining; Amber 33%–66% remaining.

Steps in the critical chain

1. Identify the constraint

The critical chain is the sequence of dependent events that prevent the project from being completed in a shorter interval, given finite resources. For a project, the critical chain is the constraint. Plan the network, resource the network, ensure that the activities have safety built in. Schedule the network with everything as late as possible.

2. Exploit the constraint

You need to ensure those activities on the critical chain have the most effort applied to them and that people hand off their work to the next person as soon as they are finished. Also, those taking over need to be warned and so be ready to accept the hand-off (this is called a resource buffer or flag). You also need to protect the entire critical chain with a safety margin (the project buffer) towards the end of the project.

3. Subordinate every other activity

Where other activities join the critical chain, protect them from delays by introducing feeder buffers.

4. Elevate the constraint

Apply more of the right resources so that key activities within the critical chain can be undertaken in parallel or in a shorter time.

5. Begin again?

Having elevated the constraint, it is probable that the critical chain will have moved. You could therefore start the process again. However, in practice this will not usually create significant gains for you unless you have created a very significant change. Generally, it is better to stick to the plan, the inefficiencies in realigning the project team to understand the new plan will far outweigh most other gains. The exeption to this is when you approaching the RED zone in your project buffer – you will need to take action and this could be one option to investigate.

The steps outlined are a central part of applying the Theory of Constraints (TOC). A full explanation of critical chain schedule management in both single and multiproject environments is to be found in *The Critical Chain* by Eli Goldratt.

Managing the Finances

The financial plan

Financial management controls

Estimating the costs

Authorization to spend funds

Recording actual costs and committed costs

Financial reporting

Just as a schedule plan is used as the baseline for measuring progress in terms of "time," the financial plan is the basis for measuring costs and financial benefits.

"We haven't the money, so we've got to think."
LORD RUTHERFORD, 1871–1937

- **Plan in summary for the full project.**
- **Base your costs on the same work breakdown as your schedule.**
- **Estimate in detail before you start work on the next stage.**
- **Once a budget is agreed, baseline it.**
- **Keep your eye on the future – forecast benefits and costs regularly.**

The financial plan

After managing time, management of the finances is the next most important and fundamental aspect of project management. Without a good schedule plan it is impossible to have a reliable financial plan. However, while the schedule is the aspect of a project most visible to outsiders, cost is often the most visible to insiders, such as your management team – sometimes it is the only aspect they see (or want to see!).

At a simple level, a financial plan will tell you:

- what each stage and work package in the project costs;
- who is accountable for those costs;
- the financial benefits deriving from the project;
- financial commitments made;
- cash flow;
- financial authorization given.

In addition, some companies also derive the net effect of the project on their balance sheet and profit and loss account.

Just as the schedule plan is used as the baseline for measuring progress in terms of "time," the financial plan is the basis for measuring costs and financial benefits. Many of the other principles I have already explained on schedule management are also applicable to the management of finances. Schedule and cost plans should share the same work breakdown structure (WBS) (see p. 133). By doing this you ensure that:

- accountability for both the schedule and cost resides with the same person;
- there is no overlap, hence double counting of costs;
- there is no "gap," i.e. missing costs.

In practice, you will develop the financial plan to a lesser level of work breakdown than you would the schedule plan.

The financial plan, like the schedule plan, is developed in summary for the full project and in detail for the next stage. There is little point in developing an "accurate" and detailed financial plan on the back of an unstable schedule plan. No matter to what level of granularity you take the calculations, they will be fundamentally inaccurate. You should take the level of accuracy and confidence forward with the schedule and related costs matching.

The costs are influenced by the following which you must take into account when drawing up your plan:

- the scope of the project;
- the approach you take to the project;
- the timescale to complete the project;
- the risks associated with the project.

Financial management controls

Financial management of a project comprises:

- estimating the costs and benefits (preparing the financial plan);
- obtaining authorization to spend funds;
- recording actual costs, committed costs;
- forecasting future costs and cash flow;
- reporting.

This is illustrated in Figure 22.1 and done in the context of the project control cycle. Tracking progress toward your objective is essential. If you don't do it you simply won't know how much the project will cost. The control cycle is exactly the same as that used for schedule management and is shown in Figure 22.2: once a financial plan has been agreed, it is necessary to measure progress against the plan, reforecast to the end, note any variances and take steps to bring the project back within budget if need be.

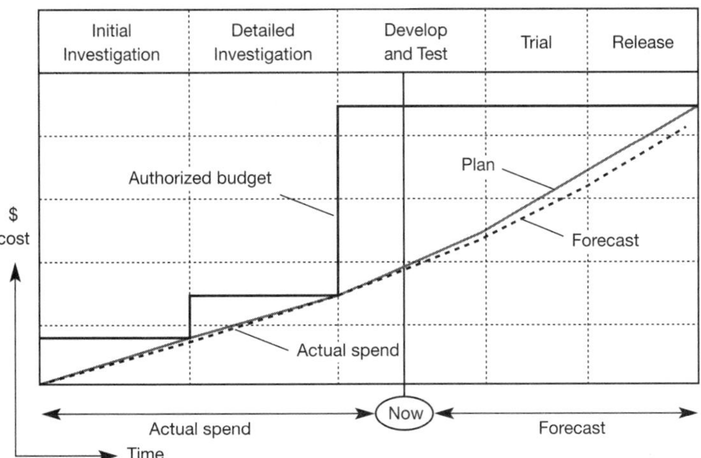

Figure 22.1 Project costs
This figure shows cumulative spend for a typical project, which includes the sum actually spent plus the forecast to completion. This can be compared against the plan (or budget). In the example, the project is forecast to be completed slightly below budget. Also shown is the authorized budget. This goes up in steps. At first a small amount of funding is given to undertake the initial investigation only. This is then increased, based on the results of the initial investigation, to cover the cost of the detailed investigation. Finally, a full business case provides the basis to authorize the remaining funds to complete the Development and Test, Trial, and Release Stages.

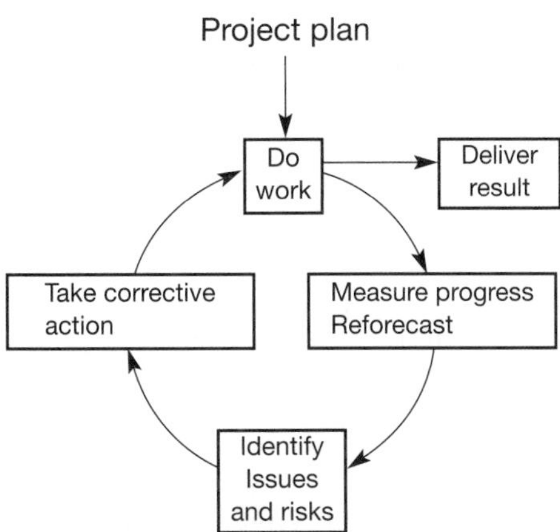

Figure 22.2 Project control cycle
The project control cycle comprises doing the work as set out in your plan, identifying any risks, opportunities or issues, and taking corrective action to keep the project on track. From time to time, results, in the form of deliverables, are generated.

BOOKKEEPING!

You should distinguish between the management of costs from a management accounting perspective and from a financial perspective The latter relates to "bookkeeping" and where the transactions appear in the formal accounts. In the management of projects, this is of little or no use. Managing the actual spend and cash flow provides far greater control.

Estimating the costs

"A little inaccuracy sometimes saves tons of explanation."

SAKI

Your cost estimates should be based on the work scope and schedule plan defined in the project definition. You should use the same work breakdown structure as the schedule plan and estimate to the same level of accuracy (summary versus detail).

Your estimate should be made up of:

- the cost of using your own employees;
- the cost of external purchases made as a result of the project.

The overall cost plan should be built up from three elements:

- the base estimate;
- scope reserve;
- contingency.

The base estimate is the total of costs for all the activities you have identified, including the cost of your own employees' time and all external purchases.

The scope reserve is an estimate of what else your experience and common sense tells you needs to be done, but has not yet been explicitly identified. This can be very large: for example, the scope reserve required in software projects can be as high as 50 percent of the base estimate.

The authority to use "scope reserve" is delegated to the project manager who should use formal change management to move funds from "scope reserve" to "base estimate."

Contingency is included in the estimate to take account of the unexpected, i.e. risks. It is ***not*** there to compensate for poor estimating. If a risk does not occur, the money put aside as contingency should not be spent. For this reason, the authorization for spending contingency rests with the project sponsor. Again, formal change management should be used to move the costs from "contingency" to "base estimate."

The proportion of your estimate divided between these elements will alter as the project moves through its life cycle stages. You should expect a higher proportion of scope reserve and contingency in the early stages than in the later stages. The accuracy of estimates also alters depending on the life cycle stage of the project. Figure 22.3 shows that in the earlier stages you expect the bulk of the cost to be "soft" except for the next stage. The next stage should be a "hard" estimate. This matches the principle of summary and detail planning. Summary plans tend to be soft, detail plans hard.

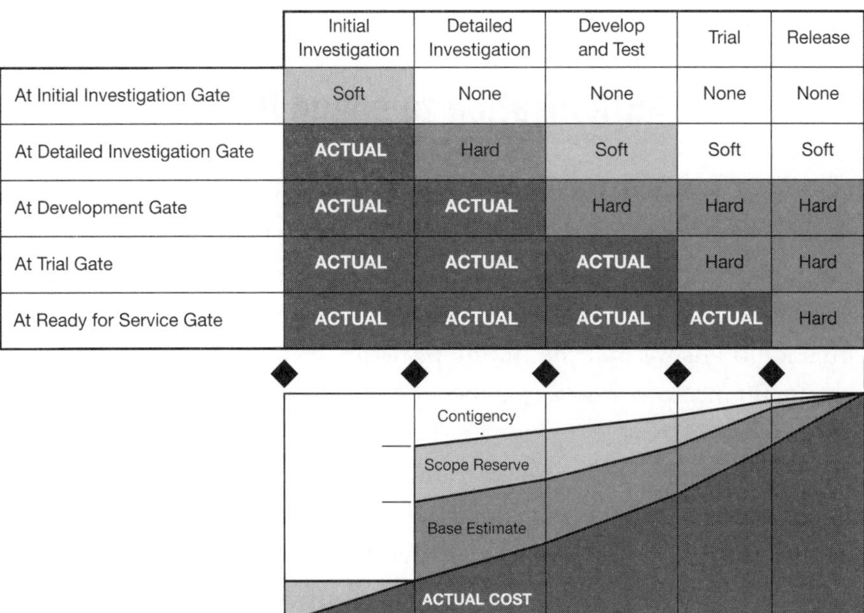

Figure 22.3 Estimating accuracy

In the earlier stages you should expect the bulk of the cost to be "soft" except for the next stage. The next stage should always be a "hard" estimate. This then alters as you roll through the life cycle stages of the project until you reach the start of the Develop and Test Stage, when your full estimate should be hard. The proportion of estimate distributed between contingency, scope reserve and base estimate also alters as you progress through the project. Toward the start you should expect a greater proportion of contingency and scope reserve than you would toward the end of the project.

A soft estimate is one to which a low level of confidence can be placed.

A hard estimate is one in which you have high confidence.

Regardless of whether your estimates are soft or hard it is important that you state any assumptions, constraints, or qualifications you have. These should be recorded in Part 1 of your initial or full business case (see p. 257).

Don't be driven solely by bookkeeping.

Authorization to spend funds

All companies have rules which prescribe who has the authority to spend money. If you are a subsidiary, such rules may be imposed on you by your parent company. Such processes can be onerous and time consuming if not matched to the project process you are using. As a minimum you should ensure that the timing of financial authorization, as laid out in your finance processes, matches the gates and review points in your project framework.

Each of the gates in the project framework offers the opportunity to allocate funds to the project. You should allocate a limited amount of money at the very start of the project (Initial Investigation Gate) to investigate the proposal so that an informed decision on whether to proceed can be made later at the Detailed Investigation Gate. Subsequently, further funds can be allocated on a stage by stage basis until the project is completed.

Alternatively, it may be more convenient to allocate funds for more than one stage, thus avoiding the need to obtain authorization a number of times and saving time on your projects. If this is done it is still part of the project sponsor's and project manager's accountabilities to undertake the gate reviews to check on the on-going viability of the project. Just because you've been given the money, it doesn't mean that you continue on blindly.

Just because you've been given the money, it doesn't mean that you continue on blindly.

For long stages it may be prudent to hold back full authorization and introduce intermediate review points, when the project is reassessed prior to further funding being authorized. Such points may conveniently be prior to major commitments such as letting a contract.

The project framework will work for whichever way you choose to arrange fund authorization. The key is to ensure that such authorization processes:

- are consistent with the principles of the project framework;
- concentrate only on substantive issues;
- are not too lengthy;
- do not duplicate other reviews or approvals.

The decision-making framework outlined in Chapter 3 (p. 53) poses three questions:

- Is the project on its own viable?
- What is its priority relative to other projects?
- Is funding available?

The control document (Business Case) used at the Detailed Investigation Gate and at the Development Gate is the same one for each question – you do not need to provide a different document for each question. This has two advantages:

- You do not need to write a number of different but similar documents.
- You can be sure that the answer to each question is based on compatible (the same!) information.

In certain circumstances you will be able to delegate all the decisions to the same person or group. This all depends on how you are organized. However, distinguishing between the key questions being addressed will help you concentrate on making the decision. For example, there is no point in prioritizing a project (question 2) which cannot stand up in its own right (question 1).

Throughout this book I have distinguished between **approval** and **authorization**. **Approval** is used when an individual accepts a deliverable as fit for purpose such that the project can continue. **Authorization** is used for allocating the funding and resources needed to carry on the project.

Approval in some form is always required before any funding is authorized. However, the converse is not true; just because authorization of funding has been given, it does not mean that *approval* has been given to complete the project. For example, you may have been given, at the detailed investigation gate, full funding to complete a simple project. Work during any of the subsequent stages may uncover issues which cannot be resolved. In which case approval at subsequent gates may not be forthcoming and the project should be terminated. In such circumstances the unused project funds should be returned to their source.

Authorization of funds is usually based on some form of investment appraisal. I do not intend to go into this in any detail. There are many books which deal with the plethora of methods which can be used. While each company will have its preferred approach, the following key points should be considered:

- Investment appraisal should be based on cash flow.
- Discounted cash flow techniques are the most favored.
- Use least cost development (lowest net present value, NPV) if you must do the project.
- Use internal rate of return for other projects.
- Concentrate on substantive elements only. If a figure is wrong and has no significant impact on the appraisal, don't waste time changing it.
- Use sensitivity analyses liberally – they give you more feel for the project than spurious accuracy in estimates.
- Use scenario analysis to check possible outcomes.

And finally:

- Do not consider financial criteria as sacrosanct. Many projects are worth doing for non-financial reasons because they support your basic strategic direction.
- Some things can't be reduced to financial terms. Just because you can't count them doesn't mean they don't count!

Some things can't be reduced to financial terms. Just because you can't count them doesn't mean they don't count!

Recording actual costs and committed costs

If you are to have any visibility over the cost of your project, you will need to have a system of capturing the costs, from wherever they originate in your company, and allocating them to the project. Similarly, you will need to have a method of capturing commitments relating to each project (see also p. 232). (Commitments are orders placed and hence the money, although not yet spent, is committed as part of an agreed contract.) If this is to have any meaning costs should be split into:

- money that stays within the company (e.g., cost of labor, drawing on internal stores);
- money that leaves the company (e.g., paid to contractors, consultants, suppliers).

In cash flow terms this distinction is critical as the former have already been "bought," but you have not yet decided what project or activity to apply them to. The latter are not spent at all if the project does not proceed.

In addition, it is essential to have the costs captured for each stage of the project so that you can confidently manage actual spend against authorized budget on a stage-by-stage basis. Many companies also capture costs at a lower level in the work breakdown structure than that.

WHAT IF I CANNOT MEASURE COSTS AS YOU SUGGEST?

Having a good project or matrix accounting system is vital if you are to reap the full benefits from business-driven project management. If you are unable to account for costs on a project-by-project basis you will have to rely on conventional cost center-based accounting or manual processes to maintain control: you have no alternative. This will mean that the balance of power remains firmly with the functions that own those cost centers and away from the project (see Figure 2.11).

It is still well worth using the tools, techniques, and guidance given in this book but you will be limited in the depth to which they can be applied and ingrained in your culture. No matter what you as managers say concerning the importance of projects, line managers will pay more attention to their cost center accounts simply because they are visible.

In Chapter 2, I pointed out that any process sits within a balance of systems, culture, and structure. You will therefore need to adapt how you apply the process to meet your system limitations while you drive towards the flexible culture you seek.

Financial reporting

The future is more important than the past. Any money you have already spent is lost and cannot be recovered. For this reason you must not only log what you have actually spent, but also forecast what is yet to be spent. The important figure to concentrate on is "what the project will have cost when it is completed."

To arrive at this figure you simply add any costs incurred to date to any cost you have yet to incur. The forecast is simply an estimate of what figures are going to appear on your project account during any particular period. So your forecasts must:

- use the same costing methods as actuals are measured;
- be forecast on at least a stage-by-stage basis;
- be timed to match the actuals (usually a monthly cut-off is used).

Figure 22.4 shows a typical report for building up the forecast.

Companies, by means of their accounting and operational systems, collect a considerable volume of data. Unless these data are converted into meaningful information, they are useless. Any reports you produce must be aimed at providing useful information which will act as a prompt for action. This implies the reports should be targeted at specific roles within your company. As the reports seek to promote action they should be:

- timely;
- as accurate as possible within those time constraints;
- forward looking.

Further, unless individuals involved in collecting the data gain some benefits themselves from them, the quality of the data will erode and the reporting will become useless.

Figure 22.5 is a typical financial report and tells you, in financial terms:

- what has been spent to date;
- the expected outcome for the project;
- the impact on the current financial year;
- the cost of work yet to be done.

In addition, you should have detailed reports which:

- list every transaction/purchase made on the project;
- detail time booked to the project.

Project: YT2Z/Triton 2000
Project Sponsor: Kelly, PJ
Project Manager: Jeffries J

PROJECT – ROLLING COST FORECAST

Period: 4 wks to 28 Sept 1997

$ 000s		ACTUAL TO DATE			COST FORECAST																
	F'cast Month	Month	Year	Life	Oct	Nov	Dec 97	Jan 98	Feb	Mar	Apr	May	Jun	Jul	Aug	Sep	Q3 O-D 98	Q4 J-M 99	Q5 A-J 99	Q6 J-S 99	Beyond	F'cast Outturn
Initial Investigation			53	53																		53
Time costs			50	50																		50
Purchases			3	3																		3
Detailed Investigation	6	7	30	55	6	7	5	5	18	10	4											110
Time costs	5	5	20	40	4	5	5	5	6	8	2											75
Purchases	1	2	10	15	2	2			12	2	2											35
Develop/Test												15	26	33	6	6	13					99
Time costs												5	25	32	5	5	12					84
Purchases												10	1	1	1	1	1					15
Trial																	13	11	2			26
Time costs																	12	10	2			24
Purchases																	1	1				2
Release																			22			22
Time costs																			18			18
Purchases																			4			4
TOTAL COST	6	7	83	108	6	7	5	5	18	10	4	15	26	33	6	6	26	11	24			310
Time cost	5	5	70	90	4	5	5	5	6	8	2	5	25	32	5	5	24	10	20			251
Purchases	1	2	13	18	2	2			12	2	2	10	1	1	1	1	2	1	4			59
CUMULATIVE COST					114	121	126	131	149	159	163	178	204	237	243	249	275	286	310	310	310	

Labor (time) costs are calculated from the "hours" forecast

For each stage you can see the labor and non-labor costs.

Total cost for the project

Total cost for the project

Figure 22.4 A typical report for building the forecast

This report gives a stage-by-stage summary of the total costs for a project and is ideally suited for building the forecast. For example, the time cost line could be derived from a manpower forecast such as that given in Figure 16.2.

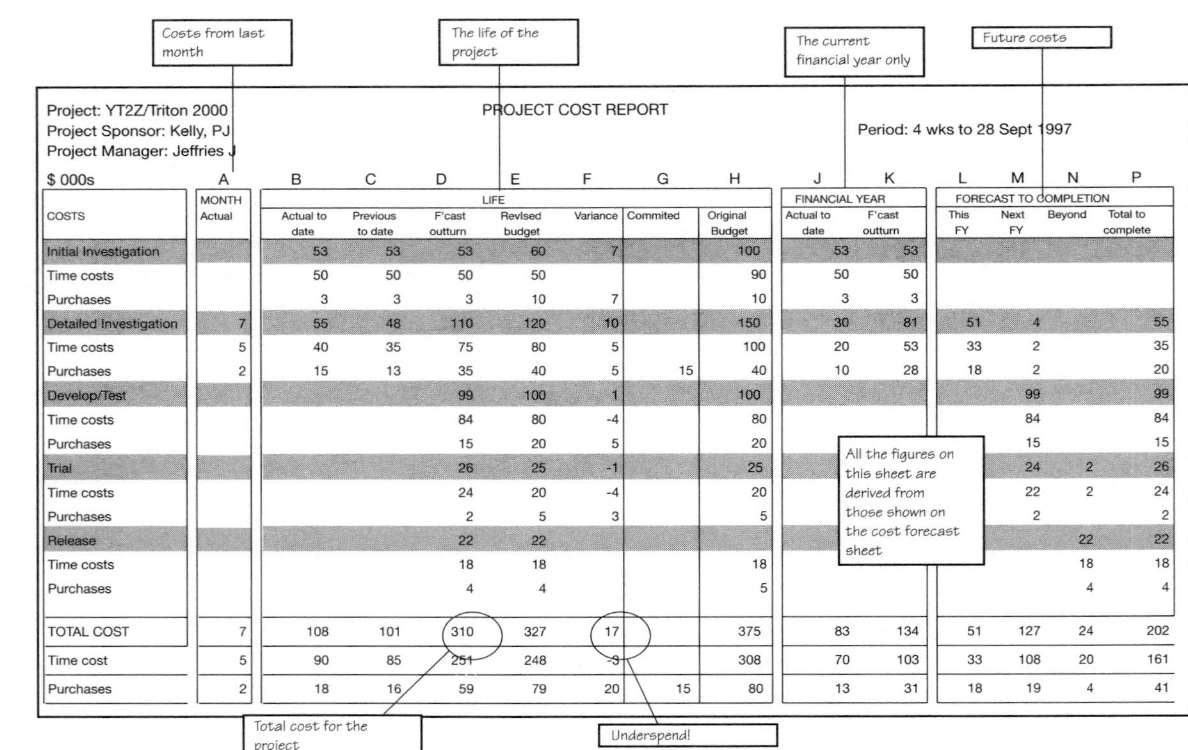

Project: YT2Z/Triton 2000
Project Sponsor: Kelly, PJ
Project Manager: Jeffries J

PROJECT COST REPORT

Period: 4 wks to 28 Sept 1997

$ 000s	A	B	C	D	E	F	G	H	J	K	L	M	N	P
	MONTH	LIFE							FINANCIAL YEAR		FORECAST TO COMPLETION			
COSTS	Actual	Actual to date	Previous to date	F'cast outturn	Revised budget	Variance	Commited	Original Budget	Actual to date	F'cast outturn	This FY	Next FY	Beyond	Total to complete
Initial Investigation		53	53	53	60	7		100	53	53				
Time costs		50	50	50	50			90	50	50				
Purchases		3	3	3	10	7		10	3	3				
Detailed Investigation	7	55	48	110	120	10		150	30	81	51	4		55
Time costs	5	40	35	75	80	5		100	20	53	33	2		35
Purchases	2	15	13	35	40	5	15	40	10	28	18	2		20
Develop/Test				99	100	1		100				99		99
Time costs				84	80	-4		80				84		84
Purchases				15	20	5		20				15		15
Trial				26	25	-1		25				24	2	26
Time costs				24	20	-4		20				22	2	24
Purchases				2	5	3		5				2		2
Release				22	22								22	22
Time costs				18	18			18					18	18
Purchases				4	4			5					4	4
TOTAL COST	7	108	101	310	327	17		375	83	134	51	127	24	202
Time cost	5	90	85	251	248	-3		308	70	103	33	108	20	161
Purchases	2	18	16	59	79	20	15	80	13	31	18	19	4	41

Figure 22.5 The financial report
A report such as this gives you, on a stage-by-stage basis, all the key financial information you should require: actual costs, forecast costs, commitments for the project as a whole and by financial year; it is derived directly from the data in Figure 22.3.

PROJECT FINANCES

1 Take the list of projects that your business is currently undertaking or, alternatively, the output from Project Workout 3.1.

2 Choose any five projects which are in the Develop and Test Stage or beyond.

3 Ask each of the following people questions (a) to (e):

- the finance manager;
- project sponsor;
- project manager.

(a) For both time costs and purchases, provide, for the project as a whole, as at the close of the last month's accounting period:

- – costs spent to date;
- – costs spent this financial year;
- – estimated cost at completion;
- – agreed budget, when the project was authorized.

(b) Answer question (a) for the current work stage.

(c) How are "time costs" calculated?

(d) Where were these data obtained from?

(e) State how easy or how difficult the information was to obtain.

4 Consider the replies. How long did it take for them to be compiled? Do they give the same information? What parts are missing? Were the same sources for the data used? If there is great consistency, fine. If not, look behind the replies. For example, if it takes a long while to compile the information or some is missing, can you reasonably expect your Project Managers to work within their budgets? Is it acceptable to make them "fly blind" without adequate instruments?

Managing What Might Go Wrong (or Right)

Risks and Opportunities

Considering possible risks and opportunities

Addressing risk at the start of the project

Addressing opportunities at the start of the project

Monitoring once the project is in progress

Tips on using the risk and opportunity log

More sophisticated risk evaluation techniques

Taking active steps to reduce the possible effects of risks is not indicative of pessimism, but is a positive indication of good project management.

"It is certain because it is impossible."

TERTULLIAN, c AD160–225

- **Risk management starts when the project starts.**
- **Reduce the likelihood of threats materializing.**
- **Contingency plan in the event that threats do materialize.**
- **Focus on the "big ones," but don't lose sight of the others.**
- **Look for opportunities to increase benefits, but not at the cost of increasing risk.**
- **Plan for the most likely opportunities**

Considering possible risks and opportunities

Risk is any potential threat or occurrence which may prevent you from achieving your defined business objectives. It may affect timescale, cost, quality, or benefits. All projects are exposed to risk in some form but the extent of this will vary considerably.

Opportunity is the possibility that your project may go better than you planned.

Figure 23.1 shows how risk and opportunity sit within the context of other project controls; a risk will become an issue if the event occurs. Issues can be resolved either within the scope of the project as currently defined or via a change to the project. An opportunity is similar to a risk but has a potentially beneficial impact rather than a negative impact. Like risk, an opportunity will become an issue if the event occurs. Figure 23.2 also shows that, once the project is well under way, the risk, or "down side" is usually bigger than any "up side" opportunities.

The purpose of risk and opportunity management is to ensure that:

- risks and opportunities on projects are identified and evaluated in a consistent way;
- risks to the project's success are recognized and addressed and significant opportunities are exploited without undue delay.

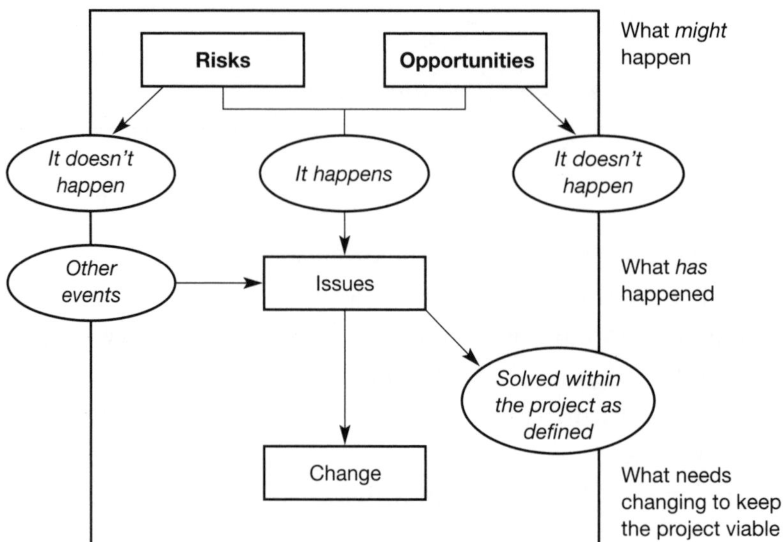

Figure 23.1 Risks, opportunities, issues, and change
A **risk** or **opportunity** will become an **issue** if the event occurs. Issues can be resolved either within the scope of the project as currently defined or via a **change** to the project.

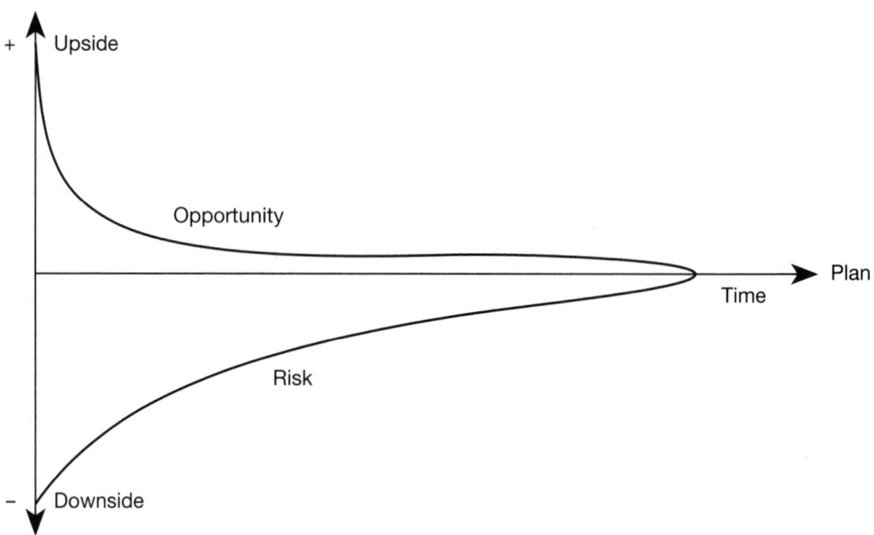

Figure 23.2 Upside and downsides to a project
Once the project is well under way, the risk, or "downside" is usually bigger than any upside opportunities. This is because people are usually optimistic.

You cannot use risk management to eliminate risk altogether, but by careful planning, you may be able to avoid it in some instances or minimize the disruption in the event of it happening in others. But what if identified risks do not materialize? What if a new approach (opportunity!) comes about which will further your business objectives better than planned? You have two options:

- You can keep to the original plan, as something quite unexpected may still go wrong and eat into the time and money you've saved.
- You can build the new found opportunity into the project and "mine it" for all it's worth.

Traditionally, the former approach is the more prudent but that does not mean it makes the most business sense in all cases.

Addressing risk at the start of the project

You should address risk when the project is first being set up during the Initial Investigation Stage. Risk is an important section within the project definition; when a project sponsor approves a project he/she does so in full knowledge of the stated risks, accepting the consequences should things go wrong.

When a project sponsor approves a project he/she does so in full knowledge of the stated risks, accepting the consequences should things go wrong.

The steps are:

- Brainstorm all the risks that may jeopardize the success of the project. Remember to include those which are under the control of the project team (e.g., completeness of project scope, quality of technical solutions, competence of project team) as well as those which are largely outside the control of the team (e.g., legislative changes, competitor activity, economic climate).
- Review each risk in turn:
  — assess the likelihood of the risk occurring;
  — assess the severity of the impact on the project if it occurs.
- Use a risk matrix such as the one that follows to determine the "risk category" (high, medium, low).
- For high risks, consider ways of reducing the impact or prepare a contingency plan.

Risk matrix	*Likelihood of event occurring*			
Severity of impact	*Unlikely* *<15%*	*Fairly likely*	*Very likely*	*Almost certain* *>85%*
1 Minor impact on project schedule or cost. No impact on benefits	Low	Low	Medium	Medium
2 Major impact on project schedule or cost. Minor impact on benefits	Medium	Medium	Medium	High
3 Major impact on project schedule or cost. Major impact on benefits	Medium	Medium	High	High

- For medium risks, prepare a contingency plan.
- For low risks, take no immediate action but continue to monitor them – they may become more significant.

Taking active steps to reduce the possible effects of risks is not indicative of pessimism, but is a positive indication of good project management.

Many possible options exist for addressing risk, including:

Prevention – where countermeasures are put in place either to stop the threat or problem occurring or prevent its having any impact.
Reduction – where the actions either reduce the likelihood of the risk occurring or limit the impact on the project to acceptable levels.
Transference – a specialist form of risk reduction where the impact of the risk is transferred to a third party such as a contractor or insurance company.
Contingency – where actions are planned or organized which will come into force as and when the risk occurs.
Acceptance – where the company decides to go ahead and accept the possibility that the risk might occur and is willing to accept the consequences.

Consider also:

- bringing risky activities forward in the schedule to reduce the impact on the project outcome if they are delayed;
- modifying the project requirement to reduce aspects with inherently high risk, e.g., new, leading edge technologies;

- allowing appropriate time and cost contingencies;
- using prototypes and pilots to test the viability of new approaches.

A project should not usually contain any high risks when first planned. If it does, the project plan should be reconsidered to lower the overall risk by using an alternative approach or by introducing ways of reducing the likely impact.

> ***A project should not usually contain any high risks when first planned. If it does, the project plan should be reconsidered to lower the overall risk.***

A convenient way of recording risk is in the form of a "log" shown in Figure 23.3.

BEWARE THE DIFFICULTIES OF "RISK CONVERSATIONS"

To raise the subject of risk is not admitting failure. If the culture in your organization is to see the discussion of risk as a failure, you must change it fast. Driving risk "underground" is not the way to deal with it. If you are truly in control, there is every benefit in sharing risks and understanding the measures you can take to manage them.

Things still go wrong. Risk management is not infallible. Something may still happen which will destroy your project. For instance, irrational behavior by individuals in your company, or from competitors, or government cannot be predicted. Emotional actions and behaviors are often the most difficult to deal with.

Risk Log

Ref No	Description of Risk	Date Raised	Probability of occurrence	Severity	Risk Category	Risk Management: Action	by
1	Seigathon may launch a new product at the same target market.	2/3/97	Unlikely	3	Medium	Monitor Seigathon market activity.	G Smith
2	The product launch relies on Project X being delivered. There is a risk that this will be delayed.	13/4/97	Unlikely	2	Medium	Monitor Project X progress.	F Kent
3	The contractor for the project is unable to deliver on time due to lack of resources and other commercial commitments.	20/6/97	Very Likely	2	Medium	Build relationship with contractor Find alternative supplier. Build contingency time into schedule	G Smith
4	The warehouse management system release will be delayed beyond the planned start of testing.	29/6/97	Certain	2	High	Provide paper based system and procedures during initial testing. (see issue log)	J Arnold
5	The credit control system release will be delayed beyond the planned start of testing.	29/6/97	Very likely	2	High	Build 3 months contingency into the schedule	F Kent

Figure 23.3 A typical risk log

A risk log is used to record the risk, the date it was recognized, its category, and risk management action (with accountability).

IDENTIFYING RISKS – 1

"If a man begin with certainties, he shall end in doubt; but if he will be content to begin with doubts, he shall end in certainties."
FRANCIS BACON, 1561–1626

This workout should be done with the project team.

1 Use brainstorming or other creative methods to generate as many possible risks as you can. You should include anything that anyone wishes to raise. By involving the team you will start to develop an idea of where their concerns lie and what confidence they have in other team members or departments. In addition, group members will hear one another's concerns and this also helps to form the team. Do not let anyone criticize or comment on any risk raised at this stage – just capture thoughts. Hint: look at any assumptions made and at any constraints (as listed in the project definition).

2 Write each risk on a Post-It Note as it is called out; ask for clarification if the risk is not understood but otherwise do not allow comments.

3 Put each Post-It Note on a board where all can see them. Carry on generating risks until the team have no more to offer.

4 By inspection, cluster the risks into similar groups. This may be around technologies, people, legal, employee relations, funding, etc. Choose any clusters that "fit" the situation.

5 Rationalize the risks, combining some, clarifying others; number each risk sequentially.

6 Evaluate each risk using the matrix on p. 000 and plot all medium and high risks onto a flip chart.

7 Take time for the team to review the output so far. Are there any themes noticeable in the risks or in the way they are clustered. Are there any particular aspects of the project which appear to be problematic?

8 Begin with the high risks: start generating possible ways of dealing with them. Allow all options to be raised. Do not evaluate, just capture the possible risk management actions for later evaluation.

9 Evaluate and agree which risk-management options should be followed and who is accountable for managing each particular risk.

Task – strive to eliminate any high risks.

- Avoid those risks you can, by using a different approach to the project for example.
- Build investigative work into your plan to drive out risks which result from having insufficient information.
- Capture your risks in a log (similar to Figure 23.3).

23.2

IDENTIFYING RISKS – 2

This workout should be done with the project team.

1 Take the output from Project Workout 21.2 (the Post-It Notes network diagram) and display it on a wall.

2 Start at the first Post-It Note and ask:

   - What can go wrong with this?
   - How likely is that to happen?
   - What effect will that have on the timescale?

3 Use the risk matrix to evaluate the risk category. Using a different colored Post-It Note, mark up the risk and its category adjacent to the relevant part of the network.

4 Repeat this until every Post-It Note in the network has been evaluated.

5 Take time for the team to review the output so far. Are there any themes or noticeable streams of the project which appear to be problematic?

6 Begin with the high risks: start generating possible ways of dealing with them. Allow all options to be raised. Do not evaluate, just capture the possible risk management actions for later evaluation.

9 Evaluate and agree which risk-management options should be followed and who is accountable for managing each particular risk.

Task – strive to eliminate any high risks.

- Look for alternative way of approaching the work which avoids sequences of risks, creates contingency time, or brings risky elements forward.

- Replan the project around these risks putting your contingency (safety) where it counts.
- Capture your risks in a risk log (similar to Figure 23.3).

Addressing opportunities at the start of the project

You should address opportunities when the project is first being set up during the Initial Investigation Stage. Like "risk," opportunities may influence your whole project strategy and plan. You should:

Like "risk," opportunities may influence your whole project strategy and plan.

- brainstorm all the opportunities that may potentially enhance the success of the project (some of these will be the converse of risks you have already identified).
- review each opportunity in turn:
  — assess the likelihood of each occurring;
  — assess the impact on the project if it occurs .
- use an opportunity matrix, such as the one that follows, to determine the "opportunity category" (major, medium, minor).

Opportunity matrix	*Likelihood of event occurring*			
Impact	*Unlikely* *<15%*	*Fairly likely*	*Very likely*	*Almost certain* *>85%*
1 Minor impact on project schedule or cost. No impact on benefits	Minor	Minor	Medium	Medium
2 Major impact on project schedule or cost. Minor impact on benefits	Medium	Medium	Medium	Major
3 Major impact on project schedule or cost. Major impact on benefits	Medium	Medium	Major	Major

- For major opportunities, consider amending your baseline plan to build the opportunity in from the start.
- For medium opportunities, prepare an outline contingency plan you could use should it happen.
- For minor opportunities, take no immediate action; stay with your current plan.

There are many possible options for you to exploit, examples include:

- modifying the project timescale such that it is possible to bring the release date, and hence benefits, forward should a risky aspect of the project proceed without undue problems;
- using time and money saved to incorporate outputs which originally had to be discarded (but make sure these really add benefit rather than are "nice to have").

A convenient way of presenting opportunities is in the form of a "log", similar to the risk log shown in Figure 23.3. This is very similar to the risk log and, in practice you may choose to use the same log for both, marking them as a risk or opportunity, as appropriate.

23.3

OPPORTUNITY – 1

"Probable impossibilities are to be preferred to improbable possibilities."
ARISTOTLE, 384–322 BC

This workout should be done with the project team. Perhaps do this after the risk workout (Project Workout 23.1) to put a more positive light on the project.

Follow the instructions for Workout 23.1, but instead of concentrating on risks, look for opportunities.

Task – build all major opportunities into the base plan.

- Set yourself up to exploit opportunities by designing the project strategy and approach accordingly without compromising your risk-management strategy!
- Build into your plan investigative work to convert medium opportunities into major ones.
- Capture your opportunities in a log (similar to Figure 23.3).

OPPORTUNITY – 2

This workout should be done with the project team. Follow the instructions for Workout 23.2, but instead of concentrating on risks, look for opportunities.

Task – strive to exploit major opportunities.

- Look for alternative sequencing of the work which allows you exploit opportunities, should they arise, without compromising your risk-management strategy!
- Replan the project around these opportunities.
- Capture your opportunities in an log (similar to Figure 23.3).

A company had to upgrade some security features of its internal data network. This involved the upgrading of the software on two major associated computer systems as well as changes to a number of nodes within the network itself. Unfortunately, the upgrading of one computer system was seen as very risky due to its inherent instability and the number of other changes being made to it at the same time. The schedule showed a 7-month duration for the remainder of the project with the critical path passing through the problem software upgrade. No work on the network codes could be started until this upgrade was done.

By following a sequence such as in Project Workouts 23.1 and 23.2 the project team identified that they could delink the network node work from the problematic software upgrade and allow it to proceed immediately (this involved a change to the upgrade specification in the second computer system). This simple change in the project approach resulted in the schedule plan of seven months having three months float in it; ample time to investigate and solve any problems on the computer system or to implement a manual alternative.

This exercise showed how team working produced a better result than any individual could – there was no one person who had the technical knowledge to devise the adopted solution. Further, the team formed a bond of understanding that stayed with them throughout the remainder of the project.

Monitoring once the project is in progress

Once the project has started, you should:

- Maintain a log of the risks and opportunities similar to the example given in Figure 23.3.
- Regularly monitor them with the team and reassess the likelihood of occurrence and seriousness of impact.
- Log, categorize, and report new risks and opportunities together with the action being taken to deal with them.
- Report new, high risks in the regular project progress report (see Chapter 19). And highlight potential, significant opportunities.

During the course of a project, either of the following can happen:

1. A risk or opportunity "event" occurs – this should be noted in the "action" column and a corresponding entry made on the issues log.
2. A risk or opportunity event is passed, i.e., the project proceeds and the event does not occur. The category should be recorded as "none."

In both cases, the log entry is "closed" and the line in the log should be shaded to show that the event no longer requires management attention.

Expect some things to go better than you expected.

A major change project undertaken by a company relied on completing a contract with a third party for out-sourcing a part of their operations. The risk of being unable to sign a mutually beneficial contract was considered highly unlikely but it was considered that negotiations could be very long, at least four to six months.

The preparatory work for hand-over to the out-source company was expected to take two months and could take place in parallel with negotiations. Rather than delay starting this preparatory work, it was decided to proceed with it immediately so in the event of the contract being signed early the company would be in a position to bring forward the implementation date (Figure 23.4).

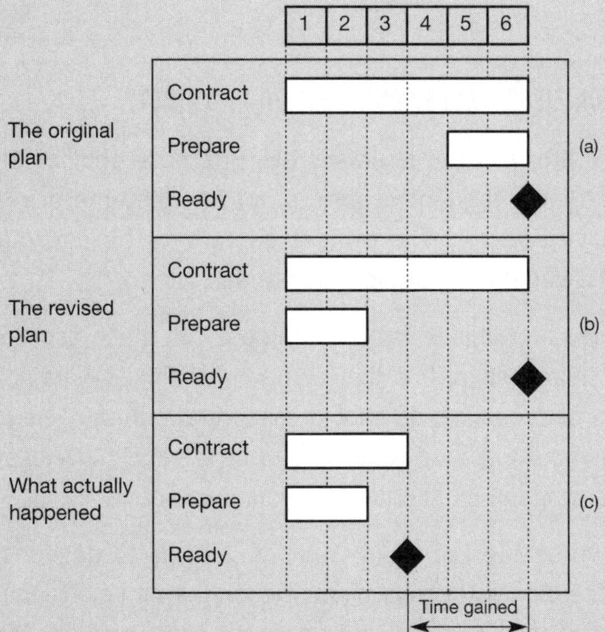

Figure 23.4 The effect of planning to create your own luck

In the original plan, (a), work was not to start on preparation until the latest possible time in order to meet the required date. However, there was a possibility that the contract could be signed early and there was little risk of failing to sign. In plan (b) the preparatory work started as soon as possible. In fact, the situation that happened is represented by (c). The contract was signed early and the company was in a position to reap the rewards earlier.

Tips on using the risk and opportunity log

- Phrase each to fit the sentence "There is a risk (or opportunity) on this project that ..."
- Only have one risk or opportunity per "line" – grouping can make managing them difficult.
- Do not add to existing entries.
- Cross-reference to the issues log when an event "happens."
- Keep all risks and opportunities visible, even those which have been passed or have happened. This acts as a check in case others' perception is different. Shading passed risks and opportunities makes it clear which are live and which are not.

RISK? OPPORTUNITIES? ISSUES? BUT WHAT DO I DO FIRST?

In managing a project you will always have to make choices about where to apply your time. Frequently there is not enough time or resources to manage every aspect of the project as fully or as rigorously as the "theory" or the benefit of hindsight demands.

Having a framework within which you can deal with these aspects of project management helps ensure that they all have visibility and are not forgotten. When under time pressure you should concentrate on the "issues" as they are now "facts on the ground" and have to be dealt with. Delegate as many as you can, leaving the most critical for your own attention.

Next apply yourself to the risks. Your mission is to deliver the project according to the plan and keeping your eye on the future. Preempting future issues is part of that. Remember some risks are potentially more dangerous than issues. They are definitely more dangerous than opportunities.

Finally, look for the opportunities.

If, as part of the Initial and Detailed Investigation Stages, you have promoted a dialog on risks and opportunities within your team (for example, by doing the workout exercises), the team itself will intuitively scan the environment for risks and opportunities on your behalf, thus sharing the workload. After all, what is a team for!

More sophisticated risk evaluation techniques

The basic approach to risk described so far in this chapter can be used by any person on any project. It requires no special tools, technical or statistical knowledge. In many cases it is the most powerful and effective approach, relying on the creativity and common sense of the team.

Nevertheless, there are occasions where other tools and techniques are very valuable for supplementing intuitive analyses.

Sensitivity and scenario analysis

So far we have looked at risk as a black and white occurrence. Either it happens or it doesn't. In practice, however, there may be a range of outcomes, with impacts ranging from the disastrously negative to the unbelievably positive. You can identify such items easily; these are your assumptions. All assumptions are risks and should be treated as such. Examples are market rates, customer usage, plant efficiency, inflation, customer demand, cost forecasts and timing.

Sensitivity analysis is used to review the impact on the project of the possible range of values for each assumption made. In this way, you will be able to decide which assumptions are substantive to the case and need to be addressed further. The steps are:

1 identify your assumptions;
2 decide on a range of values for each assumption;
3 rework your calculations (business model), using these values to see the effect on project viability on variations to that particular assumption;
4 identify those assumptions which have most impact and log them as risks;
5 decide on your response to these risks.

For example, in the following table, we see the project viability is more sensitive to percentage moves in tariff than costs.

Assumption		*–20%*	*–10%*	*+10%*	*+20%*
Change in cost	NPV ($) IRR	215k 14%	416k 32%	764k 52%	987k 67%
Change in tariff	NPV ($) IRR	10k 9%	234k 17%	865k 16%	1234k 102%

Scenario analysis takes sensitivity analysis a step further by looking at alternative futures. A scenario comprises a set of **compatible** assumptions, chosen from the risk and sensitivity analysis, which describes the future. This often requires a model to be built so that the different assumptions can be used consistently. e.g., fewer customers may lead not only to less revenue, but also less cost of sales, while fixed costs may remain the same. Three scenarios should be investigated:

1 optimistic;
2 most likely;
3 pessimistic.

Thus for a pessimistic scenario you may assume a late project completion date with a cost overrun with slower customer take-up and usage, with more severe downward price pressures than anticipated. This can be tabulated, for example:

Parameter	*Pessimistic*	*Most likely*	*Optimistic*
Timing of RFS	2 months late	On time	2 weeks early
IT cost	$450k	$340k	£320k
Customer take-up	+5%	+12%	+15%
Usage	35 minutes/day	50 minutes/day	65 minutes/day
Tariff erosion	–15% annual	–5% annual	–5% annual
IRR %	–6%	40%	87%
NPV ($k)	–1767	2990	3875
Payback	No payback	3 years	2 years

As for sensitivity analysis, the aim is to provide decision makers with an objective view of what may be the consequences of continuing the project thus enabling them to balance the possible opportunities (up side) with the associated risks (down side).

Risk simulation

Risk simulation relies on the application of a range of durations and costs associated with a particular element in a project network. This is input as:

- the lowest likely value;
- the most likely value;
- the highest probable value.

The simulation software will then analyze the network and calculate a range of likely costs and durations with a set of probabilities. The results are plotted on a chart such as that shown in Figure 23.5.

Software for critical chain scheduling (see p. 329) also includes risk and probability distributions to enable a rigorous plan to be built. Tested and rolled out.

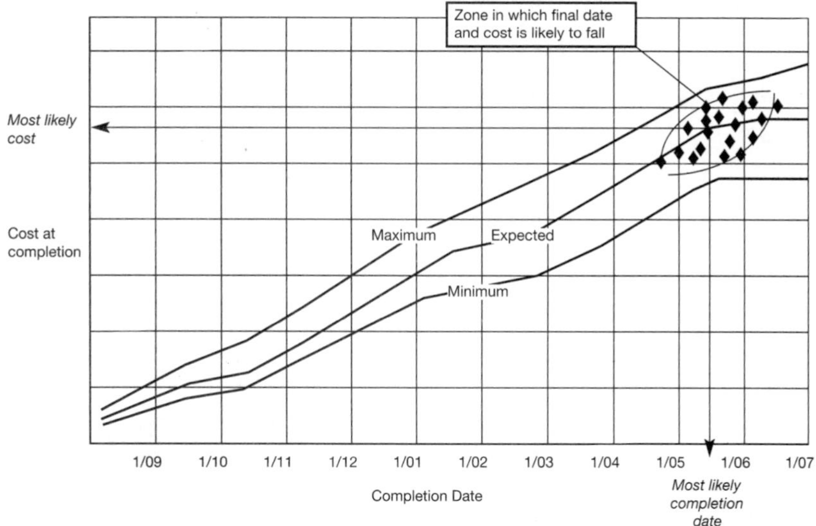

Figure 23.5 A typical output from a Monte Carlo risk simulation
The output shows the likely cost/time envelope outcomes from the project based on a simulation.

At the end of the 1990s a famous American hamburger restaurant chain decided to celebrate its birthday by providing cut-price offers on its leading product. The PR behind the event was superb. Not only did the advertising reach its target but also many news and magazine channels on radio and television as well as the press covered the forthcoming event. As it happened the consumer demand far outstripped supply to such an extent that many restaurants closed early and thousands of people had to be turned away. The event was dubbed by the press as "McBungle." Was this a success? True, the advertising was effective, but what was the real cost to the company as its supply chain failed and its customers became angry? What of the financial cost in having to provide about four times as many cut-price meals as expected? What of the cost in lost revenue as the irate customers chose to use a competitor in future?

- How do you think the marketing executives viewed this campaign?
- How do you think the operations executives viewed the campaign?
- What actions could they have taken to avoid the situation?

And remember, before you look at this with the benefit of hindsight, maybe they did do all the right things but Murphy's Law proved too strong an adversary!

Ignore risks at your peril!

Managing What Has Gone Wrong (or Right!)

Issues

What do we mean by "issues?"

When an issue is identified

Tips on using the issues log

*An issue is something that **has** happened and either threatens or enhances the success of the project. Compare this to a risk or opportunity which are things that **might** happen.*

"There are no hopeless situations: there are only men who have grown hopeless about them."

CLAIRE BOOTH LUCE

- **Be open about issues within your team – declare them.**
- **Never "sit" on an issue – escalate it if you can't deal with it.**
- **Use the team to resolve the tricky issues.**

What do we mean by "issues?"

Issues management is the process for recording and handling any event or problem which either threatens the success of a project or represents an opportunity to be exploited. Figure 24.1 shows the context: an issue occurs either as a result of an identified risk or opportunity event occurring or as a result of some unexpected event. An issue can either be dealt with within the project, as defined, or will require a change in order to keep the project viable. Examples of issues are:

Problem issues:

- the late delivery of a critical deliverable;
- a reported lack of confidence by users;
- a lack of resources to carry out the work;
- the late sign-off of a critical document or deliverable;
- a reported deviation of a deliverable from its specification;
- a request for additional functionality;
- a recognized omission from the project scope.

Opportunity issues:

- a contract negotiation is concluded early;
- a breakthrough on a new technology cuts months off the development time;
- a new, cheaper source of raw materials is located;

- the enrollment of key stakeholders happens sooner than planned;
- a contract tender comes in significantly less than the pre-tender estimate.

An issue is something that *has* happened and either threatens or enhances the success of the project. Compare this to a risk or opportunity which are things that *might* happen.

When talking to people be careful, as "issue" can also mean a "topic" or an "important point": unless you are both tuned to the same definition you may find your conversations confusing!

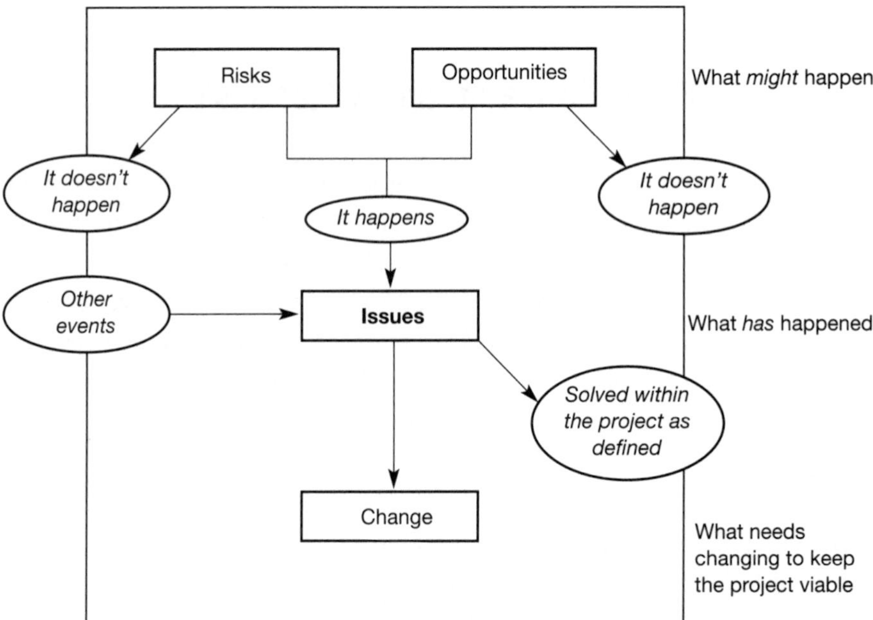

Figure 24.1 Risks, opportunity, issues, and change
An **issue** occurs either as a result of an identified **risk** or **opportunity** event occurring, or as a result of some other unexpected event. An issue can either be dealt with within the project, as defined, or will require a change in order to keep the project viable.

When an issue is identified

When an issue is identified, you should:

- Record in the issues log any issue which has been drawn to your attention for resolution. (An example issues log is in Figure 24.2.) You should:

— describe the issue;
— record who brought it up and when (date);
— rate the issue priority (1 (critical) to 4 (minor impact)).

- Decide and agree who will be accountable for managing the issue's resolution. If the issue cannot be dealt with by the project team you should refer outside the team to a person who has the necessary level of knowledge and/or authority to deal with it (to the project sponsor or project board for example). You should record, in the log:

  — the name of the person responsible for managing the resolution of the issue;
  — the date by which resolution of the issue is expected.

- Regularly update the progress commentary on the log.
- Once the issue has been resolved, record the method and date of resolution in the log. The line can then be shaded to show that the issue no longer requires attention. If the issue resolution requires an amendment to the project scope (deliverables), cost, timescales or benefits, it should be handled through the change management process (Chapter 25).
- Report new, significant issues in the regular project progress report (see Chapter 19).

Make sure you record issues, even if you have no time to address them or can not yet find a person to manage the resolution. Just making them visible is sometimes enough to start resolving them.

You should expect a large number of issues to be raised at the start of the project or at the start of a new stage within the project. These will mainly be from people seeking clarification that aspects of the project they are concerned with have been covered. This is a rich source of feedback on stakeholder concerns as well as a check on completeness of the project plan.

Make sure you record issues, even if you have no time to address them or cannot yet find a person to manage the resolution. Just making them visible is sometimes enough to start resolving them (see case study). Also, many issues cannot be resolved on their own simply because they do not reach the core problem; they are merely symptoms. Once other "symptoms" appear as issues it is possible to start making connections which can help identify the core problem. Once this is solved a number of issues can be struck off in one go.

Issues Log

1997 1 July

Ref	Description of issue	Date raised	Raised by (name)	Issue owner	Resolution date	Priority (1,2,3,4)	Comment: progress: resolution
1	The mobilisation of the 24th Legion has been delayed and it will not be ready for the start of the campaign. How can we ensure the campaign progresses on time and victory is not delayed?	1/4/97	Marcus	Lucius	2/6/97	2	From Risk 4: delay demobilization of the 19th Legion veterans
2	No time has been allocated for training recruits. How can we ensure the campaign is launched and there are sufficient legionnaires trained to take part?	5/4/97	Flavius	Keaso	15/7/97	1	
3	There is a general lack of awareness of what this campaign will do for the Roman Empire. How can we address this?	5/4/97	Trajan	Lucius	15/4/97	3	Provide an "update" in the Senate and bribe senators to vote additional funds to the campaign
4							

Priority
1: Critical – needs escalation
2: Major impact – can be handled by team
3: Medium impact
4: Minor impact

Figure 24.2 Typical issues log
The issues log contains the list of all the "happenings" which either threaten the success of the project or which may lead to an opportunity. It comprises a description of the issue, the date it was raised, who it was raised by, the name of the person accountable for resolving it, and a target date for resolution. The final column contains notes to help the reader understand that current situation or record how the issue was resolved.

A project manager was heard to say to another, after running an issues log for some months:

"This is my magic list. All I do is list the problems on it, share them with my team and . . . magic! They get resolved!"

"I don't believe you; it looks like a load of bureaucratic nonsense to me."

"Honestly. I have to work on some of the key ones quite hard myself, but many others are sorted out by the team without me. They see them written there and just act on them if they can. It's all a matter of creating your own luck."

The power of the issues log is related to its accessibility. If it is kept secret, no one will know what the problems are and hence will not be able to help. This openness does, however, carry its own risks. If seen by an uninformed stakeholder, an issues log can look like a negative and damning document for the project. You should, therefore, be very careful how you write up the issues and how you circulate or communicate them. Avoid being personal and concentrate on problems: the old saying "be tough on the problem, not on the people" is very pertinent here.

This openness does, however, carry its own risks. When seen by an uninformed stakeholder, an issues log can look like a negative and damning document for the project. You should, therefore, be very careful how you write up the issues and how you circulate or communicate it.

"I know that's a secret for it's whispered everywhere."
WILLIAM CONGREVE, 1670–1729

Murphy will strike, so learn how to handle it!

Tips on using the issues log

- Phrase the issue as a question; this is more powerful in helping to focus on a solution.
- Have only one issue per "line." Grouping a number of issues together (even if related) makes identification of a solution difficult.
- Do not add to existing issues or they will never be resolved; record a new issue if a different facet becomes apparent.
- Make cross-references between issues or refer back to the risk or opportunity logs (by a note in the "comment" column) if this is helpful.
- Keep all issues visible, even those which have been resolved, as this shows achievement in overcoming problems and exploiting opportunities. It also acts as a check in case the same issue resurfaces later. Shading completed issues makes it clear which are live and which are resolved.
- If the resolution of the issue requires a project "change," put a cross reference to the change log in the resolution column.
- Be open with your issues log; share it with the project team and others on whom the project will have an impact.

A manufacturing company was relocating its works. It was intended that the existing plant would be moved and operated in the new location. After the site was acquired and construction was almost completed an issue was raised under European legislation that the old plant would not be allowed to run in the new location. It was deemed to be a new site and hence all plant had to conform to new emission restrictions immediately.

An issue was logged and immediately escalated to the project sponsor as the project manager had no knowledge or power to deal with this. The project sponsor quickly circulated the problem among various contacts within the company. Very soon a specialist unit was identified in the head office that was able to review the issue. It found that the issue was a misinterpretation of the legislation and was not valid. The issue was potentially a show stopper for the project. However, by identifying it, and describing it accurately, the issue was able to be circulated and resolved (or in this case dissolved). A potentially very expensive change to the project was thus avoided.

POINTS OF INTEREST

Remember, an issue can be raised at any time by anyone and is the means of making a problem visible and having it escalated to the level where it can be resolved.

RESOLVING ISSUES – FROM BREAKDOWN TO BREAKTHROUGH 24.1

The following process, if used in full, is a very effective and powerful driver for resolving issues. Followed rigorously it will enable you to "breakthrough" an issue which is blocking your project or program. The toughest part is to declare that you do in fact have a problem. Doing this puts you in a position of responsibility which will enable you to proceed. Be careful however; the natural tendency will be for you to dwell on what's wrong: what's wrong with you, or with the project, or with "them." Steps 3 to 8 should be done with those who have a stake in the issue in a facilitated, workshop setting, recording the input from the group on flip charts. Do all the steps and do them in the right order. Do not jump ahead.

1 **Declare that you have an issue!**
Tell everyone who could possibly have an impact on resolving the issue, particularly those you do not want to know about it. Don't hide the issue. Merely putting it on your issues log is not enough. Actively tell people!

2 **Stop the action**
Call everything around the issue to a halt. Don't react. Don't try to fix it. Relax.

3 **What, precisely is the issue?**
Exactly what did or didn't happen? When? Distinguish between facts and rumors. Then describe the issue in one sentence. This is the sentence you should write in the issues log.

4 **What commitments are being thwarted?**
Which of your commitments is being thwarted, stopped, or hindered by the issue? Remind yourself of the reasons for the project in the first place and the drivers for action.

5 What would a breakthrough make possible?

What would the resolution of the issue, under these circumstances, look like? What would it make possible? Are you really committed to resolving this and furthering these possibilities? If so, continue.

6 What's missing? What's present and in the way?

Take stock of the entire project. What's the situation now (stick to facts!)? What's missing, that if present, would allow the action to move forward quickly and effectively? What's present and standing in the way of progress?

7 What possible actions could you take to further your commitments?

Leave the facts of the current situation and what is missing in the background. Stand in the future, a breakthrough having been accomplished, and create an array of possible actions. Look outside your paradigm. Think laterally.

8 What actions will you take?

Next, narrow down the possibilities to those with the greatest opportunity and leverage. Not necessarily the safest and most predictable! Then choose a direction and get back into action. Make requests of people and agree the actions needed. Hold them to account on those actions.

(Adapted, with kind permission of the London Peret Roche Group, from their "Breakdown to Breakthrough" technology. Copyright © 1992, N J.)

Let's Do it Differently!

Change Management

Changes are an inevitable fact of project life. Unless you manage these changes effectively you will soon lose sight of the objectives and scope and thereafter lose total control of the project.

"Change is certain. Progress is not."

E H CARR

- **Change is inevitable – manage it.**
- **Have a clear, simple process for introducing changes.**
- **Assess the impact of proposed changes.**
- **Only include beneficial changes.**

Managing change

Changes are an inevitable fact of project life (Figure 25.1). Seldom does a project go exactly to plan. Unless you manage these changes effectively you will soon lose sight of the objectives and scope and thereafter lose total control of the project.

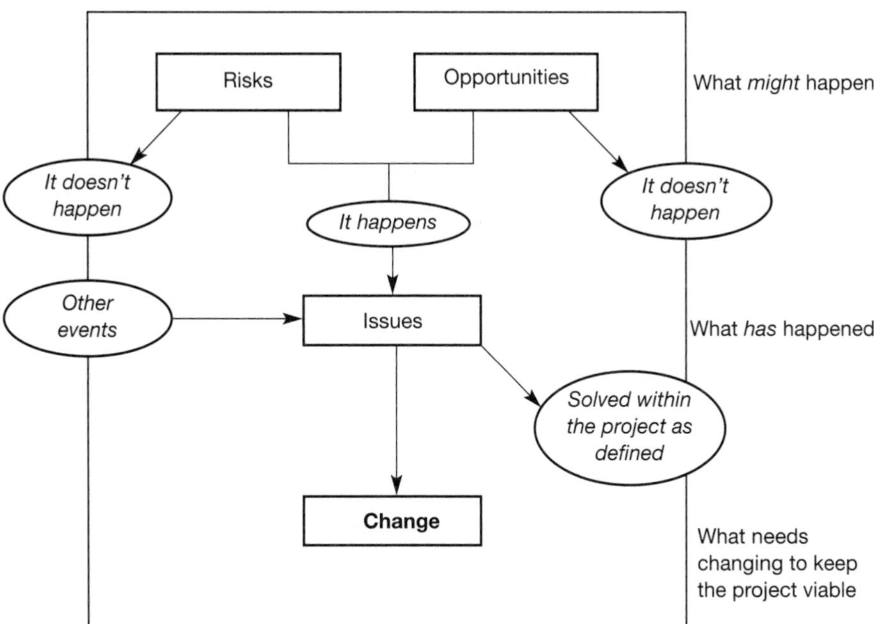

Figure 25.1 Risks, opportunity, issues and change

A **risk** or **opportunity** will become an **issue** if the event occurs. Issues can be resolved either within the scope of the project as currently defined or via a **change** to the project. If this "issue" is to be resolved by a change to the defined project, the impact of this change should be assessed, particularly with respect to the expected benefits.

Managing change does not mean preventing change, but rather allowing only beneficial changes to be adopted and included in the project.

Change management is related to risk, opportunity, and issue management; a risk or opportunity will become an issue if the event occurs. Issues can be dealt with either within the scope of the project as currently defined or via a change to the project. If this "issue" is to be resolved by a change to the defined project, the impact of this change should be assessed, particularly with respect to the expected benefits. (see Figure 25.1).

Change may result from a number of sources:

- changes in business needs/requirements driven by the project sponsor or other stakeholders;
- changes in the business environment (e.g. economics, social factors, competitor action);
- problems or opportunities which occur during the course of the project;
- modifications or enhancements identified by the project team (beware of these!);
- faults detected by the project team or users (these must be addressed).

Change, in the context of a project, is any modification to the benefit, scope, time, or cost targets that have previously been approved. This means that there can only be a "change" if there is an approved standard or "baseline." The baseline is provided by the project definition (included in the initial and full business case) which defines the:

- benefits to be delivered by the project;
- scope of work and detail for each deliverable;
- project timescale and intermediate milestone dates;
- project cost.

Change management is the process through which changes to a project (to cost, schedule, scope, or benefits) are introduced and evaluated prior to their adoption or rejection.

"Scope creep" is a phenomenon where a project overruns its agreed timescale and budget due to many extra (often minor) "requirements" being added in an uncontrolled manner. For this reason it is often easier to bundle a number of small changes together and assess them as a whole, choosing to implement only those which will further the objectives of the project. At the other end of the scale it is wise to consider delaying the addition of a major change until after the project is completed and introduce it as a second phase project.

"Scope creep" is a phenomenon where a project overruns its agreed timescale and budget due to many extra (often minor) "requirements" being added in an uncontrolled manner. For this reason it is often easier to bundle a number of small changes together and assess them as a whole, choosing to implement only those which will further the objectives of the project.

Remember, the primary aim of a project is to fulfill a stated business need. As long as this need is satisfied, fine tuning, enhancing, or embellishing the outputs is a potential waste of resource and time.

Inevitably, a time will come when an issue will arise on a project which cannot be resolved while still keeping the project viable. Either a time window will be missed or costs will be so high that even a marginal cost analysis leads to the conclusion that it is not worth continuing. In these cases, the impact assessment will result in a recommendation to terminate the project. Such an outcome should be treated as a success, as there is little point in continuing with a project which is not viable in business terms (for more on termination, see pp. 398, 413).

Don't make decisions on changing the project without assessing the impact.

The change management process

Because of the potential for changes to reduce projects to chaos, it is preferable to adopt a formal approach to assessing and authorizing change right from the start (Figure 25.2):

- Note the proposed change in the change log (see Figure 25.3, for an example).
- Assess the impact of the change on the project and any interdependent projects. (See Figure 25.4 for a summary impact assessment form.)
- If within the project manager's authority, reject or accept the change proposal.
- If it is outside the project manager's authority, refer the decision (with a recommendation) to the appropriate level for a review and decision.

The change proposal may be:

- accepted for immediate implementation;
- accepted, subject to certain conditions being met;
- accepted but implementation is deferred to a later date;
- rejected (with/without recommendation to include in a later project).

Once the decision has been made, the project manager should:

- obtain further financial authorization (if needed);
- record the outcome in the change log.
- If the change was accepted:
  — implement the change;
  — update the project documentation;
  — inform all interested parties about the change;
- inform the originator of the outcome and, if rejected, give the reason for the decision.

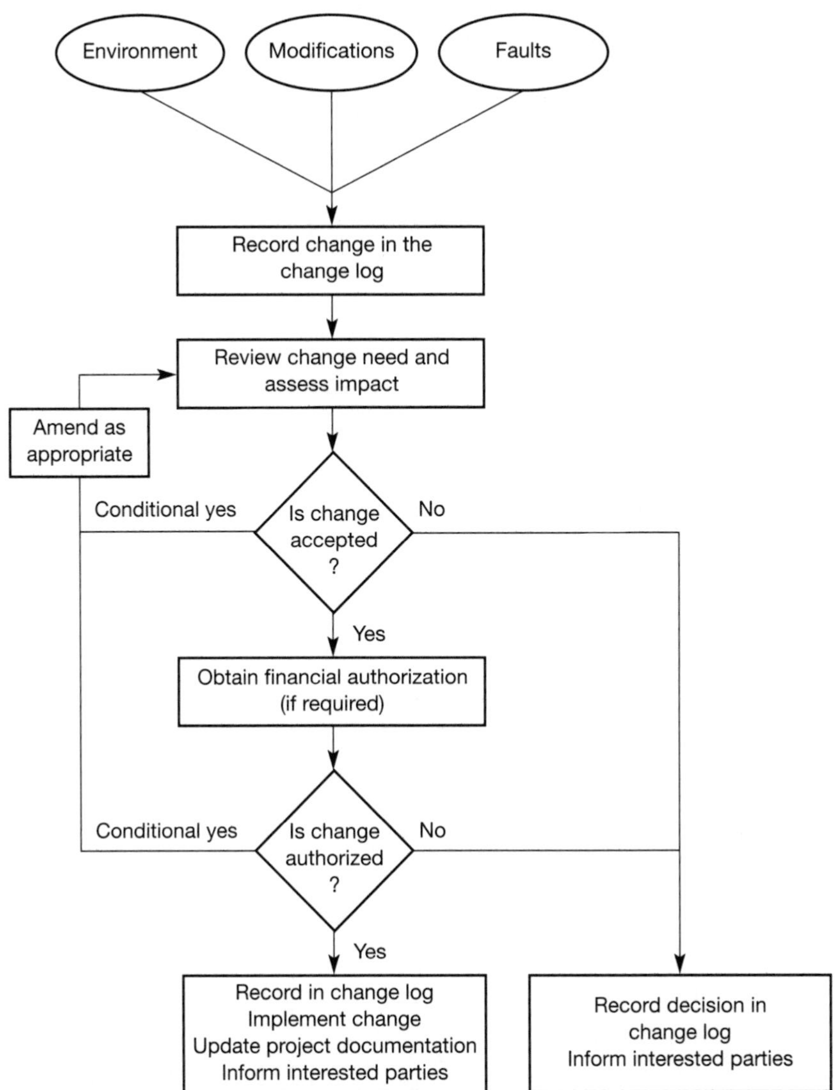

Figure 25.2 The change management process

The change management comprises capturing the proposed changes, assessing the impact on time, costs, benefits, and scope, making a decision on whether to approve the change, and obtaining further funding, if required.

Project change log

Ref No	Description	Originator	Date raised	Impact assessment by (name)	Approval by	Approved Yes/No	Date approved	Date authorized	Comments
1	Extend scope of tracking system to include all customers	J Philips	3/8/97	LR Reagan	G Large	Yes	3/10/97	5/10/97	No impact on timescale Extra $12K required Funded from contingency
2	Change process for communicating to customers	S Stone	1/10/97	TD Hepper	K Mason (Project manager)	Not required			Required as a result of legal and regulatory issues which were not taken into account at the start of the project Extra $2K cost Funded from scope reserve
3									

Figure 25.3 A typical change log
The change log supplements the initial or full business case by recording all potential and approved changes to the project.

Accountabilities for change decisions

All proposed changes need to be reviewed and their impact assessed before they are implemented or rejected. A project may have several levels for the review and authorization of changes, depending on how serious or far reaching the change will be. The following table suggests such levels.

Notice that the first two levels of authority lie within the project itself as the impacts do not affect other projects. Once other projects are affected, it is necessary to have the change reviewed and authorized by a higher authority that can balance the conflicting needs of different projects and sponsors.

The impact levels should be defined and agreed when the project is authorized. This should be documented in the Initial or Full Business Case.

Impact of change	*Approval required by*
No impact on overall schedule, cost or benefits Allocation of scope reserve	Project manager (record in change log)
Minor impact. Change affecting schedule or costs which can be accommodated without affecting other projects and are within the authority (tolerance) delegated to the project sponsor Allocation of contingency	Project sponsor (use change request form and record in change log)
Major impact. Change affecting scope, objectives, benefits, schedule, or costs which can not be accommodated within the authority (tolerance) delegated to the project sponsor or which affect other projects	Project review group (use change request form and record in change log) In some cases a business program board may have delegated authority which would normally be at project review group level

The change request form

If a change is minor in nature and can be approved by the project manager, this may be noted directly in the change log. If approval is required by higher authority it is recommended that a change request form is used to ensure the relevant information is captured prior to completing the log.

A change request form is used to:

- document requested changes;
- summarize the impact of the change;
- formally record the decision regarding the change.

An example is given in Figure 25.4. While this is a "paper-based" example, the logic lends itself to electronic-based workflow systems.

The project manager should:

- enter the relevant data into the change log (change reference number, description, originator, date raised, impact assessment by, assessment due);
- complete Part I of the change request form;
- assess (with the help of others) the impact of the change and complete Part II (impact) of the form;
- pass the form (with any supporting information) to the higher authority as appropriate (see p. 387) for approval. Any necessary financial authorization documents should also be prepared.

The "approver" should:

- review the proposed change and complete Part III as appropriate;
- return the form to the project manager.

The project manager should complete the entry in the change log.

Change Request Form			
Project number:			
Project title:			
Change number:			
PART I Proposed change (to be completed by the Project Manager)			
Description of change requested			
Reason for/benefits of the proposed change			
Approval required from:		**By (date)**	
PART III Decision (to be completed by the "Approver")			
* ❑ The change is accepted ❑ The change is accepted subject to the comments noted below: ❑ The change is rejected **Tick appropriate box*		**Name** **Date**	
Action required / Comments			

Figure 25.4 A change request form (page 1)

This sheet describes the change, reason for it and records approval.

PART II Summary of impact

(to be completed by the Project Manager)

Quantifiable Benefits	
Estimated incremental cost of change	
Effect on timescales	
Additional resources required	
Effect on other projects/activities	
Additional risks	
Recommendation	**Change should be accepted / Change should be rejected**
Assessment done by	
Date	

Figure 25.4 A change request form (page 2)

This sheet summarizes the impact of the change on the project.

DO YOU MANAGE CHANGE ON YOUR PROJECTS?

25.1

1 Take any one of your longer running projects which is in the Develop and Test Stage or beyond. From the documentation which authorized the project extract the following data:

- the total budgeted cost;
- the baseline completion date (or other identifiable milestone);
- the scope;
- the expected benefits.

2 From the most recent project progress report extract the following data:

- total forecast cost;
- forecast completion date (or other identifiable milestone);
- the current scope;
- the current expected benefits.

3 Compare your answers from 1 and 2. If there are differences, are they due to time slippage or cost overruns? Or are they due to a deliberate decision to change one of the four key control aspects of a project? If the latter, how do you know?

HARNESSING IT FOR RISK, ISSUES AND CHANGE

Now that many organizations have IT capabilities on virtually every desktop, the opportunity now exists to streamline the project control logs. Many companies are now building database tools which integrate the risk, opportunity, issue and change logs into a single tool. In addition meeting notes, action and lessons learned are also often included. Such tools can greatly simplify administration. However, always remember you do need to communicate these logs/reports and therefore unless all your team members and stakeholders are equipped, you risk "cutting them off."

Reviews and More Reviews

Keeping sight of the objectives

Review when a proposal is raised

Review at the detailed investigation gate

Reviews during the project

Project closure review

Post-implementation review

Recording agreement when you need to

You should always welcome reviews as they are the opportunity to correct any shortcomings or improve those things which are going well to make them even better.

"One sees great things from the valley; only small things from the peak."

G K CHESTERTON

- **You, as project sponsor, should initiate the reviews.**
- **Focus on the business objectives and benefits.**
- **If the project is no longer viable – terminate it!**
- **Don't assume performance to date is an indicator of future performance.**
- **Be forward looking; don't dwell on past problems and failures.**
- **Agree an action plan and see it through.**

Keeping sight of the objectives

Your project is underway and may have been running for a long time. The team will be immersed in the day-to-day work of building and delivering the required outputs. This is when you are in danger of losing focus on the real business objectives which initiated the project in the first place. It is vital that you lift yourself above the day-to-day workload and **review** whether:

- the project still serves your business objectives;
- the conditions of satisfaction are clearly understood and are being pursued;
- continuation of your project is still justified before further costs are committed to (e.g., signing a major contract);
- your project is being effectively managed and the team is confident that the project will be completed.

Such reviews are an indispensable part of good project management, reassuring you, if you are the project sponsor, that the benefits you require will in fact be delivered and, if you are the project manager, giving you an independent view on the effectiveness with which you are running the project. You should always welcome reviews as they are the opportunity to correct any shortcomings or improve those things which are going well to make them even better.

> ***The team will be immersed in the day-to-day work of building and delivering the required outputs. This is when you are in danger of losing focus on the real business objectives which initiated the project in the first place.***

If a review is to be welcomed in this way you will have to make sure that it is conducted in an open and honest way with "fault" and "blame" being rarely, if ever, used. Witch hunts during the course of a project rarely benefit anyone – be tough on the problem, not on the people. If you can foster this atmosphere of trust an open and honest review will:

Witch hunts during the course of a project rarely benefit anyone.

- give you the confidence that your money is being well spent to provide clear business benefits and that these will be achieved (or conversely that a project which is no longer viable is terminated);
- give the project manager and team confidence that what is being done is really supported by the business.

Conversely, a review conducted in an atmosphere of retribution, fear, and blame will not uncover a reliable picture of the status of the project.

It is important to distinguish between a "review," a "decision," and a "progress check." A **review** is when advice and comment is requested. Such advice may or may not be followed. A **decision** follows a review and is a choice between possible futures. Such a decision may draw on the collective "wisdom" of the reviewers, but ultimately rests with the person making the choice. The role of the reviewers is to ensure that decision makers make informed choices. A **progress check** differs from a review in that it is conducted by the project manager and focusses on the execution of the project (what, when, how much) rather than its overall objective (why). In summary a review gives you the opportunity to:

- recall why you are doing the project;
- check that what you are doing is still appropriate;
- assess how you are going about it;
- confirm when it is going to be completed;
- confirm how much it will cost you;
- and . . . whether you still need it!

When should you have a review?

You should hold a review prior to making any key decisions affecting the future of the project. Typically these will be:

- at the Initial Investigation Gate when a proposal has been submitted;

- at the Detailed Investigation Gate when the initial business case is approved and the project is committed into your project portfolio;
- during the course of the project:
  — at the gates prior to starting key stages of the project:
    — Development Gate;
    — Trial Gate;
    — Ready for Service Gate;
  — when major contracts are to be let;
  — when major deliverables are to be accepted;
  — during stages which are inherently risky;
  — when a "show-stopping" issue has been identified;
  — when the risks become unacceptably high;
- at the "close" of the project (whether completed or terminated);
- at an appropriate time after the project completion so that achievement of the benefits can be assessed (Post-Implementation Review).

Notice that all these reviews are event driven and occur when a particular point in the project has been reached. They are not driven by calendar lapse time. You should plan the reviews into the project schedule in advance except for those which are driven by unplanned events (risks and issues).

Who is accountable for ensuring a review happens?

There is little point in the project manager completing a project on time, within budget and to the expected standard, only to find it is no longer needed. Consequently, it is the project sponsor who is accountable for that ensuring all reviews take place.

The project sponsor is accountable for the business benefits and it is, therefore, in his/her interest that reviews take place. There is little point in the project manager completing a project on time, within budget and to the expected standard, only to find it is no longer needed. Consequently, it is the project sponsor (or higher authority, e.g. business program sponsor) who is accountable for ensuring that all reviews take place.

You must be clear on the purpose of each review and know:

- the scope of each review (total project, subpart, etc.);
- driver for the review (the event which triggers the review);
- the names of the review leader and team members;
- evaluation criteria to be used (checklists, etc.).

Except for names and actual dates, these are all predefined in the staged framework for the gate reviews, closure review and Post-Implementation Review.

Generally, all reviews assess the deliverables, documentation, and performance of the project to date. This is coupled with interviews with the project team, users, customers, third parties, suppliers, and functional managers so that you can gain different perspectives on and perceptions of the project from the different stakeholders. Do also include the project manager. If the review comes up with recommendations concerning the running of the project it is important that the project manager is enrolled to implement them.

Unless included in formal gate deliverables, the review team leader should record and communicate his or her findings in a brief report covering:

- the key findings from the review;
- recommendations for improvements/changes needed together with who should be actioned to implement them;
- areas where the project has performed well.

This report should be sent to the project sponsor (and project board if there is one) who should agree with the project manager which recommendations should be incorporated into the project, by when, and by whom. If there are lessons which could usefully benefit other projects or which provide useful feedback on the project processes, these should be recorded and sent to the relevant people.

TERMINATING PROJECTS IS NOT INDICATIVE OF FAILURE

In some circumstances it is apparent that the project is no longer likely to meet its stated objectives and should be stopped. This may be because:

- the business need no longer exists;
- an issue has arisen which cannot be resolved;
- risks are unacceptably high;
- any prescribed criteria noted in the business case have been encountered.

Such circumstances should always be considered within any review and stopping projects as a result should not be treated as a "failure."

Review when a proposal is raised

The staged framework prescribes that any proposal for a new project is formally written up, sponsored, and registered at the Initial Investigation Gate. The key question facing you at this point is "Is this proposal worth consuming resources and money on undertaking an initial investigation?" Is the objective compelling? While information on costs, timescale, and impact may be very sketchy, it should be possible to decide if the proposal fits within the current strategy. If this is not possible, the proposal should proceed no further.

Review at the Detailed Investigation Gate

One of the key lessons of project management is that if high emphasis is placed on the early stages of a project, the likelihood of project success is increased considerably. A thorough review at the time the project is formally committed into the project portfolio (at the Detailed Investigation Gate) is, therefore, essential as it is at this point that the proposal of "what we **want** to do" becomes a project, i.e. "what we are **going** to do." The project sponsor is, in effect, stating he/she can be held accountable for all subsequent costs and benefits associated with the project no matter where they are spent or earned within the company.

The review is intended to ensure that all interested parties understand the objectives of the project, what they are accountable for during its execution and how it will affect them once it is implemented. The review should confirm that the correct project is being started at the right time; if the review finds otherwise, then the project should be terminated or postponed.

Project Workout 26.1 comprises a "health check" which may be used to aid this review. This tool is designed to give an overall assessment of the supporting environment, within which the project will live and an associated "risk" rating.

Reviews during the project

Reviews during the execution of the project provide additional check points where the objectives and general "state of health" of the project can be assessed.

Reviews related to stages and gates

For long stages, intermediate reviews should be planned into the project schedule. These should usually be event driven (i.e., a particular milestone has been reached such as signing a major contract) rather than time driven.

Within the staged framework these are at the gates prior to starting new stages, for example, at the Development Gate, the Trial Gate and the Ready for Service (RFS) Gate. In such cases, the review should focus on the decision to proceed with the project (or not) and, if so, check the adequacy of preparation for the next part or stage of the project.

For long stages, intermediate reviews should be planned into the project schedule. These should usually be event driven (i.e., a particular milestone has been reached such as signing a major contract) rather than time driven. It is good practice to plan reviews such that one is due approximately every three months. Notwithstanding this, it may also be appropriate to review a project prior to the regular quarterly business refracts. These reviews should confirm that the costs, timescales, and project targets remain achievable and that the expected benefits will be delivered to the business.

Finally, the project management practices should always be assessed to confirm that they are being implemented effectively. The "health check" tool included in Project Workout 26.1, later in this chapter, can be used to assist in this.

Reviews related to deliverables

When project deliverables are produced, they need to be reviewed and approved against predetermined criteria. It may be appropriate to link a review of the entire project to a key project deliverable.

Reviews related to risks or issues

You cannot predict when these are needed. They are the most difficult to set up and manage as there is the persistent hope that all will come right in the end, especially if you don't have to waste time doing a review! Realism, honesty, and openness are what are called for. The project manager needs to recognize when circumstances are conspiring against the project and the project sponsor needs to be made aware. The project sponsor also needs to recognize that the benefits he or she seeks may not be delivered by this project. In such cases it is important to focus on **why** the project was started and look at what else could be done to meet those same objectives.

> ***There is the persistent hope that all will come right in the end, especially if you don't have to waste time doing a review!***

Project closure review

A project can be closed either when it has been completed or if it is terminated. (Any review examined here may lead to termination!) It is important that a project is closed down in a controlled way and that all accountabilities relating to it are discharged and lessons learned. The **closure review** aims to fulfill this and is described more fully in Chapters 10 and 27. It should:

- review the efficiency of the project in terms of meeting the original time, cost, and resource targets;
- confirm that the benefits have been built into the business forecast;
- record and communicate any lessons which can be beneficial to future projects.

As far as the project sponsor is concerned, either the project has been completed and he/she can now expect to benefit from it, or the project has been terminated. In the latter case, this may be because the original business need no longer exists, but, if it does, the project sponsor will need to take action to address the unresolved business need which initiated the project in the first place.

Post-implementation review

Between three to six months after the project has been completed, you should undertake a formal review to assess whether the project has, in fact, met its stated business objectives or is on course to achieve them. This is called a **Post-Implementation Review** (see also Chapter 11). It should:

- assess the benefits which have already been achieved and compare them with those originally planned;
- assess how well the outputs for the project are working in practice;
- make recommendations for corrective actions (if any);
- record and communicate any lessons which may be useful for future projects.

It is important that the review is considered from the differing viewpoints of the various stakeholders involved, for example:

- project sponsor;
- benefitting functions and units;
- operational users;
- third parties;
- customers.

"Almost complete" is often not enough.

Recording agreement when you need to

Obtaining agreement to key deliverables during the project is essential. However, it can often prove to be a difficult task to:

- identify those who need to be involved;
- engage them in taking time to address the review;
- be certain that a review has, in fact, been done.

For these reasons, it is often useful to follow a formal process for checking, agreeing, and documenting the review and acceptance of project deliverables. This is key for final deliverables, but applies just as much to intermediate deliverables (i.e., those developed during the project) which set the "agenda" for the next stage of work to be formally reviewed and signed off. Unless this is done, there is a danger that work may proceed on a premise which does not have the support of the users or other stakeholders.

The following is a recommended procedure where alternative formal processes have not been adopted.

Standard record for reviews and approvals

A standard form (such as given in Figure 26.1) may be used instead of a memo or letter as it provides a concise and recognizable document which clearly states what is required of the recipient. For example, some individuals may receive a deliverable for comment on particular points only, while others will receive a "final" deliverable and will be required to accept (approve) it.

The project documentation should list the key deliverables from the project, stating who has responsibility for reviewing and accepting them. If a deliverable is not readily portable, alternative methods of review (demonstrations, tests, etc.) should be arranged.

Procedure

1 The originator of the deliverable (or project manager) sends the deliverable under cover of a request form (with Part I completed) to the reviewer.

2 The reviewer carries out the action noted under "review and sign-off criteria," completes Part II of the form and returns it to the originator. It is not usually necessary to have a real signature, as e-mail or electronic signatures are generally adequate.

<table>
<tr><th colspan="4">Review/Approval Record</th></tr>
<tr><td colspan="4">Project number</td></tr>
<tr><td colspan="4">Project title</td></tr>
<tr><td colspan="4">PART I Request (to be completed by the person making the request)</td></tr>
<tr><td>Reviewer (name):</td><td></td><td>Review requested by: (name):</td><td></td></tr>
<tr><td>Issued to Reviewer on (date):</td><td></td><td>To be returned to by (date):</td><td></td></tr>
<tr><td colspan="4">Deliverable to be reviewed</td></tr>
<tr><td colspan="4"></td></tr>
<tr><td colspan="4">Review criteria</td></tr>
<tr><td colspan="4"></td></tr>
<tr><td colspan="4">PART II Response (to be completed by the Reviewer)</td></tr>
<tr><td colspan="4">I have reviewed the above deliverable on behalf of</td></tr>
<tr><td colspan="4"></td></tr>
<tr><td colspan="4">*❑ The deliverable is accepted
❑ The deliverable is accepted to subject to inclusion of the comments noted below
❑ The deliverable is rejected for the reasons noted below
*Tick appropraite box</td></tr>
<tr><td colspan="4">Reviewer's comments</td></tr>
<tr><td colspan="4"></td></tr>
<tr><td>Name</td><td></td><td>Function</td><td></td></tr>
<tr><td>Signature</td><td></td><td>Date</td><td></td></tr>
</table>

Figure 26.1 An example of a sign-off form

PROJECT HEALTH CHECK

26.1

This tool is a useful analytical device to assess the current "health" of a project. It looks at the full project environment and using a set of key questions results in an assessment of the overall risk associated with the project. As such it fulfills two roles:

- as a checklist;
- as a tool to indicate where a project manager's efforts should be directed.

It is recommended that the "health check" is carried out as a part of every project review and at least quarterly.

Instructions

1 Answer each set of the following questions with a grading –4 to +4:

–4	=	strongly disagree or don't know
–2	=	disagree
0	=	neutral
+2	=	agree
+4	=	strongly agree.

2 Enter the total score from each section in the summary section.

3 Add the scores together.

4 Use the key to assess the overall health of your project and hence the risk associated with it.

Project plan	☐	P score
Resources	☐	R score
Ownership	☐	O score
Justifiable case	☐	J score
Expertise	☐	E score
Clear specification	☐	C score
Top level support	☐	T score
Total score	☐	

Key: degree of risk

☐ +14 to +7 = low ☐ + 7 to 0 = medium

☐ 0 to –7 = high ☐ –7 to –14 = impossible

(Adapted with the kind permission of the Strategic Management Group, based on the Project Implementation Profile by Jeffrey K Pinto and Dennis P Slavin.)

PROJECT PLAN

There is a detailed plan (including critical path/chain schedule, milestones manpower, etc.) for at least the current stage of the project and an outline plan to the end.

There is a detailed cost plan for at least the current stage of the project and a summary cost plan to the end.

Key personal accountabilities (who, when) are specified in the project plan.

We know which activities contain float for time and which resources can be used in other areas for emergencies.

There are contingency plans in case the project is off schedule or off budget or if benefits are forecast to decline.

Total

P score = total/10

RESOURCES

There is sufficient manpower to complete the project.

The appropriate technology is available throughout the project life cycle.

The technology to be used to support the project works and is fully supported.

Specific project tasks are well managed.

Project team personnel understand their role.

Total

R score = total/10

OWNERSHIP

The stakeholders were given the opportunity to make an input early in the project.

The stakeholders accept ownership of project actions.

Measures of success have been agreed with the stakeholders.

Stakeholders understand the limitations of the project (what the project is not supposed to do).

Stakeholders understand which of their requirements are included in the project.

Total

O score = total/10

JUSTIFIABLE CASE

The project has been fully costed and budgets agreed with the project sponsor.

Estimates of the financial and commercial benefits of the project have been made.

The project promises benefit to the company and a clear return on investment.

Conditions of satisfaction have been defined and measurement processes put in place.

Adequate funding is available for the duration of the project.

Total

J score = total/10

EXPERTISE

All members of the project team possess the appropriate levels of expertise.

Stakeholders and users understand the project and are capable of using its deliverables.

Personnel on the project team understand how their performance will be evaluated.

Project role descriptions for team members have been written and understood.

Adequate training (and time for training) has been built into the project schedule.

Total

E score = total/10

CLEAR SPECIFICATION

The objectives of the project are clear to all stakeholders.

The goals of the project are in line with corporate goals and corporate standards.

I am enthusiastic about the chances of success for this project.

There is adequate documentation of the requirements and the measures of success.

An adequate presentation of the project aims and objectives has been given to stakeholders.

Total

C score = total/10

TOP LEVEL SUPPORT

Top management shares responsibility with the project team for ensuring the project's success. ☐

Management is responsive to requests for additional resources, if the need arises. ☐

Terms of reference, authority levels, and accountabilities have been agreed. ☐

There is confidence that management can be called upon to help when necessary. ☐

The project sponsor is fully committed to the project's success. ☐

Total ☐

T score = total/10 ☐

27

Closing the Project

It is the project sponsor's role to approve the closure of a project. However, if a project is to be closed part way through and other projects are affected (the project definition will define interproject interdependencies), approval may need to be given by a higher authority or agreed with other affected parties.

"Yes, in the old days that was so, but we have changed all that."

MOLIÈRE 1622–1673

- **Closure is the project sponsor's decision.**
- **Check interdependent projects before terminating yours.**
- **Make project closure explicit.**
- **Communicate closure to the stakeholders.**
- **Learn the lessons and share them.**

Project closure

The objective of project closure is to ensure that:

- a project is closed down in a controlled and organized way;
- all accountabilities relating to it have been discharged or handed over to the line or to another project.

Closure is the formal "end-point" of a project, either because it is **completed** or because it has been **terminated**. Termination may occur because the project is no longer viable or because the risks associated with it have become unacceptably high. The closure review should:

- review the efficiency of the project in terms of meeting the original time, cost, and resource targets;
- confirm that the benefits have been built into the business forecast;
- record and communicate any lessons which can be beneficial to future projects.

As far as the project sponsor is concerned, either the project has been completed and he/she can now expect to benefit from it, or the project has been terminated. In the latter case, this may be because the original business need no longer exists, but if it does, the project sponsor will need to take action to address the unresolved business need which initiated the project in the first place.

There are three key steps to closing a project:

1 Prepare the closure report.
2 Formally close the project.
3 Close down and communicate.

The closure report

It is the project sponsor's role to approve the closure of a project. However, if a project is to be closed part way through and other projects are affected (the project definition will define any project interdependencies) approval may need to be given by a higher authority or agreed with other affected parties.

When a project is to be closed, you, as project manager, should:

- Check the status and completeness of the Business Case (including the project definition), the change and issues logs, the most recent progress report, and any papers referring to early cancellation of project. (Do this using Project Workout 27.1.)
- Prepare a draft project closure report with the team, including the terms of reference for Post-Implementation Review (PIR).

The purpose of the closure report is expected to record the reason for closure, the benefits the project achieved, and any outstanding accountabilities which need to be handed over. It also documents any lessons learned regarding how the project was conducted and the efficacy of the supporting processes.

The project closure report should include the following sections:

1 Business objectives.
2 Closure statement.
3 Benefits measurement.
4 Outstanding issues and deliverables.
5 Project efficiency.
6 Lessons learned.
7 Acknowledgments.

An appendix can give the terms of reference for a Post-Implementation Review, if one is required.

Contents of a project closure report

1. *Business objectives*

Restate the business objectives as given in the Business Case, including any changes that have been approved since the sign-off (see p. 262). If there have been any changes, state the reasons.

2. *Closure statement*

State the circumstances under which the project is being closed as one of the following:

- the project has been successfully completed;
- the project has been terminated prior to completion.

If the latter is the case, describe the reasons for termination and indicate the current likelihood of resurrection.

3. *Benefits measurement*

Restate the tangible benefits (given in the business case; see p. 262) which the project will provide and how these will be measured, together with who will be accountable for measuring them. In addition:

- state whether the current business plan/forecast reflects the project benefits;
- include defined review periods for measurements of benefits.

4. *Outstanding risks, issues and deliverables*

List any issues or key deliverables not yet accepted. For each give:

- the nature of the risk and/or issue or reason for non-acceptance;
- who has agreed to be accountable;
- the proposed resolution (including date).

5. *Project efficiency*

State the actual cost and resources consumed as well as the actual schedule achieved compared with the plan.

Cost (£,000)	Resource (man days)	Trial Gate date	RFS Date	Release Date	Project complete date
Original baseline					
Current baseline					
Actual					
Variance					

6. *Lessons learned*

Referring to project efficiency and the project team's experiences, (e.g., major issues encountered, changes of strategy) state what could have been done better:

- Identify areas where time, money, or resource could have been better utilized.
- Recommend courses of action for future projects to help eliminate any inefficiencies found.
- Identify what worked well and recommend methods, processes, procedures, and tools which other projects may find of use in the future.

7. *Acknowledgments*

Acknowledge all individuals who have made special contribution to the project.

Appendix A: terms of reference for PIR

The Post-Implementation Review (PIR) is designed to measure the benefits delivered by the project against the conditions of satisfaction given in the Business Case (see also p. 262).

If a Post-Implementation Review is required, state:

- who is accountable for organizing and chairing it;
- when it will occur;
- which functional areas and stakeholders who are required to participate.

The closure meeting

You should invite key individuals to a meeting at which the project is formally approved for closure by the project sponsor. By drawing the group together, the project manager has an opportunity to:

The quality and sharing of feedback is always greater when done in a group than when conducted in isolation.

- acknowledge the team and celebrate;
- assign accountabilities for outstanding issues;
- ensure feedback reflects the differing viewpoints of those involved.

The quality and sharing of feedback is always greater when done in a group than when conducted in isolation.

A suggested agenda for a closure meeting follows and detailed in Figure 27.1:

1 Deliverables.
2 Outstanding issues.
3 Benefits and business plan.
4 Post-Implementation Review.
5 Acknowledgments.
6 Formal closure.
7 Lessons learned.

The draft project closure report, which should be circulated prior to the meeting, provides the briefing for the attendees. This will be amended based on the discussions and feedback received at the meeting.

Small projects

If the project is small or if the project sponsor and project manager do not believe a meeting will add value, formal closure should be agreed by the project sponsor after a review of the closure report by the relevant individuals.

Large projects

It may be advisable to hold two meetings for large projects; the first to cover items 1 to 6 and the second to cover item 7. This is particularly of value when it is known that the project can contribute greatly to the company's corporate learning.

PROJECT CLOSURE MEETING
AGENDA

1 **Deliverables**

Confirm that all deliverables have been approved and accepted by the business.

2 **Outstanding issues**

Review outstanding issues; for each issue, obtain agreement from a named person in the line or in another project that they will "own" the issue and its resolution.

3 **Benefits and business plan**

Confirm that the benefits have already been built into the business plan or are due to be included in the next forecast.

Accountability for the monitoring of benefits should be agreed together with a timetable of defined review points.

4 **Post-Implementation Review**

If a PIR is required, the terms of reference should be agreed together with a timetable and named participants. The accountability for the review must be agreed.

5 **Acknowledgments**

Acknowledge all contributions to the project.

6 **Formal closure**

Assuming all the preceding business has been conducted, the project manager and project sponsor should "sign-off" closure of the project.

7 **Lessons learned**

What worked well on the project? What did not? Were all the controls effective and useful? What would we use again? What would we do differently next time?

Suggested attendees:

- Project sponsor.
- Project manager.
- Project board members.
- Key team members.
- Functional line/process managers accountable for signing off key deliverables.
- Functional line/process managers who will accept accountability for outstanding issues.
- Project manager from any related projects who will accept account ability for any outstanding issues.

Figure 27.1 A suggested agenda for a project closure meeting

Closure actions

Following approval to close the project from the project sponsor, the project manager should:

- finalize the project closure report;
- prepare a communication, enclosing the approved project closure report to the project sponsor, project team, and stakeholders, confirming the decision to close the project;
- complete any outstanding closure actions;
- feed back any suggested process improvements to the relevant project offices and/or process support group.

A full checklist is included in Project Workout 27.1.

WHAT HAPPENS TO THE LESSONS?

Collecting the lessons learnt from each project and focussing on them at project closure will ensure those involved in the project are less likely to fall into the same traps twice. It will not, however, ensure no one else does! If your company as a whole is to benefit, you need to be able to make these lessons more widely available. In large companies this can be problematic as the volume of information can be daunting. Don't fall into the trap of just listing each lesson in a long document; no one will find anything. You must invest some time in making the lessons accessible and relevant. Think of a cookery book. It is not merely a set of recipes that the author has cooked over the past year. It is carefully divided up and indexed to make it as easy as possible for the reader to find what is needed. Your lessons learnt should be the same. Intranet capabilities are also invaluable in helping you distribute the lessons.

Make sure you tell them it's over.

27.1

CLOSURE CHECKLIST

1 Deliverables

- ☐ Have all project deliverables been approved and handed over to on-going "owners?"
- ☐ Has accountability for outstanding deliverables been agreed?

2 Issues

- ☐ Have all issues been resolved?
- ☐ Has ownership of each outstanding issue been accepted by a named person in the line or in another project ?

3 Business forecast

- ☐ Have the functions and business units updated their plans to take into account the operational resources, costs and benefits relating to the project?
- ☐ Has the business forecast been updated or will it be?
- ☐ Has a person accepted accountability for monitoring the benefits?
- ☐ Have review points for measuring the benefits been defined?

4 Post-Implementation Review (PIR)

- ☐ Has a decision been made to have a PIR?
- ☐ Have the timing and terms of reference for the PIR been agreed?
- ☐ Has it been agreed who is accountable for ensuring the PIR takes place?

5 Team and stakeholders

- ☐ Have all who need to know about the closure of the project been informed?
- ☐ Have all team members been reassigned to other activities?
- ☐ Have project team appraisals relating to the project been completed?
- ☐ Have those who deserve special acknowledgment been acknowledged?

6 Project documentation

- ☐ Has all documentation pertaining to this project been filed, archived, and referenced?

7 Facilities

- ☐ Have all project facilities (desks, computers, office space, etc.) been released?
- ☐ Have all facilities reserved for the project outputs or contracts raised been canceled?

8 Project accounting and other systems

- ☐ Has the project account been closed such that no further expenditure can be attributed to the project?
- ☐ Have other corporate or functional project tracking systems and registers been updated?

Part Five

IMPLEMENTING THE FRAMEWORK

Implementing the Framework

Advice from other companies

Finding help in implementing a project's approach

A strategy for implementation

The implementation task is very large but not so large that you should give up now! Implementing a project's approach is not a single project.

"If there are obstacles, the shortest line between two points may be a crooked one."

BERTOLT BRECHT

You've read and understood the book, bought into the principles, and now you want to apply them to your company. You've some projects going on but you are not quite sure how many. You do not know what stage in the project framework they are. You might not know who wants the benefits or even who is managing them. You now want to do something about it – but what?

Advice from other companies

I asked a number of companies what their advice would be to anyone embarking on the introduction of a projects approach to business in their company, be it for the company as a whole or for one particular cross-functional activity such as product development. All the advice given matched that which you would find in any good book on the management of change. However, despite this body of common sense much of this advice had been ignored by many of the companies ... to their cost!

"It is the true nature of mankind to learn from mistakes, not from example."

FRED HAYLE

"Top management" support was always stated as essential, particularly as the "project approach" relies on them as decision makers. This is one of the few business processes where they are required to "live" the process rather than monitor it. Where they are not the fire-fighting problem solvers but a key link in the chain. If they don't perform by making good, timely decisions, it will slow projects down at best or set off the wrong projects at worst. One chief executive of a major engineering group held back his implementation for six months until he was convinced that his board was really committed. This was in an organization where cross-functional working and project management were already well established.

COMMITMENT OR INVOLVEMENT?

Consider the great British breakfast of bacon and eggs. The hen is involved but the pig is committed.

Other valuable advice included:

- Don't underestimate the training and coaching effort needed.
- Don't underestimate the resources needed to support your implementation.
- Use champions embedded in the business to promote the process.
- Roll it out in parts – you can't do all of it at once.

Finally, keep any supporting documentation simple. One company had the basic process written on just ten sheets of paper. This was supported by a number of more detailed guides to aid the users with particular aspects.

Of course, you have to direct and manage your business regardless of whether you have a project process to aid you or not. Many companies have operated as functional hierarchies for years and not even heard words such as "cross-functional" or "project." By the same token, there are companies today where the use of the word "cross-functional" is no longer needed. They always work in teams, drawing on the most appropriate people from across the organization to work together in pursuit of objectives. They can't conceive of any other way to work effectively. I know which sort of company I'd rather work in!

A projects approach will give you the capability to know:

- what you are doing to change your business in pursuit of your strategy;
- the interdependencies between your programs and projects;
- the benefits and risks you are signed up to.

It does this by making projects, and hence the implementation of strategy, very visible. It does not reduce or affect your discretion to manage and direct your business as you see fit. In fact, it gives you the knowledge to enable you to make better informed decisions. It also allows you to delegate more than you ever have before. You can assign programs or projects to your colleagues and subordinates but, because they are visible and defined, you do not lose sight of them.

Implementing a projects approach entails introducing complex changes encompassing processes, systems, structure, and culture. This book gives you an insight into the processes, the systems, structures, and cultures that have been shown to work best. But it is impossible to be prescriptive about how it will look in your own company. The easier parts to implement are the processes and systems. These are tangible things, they can be written down and created. However, structure and culture are another matter. As soon as you start changing the structures, for example, relating to decision making, the defence mechanisms of those who feel threatened will rise. Similarly, just because you have a process, it doesn't mean that some will do anything but play lip service to it. You have to grow a culture which wants to play the game and enrolls all your people from top to bottom. Earlier in this book I talked about the company which always looked to "people problems" when their process broke down. They had learned that this was usually the root cause of breakdowns rather than the process itself. We also discovered that project management is one of the few business processes which senior management take a part in rather than watch from afar. It is therefore vital that your implementation includes full briefing of the roles that those key people are to take.

You have to grow a culture which wants to play the game and enrolls all your people from top to bottom.

Finding help in implementing a projects approach

Finding help in putting the principles and practice outlined in this book into effect can be a daunting first step. The options include:

- asking a consultant to advise you;
- asking your in-house experts to investigate;
- finding out how others solve this problem (benchmarking).

Employing an outside consultant is an obvious and frequently used choice. However, their solutions may be resisted from within the organization. "We're different," "That's too theoretical," and "You don't understand how complicated our business is" are commonly heard. Unfortunately, much good experience, advice and money are wasted if an organization lacks trust and belief in what its consultants are saying. However, before you ignore the complaints of your people, consider whether the consultants you have chosen (or propose to use) really do know what they are doing. Check a number of consultancies and check their former clients for references. Making a wrong move at the start could be catastrophic.

Many organizations use their own people. They are cheaper than consultants and may even have been recruited from the best consulting firms in the first place. However, if they are seen as a "prophet in their own country who is not believed," the result may be that they have less credibility than an external consultant. If you propose to use your own people, check them out as thoroughly as you would an external consultant. Look for evidence that they really know what they are talking about *and* that they can deliver the goods.

Nowadays the use of "benchmarking" is becoming commonplace and is invaluable both to the commercial and the non-commercial sectors in improving performance and finding better ways of structuring and running organizations. Looking at other organizations enables you to look beyond your own immediate local problems and see how others really work.

Using a combination of consultants, internal staff, and benchmarking is often the most productive route into the implementation maze if trust in the proposed solutions is to be generated:

- Consultants can give a dispassionate view based on their own specialist knowledge and bring to bear considerable experience in a particular field.
- In-house experts will know their own company, its culture and style; they will also have to live with any solutions which are adopted.
- Benchmarking gives you a wider perspective. ("Other companies really do it that way!")

It is as comforting to know you are on the right track as it is to be put on the right track.

Often benchmarking may merely confirm that the approach being taken is correct but always has the additional benefit that it may also suggest alternative and illuminating approaches and experiences. Both are very valuable and it is as comforting to know you are on the right track as it is to be put on the right track.

Remember, if benchmarking is to work, you must be receptive to new ideas and even old ones you may have previously discarded. Benchmarking findings may otherwise be lost in a fog of mistrust, as may the wisdom of consultants and in-house experts.

A strategy for implementation

Boil the ocean and eat an elephant

> ***Use the tools, techniques, lessons, and principles in this book. What better test is there for a projects framework than to use it in its own creation!***

The implementation task is very large but not so large that you should give up now! Implementing a projects approach is not a single project. You cannot do it all at once, the scale of the changes needed are too extensive. You, therefore, need to split the project up into smaller parts, each of which will satisfy a particular need and give you some definite benefit. Each of these parts should be run as a project, using all the discipline that a projects approach entails. You can then ease your way forward a step at a time and start reaping the rewards early. As a start you could use the tools, techniques, lessons, and principles in this book. What better test is there for a projects framework than to use it in its own creation!

WITHOUT TRUST IN THE SOLUTIONS, THE SOLUTIONS WILL NOT WORK

A board of senior managers was listening to a presentation on the findings from a benchmarking study (Part One of this book!). A few of them were shaking their heads, commenting that "The approaches being presented were not used in the 'real world.'" The chief executive stopped the presentation stating: "You may think these approaches don't work but the companies we talked to are highly respected and successful and they do use them. This is the real world: forget about what you think we could or could not do in this company and *listen*."

One word of warning: you will need to be very firm on maintaining the principles that a projects approach relies on. As the framework starts to bed in it will throw other processes and procedures within your company into sharp relief. Sometimes it will show them up to be inadequate. This is not necessarily the fault of the new projects process – the other procedures may always have been inadequate, it's just that they were hidden.

One word of warning: you will need to be very firm on maintaining the principles that a projects approach relies on. As the framework starts to bed in it will throw other processes and procedures within your company into sharp relief. Sometimes it will show them up to be inadequate.

Alternatively, it may be that the side effects of the new project process had been missed during your trial stage. The temptation is always to stop and fix every "new problem." Resist this. Keep on implementing the parts you decide to implement. If the "new" problems have been with you for a number years lying unnoticed, a few more months will do no great harm. If you stop what you are doing to fix everything you find, however, you will end up being diverted to do more and more until you will indeed be trying to eat the elephant.

The design of the basic staged project framework was completed. It was agreed. It was ready to be introduced. However, one small question was raised:

Executive: "The gates require us to make decisions – how do we do that? Could you design a decision-making process? We need that before we go any further. We need to know how to prioritize."

Project champion: "Why do you need that now? All I've done is design a management framework for projects. I haven't touched decision making. You make decisions on these things now, so continue the same way until we work out a better way."

What had in fact happened, was that by rationalizing one part, the fundamental aspect of decision making was shown to be lacking. You can't "process" decision making, only process the points when they need to be made. You can however, provide a capability to provide information to enable you to make informed decisions – but that relies on having a basic framework within which to manage in the first place. Delaying the implementation of the staged process until decision making is in place would not necessarily solve the problem and would probably lead to implementation being delayed until *all* process components (resources, business planning, fund management, etc.) were defined and approved. In practice, this probably means that nothing is ever implemented.

Building your implementation strategy

When undertaking complex change or business process reengineering we are often advised that it should be done in phases, moving from one "temporary mode of operation" or "island of certainty" to another. Put some change in place, let it settle, put some more in place. This assumes a linear and sequential transition from one state to another. It also assumes that you can plan the overall implementation order and configurations at the islands, in advance (see a in Figure 28.1).

The advice to split the implementation up into projects and hence manage them as a program is sound. However, the concept of progressing from one planned state to another is unrealistic.

The advice to split the implementation up into projects and hence manage them as a program is sound. However, the concept of progressing from one planned state to another is unrealistic. The implementation will not be a "paint by numbers" program. Overall, it will start off as a fog and you will need to

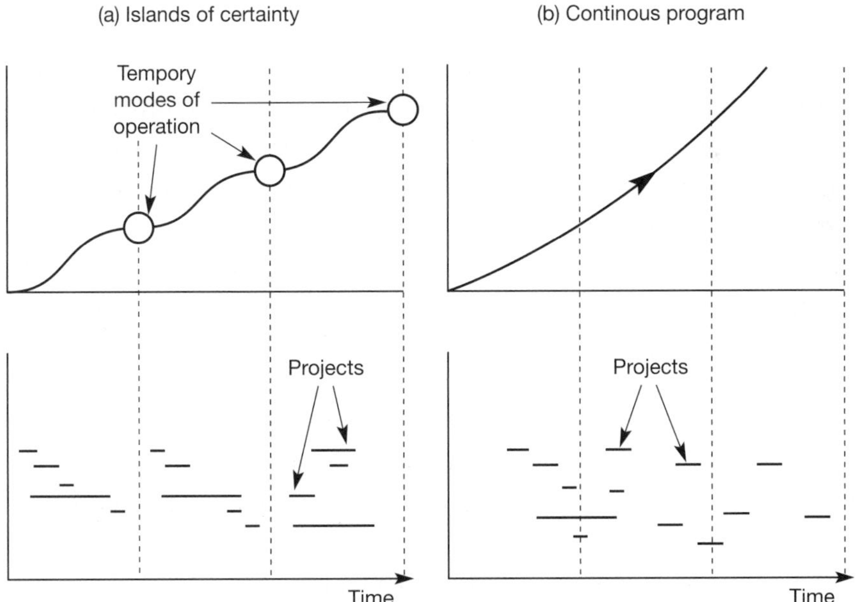

Figure 28.1 Islands of certainty and progressive change
Often the advice on implementing complex change is undertake a first tranche of changes, pause to allow the new changes to bed in (island of certainty or temporary mode of operation), and then move on with the next set of changes. In contrast using a strategy of continuous change, moving from configuration to configuration, will give you the freedom to choose whether to carry on without limiting yourself to what may be arbitrary islands.

feel your way forward. Further, even if you did create a road map detailing your islands of certainty, you may impose constraints on your freedom to capitalize on implementation opportunities as they arise. Using a strategy of continuous change, moving from configuration to configuration, will give you the freedom to choose whether to push forward or pause every time a new project is set off (b in Figure 28.1). Such decisions must be taken in the knowledge of the prevailing workload in the company and level of acceptance you have achieved so far.

Assume that you have decided to split your implementation up into projects as follows:

- high level design of the final state;
- staged framework and project management;
- decision making;
- strategic alignment;
- fund management;
- release management.
- resource management;
- business planning and forecasting.

Depending on where your company is now, you will have a certain amount of confidence in your current operational capabilities for each area of implementation covered by these projects. For you, some of the projects listed here will be paint by numbers, some will be quests and others may even be fogs.

If you start with the paint by numbers projects, you will have more confidence in delivery and hence in securing some benefits. As for the others, you will not know how long they will take or the order in which they can be completed. Neither will you really be sure on the timing, as much of the change relies on the development of a projects culture. So you cannot predict any further islands of certainty – you are in uncharted territory. Your starting point has affected your implementation strategy from the very first day.

A possible implementation strategy would be:

Project set 1. Build a high level picture of what you ultimately want to achieve and define a program of possible projects – classify them as paint by numbers, fog or quest.
Project set 2. Implement the staged framework and project management.

Project set 3. Implement any other paint by numbers projects you have identified. You must look for early benefits if the program is to be seen as credible.

Project set 4. Work on the remaining quests and fog projects as soon as you can make resource available, implementing them as soon as they become clear and the conditions in the company are right.

The overall design (Project set 1) is critical to sound implementation. This book is a reference to help you identify and design the elements of the framework for your company. You will also need to know how you are currently dealing with all the activities which will be a part of your future project framework (your present mode of operation). Do not spend too long on this. You need only know sufficient to make sure that your new framework fits into the company and that there are no gaps. Designing the new framework can be dealt with on an iterative basis. You will not design it correctly the first time; you are bound to make a few mistakes. Accept this and plan for it. A very effective way of designing and validating the framework is to take a part of it and trial it on a number of projects. Use the learnings from these to refine the process before moving into wider implementation.

"A man who makes no mistakes does not usually make anything."
EDWARD JOHN PHELPS, 12 January 1899

After completing your overall design you should implement the staged framework itself (Project set 2). The benefit of putting this in place first is that it provides the fundamental foundation block and hooks that all the associated processes need to lock onto. The teams undertaking the other projects will have a known reference point to join onto (look back at Figure 14.2). They cannot help but align to each other as they are all referenced to the same anchor or plank. The work scope for this set should include basic guides outlining the framework, together with foundation training for project sponsors, project managers, line managers, and team members. You should also have project coaches available to guide newcomers through the framework – training, on its own, is seldom sufficient.

After completing your overall design you should implement the staged framework itself. The benefit of putting this in place first is that it provides the fundamental foundation block and hooks that all the associated processes need to lock onto.

The choice of the next implementation projects is critical (Project set 3). They must be those you know how to do and what to do *and* which will remain stable once in place. They should be ones which, when coupled with those that follow, will ensure you progress up the benefits chain. In this way, you build a launch pad very quickly from which you can progress the remainder of the implementation. Decision making and establishing a project list should be a high priority.

You may then undertake your remaining projects (Project set 4) in any order, at any time, creating continual change toward your objective rather than moving from island to island in any predesigned order. This does not mean to say that there will be no critical dependencies between projects nor any overall program plan. On the contrary, in order to have this flexibility you must be sure of your high level design and of the possible configurations you may pass through on the way. It may also be that the particular systems or related processes in your company will require some elements to be completed before others. You need to consider this in the investigative stages of each project and design your operational configurations accordingly. To do this, you may need to implement temporary systems, structures, and processes along the way. For example, you will need to have a project portfolio list very soon after putting the staged framework in place, if you're to maintain control. That does not mean you must have the finished database, fully networked and operating on everyone's desk. A simple spreadsheet may be sufficient to start you off. It could even be beneficial as a prototype to help you decide the design requirements for the final system.

You should also try to ensure that one of the early projects provides management information and reporting which will be useful to the decision makers and others involved in the process. Reporting makes the process visible and serves as a driver of behavior. Again, this helps set the scene for a cultural shift. Provided you use the new found knowledge responsibly, the shift will be in the right direction. If you use the new information to expose "wrong doers" and punish them, do not be surprised if people become less enthusiastic about the process and work to undermine it.

When undertaking any of the projects, do not assume you need do them throughout your whole organization at the same time. It is usually better to implement the new way of working on a particular portfolio of cross-functional projects, for example, product development. Use this as the vehicle to refine and bed in the new processes, systems and structures, and to start growing the new culture. Remember that business projects are usually by nature cross-functional, therefore, you will not be able to implement the framework on a phased basis, function by function. Do take into account, however, that if you implement in a phased way, you will probably come across some boundary issues where people will insist that certain projects are "outside the new process." Expect and accept this. Many people will take the opinion that they can move their projects forward quicker outside the project framework and a few of them may be right, in the short term at least. As the disciplines become better established the advantages of working within a known framework will become obvious – projects will meet their objectives.

As some of your process infrastructure may be broken before you even start, it does not matter in which order the remaining projects are introduced. You choose the order which suits your own circumstances and the timing of when the quest and fog projects come to fruition (Figure 28.2). At the start you will notice inefficiencies but these will reduce as more of the "final configuration" comes into being. People may even start to solve some problem areas outside the formal program. As they will be aligned to the core staged framework there will be little danger of conflict. In this way, certain parts of the company can adopt certain elements before others if it suits their needs at that point in time. The fact that people do this is evidence that the approach is naturally gaining acceptance and that part of the cultural shift is happening.

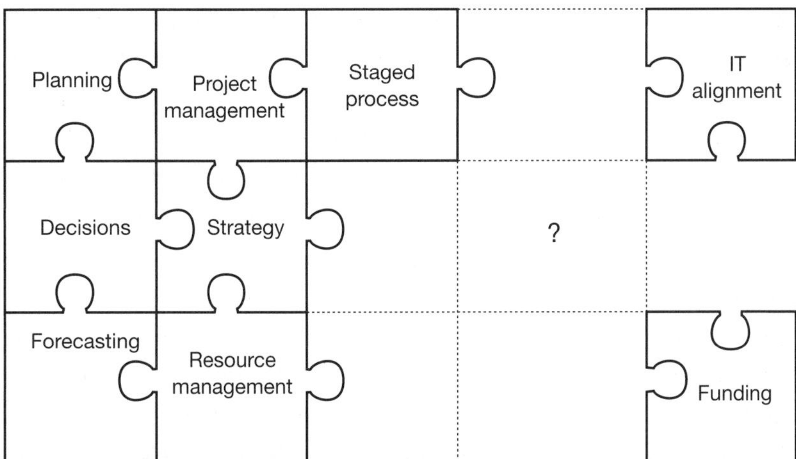

Figure 28.2 Implementation of a projects approach

Think of the implementation of a jigsaw. The work from Project set 1 will give you a view of the final picture, although some parts may be fuzzy. Fill in the new pieces as projects are completed. The picture will become clearer as more of the pieces are in place. Do not think of it as building a wall. In a wall it is not possible to put the coping stone on until the bricks below are in place. With a jigsaw, you can put any pieces in place as, and when, you see fit.

WHAT DO I DO WITH THE EXISTING PROJECT PROCESSES? A CONVERGENT STRATEGY

You will most probably have some parts of your organization already using a projects approach. They may also be backed up by excellent good practice tools and guides. Should you ask them to throw these away in favor of a company-wide approach which is as yet unproven? If you try this you will meet resistance. Your aim is ensure that change in your business is managed well and properly directed. Your aim is not to force people into a straitjacket process. Make sure you involve the key players who are champions of their local project processes. Have them design the detail of the new process adding whatever they can from their own toolkits. Don't insist they follow the new process from day one. Start off by saying it is for those people in the organization who have nothing and it is for the senior managers who will act as project sponsors or project board members. You can then ask them to show how their local processes align to the new one. Where possible, ask them to adopt any new terminology (especially stages, gates and key roles) and any templates. Over time, the local processes will converge on a single "best way."

How long will this take?

The time taken to establish a viable project framework depends very much on your starting point. If you are an organization that is used to cross-functional working and puts more emphasis on role than formal job description, much of the culture will already have been established. If, however, your organization is a very functional-led hierarchy where rank is highly prized, the change will be a shock. If you have stable leadership, the speed with which you can move forward will be greater than if your leadership suffers frequent change. In fact, if your company is one where change is relentless, make sure that you implement in bite-sized chunks so that at least part of the jigsaw is established prior to a change at the top. Many implementations have failed as they never quite got there before the old top team went. Nevertheless, a period of three to five years for fully establishing a project framework, fully integrated into the business (shown on pp. 162–4) would not be uncommon.

A staged process together with its associated documentation and training can be launched within three to six months of a decision to move forward. After that aim to have another major piece of the jigsaw in place every three to six months. Remember that one factor which will influence your rate of change is the state of the business processes and culture in aspects which influence projects. The better they are, the quicker you can move forward.

BEING HELD ACCOUNTABLE

If you are an invisible project manager on an invisible project which few people know exists, let alone what it is for, you may take your accountabilities less seriously than if your name is published to the company in a list against the project with key milestones appended. In the former case failure can be hidden, objectives can be recast to suit performance. However, in the latter you are being asked to deliver on a "promise" and being held accountable. This may sound hard, but remember that the project has been approved in full knowledge of the risks and that stopping the project, if circumstances dictate it, is a success – you are not expected to be Superman.

A final thought ...

Books are not enough. They educate. They inform. They enlighten. But ...

> *"People create change ... people constrain change."*
>
> EDDIE OBENG'S THIRD LAW OF CHANGE

Doing it by the book is *never* enough.

Appendix A
Brainstorming

"He objected to ideas only when others had them."

A J P TAYLOR

Brainstorming is a very popular technique for generating ideas in a group. Despite its popularity it is often poorly practiced. The technique was developed by Alex Osborn in the 1930s and had five basic principles:

Osborn's Five Basic Principles

1 **Defer judgment**
   Do not criticize any ideas generated as part of a brainstorm. If each idea is analyzed as it is created, few ideas will actually surface and many will be suppressed. This will either be because you will run out of time or because a proposer of an idea may not want to appear "silly." It is exactly the "silly" ideas which trigger unique and creative solutions. Never mix idea generation and analysis.

2 **Quantity breeds quality**
   By deferring judgment, you will increase the quantity of ideas. This in turn leads to an increase in the probability of delivering more creative solutions.

3 **The wilder the idea, the better**
Divergent thinking requires a certain amount of risk taking. Breakthrough ideas are hardly likely to come from "safe" propositions. Remember at this stage you are hardly taking a risk by calling out something which may make you look foolish. The bigger risk is that you are quiet and the killer solution never sees the light of day.

4 **Combine and improve ideas**
Build on what has gone before. Most ideas are not new; they are built on what went before by modifying and evolving.

5 **Take a break from the problem**
Idea generation is tiring. Tired people do not perform well. Keep the idea generation sessions to about 10 to 15 minutes.

A Blueprint for a Brainstorming Session

1 **Define the subject**
Write the subject on a flip chart. Make sure everyone can see it and understands it.

2 **Choose a facilitator**
This person will not take part in the idea generation session. He should start by reminding everyone of the principles and should ensure these principles are upheld and act as the scribe. He may only contribute if the flow has stopped and he needs to get the group started again.

3 **Generate ideas**
Ask the group to contribute ideas by calling them out. The facilitator should write them on Post-It Notes and display these prominently, where everyone can see them.

4 **Evaluate the ideas**
Cluster the ideas into groups (hence the use of Post-It Notes) to aid the selection and analysis of the ideas.

Variants

To add variety to the sessions and get the group mobile if they've been sitting at a meeting table too long:

- Ask people to write their ideas on Post-It Notes themselves and stick them on the wall. (The silent brainstorm).
- Divide the group into subgroups of two or three people. Give each subgroup a flip chart on which they post their ideas. Swap flip charts every few minutes until each group has visited each flip chart twice to add their ideas.
- Divide the group into subgroups of two or three people and ask them to draw, on a flip chart (or several stuck together), a picture or cartoon of the problem or issue at stake.

Appendix B Glossary

All cross references are shown in *italics*.

Accountability What you can count on a person doing. That person and only that person can be called to account if something they have accountability for is not done.

Activity Individual components of work that must be undertaken to complete the stages of the project. Each activity should be defined in terms of its start and end dates and the name of the person accountable for its completion.

Approval The term used when an individual accepts a deliverable as fit for purpose such that the project can continue.

Authorization The decision which triggers the allocation of the resources funding and needed to carry on the project.

Bar chart Graphical representation of activities within a project over time. Each activity's duration is shown as a bar, the ends of which correspond to the start and end dates. A bar chart is also known as a Gantt chart.

Baseline The original project plan you use to track progress against during a project. The baseline plan includes, start and finish dates of activities and budget costs. The baseline cost is often called a *project budget*.

Benefits Quantified increases in revenue, decreases in costs, reductions in working capital and/or increase in performance which occur directly as a result of a project.

Brainstorming A technique for generating ideas in a group.

Budget Planned, approved cost for the project. See also *baseline*.

Business case A document providing the justification for undertaking (or for continuing) a project, defining the financial and other benefits which the project is expected to deliver together with the schedule and other constraints within which the project is to operate. This is usually prepared in two stages. The first is the initial business case which is prepared for the Detailed Investigation Gate review. The second is the full business case which is prepared for the Development Gate review.

Business Program A Business Program comprises current benefit generating business activities togther with a loosely coupled but tightly aligned *portfolio* of programs and projects, aimed at delivering the benefits of part of a business plan or strategy.

Capabilities Building blocks of systems, process, and competence which are combined with other capabilities to provide an operational capability.

Capacity buffer A *Critical Chain* term. Protective time placed between projects within the drum resource.

Change management The formal process through which changes to the *project plan* are introduced and approved. Changes are recorded on a change log. (Do not confuse with the *management of change*.)

Closure Formal "end point" of a project either because it is completed or because it has been *terminated* early. Closure is formally documented in a closure report.

Constraint Defined restriction or limitation imposed on a project.

Contingency plan Plan of action to minimize or negate the adverse effects of a risk should it occur.

Cost plan Document detailing items of cost associated with a project, in categories (work packages) relating to the schedule plan. See also *budget* and *baseline*.

Critical chain The critical chain of a single project is the sequence of dependent events that prevents the project from being completed in a shorter interval, given finite resources.

Critical path The path through a series of activities, taking into account dependencies, in which late completion of activities will have an impact on the project end date, or delay a key *milestone*.

Culture Culture comprises two elements:

1. The norms and behaviors of a group (the way we do things here!)
2. Unconscious programming of the mind leading to a set of similar collective habits, behaviors, and mindsets.

Deliverable Output produced by the project in the process of achieving the business objectives, e.g. a report, system or product. Each key deliverable should be defined in the *project definition* section of the initial or full *business case* document and represented by a *milestone* on the project plan.

Dependency A constraint on the sequence and timing of activities in a project. Activities may be dependent on other activities within the same project (internal dependency) or on activities/deliverables from other projects (*interdependency*).

Detailed plan Developed throughout the project, from the *summary plan*, breaking down the forthcoming stage into manageable work packages and activities.

Detailed investigation stage The second stage within the staged project framework when a detailed study is undertaken to evaluate a number of possible project options and to recommend a particular course of action.

Duration The amount of time required to complete an *activity*. It is calculated as the finish date – the start date.

Emergency project A project which is required as a result of a business issue which will severely damage the company if not addressed without delay. These projects may cause previously committed projects to be allocated a lower priority or to be *terminated* in order to release resources.

Escalation To increase the awareness and ownership of a problem or *issue* to a level in the company where the required resources, expertise and/or authority can be applied in order to resolve that issue.

Feeding buffer A feeding buffer protects the start of a *Critical chain activity* from a delay of an upstream dependent non-critical chain activity. A project can have many feeding buffers.

Fog Project (walking in a fog) Formally known as an open project, this type of project occurs when you are unsure of both what is to be done and how.

Gate The point, preceding each stage, at which all new information converges and which serves for:

- quality control checks
- prioritization
- a point from which to plan forward
- a Go/No go decision point.

Health check A tool used in project reviews to assess the overall risk associated with the project.

Idea A possibility for a new or enhanced capability, system, service, or product. This is written up as a *proposal*.

Impact assessment A study undertaken to determine the effect of an *issue* on the project. An impact assessment is required as part of *change management*.

Interdependency If Project B requires a *deliverable* from Project A in order to achieve its objective, project B is dependent on project A. Dependency is when a deliverable is passed from one project to another.

Issue A circumstance (event, lack of knowledge, etc.) that has occurred and which will jeopardize the success of a project. They are recorded on an issues log. Issues can either be resolved within the project as defined or a change may be required to accommodate it.

Late activity An *activity* which is forecast to end later than the *baseline* plan finish date. This is reported on a late activities report.

Life cycle A sequence of defined *stages* over the full duration of a project, i.e. initial investigation, detailed investigation, develop and test, trial, release.

Link A relationship between *dependent* activities.

Management of change A name often used to describe the process of transforming and organization from one state to another. Not to be confused with *change management* which is a technique used on projects to ensure that alterations to the project time, scope, *benefits*, and cost are introduced in a regularized way.

Milestone A major event (often representing the start of a *stage*) which is used to monitor progress at a summary level. Milestones are activities of zero duration.

Movie project (making a movie) Formally a semi-open project, where the means are known but not the output.

Network chart A diagram which shows dependencies between project *activities*. Activities are represented as boxes or nodes and the activity relationship is shown by arrows connecting the nodes. Often called a PERT chart.

Opportunity The opposite of a *risk*. An opportunity is a possibility to enhance the project *benefits*. Opportunities are recorded on an opportunity log.

Originator The person who conceives an "*idea*" or need for a new development or enhancement and publishes it in the form of a *proposal*. This person can come from any function or level in the company.

Output definition document The fundamental sourcebook describing the project output in terms of "feel," technology, commercial, and customer / user needs. It is the document which integrates all the individual system, process, and platform requirements and specifies how they will work together.

Pilot A pilot is the ultimate form of testing a new development and its implementation plan prior to committing to the full release. It is undertaken using a sample of potential customers and users. This would normally take place in the trial stage although may, in some cases, be treated as a limited release.

Portfolio A grouping or bundle of projects which are collected together for management convenience, e.g. the collection of projects sponsored by an individual is his or her sponsorship portfolio; those project managed by a person is a management portfolio; the full set of projects within a company is the company portfolio.

Post-Implementation Review (PIR) A review, three to six months after the end of the project, to assess whether the expected *benefits* and performance measures are being achieved. This checks the effectiveness of a project as opposed its efficiency which is reviewed as part of project *closure*.

Program Programs are a tightly coupled and tightly aligned grouping of projects.

Progress bar chart A bar chart which shows the actual and forecast dates for each *activity* compared with the *baseline* plan dates.

Progress report Regular report from the project manager to the project sponsor and other stakeholders summarizing the progress of a project including key events, milestones not achieved, and issues.

Project A project, in a business environment, is:

- a finite piece of work (i.e. it has a beginning and an end)
- undertaken within defined cost and time constraints
- directed at achieving a stated business benefit.

Project board Body established to monitor the project and to assist the project sponsor in delivering the benefits and the project manager in achieving the deliverables. Sometimes called a steering group.

Project buffer The project buffer protects the project end date from viability in the duration of the tasks in the *critical chain*. For a single project the size of the buffer depends on the number and duration of the critical chain activities and on the degree of risk associated with each. See also *feeding buffers*.

Project definition A section within the Initial and full *business case* which defines a project, i.e. what will be done, how it will be delivered and what business need the project supports.

Project manager Person accountable for managing a project on a day-to-day basis, from start to finish, to ensure successful implementation within agreed cost, schedule, and quality targets.

Project plan The supporting detail to the *project definition* which details the schedule, resource and costs for the project. It can be in outline or detail.

Project review group A company-wide cross-functional group accountable for project priorities, issue escalation and resource allocation for a portfolio of projects.

Project sponsor The person who sees a commercial possibility in an idea and who agrees to take ownership of the proposal. Once a project is approved, the project sponsor is accountable for delivering the benefits to the business. Typically, he/she will:

- chair the *project board*
- appoint the *project manager*
- represent the business and users in key project decisions
- approve key *deliverables*
- resolve *issues* which are outside the project manager's control
- ensure that the delivered solution matches the business needs.

Proposal A short document prepared, by the *originator*, for the initial investigation gate review, which outlines the proposed project, its fit with current strategy and, if known, the impact on the organization, broad estimates of benefits and cost, and expected time to completion.

Quest project (going on a quest) Quest projects are formally known as semi-closed projects. You are clear what is to be done but have no idea about how to do it.

Ready for Service (RFS) The *milestone* prior to the *release stage*, by when all prerequisite project work, testing, and trials have been completed and full operational support is in place.

Release Generic term used to denote when an output from a project is put into service, e.g. a product can be used by a customer under standard terms and conditions (i.e. not trial agreement), handover of a customized service for the customer to start using, a system started to be used, new process operational. It must not be confused with *ready for service* which is the point when all capabilities are ready to use but have not yet been put to use.

Release stage The final stage in the staged project framework during which the final output is launched and put into service.

Resource buffer A resource buffer is used in critical chain schedule management to provide early warning, from one *critical chain* activity to another critical chain activity, for an activity to start.

Resource manager A person in each unit and function who is accountable for knowing the future assignment of resources to processes and projects.

Responsibility What a person is or feels, responsible for. It assumes they have a commitment, beyond their own *accountabilities*, to act responsibly to ensure the project objectives are met.

Review A process used as a check point at which a deliverable or the project in full, can be evaluated against its business objectives. *Gates* are a special review point. Reviewers are contributors to a decision and do not actually make the decisions. See *sign off*.

Risk Potential occurrences or threats that would jeopardize the success of a project. Risks are continuously assessed and recorded on a risk log.

Sign off The formal process for making a decision (e.g. proceeding to the next stage, accepting a *deliverable*). It is preceded by a review.

Simple project A project where the end point can be seen clearly from the detailed investigation gate and which, if started, will not compromise future, more beneficial projects. Typically simple projects consume little resource or have their own separate resources which cannot be allocated to other projects.

Single point accountability The concept that any *activity*, or *work package*, at any level in the *work breakdown structure* has only one, named person accountable for it.

Slippage *See* **Late activities**.

Sponsor *See* **Project sponsor**.

Stage The natural high level breakpoints in the project *life cycle* (e.g. initial investigation, detailed investigation, develop and test, trial and release).

Stakeholder Any person or group who has an interest in the project. Typically some support it, some are neutral and other are antagonists.

Stakeholder Influence Map A diagram used to depict the influence that individual stakeholders have on others. The objective is to identify the routes by which key influencers and decision makers can be enrolled in the project's objectives.

Subproject A tightly aligned and tightly coupled part of a project. Subprojects are usually run to their own staged *life cycle*.

Summary plan Initial part of the evolution of the schedule, resource, and cost plan, developed at the start of the project, defining the overall targets and key dates.

Termination The premature *closure* of a project due to an issue which cannot be addressed or because the risks have become too high.

Theory of constraints The theory expounded by Eli Goldratt which led to the development of *critical chain* schedule management.

Trial stage A trial of a capability in same environment as the customer or user will use it. This is done as part of the trial. Often denoted as a beta trial under special trial agreements.

White space Unassigned resources which are available to work on future projects. White space is required at short notice for initial investigations and at medium notice to resource future projects after the detailed investigation gate. Without white space, companies are unable to change themselves without taking resource from previously authorized and committed work.

Work Breakdown Structure (WBS) A structured hierarchy of *work packages*.

Work Package Generic term used to describe a grouping of *activities*, *stages*, etc. each of which has a defined scope, timescale, cost and a single person accountable for it.

Appendix C
A project process framework

"Life is one long process of getting tired."
SAMUEL BUTLER (1612–1680)

Teach me to cheat

How to document and organize your processes can pose a number of problems. In one company I visited, they proudly showed me their process documentation (all to ISO 9000 standards), in Lever Arch files covering about 5 yards of shelves. I was not impressed and, in fact, they were hoping I wouldn't be. This collection of files was their process before they reorganized it. After a pause, they pulled from the shelf a single, slim volume which was now the process documentation for the entire company. I asked how they managed this remarkable reduction. They told me they "cheated" and would show me how to do the same.

Their documentation was divided into three basic types:

1 Processes
2 Guides
3 Templates.

The processes were very simple tabulations stating the activity, who is accountable, the deliverable and who it goes to. In addition, they have a further column which referred to any relevant templates or guides. Flow charts were only used, if necessary, for clarification. The documents were kept very brief and factual with no explanation or guidance of any sort.

The guides were the "education" documents. They contained the principles, the methods, best practice and checklists.

The templates were the actual documents. They not only contained the titles of each document but also described what each section was for, rather like I have on page 281. Each template also had a size guide and described what its purpose was.

The slim document I was shown was in fact the processes only. The remaining documents were the guides and templates. These were all very necessary documents but not needed all the time. Most users could work from the process alone; if they needed more, the cross-reference was supplied. Another advantage is that the system requires very little administration and also lends itself to intranet publication with the process at the core and the guides and templates hotlinked in the appropriate places.

Process framework – the component parts

The component parts of the process are included in Figure C.1, which shows, on a single sheet, how the key accountabilities on a project interact and what deliverables pass between them. If you have tabulated your own process correctly, you should be able to create a similar summary diagram.

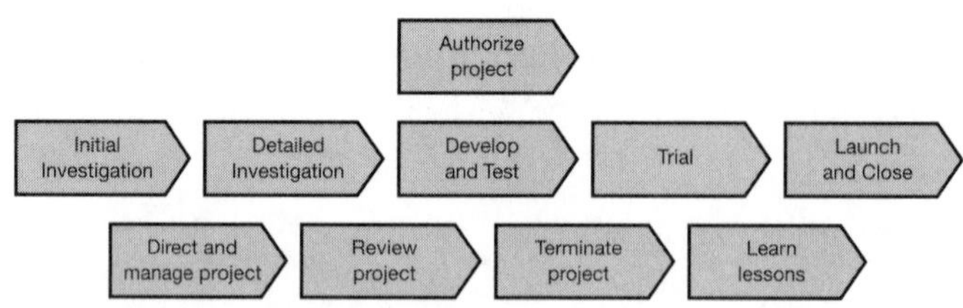

Figure C.1 Process components

Top row: the authorization process should be a stand alone document.
Second row: the staged framework should follow the stages which define what happens throughout, similar to those in Part 2.
Third row: the remaining processes can be called on at any time during the project.

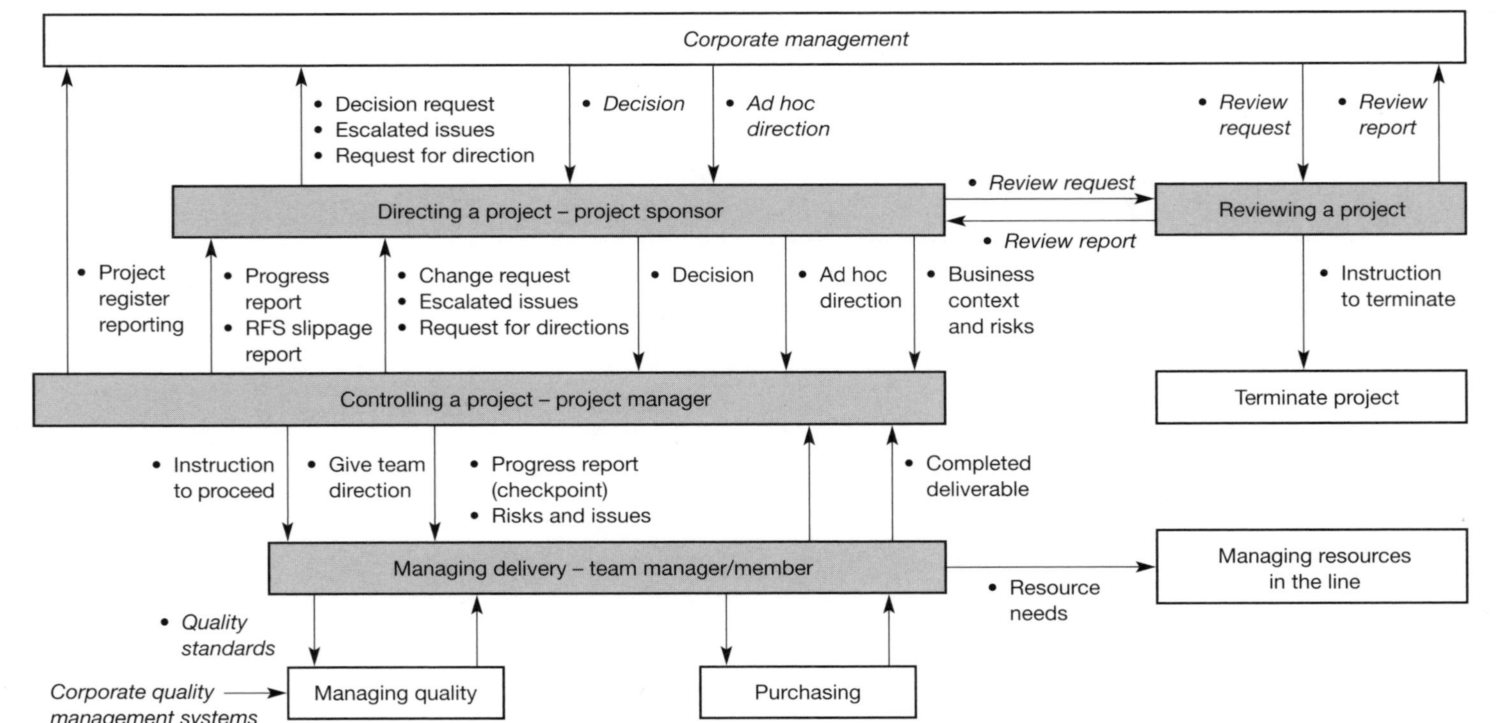

Figure C.2 Direct and manage a project
The overall design shows, in a single diagram, the key interactions between the corporate center (e.g. Business program, Project review group), the project sponsor, project manager and team managers and members. The arrows flowing between the blocks describe the deliverables. Compare this to the accountabilities in Chapter 4.

Index